T0301588

Additional Praise for
*Quantitative Credit Portfolio Management*

"A first-class work on credit risk modeling and credit portfolio management. This book addresses real-world challenges that we face every day using extensive theoretical and empirical analysis. I strongly recommend the book to anyone who wants to understand how credit markets work and how to work in credit markets."

—Benjamin Deng, Group Head of Investment Analytics,
AIA Group, Hong Kong

"For many years this quantitative research team has offered new insights and helpful support to many institutional investors such as APG. Based on the extensive data base available to them and the truly two-way dialogue they have with end-investors like us, many empirical questions and dilemmas have been tackled. By introducing concepts such as Duration Times Spread and liquidity scores, the authors have improved our understanding of risk. Moreover, by applying these concepts to the portfolio construction process, we have gained more confidence in the robustness of our portfolios."

—Eduard van Gelderen, CIO Capital Markets,
APG Asset Management, Netherlands

"A must-read for all future and current credit portfolio managers. The book is a comprehensive review of the quantitative tools available to better manage the risks within a credit portfolio and combines the right amount of statistical work with practical answers to questions confronting credit managers."

—Curtis Ishii, Head of Global Fixed Income,
California Public Employees' Retirement System, USA

"For investors who struggled with managing credit risk through the 2007–2009 crisis, *Quantitative Credit Portfolio Management* offers practical answers to vexing questions. Duration Times Spread as a risk measure is one of those elegant innovations in finance that seem obvious in retrospect but have eluded the grasp of previous analysts. The liquidity analysis is the first robust attempt I have seen at quantifying this important factor in the OTC market of corporate bonds. All in all, a strong effort by what is arguably the best team of fixed income research analysts on the Street."

—Randolph E. Wedding, Senior Managing Director, Fixed Income,
Office of the Treasurer of the Regents, University of California, USA

"Lev Dynkin and his coauthors offer insights and practical solutions to critical issues in corporate bond risk analysis. In particular, the measurement of credit spread risk using Duration Times Spread is a powerful tool and a significant improvement over prior market practice. This book reflects top caliber analysis and has many useful applications."

—John Brennan, Portfolio Manager, DB Advisors, USA

"The practical orientation of this book on institutional credit portfolio management makes it particularly useful for practitioners. All key areas of interest are well covered. An excellent effort by a team with extensive industry experience."

—Lim Chow Kiat, President, GIC Asset Management, Singapore

"As an investor coming out of the financial crisis of 2007–2009, I began to wonder if our traditional risk models and fixed income assumptions about portfolio construction and diversification were obsolete. Was this crisis the financial market's equivalent of discovering that the earth is round, or that the earth is not really the center of the universe? As practitioners rethink traditional credit views, it's a perfect time for a fresh approach and some new concepts backed fully by empirical evidence and, most importantly, common sense. It's no longer enough to demonstrate that a risk management framework is empirically sound based on historical data from more 'normal' times. In *Quantitative Credit and Portfolio Management*, the authors apply techniques developed prior to the crisis and pose the question: Would those measures provide insight to events that happened during the crisis itself?

"In short, the ideas presented here simply make sense. Risk managers, portfolio managers and credit specialists can benefit from this book, not to mention inquisitive CIOs. I found the recommendations to be theoretically sound and fundamentally practical to implement."

—Ron Joelson, CIO, Genworth Financial, USA

"This book provides enormous insights for beginning practitioners looking to learn the most advanced credit management techniques. For experienced professionals, it provides a great update and advancement. The empirical evidence and discussion of metrics, such as DTS and Liquidity Cost Scores (LCS), illustrate how these should be used to better manage credit risk as well as liquidity risk in portfolios. The global financial crisis of 2007–2009 and the ongoing sovereign crisis have taught us that the world has changed and more focus should be put on liquidity. Applying and testing their findings in the recent market turmoil strengthens the authors' conclusions and offers many critical tips for managers. The book is a must read for all active players in credit markets given the changes after the recent crisis."

—Jan Straatman, Global CIO,
ING Investment Management, Netherlands

"Lev Dynkin and his team are of the highest authority on fixed income portfolio analytics. Their thoughtful and rigorous quantitative research, unparalleled access to high-quality data, and cooperative approach with leading fixed income managers sets them apart. This book provides the reader with new ideas to improve both risk management and alpha capture in credit portfolios."

—Carolyn Gibbs and Rich King, Co-heads of U.S. Taxable
Fixed Income and Global High Income, Invesco, USA

"Quickly and accurately identifying and measuring the risk exposures of credit portfolios has become even more critical in the post-crisis era of low government bond yields. As clients increasingly want pure credit exposure, divorced from the interest rate environment, the techniques described in this book are an important advance in successfully managing fixed income credit portfolios. I recommend this book for managers looking to outperform credit fixed income benchmarks."

—Lisa Coleman, Head of Global Investment-Grade Credit,
J.P. Morgan Asset Management, USA

"*Quantitative Credit Portfolio Management* is a one of a kind book addressing everyday issues and topics submitted by investors and practitioners to the QPS team. It presents a decade of research in a single volume. It is a must for portfolio managers willing to understand the nature of corporate bond spread risk (systematic, issuer specific, and liquidity). It introduces the concept of DTS, a superior measure of bond spread risk, and tests its validity across a wide spectrum of asset classes and time periods, including the recent crisis. The practical instructions advocated in this book are best practices that we already rely on in our credit investment process for superior active management."

—Ibrahima Kobar, CIO Fixed Income,
Natixis Asset Management, France

"This is a convergence of in-depth analytical research and practical applications to comprehensively understand and quantify systematic and nonsystematic risks in credit and sovereign portfolios and benchmarks. This book is essential reading for investment professionals, portfolio managers, hedge fund managers, pension fund managers, and students of the industry in the post–global financial crisis environment. It shows the way to more effectively manage liquidity, downgrade, default, and derivative risks."

—Susan Buckley, Managing Director, Global Fixed Interest,
Queensland Investment Corporation, Australia

"The Quantitative Portfolio Strategy Group led by Lev Dynkin is considered by the fixed income industry to be the leader in the field of quantitative bond investing research. The strength of this book is that all the concepts described are not just theoretical but are used in practice. In addition, many of them, such as liquidity scores, empirical duration, issuer diversification, and fallen angels as an asset class are very topical in today's management of credit portfolios. We consider the joint effort that led to the development of the DTS concept as a breakthrough in the field of credit risk management. The DTS concept has improved our understanding of credit risk and led to better assessment of value in credit markets by our portfolio managers."

—Edith Siermann, CIO Fixed Income, Robeco, Netherlands

"The authors' team has been a solid lighthouse for portfolio managers amid the rough seas of fixed income markets. Its gleam has never died, even in the recent credit turmoil, and guided us to a safe harbor. This book covers their new findings and developments on managing credit portfolios tested in practice during the 2007–2009 crisis, which all practitioners must read regardless of whether they are involved in corporate credit or sovereign markets."

—Seiichiro Nemoto, Head of Pension Research Center,
Sumitomo Trust & Banking Company, Japan

"This book addresses many of the questions every fixed income professional is faced with today, which includes optimal diversification, price behavior during rating changes, and measures of liquidity. The authors are especially well known for introducing the concept of Duration Times Spread for managing credit spread risk. This newest book shows a wide range of potential uses of DTS in constructing and managing a credit portfolio by looking at the results achieved with DTS in the recent crisis. I strongly recommend this book to every bond portfolio manager in the current environment of heightened credit risk even in the sovereign space."

—Sandro Streit, Head of Asset Management,
Swiss National Bank, Switzerland

"The authors ... industry leaders from Barclays Capital ... have done it again! Following up on their excellent book, *Quantitative Management of Bond Portfolios* (2006), which brought tremendous insight in the management of multisector bond funds, they have now done an even deeper dive into managing credit portfolios, which is not an easy task to be sure! They not only delve into improved risk management metrics, but also reveal helpful strategies to improve both passive and active fund management. Once again, this team is taking our business to new levels of excellence."

—Ken Volpert, CFA, Head of Taxable Bond Group, Vanguard, USA

"This book tackles the Big C—CREDIT. Market relationships and yield spreads of corporate, sovereign and emerging market debt have morphed nearly beyond recognition over the last 15 years, culminating with the enormous devastation of the global financial crisis. Institutional bond investors have long known to go to Lev and his team with their thorniest and most complex portfolio problems. Here they lay out a very straightforward exposition of best practices in credit portfolio management. This is a must read for those charged with navigating today's global capital markets."

—Ken Leech, former CIO, Western Asset Management Company, USA

"This is another terrific contribution by an established team of Wall Street researchers. In their characteristic style, they masterfully combine rigorous empirical work with practical wisdom and clear intuition. This book should be of great value to both practitioners and academics interested in the cutting edge of thinking in the area of credit risk and portfolio management."

—Leonid Kogan, Nippon Telegraph and Telephone Professor of Management, Sloan School of Management, MIT, USA

"Clients of credit portfolio managers typically ask: What caused the performance and unexpected high volatility during the financial crisis? What have you learned? What changes have you made to your investment process so it doesn't happen again? The right answers lie in this comprehensive book of applied research. It will be required reading for credit portfolio managers interested in risk management, superior performance, and high information ratios."

—Stanley J. Kon, Editor, *Journal of Fixed Income*, USA

"This volume will quickly become an indispensable reference for any fixed income investor. The authors are seasoned practitioners with many years of experience in helping clients manage risk, optimize expected returns, and solve real-world problems using the most sophisticated tools of financial engineering. The profession should be grateful that they're willing to share their insights with the rest of us."

—Andrew W. Lo, Harris & Harris Group Professor, Sloan School of Management, MIT, USA

# Quantitative Credit Portfolio Management

# The Frank J. Fabozzi Series

*Fixed Income Securities, Second Edition* by Frank J. Fabozzi
*Focus on Value: A Corporate and Investor Guide to Wealth Creation* by James L. Grant and James A. Abate
*Handbook of Global Fixed Income Calculations* by Dragomir Krgin
*Managing a Corporate Bond Portfolio* by Leland E. Crabbe and Frank J. Fabozzi
*Real Options and Option-Embedded Securities* by William T. Moore
*Capital Budgeting: Theory and Practice* by Pamela P. Peterson and Frank J. Fabozzi
*The Exchange-Traded Funds Manual* by Gary L. Gastineau
*Professional Perspectives on Fixed Income Portfolio Management, Volume 3* edited by Frank J. Fabozzi
*Investing in Emerging Fixed Income Markets* edited by Frank J. Fabozzi and Efstathia Pilarinu
*Handbook of Alternative Assets* by Mark J. P. Anson
*The Global Money Markets* by Frank J. Fabozzi, Steven V. Mann, and Moorad Choudhry
*The Handbook of Financial Instruments* edited by Frank J. Fabozzi
*Collateralized Debt Obligations: Structures and Analysis* by Laurie S. Goodman and Frank J. Fabozzi
*Interest Rate, Term Structure, and Valuation Modeling* edited by Frank J. Fabozzi
*Investment Performance Measurement* by Bruce J. Feibel
*The Handbook of Equity Style Management* edited by T. Daniel Coggin and Frank J. Fabozzi
*Foundations of Economic Value Added, Second Edition* by James L. Grant
*Financial Management and Analysis, Second Edition* by Frank J. Fabozzi and Pamela P. Peterson
*Measuring and Controlling Interest Rate and Credit Risk, Second Edition* by Frank J. Fabozzi, Steven V. Mann, and Moorad Choudhry
*Professional Perspectives on Fixed Income Portfolio Management, Volume 4* edited by Frank J. Fabozzi
*The Handbook of European Fixed Income Securities* edited by Frank J. Fabozzi and Moorad Choudhry
*The Handbook of European Structured Financial Products* edited by Frank J. Fabozzi and Moorad Choudhry
*The Mathematics of Financial Modeling and Investment Management* by Sergio M. Focardi and Frank J. Fabozzi
*Short Selling: Strategies, Risks, and Rewards* edited by Frank J. Fabozzi
*The Real Estate Investment Handbook* by G. Timothy Haight and Daniel Singer
*Market Neutral Strategies* edited by Bruce I. Jacobs and Kenneth N. Levy
*Securities Finance: Securities Lending and Repurchase Agreements* edited by Frank J. Fabozzi and Steven V. Mann
*Fat-Tailed and Skewed Asset Return Distributions* by Svetlozar T. Rachev, Christian Menn, and Frank J. Fabozzi
*Financial Modeling of the Equity Market: From CAPM to Cointegration* by Frank J. Fabozzi, Sergio M. Focardi, and Petter N. Kolm
*Advanced Bond Portfolio Management: Best Practices in Modeling and Strategies* edited by Frank J. Fabozzi, Lionel Martellini, and Philippe Priaulet
*Analysis of Financial Statements, Second Edition* by Pamela P. Peterson and Frank J. Fabozzi
*Collateralized Debt Obligations: Structures and Analysis, Second Edition* by Douglas J. Lucas, Laurie S. Goodman, and Frank J. Fabozzi
*Handbook of Alternative Assets , Second Edition* by Mark J. P. Anson
*Introduction to Structured Finance* by Frank J. Fabozzi, Henry A. Davis, and Moorad Choudhry
*Financial Econometrics* by Svetlozar T. Rachev, Stefan Mittnik, Frank J. Fabozzi, Sergio M. Focardi, and Teo Jasic
*Developments in Collateralized Debt Obligations: New Products and Insights* by Douglas J. Lucas, Laurie S. Goodman, Frank J. Fabozzi, and Rebecca J. Manning
*Robust Portfolio Optimization and Management* by Frank J. Fabozzi, Petter N. Kolm, Dessislava A. Pachamanova, and Sergio M. Focardi
*Advanced Stochastic Models, Risk Assessment, and Portfolio Optimizations* by Svetlozar T. Rachev, Stogan V. Stoyanov, and Frank J. Fabozzi
*How to Select Investment Managers and Evaluate Performance* by G. Timothy Haight, Stephen O. Morrell, and Glenn E. Ross
*Bayesian Methods in Finance* by Svetlozar T. Rachev, John S. J. Hsu, Biliana S. Bagasheva, and Frank J. Fabozzi
*Structured Products and Related Credit Derivatives* by Brian P. Lancaster, Glenn M. Schultz, and Frank J. Fabozzi
*Quantitative Equity Investing: Techniques and Strategies* by Frank J. Fabozzi, Sergio M. Focardi, andPetter N. Kolm
*Introduction to Fixed Income Analytics, Second Edition* by Frank J. Fabozzi and Steven V. Mann
*The Handbook of Traditional and Alternative Investment Vehicles* by Mark J. P. Anson, Frank J. Fabozzi, and Frank J. Jones
*The Theory and Practice of Investment Management, Second Edition* edited by Frank J. Fabozzi and Harry M. Markowitz

# Quantitative Credit Portfolio Management

*Practical Innovations for Measuring
and Controlling Liquidity, Spread,
and Issuer Concentration Risk*

ARIK BEN DOR
LEV DYNKIN
JAY HYMAN
BRUCE D. PHELPS

WILEY

John Wiley & Sons, Inc.

Published by John Wiley & Sons, Inc., Hoboken, New Jersey.
Published simultaneously in Canada.

For general information on our other products and services or for technical support, please contact our Customer Care Department within the United States at (800) 762-2974, outside the United States at (317) 572-3993 or fax (317) 572-4002.

Wiley also publishes its books in a variety of electronic formats. Some content that appears in print may not be available in electronic books. For more information about Wiley products, visit our web site at www.wiley.com.

*Library of Congress Cataloging-in-Publication Data:*

Quantitative credit portfolio management : practical innovations for measuring and controlling liquidity, spread, and issuer concentration risk / Lev Dynkin . . . [et al.]. – 1st ed.
        p. cm. – (Frank J. Fabozzi series ; 202)
    Includes index.
    ISBN 978-1-118-11769-9 (hardback); 978-1-118-16742-7 (ebk);
    978-1-118-16736-6 (ebk); 978-1-118-16738-0 (ebk)
    1. Credit derivatives.  2. Portfolio management.  3. Investment analysis.  I. Dynkin, Lev, 1957–
    HG6024.A3.Q36 2011
    332.63′2–dc23

                                                                          2011039273

Printed in the United States of America.

10  9  8  7  6  5  4  3  2  1

# Acknowledgments

The authors would like to thank several colleagues at Barclays Capital Research for their contributions to this book and help with the manuscript:

Albert Desclée for his long-term leadership in the group's research in Europe and his contribution to several chapters; Ariel Edelstein, Vadim Konstantinovsky, Simon Polbennilov, Anando Maitra, Kwok Yuen Ng, and Jason Xu for their contribution to several chapters; and Ariel Edelstein, Vadim Konstantinovsky and Yael Eisenthal-Berkovitz for their help in reviewing and editing the manuscript.

The authors would also like to acknowledge former colleagues Madhur Ambastha, Siddhartha Dastidar and Professor Leonid Kogan for their past contributions to the research of the group and useful discussions of the material of this book.

The authors are very grateful to Larry Kantor for his initiative to support and enhance the group's research effort, which made this book possible.

The authors would like to recognize Jerry Del Missier for his sponsorship of investor-oriented research at Barclays Capital and of our group's focus on issues important to investment practitioners.

The authors are also grateful to Guglielmo Sartori di Borgoricco, David Campbell, Neil Cummins, Nick Howard, Stephen Lessing, John Stathis, Brett Tejpaul, and Kashif Zafar for their interest and consistent support of our work, and for including us in their dialogues with institutional investors that motivated the studies contained in this book.

Finally, the authors would like to thank their families for bearing over several years the sacrifices of family time necessary to produce the research in this book and prepare it for publication.

# Contents

Foreword                                                                xvii

Introduction                                                            xix

Notes on Terminology                                                   xxvii

## PART ONE
### Measuring the Market Risks of Corporate Bonds

### CHAPTER 1
### Measuring Spread Sensitivity of Corporate Bonds                       3
Analysis of Corporate Bond Spread Behavior                                5
A New Measure of Excess Return Volatility                                20
Refinements and Further Tests                                            25
Summary and Implications for Portfolio Managers                          30
Appendix: Data Description                                               34

### CHAPTER 2
### DTS for Credit Default Swaps                                         39
Estimation Methodology                                                   40
Empirical Analysis of CDS Spreads                                        41
Appendix: Quasi-Maximum Likelihood Approach                              51

### CHAPTER 3
### DTS for Sovereign Bonds                                              55
Spread Dynamics of Emerging Markets Debt                                 55
DTS for Developed Markets Sovereigns: The Case of Euro
   Treasuries                                                            59
Managing Sovereign Risk Using DTS                                        66

**CHAPTER 4**
**A Theoretical Basis for DTS**                                              **73**
The Merton Model: A Zero-Coupon Bond                              74
Dependence of Slope on Maturity                                      77


**CHAPTER 5**
**Quantifying the Liquidity of Corporate Bonds**                            **81**
Liquidity Cost Scores (LCS) for U.S. Credit Bonds                82
Liquidity Cost Scores: Methodology                                88
LCS for Trader-Quoted Bonds                                       92
LCS for Non-Quoted Bonds: The LCS Model                          96
Testing the LCS Model: Out-of-Sample Tests                      102
LCS for Pan-European Credit Bonds                                113
Using LCS in Portfolio Construction                             123
Trade Efficiency Scores (TES)                                   129


**CHAPTER 6**
**Joint Dynamics of Default and Liquidity Risk**                           **133**
Spread Decomposition Methodology                                138
What Drives OAS Differences across Bonds?                       139
How Has the Composition of OAS Changed?                         141
Spread Decomposition Using an Alternative Measure of
    Expected Default Losses                                     145
High-Yield Spread Decomposition                                 147
Applications of Spread Decomposition                            147
Alternative Spread Decomposition Models                         150
Appendix                                                        152


**CHAPTER 7**
**Empirical versus Nominal Durations of Corporate Bonds**                  **157**
Empirical Duration: Theory and Evidence                         159
Segmentation in Credit Markets                                  173
Potential Stale Pricing and Its Effect on Hedge Ratios          173
Hedge Ratios Following Rating Changes: An Event Study
    Approach                                                    179
Using Empirical Duration in Portfolio Management
    Applications                                                186

**PART TWO**

**Managing Corporate Bond Portfolios**

**CHAPTER 8**
**Hedging the Market Risk in Pairs Trades**     **197**
Data and Hedging Simulation Methodology     199
Analysis of Hedging Results     200
Appendix: Hedging Pair-Wise Trades with Skill     208

**CHAPTER 9**
**Positioning along the Credit Curve**     **213**
Data and Methodology     214
Empirical Analysis     217

**CHAPTER 10**
**The 2007–2009 Credit Crisis**     **229**
Spread Behavior during the Credit Crisis     229
Applications of DTS     234
Advantages of DTS in Risk Model Construction     244

**CHAPTER 11**
**A Framework for Diversification of Issuer Risk**     **249**
Downgrade Risk before and after the Credit Crisis     250
Using DTS to Set Position-Size Ratios     257
Comparing and Combining the Two Approaches to Issuer
    Limits     260

**CHAPTER 12**
**How Best to Capture the Spread Premium of Corporate Bonds?**     **265**
The Credit Spread Premium     266
Measuring the Credit Spread Premium for the IG Corporate
    Index     266
Alternative Corporate Indexes     279
Capturing Spread Premium: Adopting an Alternative Corporate
    Benchmark     288

**CHAPTER 13**
**Risk and Performance of Fallen Angels**     **295**
  Data and Methodology    298
  Performance Dynamics around Rating Events    303
  Fallen Angels as an Asset Class    319

**CHAPTER 14**
**Obtaining Credit Exposure Using Cash and Synthetic Replication**     **337**
  Cash Credit Replication (TCX)    338
  Synthetic Replication of Cash Indexes    351
  Credit RBIs    358

**References**     **367**

**Index**     **371**

# Foreword

The financial market crisis that began in 2007 delivered a rude shock to corporate bond investors, a constituency whose numbers had been swelled by an extended period of low interest rates and plentiful liquidity. The corporate bond asset class had offered coupon levels seemingly well in excess of any likely defaults, as well as a price volatility relative to government bonds, that was naturally dampened by the cyclical nature of credit quality. Enhanced by structural rigidities that offered well-known opportunities for active managers, these characteristics warranted a nearly permanent overweighting of corporate bonds. This worked until the credit crisis. Ever since, the corporate bond markets have misbehaved dramatically when viewed through traditional lenses, and the havoc wrought to investment portfolios is obvious given the strikingly poor performance delivered by active managers in 2007–2008.

So, is this asset class irreparably damaged? Or do we simply need to address it differently?

In this book, the authors demonstrate convincingly that the deployment of new tools enables investors to continue to harvest the benefits of corporate bond investing whose origins go back as far as the nineteenth century. Indeed, many of these tools were already available and others have been developed in response to investor experience in more recent times. While the approach here is strongly grounded in investment theory, it is also tethered to real-world experiences and does not stray into a merely academic consideration. The authors make extensive use of the rich databases available now to both develop and test the tools they recommend. These applications are eminently capable of practical deployment in day-to-day portfolio management—and I have first-hand experience in their successful utilization.

The symptoms of investor distress provided a natural "to do" list, for which the authors have supplied the remedies. The volatility of individual corporate bonds bore little relation to that suggested by traditional risk measures. The impact of interest rate duration was often surprising. The relationship between the cash markets and derivatives was bent out of shape to the degree that risk-free arbitrage was seemingly on offer. Finally, market liquidity varied widely but uniformly deteriorated. An inability to quantitatively measure trading liquidity had led the industry to ignore this risk dimension with the result that investors were ill-prepared to manage their way through the market volatility. These symptoms were not limited to active portfolio managers. Investors who simply wished to build representative exposure to the asset class were equally challenged.

This book provides practical tools to address these issues and demonstrates new ways to manage well-established strategies in corporate bond markets. Of course, in this era of impaired national balance sheets, credit worthiness is no longer the exclusive preserve of the corporate bond investor. For this reason, the authors explore how sovereign credit risk can be better approached. With the concept of risk-free investing under threat, providing smarter tools for the management of credit risk could not be timelier.

Paul Abberley
Chief Executive
Aviva Investors
London, U.K.

# Introduction

For more than 20 years, the Quantitative Portfolio Strategy Group (QPS) has been a part of Fixed Income Research at Barclays Capital and Lehman Brothers, two dominant providers of bond market indexes and fixed income analytics for institutional investors. Throughout this time, we have been actively involved in all aspects of index design and analytics, and engaged in a frequent dialog with investors benchmarked to both standard and customized indexes as well as managers with pure total return mandates. The benefit of ready access to detailed security-level historical data for index constituent securities has allowed us to address our clients' needs for sensible and implementable solutions to problems arising in managing their portfolios.

Our group's goal since its inception has been to offer objective solutions based on innovative modeling and empirical data analysis. Constant dialog with practitioners from around the globe has kept our research topics firmly grounded in the realities of asset management. In 2007, we published *Quantitative Management of Bond Portfolios* (Princeton University Press) in which we presented some of our most relevant methodologies and findings across a broad spectrum of issues covering portfolio construction, risk management, performance evaluation, and benchmark customization. Since then, the capital markets have suffered the worst calamity since the Great Depression. The tumultuous period of 2007–2009 not only raised many new questions for portfolio managers but also starkly revealed previously overlooked sources of risk and performance. Perhaps most importantly, this period provided quantitative analysts with valuable observations of extreme behavior of fixed income securities. Analysts can now base their studies on a rich historical fixed income data set that includes several "crisis" and "normal" market periods.

In this book, we focus exclusively on management of credit portfolios. Credit portfolio managers traditionally rely on fundamental research for decisions on issuer selection and sector rotation. Quantitative researchers tend to use mathematical techniques for the purpose of pricing and quantifying credit risk. Our research bridges the two approaches. Each chapter in this book is based on questions brought to our attention by credit portfolio managers and reflects our original research aimed at answering them in an objective, quantitative way. Despite our quantitative orientation, we present all our conclusions and recommendations in an intuitive way that is implementable by all credit managers.

The book is structured in two parts. In the first part, we focus on new measures of spread risk, liquidity risk, and Treasury curve risk. We present empirical and theoretical evidence of the benefits these measures offer to portfolio managers compared to established approaches. In the second part, we turn our attention to portfolio management applications of these new risk measures as well as some new ideas for capturing more of the spread premium in credit portfolios. Throughout the book, we maintain a sharp focus on new research results and their practical implications, especially during the 2007–2009 credit crisis, and do not present a complete overview of existing approaches to each topic. Individual chapters, while often cross referenced, were written such that they can be read independently even if this meant some repetition of earlier material.

## PART ONE: MEASURING THE MARKET RISKS OF CORPORATE BONDS

Yields offered to investors holding credit securities compensate them for assuming a variety of different risks together with the complexities of their interdependence. Changes in prices of corporate bonds reflect the impact of the Treasury yield curve movement on the present value of their future cash flows. They also reflect mark-to-market risk resulting from fluctuations in credit spreads to the yield curve (be it Treasury or LIBOR curve) as well as market expectations for "jumps to default" without the interim spread widening. Credit spread fluctuations, in turn, reflect changes in market expectations of future default probabilities and the compensation demanded by credit investors for giving up a certain degree of liquidity. Prices of bonds with embedded options based on call, put, or optional sink provisions are also sensitive to additional factors, such as changes in interest rate volatility.

Established market conventions exist for measuring the sensitivity of corporate bonds to most of these risk factors such as changes in yield curve, spread level, and interest rate volatility. The material in the first part of this book is by no means an overview of these conventions and cannot serve as an introduction to the topic. The issue of interdependence of the risk factors, for example, was addressed in our previous book in the context of the multifactor risk model and is not covered here. Rather, we present some new results and risk measures that we developed to overcome shortcomings of the existing methodologies.

We start by focusing on the behavior of credit spreads and the best approach to capturing a portfolio's exposure to spread changes. Since 2005, we have studied the dynamics of spread change across a broad spectrum of credit asset classes. We found strong empirical evidence that credit spreads do not move in parallel, but rather change in linear proportion to spread levels. In simple terms, when bad news hits a sector, the weakest credits in that sector widen the most. We have shown that while the volatility of absolute spread changes through time is very high, relative spread changes are much more stable, and the difference is at times striking. For instance, while the absolute volatility of the sovereign spread of Greek bonds increased tenfold as a result of the sovereign crisis that started in 2009, the relative spread volatility remained nearly unchanged. Given this evidence, we advocated that a portfolio's sensitivity to spread change should not be expressed simply as contributions to spread duration—a measure of price sensitivity to a parallel shift in spreads—but rather by Duration Times Spread (DTS), representing price sensitivity to a percentage change in spread (Chapters 1 to 4). To demonstrate the out-of-sample predictive power of the DTS approach to forecasting spread changes and managing risk in credit portfolios, we present our empirical findings in each chapter over the time period covered by the original study, rather than update all of the analysis to the present. For instance, we use the spread volatility relationship to spread calibrated to data prior to 2005 from our first DTS study and examine how well it predicted the spread volatility during the 2007–2009 crisis.

The empirical and theoretical support for the DTS approach to credit risk management and its relevance to many portfolio applications (discussed in Part Two) are very compelling. Most of our institutional clients adopted it, benefiting from it greatly, especially during the 2007–2009 crisis. In the DTS framework, a wider spread points to an instantly and proportionally higher spread volatility without the built-in delays of conventional volatility measures based on historical spread variability. As spreads widened rapidly at the start of the 2007–2009 crisis and tightened at its tail end, this instant risk adjustment served investors well in structuring credit portfolios. Practitioners always realized that the spread durations of two portfolios representing the same sector and credit quality cannot be compared if the spreads of their constituent securities are very different. Many investors resorted to empirical beta-adjusted durations obtained by regressing excess returns of a security on the excess return of its peer group—the market. Like any historically based risk measure, these betas are sensitive to the calibration period and adapt slowly to changing markets. We advocate the use of DTS in place of the beta-adjusted spread duration, as we argue that the spread itself is the best beta measure. (This comparison is addressed specifically in Chapter 8.)

We continue by examining a critical source of risk that was often over-looked prior to 2007 but was put front and center in the minds of credit investors by this crisis—liquidity risk. As the crisis unfolded, asset managers approached us with a request to quantify the cost of portfolio liquidation, especially in credit, so their investors could be given advance quantitative guidance as to the liquidity implications of their investment choices. In Chapter 5, we introduce Liquidity Cost Scores (LCS), a security-level numeric measure which represents the cost of a roundtrip transaction in a normal institutional size. LCS is based on bid-offer indications from traders, which have been captured historically as part of the pricing process of Barclays Capital bond market indexes. These quotes cover a significant percentage of securities in the Credit Index. We then calibrate a model to all available quotes and use it to estimate LCS for all non-quoted bonds based on attributes relevant to liquidity. The behavior of LCS through time, cross-sectionally and out-of-sample, strongly suggests that these scores capture market realities. In Chapter 6, we apply this new measure to the task of de-composing credit spreads into liquidity and default components and show the results to be intuitive and informative. We also employ the LCS measure in a variety of portfolio applications discussed in Part Two.

In 2003, we began to investigate the relationship between analytical durations based on theory and empirical durations based on practically observed sensitivities of corporate bonds to Treasury yield curve movement. We have examined this relationship across the spectrum of credit qualities, and through time. Our work focused initially on high-yield bonds. Investors drew our attention to the fact that with high-yield spreads at that time (2002) being historically tight, portfolio managers shouldn't ignore the Treasury durations of this asset class. To understand under what conditions empirical and analytical durations may differ, we first derive in Chapter 7 an explicit theoretical linkage between the two. This linkage suggests that empirical durations depend on the spread level and that they should decline as spreads widen. Indeed, we found that empirical durations of high-yield securities exhibit considerable variation, reaching numbers as high as 40% of the theoretical durations when spreads were at their lows and zero or even negative when high-yield spreads were wide.

We further show that an empirical duration of 25% of the theoretical duration often used by practitioners is, indeed, a good long-term estimate. During the 2007–2009 credit crisis, investment-grade spreads widened beyond levels of high-yield spreads in prior years. Naturally, the question we received from investors was whether at such levels of spread investment grade securities will exhibit the yield curve sensitivity commonly seen for high-yield bonds. Our analysis shows that this was not at all the case. It appeared that investment grade bonds remain highly sensitive to the yield curve movement even at very wide spreads, while high-yield bonds are much less sensitive even at very tight spreads. The second part of Chapter 7 examines several possible explanations for the segmentation and shows that it is not driven by the differences in pricing conventions, liquidity, or bond characteristics of the two markets. Rather, it represents the market reality and an opportunity for investors to exploit it.

## PART TWO: MANAGING CORPORATE BOND PORTFOLIOS

In the second half of the book, we turn our focus to portfolio management issues. We demonstrate how the new risk measures and sensitivities introduced in the first half of the book can be used for constructing, managing, and hedging credit portfolios. This part is structured in three segments, pertaining to the management of spread risk, issuer-specific risk, and liquidity risk.

In the first segment, we apply the concept of DTS introduced in Part One to focus on market risk in a number of portfolio applications. The paradigm shift resulting from the DTS concept has an impact on many decisions for portfolio managers, both in terms of how they manage exposures to systematic risk (industry and quality factors) and their approach to issuer exposures (non-systematic or idiosyncratic risk).

In Chapter 8, we explore the use of DTS in hedging issuer-specific trades. Within the context of long–short pairs trading in the credit default swap (CDS) market, we compare DTS-based hedging with both pure spread duration hedging and with an approach based on empirical betas. We find that the DTS approach is superior at reflecting and neutralizing the systematic spread risk exposures in these trades.

Chapter 9 addresses the use of DTS in risk-neutral positioning of a credit portfolio along the credit curve to maximize carry. For a given DTS, and, consequently, a given level of expected risk (volatility of excess return over duration-matched treasuries), short-dated portfolios offer higher excess returns than long-dated portfolios. Practitioners have long been aware of the superior Sharpe ratios of short-dated corporate bonds. As is often the case with carry trades, the combination of a long position in short-dated corporates and a short position in long-dated corporates generates high information ratios much of the time, but suffers during "tail" events when default expectations rise and the overweight to the short end leads to underperformance.

In Chapter 10, we view the credit crisis of 2007–2009 as a severe out-of-sample test of the DTS model. We revisit the empirical results from Chapter 1 and test how they held up under the extreme stresses of the crisis. We find that the relationship between spread and spread volatility remains strongly linear, albeit with a steeper slope. We show that forward-looking estimates of relative excess return volatility based on DTS (even without updating the spread volatility versus spread slope) were more accurate than those based on absolute spread volatility. In an index replication exercise, we find that matching sector-quality allocations of a credit index in terms of contributions to DTS leads to improved tracking compared with matching the contributions to spread duration. The DTS-based approach to portfolio construction can help to not only replicate an index but also more accurately express active portfolio views. Using DTS to measure spread risk can enhance portfolio risk models in several ways, as discussed at the end of this chapter.

In the second segment of Part Two, we focus on several aspects of optimizing issuer-specific risk in credit portfolios. In Chapter 11, we compare and contrast two different approaches to setting issuer limits. The first is based on an event study of the return implications of an issuer downgrade in the months leading up to it. Observing the severity of the underperformance of a downgraded issuer versus its peers prior to the downgrade helps us derive an optimal position diversification ratio needed to minimize this underperformance. Over the last 20 years, this optimal diversification ratio by the original credit rating changed significantly. In the early 2000s, the return implications of a downgrade were much more severe for issuers initially rated Baa than for those with higher initial ratings. Our study then argued for disproportional diversification of Baa positions and relatively concentrated holdings in issuers rated Aa or A. However, the market experience during the 2007–2009 crisis argues for stricter limits on higher-rated issuers, as a number of financial institutions experienced distress or even default directly from an A rating or better. Instead of relying on historical return data, a second approach to issuer diversification would be to use DTS as the basis for setting position limits. To test this, we use the average DTS of each credit quality bucket to determine its position limit. The diversification ratios by credit quality obtained by this method change over time in a way that is consistent with the results of the first model. We review the relative strengths of the history-based and DTS-based approaches to optimal diversification of issuer-specific risk and recommend using a blend of the two.

Constraints can have a strong influence on the issuer composition of a portfolio. In Chapter 12, we examine the performance implications of certain constraints, often overlooked by investors, embodied in the definition of investment-grade credit benchmarks. Over the past two decades, the excess returns of investment-grade corporate bonds over duration-matched treasuries have been substantially lower than those implied by their spreads at the beginning of the period, adjusted for realized defaults. We find strong empirical evidence that much of the observed underperformance of investment-grade corporate bonds can be traced to the constraints implicit in the index definition. Index rules, like many investment mandates, require the sale of any securities downgraded to high yield. This rule causes the investment-grade index to lock in the loss of value in the downgraded security at the time it experiences strong, transient selling pressure. Many of these securities eventually proceed to recover, but only after they have been sold out of the index. While this effect benefits the high-yield index, especially its Ba segment, the investment-grade index loses as much as half of its excess return due to this forced selling. We show that adopting a "downgrade-tolerant" investment-grade index can nearly double the reported excess return without any observed increase in risk.

In Chapter 13, we focus on the performance of the "fallen angels" and show that they represent an attractive asset class in its own right. We present strong empirical evidence of the transient price pressure experienced by these securities due to forced selling driven by investment constraints. A study of the time course of this effect shows that this price pressure tends to peak about three months after the downgrade. Over a period of one to two years following the downgrade, most securities recover. A simple rules-based strategy of buying fallen angels immediately after the downgrade and holding them long enough to benefit from this recovery generates high risk-adjusted performance, even after transaction costs.

Finally, in the third segment of Part Two, we explore the issue of replicating the credit index with a liquid portfolio of synthetic or cash securities. Synthetic instruments (CDS baskets and interest rate swaps) remained highly liquid through the 2007–2009 crisis, in stark contrast to cash corporates. This created a high and volatile basis risk between the two as the arbitrage relationship broke down due to a lack of financing on the cash side. As a result, synthetic replicating portfolios tracked cash credit indexes very poorly on a monthly basis as the spread of illiquid cash corporate bonds widened to new highs and then tightened when liquidity returned to the market. Synthetic replication remains a viable liquid alternative for long-horizon replication of credit index returns, as the basis between cash and synthetic corporate securities tends to gradually revert to its mean. For investors who need to replicate the index over short horizons, we discuss the very attractive alternative of creating a fully rules-based basket of a small number of corporate bonds. First, we select a universe of very liquid bonds using our LCS measure; weights are then set according to a transparent and replicable stratified sampling scheme that matches the DTS contribution of the index to broad sector-duration cells. We create a family of portfolios—TCX (tradable credit index)—and show that they tracked the index very closely on a monthly basis (even during the 2007–2009 crisis), incurred modest turnover, and kept the credit allocation much more liquid than the index itself without a significant deviation in cumulative performance. With the LCS measure built into the portfolio construction process, credit investing need not automatically mean giving up liquidity.

In conclusion, we would like to stress again that all the new ideas and methodologies discussed in this book were developed as a result of inquiries we received from portfolio managers. We consider it a privilege our team enjoyed for decades to be in constant contact with practitioners and be able to stay abreast of their current issues. We are constantly working on developing further and refining all of the risk measures and frameworks discussed here. Topics we have targeted for further research include the applicability of the DTS framework to additional asset classes, term structure effects in relative spread volatility, and finding the best ways to balance market-driven DTS-based portfolio management with minimizing portfolio turnover. We produce monthly LCS reports to give investors a sense of changes in the liquidity profile of various segments of the global bond market. We are looking for ways to quantify the market impact of trades in addition to quantifying the cost of a "normal" size transaction. We hope that credit market practitioners—portfolio managers and research analysts alike—will find the methodologies outlined in this book useful and relevant to their portfolio management needs. As always, we welcome inquiries and challenges to our work as these discussions help us advance the applicability and rigor of our future research.

# Notes on Terminology

This book is based in large part on empirical studies of global credit markets, and makes extensive use of bond index data from Barclays Capital. To avoid undue repetition in the text and keep the writing simple, the following conventions are followed throughout the book.

## INDEX, PRICING, AND ANALYTICS

All indexes mentioned (e.g., U.S. Corporate Index, Aggregate Index, etc.) are published by Barclays Capital unless otherwise specified. Similarly, all pricing data and the various analytics are based on Barclays Capital index data.

## CREDIT RATINGS

Credit ratings reflect the index methodology for determining a bond's credit rating, which may vary from one market to another and change over time. For U.S. investment-grade credits, in particular, the rules have evolved as follows. Prior to October 2003, the index rating was set equal to Moody's, or the equivalent S&P ranking if Moody's was unavailable. From October 2003 to July 2005, it was the lower of Moody's and S&P. The rule in place since July 2005 uses the middle rating of Moody's, S&P, and Fitch. The index convention, adopted in this book as well, is to use the Moody's nomenclature regardless of the source of the rating. Thus, for example, an index rating of Baa can refer to a Moody's rating of Baa or an S&P rating of BBB.

## EXCESS RETURN

The *excess return* of a bond is defined relative to a hypothetical portfolio of treasury bonds with the same duration exposures along the curve. The precise computational methodology follows index rules, which may vary by currency.

## SPREAD

Unless otherwise indicated, the term *spread* refers to option adjusted spread (OAS) relative to the treasury curve.

# Measuring the Market Risks of Corporate Bonds

# Measuring Spread Sensitivity of Corporate Bonds

## Duration Times Spread (DTS)

The standard presentation of the asset allocation in a portfolio or a benchmark is in terms of percentage of market value. It is widely recognized that this is not sufficient for fixed income portfolios, where differences in duration can cause two portfolios with the same allocation of market weights to have extremely different exposures to macro-level risks. A common approach to structuring a portfolio or comparing it to a benchmark is to partition it in homogeneous market cells comprised of securities with similar characteristics. Many fixed income portfolio managers have become accustomed to expressing their cell allocations in terms of contributions to duration—the product of the percentage of portfolio market value represented by a given market cell and the average duration of securities comprising that cell. This represents the sensitivity of the portfolio to a parallel shift in yields across all securities within this market cell. For credit portfolios, the corresponding measure would be contributions to spread duration, measuring the sensitivity to a parallel shift in spreads. Determining the set of active spread duration bets from different market cells and issuers is one of the primary decisions taken by credit portfolio managers.

Yet all spread durations were not created equal. Just as one could create a portfolio that matches the benchmark exactly by market weights, but clearly takes more credit risk (e.g., by investing in the longest duration credits within each cell), one could match the benchmark exactly by spread duration contributions and still take more credit risk—by choosing the securities with the widest spreads within each cell. These bonds presumably trade wider than their peer groups for a reason—that is, the market consensus has determined that they are more risky—and are often referred to as *high beta*, because their spreads tend to react more strongly than the rest of the market to a systematic shock. Portfolio managers are well aware of this, but many tend to treat it as a secondary issue rather than as an intrinsic part of the allocation process.

To reflect the view that higher spread credits represent greater exposures to systematic risks, we introduce a new risk sensitivity measure that utilizes spreads as a fundamental part of the credit portfolio management process. We represent sector exposures by contributions to *duration times spread* (DTS), computed as the product of market weight, spread duration, and spread. For example, an overweight of 5% to a market cell implemented by purchasing bonds with a spread of 80 basis points (bps) and spread duration of three years would be equivalent to an overweight of 3% using bonds with an average spread of 50 bps and spread duration of eight years.

To understand the intuition behind this new measure, consider the return, $R_{\text{spread}}$, due strictly to change in spread. Let $D$ denote the spread duration of a bond and $s$ its spread; the spread change return is then:[1]

$$R_{\text{spread}} = -D \cdot \Delta s \tag{1.1}$$

Or, equivalently,

$$R_{\text{spread}} = -D \cdot s \cdot \frac{\Delta s}{s} \tag{1.2}$$

That is, just as spread duration is the sensitivity to an absolute change in spread (e.g., spreads widen by 5 bps), DTS ($D \cdot s$) is the sensitivity to a relative change in spread. Note that this notion of relative spread change provides for a formal expression of the idea mentioned earlier—that credits with wider spreads are riskier since they tend to experience greater spread changes.

In the absolute spread change approach shown in equation (1.1), we can see that the volatility of excess returns can be approximated by

$$\sigma_{\text{return}} \cong D \cdot \sigma_{\text{spread}}^{\text{absolute}} \tag{1.3}$$

while in the relative spread change approach of equation (1.2), excess return volatility follows

$$\sigma_{return} \cong D \cdot s \cdot \sigma_{spread}^{relative} \tag{1.4}$$

Given that the two representations above are equivalent, why should one of them be preferable to another?

In this chapter, we provide ample evidence that the advantage of the second approach, based on relative spread changes, is due to the stability of the associated volatility estimates. Using a large sample with over 560,000 observations spanning the period of September 1989 to January 2005, we demonstrate that the volatility of spread changes (both systematic and idiosyncratic) is linearly proportional to spread level.[2] This relation holds for both investment-grade and high-yield credit irrespective of the sector, duration, or time period. Furthermore, these results are not confined to the realm of U.S. corporate bonds, but also extend to other spread asset classes with a significant default risk. The next two chapters, for example, contain similar results for credit default swaps, European corporate and sovereign bonds, and emerging market sovereign debt denominated in U.S. dollars. Indeed, as we show in Chapter 4, even from a theoretical standpoint, structural credit risk models such as Merton (1974) imply a near-linear relationship between spread level and volatility. This explains why relative spread volatilities of spread asset classes are much more stable than absolute spread volatilities, both across different sectors and credit quality tiers, and also over time. In Chapter 10, we present more recent empirical evidence showing the benefits of using DTS during the 2007–2009 credit crisis.

The paradigm shift we advocate has many implications for portfolio managers, both in terms of the way they manage exposures to industry and quality factors (systematic risk) and in terms of their approach to issuer exposures (non-systematic risk). Throughout the chapter, we present evidence that the relative spread change approach offers increased insight into both of these sources of risk. Furthermore, in Chapter 5, we also show that DTS is an important determinant of corporate bond liquidity.

## ANALYSIS OF CORPORATE BOND SPREAD BEHAVIOR

How should the risk associated with a particular market sector be measured? Typically, for lack of any better estimator, the historical return volatility of a particular sector over some prior time period is used to forecast its volatility for the coming period.[3] For this approach to be reliable, these volatilities have to be fairly stable. Unfortunately, this is not always the case.

As an example, Figure 1.1 shows the 36-month trailing volatility of spread changes for various credit ratings comprising the U.S. Corporate Index between September 1989 and January 2005. It is clear from the chart that spread volatility decreased substantially until 1998 and then increased significantly from 1998 through 2005. The dramatic rise in spread volatility since 1998 was only a partial response to the Russian Crisis and the

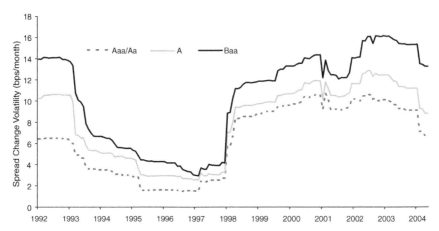

**FIGURE 1.1**   Spread Change Volatility by Credit Rating (trailing 36 months;
September 1989–January 2005)
*Source:* Barclays Capital.

Long-Term Capital Management debacle as volatility did not revert to its
pre-1998 level.

If the investment-grade corporate universe is partitioned by spread levels, we find that the volatilities of the resulting spread buckets are considerably more stable, as seen in Figure 1.2. After an initial shock in 1998,

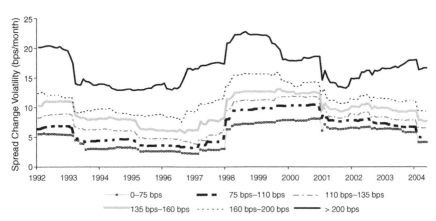

**FIGURE 1.2**   Spread Change Volatility by Spread Range (trailing 36 months;
September 1989–January 2005)
*Source:* Barclays Capital.

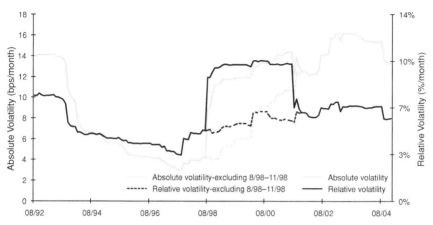

**FIGURE 1.3** Absolute and Relative Spread Change Volatility of Baa-Rated Bonds (trailing 36 months)
*Source:* Barclays Capital.

the volatilities within each spread bucket revert almost exactly to their pre-1998 level (beginning in August 2001, exactly 36 months after the Russian crisis occurred). In this respect, one could relate the results of Figure 1.1 to an increase in spreads—both across the market and within each quality group.

As suggested by equation (1.4), a potential remedy to the volatility instability problem is to approximate the absolute spread volatility (bps/month) by multiplying the historically observed relative spread volatility (%/month) by the current spread (bps). This improves the estimate if relative spread volatility is more stable than absolute spread volatility. The results in Figure 1.2 point in this direction and indicate a relationship between spread level and volatility.

Figure 1.3 plots side-by-side the volatility of absolute and relative spread changes of the Corporate Baa index (relative spread changes are calculated simply as the ratio of spread change to the beginning of month spread level). The comparison illustrates that a modest stability advantage is gained by measuring volatility of relative spread changes; however, the improvement is not as great as we might have hoped, and the figure seems to show that even relative spread changes are quite unstable. This apparent instability, however, is only due to the dramatic events that took place in the second half of 1998. When we recompute the two time series excluding the four observations representing the period of August 1998 to November 1998, the difference between the modified time series is striking. From a low of

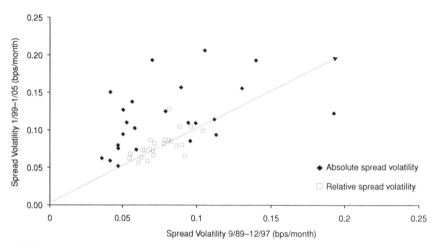

**FIGURE 1.4** Absolute and Relative Spread Change Volatility before and
after 1998
*Notes:* Based on a partition of the U.S. Corporate Index, 8 sectors × 3 credit
ratings. To enable the two to be shown on the same set of axes, both absolute and
relative spread volatility are expressed in units with similar magnitudes. However,
the interpretation is different: An absolute spread change of 0.1 represents a 10 bps
parallel shift across a sector, while a relative spread change of 0.1 means that all
spreads in the sector move by 10% of their current values (e.g. from 50 to 55, from
200 to 220).
*Source:* Barclays Capital.

3 bps/month in mid-1997, absolute spread volatility increases steadily
through a high of 16 bps/month in 2002–2003, growing by a factor of
five. In contrast, relative spread volatility increases more modestly over the
same time period, from 3%/month to 7%/month.

Another demonstration of the enhanced stability of relative spread
changes is seen when comparing the volatilities of various market segments
over distinct time periods. We have already identified 1998 as a critical turn-
ing point for the credit markets, due to the combined effect of the Russian
default and the Long-Term Capital Management crisis. To what extent is
volatility information prior to 1998 relevant in the post-1998 period?

Figure 1.4 depicts two different measures of volatility based on absolute
and relative spread volatilities over two distinct periods: pre-1998 (x-axis)
and 1999 to 2005 (y-axis). The Corporate Index is divided into a 24-cell
partition (8 sectors by 3 credit qualities), and each observation shown on
the graph represents a particular sector-quality combination.[4] Points along
the diagonal line reflect identical volatilities in both time periods.

Two clear phenomena can be observed here. First, most of the observations representing absolute spread volatilities are located far above the diagonal, pointing to an increase in volatility in the second period of the sample despite the fact that the events of 1998 are not reflected in the data. In contrast, relative spread volatilities are quite stable, with almost all observations located on the 45-degree line or very close to it. This is because the pick-up in volatility in the second period was accompanied by a similar increase in spreads. Second, the relative spread volatilities of various sectors are quite tightly clustered, ranging from 5% to a bit over 10%, whereas the range of absolute volatilities is much wider, ranging from 5 bps/month to more than 20 bps/month.

These results clearly indicate that absolute spread volatility is highly unstable and tends to rise with increasing spread. Computing volatilities based on relative spread change generates a more stable time series. These findings have important implications for the appropriate way of measuring excess return volatility and demonstrate the need to better understand the behavior of spread changes.

To analyze the behavior of spread changes, we first examine the dynamics of month-to-month changes in spreads of individual bonds. When spreads widen or tighten across a sector, do they tend to follow a pattern of parallel shift or one in which spread changes are proportional to spread levels? The answer to this question should determine how we measure exposures to systematic spread changes.

As a next step, we look at systematic spread volatility. If spreads change in a relative fashion then the volatility of systematic spread changes across a given sector of the market should be proportional to the average spread of that sector. This is true when comparing the risk of different sectors at a given point in time, or when examining the volatility of a given sector at different points in time.

To complete our analysis, we also examine issuer-specific (or idiosyncratic) spread volatility. Does the dispersion of spread changes among the various issuers within a given market cell, or the extent by which the spread changes of individual issuers can deviate from those of the rest of the sector, also tend to be proportional to spread?

We investigate each of these issues using historical data underlying the U.S. Corporate Index spanning more than 15 years, from September 1989 through January 2005. The data set contains monthly spreads, spread changes, durations, and excess returns for all constituents of the Corporate Index. For the sections of our analysis that also include high-yield bonds, we augment the data set with historical data from the U.S. High Yield Index. A more detailed description of the data set can be found in the appendix at the end of this chapter.

## The Dynamics of Spread Change

In order to understand why absolute spread volatility is so unstable, we first need to examine at a more fundamental level how spreads of individual securities change in a given month. One basic formulation of the change in spread of some bond $i$ at time $t$ is that the overall change is simply the sum of two parts, that is, systematic and idiosyncratic:

$$\Delta s_{i,t} = \Delta s_{J,t} + \Delta s_{i,t}^{idiosyncratic}; i \in J \tag{1.5}$$

where $J$ denotes some peer group of bonds with similar risk characteristics (e.g., Financials rated Baa with duration of up to five years). This formulation is equivalent to assuming that spreads change in a parallel fashion across all securities in a given market cell $J$ (captured by $\Delta s_{J,t}$). Alternatively, if changes in spreads are proportional to spread level then we have (omitting the subscript $t$ for simplicity):

$$\frac{\Delta s_i}{s_i} = \frac{\Delta s_J}{s_J} + \frac{\Delta s_i^{idiosyncratic}}{s_i}$$

or

$$\Delta s_i = s_i \cdot \frac{\Delta s_J}{s_J} + \Delta s_i^{idiosyncratic} \tag{1.6}$$

Equation (1.6) reflects the idea that systematic spread changes are proportional to the current (systematic) spread level and that the sensitivity of each security to a systematic spread change depends on its level of spread. Higher-spread securities are riskier in that they are affected more by a widening, or tightening, of spreads relative to lower-spread securities with similar characteristics.

In order to analyze the behavior of spread changes across different periods and market segments, we use equations (1.5) and (1.6) as the basis of two regression models. The first model corresponds to the parallel shift approach shown in equation (1.5):

$$\Delta s_i = \alpha + \varepsilon_i \tag{1.7}$$

The second model reflects the notion of a proportional shift in spreads as in equation (1.6):

$$\Delta s_i = \beta \cdot s_i + \varepsilon_i \tag{1.8}$$

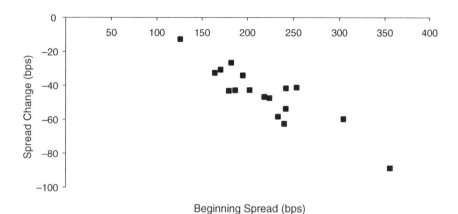

**FIGURE 1.5** Average Spreads and Spread Changes for Key Issuers in the Communications Sector (January 2001)
*Source:* Barclays Capital.

Comparing equation (1.8) to (1.6) reveals that the slope coefficient $\beta$ that we estimate using data from a given sector $J$ corresponds to the proportional systematic spread change $\Delta s_J / s_J$. These two models are nested in a more general model that allows for both proportional and parallel spread changes to take place simultaneously:

$$\Delta s_i = \alpha + \beta \cdot s_i + \varepsilon_i \qquad (1.9)$$

Before we proceed with a full-scale estimation of the three models, we illustrate the idea with a specific example. Figure 1.5 shows changes in spreads experienced by key issuers that were part of the Communications sector of the Corporate Index from their beginning-of-month spreads in January 2001.[5] It is clear that this sector-wide rally was not characterized by a purely parallel shift; rather issuers with wider spreads tightened by more.

Table 1.1 reports the regression results when the three general models of spread change are fitted to the data in this specific example. The results verify that spreads in the Communication sector in January 2001 changed in a proportional fashion. The slope estimate is highly significant and the high $R^2$ (97.1%) indicates that the model fit the data well.[6] The combined model, which allows for a simultaneous parallel shift, achieves only a slightly better fit (97.7%) and yields a somewhat unintuitive result: It shows that the sector widens by a parallel shift of 16 bps and simultaneously tightens by a relative spread change of –28%. We therefore estimate a fourth model, which is

**TABLE 1.1** Regression Estimates of Various Models of Spread Change

| | | Coefficients | | t-statistics | | $R^2$ | |
|---|---|---|---|---|---|---|---|
| Model | Equation | Shift (bps) | Slope (%) | Shift | Slope | Jan-01 | Aggregate |
| Parallel | 1.7 | −45 | | −10.9 | | 88.2% | 16.9% |
| Relative | 1.8 | | −21% | | −23.2 | 97.1% | 33.0% |
| Combined | 1.9 | 16 | −28% | 2.0 | −7.9 | 97.7% | 35.2% |
| Combined with normalized spread | 1.10 | −45 | −28% | −24.1 | −7.9 | 97.7% | 35.2% |

*Note:* Based on data for large issuers in the Communication sector of the Corporate Index, as of January 2001. The $R^2$ values reported in the last column are based on 1,480 individual regressions (185 months × 8 sectors).
*Source:* Barclays Capital.

essentially a variant of the "combined" model:

$$\Delta s_i = \bar{\alpha} + \beta \cdot (s_i - \bar{s}) + \varepsilon_i \qquad (1.10)$$

Normalizing spreads by subtracting the average spread level in equation (1.10) yields identical slope coefficients and $R^2$ to those generated by the "combined model," but now the intercept $\bar{\alpha}$ represents the average spread change in the sample. This model expresses the month's events as a parallel tightening of 45 bps coupled by an additional relative shift, with a slope of −28%, that captures how much more spreads move for issuers with above-average spreads, and how much less they move for issuers with below-average spreads.

We conduct a similar analysis to the one presented in Table 1.1 using individual bond data in all eight sectors and 185 months included in the sample. Our hypothesis that the relative model provides in general an accurate description of the dynamic of spread changes has several testable implications. First, the aggregate $R^2$ for the relative model should be significantly better than that of the parallel model, and almost as good as that of the combined model. Second, we would like to find that the slope factor is statistically significant (as indicated by the t-statistic) in most months and sectors. Third, the realizations of the slope and the parallel shift factor in the combined model with normalized spread should be in the same direction, especially whenever the market experiences a large move. That is, in all significant spread changes, issues with wider spreads experience larger moves in the same direction.

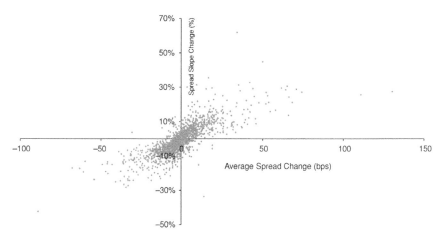

**FIGURE 1.6**   Regression Coefficients for Shift and Slope Factors
*Source:* Barclays Capital.

We find support for all three implications. The last column of Table 1.1 reports the aggregate $R^2$ for these regressions across all sectors and months. The relative model explains twice the variation in spreads (33%) as the parallel shift model (16.9%) and almost as much as the less restrictive combined model. The fact that only about a third of spread movements are explained is due to the fact that, in many months, there is little systematic change in spreads, and spread changes are largely idiosyncratic. Still, the slope factor was statistically significant 73% of the time.

Figure 1.6 shows that large spread changes are accompanied by slope changes in the same direction (the correlation between the two is 80%). Rising spread curves tend to steepen and tightening spread curves tend to flatten. That is because bonds that trade at wider spreads will widen by more in a sell-off and tighten by more in a rally. There are essentially no examples of large parallel spread movements in which the slope factor moves in the opposite direction. This clear linear relationship between the shift and slope factors serves as an additional validation of the relative model.

## Systematic Spread Volatility

The security-level analysis established that systematic changes in spreads are proportional to the systematic level of spread, consistent with equation (1.6). We now proceed to examine the relation between systematic spread volatility and the level of spreads. To do this, we would like to partition our data set by spread level, separately measure the volatility of each spread bucket, and examine the relationship between spread level and spread volatility.

However, the nature of the data set presents several challenges. First, it is far from homogeneous—it contains bonds from different industries, credit qualities, and maturities. Second, the spreads of corporate bonds have changed quite substantially during the course of the period studied, so that the populations of any fixed spread buckets vary substantially from one time period to another. Our goal was to design a partition fine enough that the bonds in each cell share similar risk characteristics, yet coarse enough so that our cells are sufficiently well populated to give statistically meaningful results.

We first partition the Corporate Index rather coarsely by sector (financials, industrials, and utilities) and duration (short, medium, and long). To ensure that every sector-duration cell is well-populated each month, we do not use prespecified duration levels but rather divide each sector into three equally populated duration groups.[7] In the last step, bonds in each sector-duration cell are assigned to one of several buckets based on spread level. To allow a detailed partitioning of the entire spread range, while minimizing the number of months where a bucket is sparsely populated, the spread breakpoints differ from sector to sector. In addition, the financial and industrial sectors are divided into six spread buckets whereas the utilities sector has only five spread buckets (a more detailed description of the partition and sample population can be found in this chapter's appendix).

The systematic spread change in cell $J$ in month $t$ can be represented simply as the average spread change across all bonds in that bucket in month $t$. Therefore, for each of the cells in the partition, we compute every month the median spread, the average spread change, and the cross-sectional standard deviation of spread change. This procedure produces 51 distinct time series data sets; each consists of a fairly homogeneous set of bonds for which we have monthly spreads and spread changes. We then calculate the time series volatility of these systematic spread changes.[8] Similarly, the spread level for bucket $J$ is calculated as the time series average of the monthly median spread (rather than the average spread).

The relation between the volatility of systematic spread changes and spread level is plotted in Figure 1.7, where each observation represents one of the 51 buckets in the partition. The chart illustrates a clear relationship between spread volatility and spread level. Higher spreads are accompanied by higher volatilities for all sector-duration cells. Relatively minor differences can be seen between industrials and the other two broad sectors. Similarly, duration does not seem to have any significant systematic effect on the results.[9]

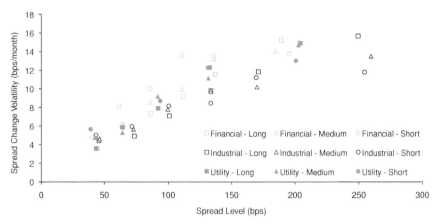

**FIGURE 1.7** Time Series Volatility of Systematic Spread Changes versus Spread Level (September 1989–January 2005)
*Source:* Barclays Capital.

Nonetheless, the results shown in Figure 1.7 do not perfectly corroborate our hypothesis of proportional spread volatility, which would predict that all of our observations (or at least all observations within a given sector) should lie along a diagonal line that passes through the origin of the form:

$$\sigma_{\text{spread}}^{\text{absolute}}(s) \cong \theta \cdot s \qquad (1.11)$$

While the points at the left side of Figure 1.7 seem to fit this description, the points to the right, representing higher spread levels, do not seem to continue along this line. Rather, volatility seems to flatten out beyond the 200 to 250 bps range. Is it possible that spread volatility does not continue to grow linearly when spreads increase beyond a certain point?

Before we reject our hypothesis, one may question the significance of these few highest-spread observations. In most time periods, the 250 to 300 bps spread region represents the boundary between investment-grade and high-yield bonds. For a good part of the time period of our study, these spread cells are very lightly populated by our investment-grade bond sample. Due to our policy of excluding any month when a cell has less than 20 bonds, the summary results for these cells may be less robust than desired.

To examine the relation between systematic spread change volatility and spread level beyond the 250 bps level, we repeat the analysis including all bonds rated Ba and B. This increases the sample size by roughly 35%

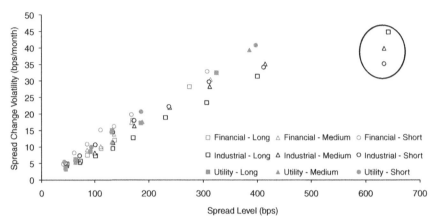

**FIGURE 1.8**   Systematic Spread Volatility versus Spread Level (Investment-Grade + High-Yield bonds)
*Note:* Based on monthly observations for all bonds rated Aaa to B (September 1989–January 2005).
*Source:* Barclays Capital.

to 565,602 observations. We employ the same Sector × Duration × Spread partition, with the addition of several spread buckets to accommodate the widening of the spread range (the number of cells increases to 66).

Figure 1.8 plots the relationship between systematic spread volatility and spread level using both investment-grade and high-yield data. The linear relationship between the two now extends out through spreads of 400 bps. As before, the three observations that represent the highest spread bucket in industrials (circled) have somewhat lower than expected spread volatility. The statistical relevance of these most extreme data points is highly questionable.

The simple linear model of equation (1.11) provides an excellent fit to the data, with $\theta$ equal to 9.1% if we use all observations or 9.4% if we exclude the three circled outliers. Hence, the results suggest that the historical volatility of systematic spread movements can be expressed quite compactly, with only minor dependence on sector or maturity, in terms of a relative spread change volatility of about 9% per month. That is, spread volatility for a market segment trading at 50 bps should be about 4.5 bps/month, while that of a market segment at 200 bps should be about 18 bps/month.

### Idiosyncratic Spread Volatility

To study the spread dependence of idiosyncratic spread volatility, we employ the same partition we used for the study of systematic spread volatility.

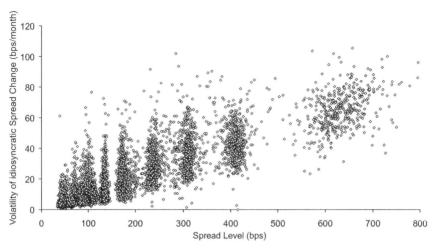

**FIGURE 1.9** Volatility of Idiosyncratic Spread Change versus Spread Level
*Note:* Monthly calculations (September 1989–January 2005) using all bonds rated
Aaa to B; computed separately by sector, duration, and spread bucket (N = 7,250).
*Source:* Barclays Capital.

Instead of the average spread change experienced within a given cell in a
given month, we examine the dispersion of spread changes within each cell.

The idiosyncratic spread change of bond $i$ in market cell $J$ at time $t$ is
defined as the difference between its spread change and the average spread
change for the cell in that month:

$$\Delta s_{i,t}^{\text{idiosyncratic}} = \Delta s_{i,t} - \Delta s_{J,t} \qquad (1.12)$$

The volatility of idiosyncratic spread changes is then exactly equal to
the cross sectional standard deviation of total spread changes.[10] Figure 1.9
shows a scatter plot of the cross-sectional volatility from all months and
spread buckets including high-yield bonds. This plot clearly shows the general pattern of volatilities increasing with spread, as well as the relative
paucity of data at the higher spread levels.

To obtain a single measure of idiosyncratic spread volatility for each
bucket, we pool all observations of idiosyncratic risk within a given market
cell $J$ over all bonds and all months, and compute the standard deviation.
This pooled measure of idiosyncratic spread volatility per market cell is
plotted in Figure 1.10 against the median spread of the cell.

The linear relationship between spread and spread volatility is strikingly
clear. Observations that represent buckets populated almost exclusively by

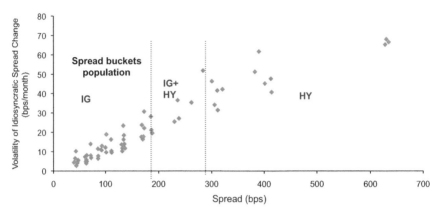

**FIGURE 1.10** Pooled Idiosyncratic Spread Volatility versus Spread Level
*Note:* Each observation represents the standard deviation of idiosyncratic spread changes aggregated across all sample months separately by sector, duration, and spread bucket for all bonds rated Aaa to B (September 1989–January 2005).
*Source:* Barclays Capital.

high-yield bonds exhibit more variation than those representing investment-grade bonds, but follow the exact same pattern. The regression results indicate a zero intercept, but the estimated slope coefficient (the relative volatility of idiosyncratic yield change) is somewhat larger than estimated previously, 11.5% versus 9.1%.

## Stability of Spread Behavior

We have established that spread volatility is linearly proportional to the level of spread. We now investigate the magnitude of time variation in the spread slope or the change in spread volatility as spreads vary.

For each bucket, we compute the yearly systematic spread volatility and corresponding average spread level (i.e., using 12 months of average spread change).[11] We then regress these estimates of systematic spread volatility against an intercept and a spread slope factor. We follow the same approach for idiosyncratic spread volatility except that we use the monthly cross-sectional volatility estimates.

Figure 1.11 presents the yearly spread slope estimates and corresponding adjusted $R^2$. The results are plotted two ways, using only investment-grade credit, or including high-yield securities as well. The estimated coefficients are all highly significant, with $t$-statistics ranging between 15 and 30 for both systematic and idiosyncratic spread volatility. Not surprisingly,

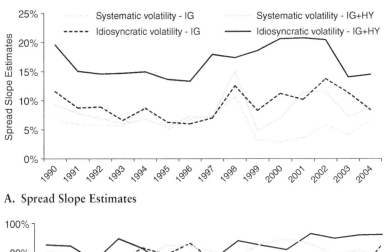

**A. Spread Slope Estimates**

**B.** *R*-squared

**FIGURE 1.11** Yearly Regression of Spread Volatility against Spread Level
*Source:* Barclays Capital.

Figure 1.11(A) reveals that including high-yield data generally increases the spread slope estimate for both systematic and idiosyncratic volatility. The spike in volatility caused by the 1998 Russian crisis is evident in the large estimate of spread slope in 1998 (except for the case of idiosyncratic volatility with high-yield). Excluding 1998, the spread slope estimates are remarkably stable in light of the small number of months used in each estimation.

Figure 1.11(B) reveals that the explanatory power of the regressions is higher and more stable when high-yield securities are included. When we analyze investment-grade data only, the $R^2$ of our regressions goes as low as 40% for systematic volatility and 30% for idiosyncratic volatility. When we include high-yield data as well, the regression $R^2$ values are consistently over 70% for systematic volatility and 60% for idiosyncratic volatility.

Overall, this pattern confirms that relative spread changes characterize both investment-grade and high-yield credit.

## A NEW MEASURE OF EXCESS RETURN VOLATILITY

What are the implications of spread proportionality? Which measure is more appropriate for representing the risk of credit securities, DTS or spread duration? In this section, we demonstrate that excess return volatility increases linearly with DTS, consistent with the formulation in equation (1.4). Furthermore, portfolios with very different spreads and spread durations but with similar DTS exhibit the same excess return volatility. For example, a portfolio with a weighted spread of 200 bps and spread duration of two years is equally risky as a portfolio with a spread of 100 bps and spread duration of four years. We also show that using DTS generates improved estimates of future excess return volatility when compared with those calculated by simply employing spread duration.

### DTS, Spread Duration, and Excess Returns

If the volatility of both systematic and idiosyncratic spread changes is proportional to the level of spread, then the volatility of excess returns should be linearly related to DTS, with the proportionality factor equal to the volatility of relative spread changes over the corresponding period (see equation 1.4).

To examine this prediction, each month bonds are assigned to quintiles based on their DTS value. Each of these quintiles is further subdivided into six buckets based on spread. Every month the average excess returns and median DTS are calculated, and then the time series volatility of excess returns and average DTS is calculated separately for each bucket. This formulation yields two empirical predictions:

> Prediction 1: Excess return volatility should increase linearly with DTS, where the ratio of the two (or slope) represents the volatility of relative spread changes we previously estimated.
>
> Prediction 2: The level of excess return volatility should be approximately equal across portfolios with similar DTS values.

The results of the analysis, presented in Figure 1.12, strongly support both empirical predictions despite the fact that we do not control for industry, quality, maturity, or any other effect.

First, it is clear that excess return volatility increases with the level of DTS and that a straight line through the origin provides an excellent fit.

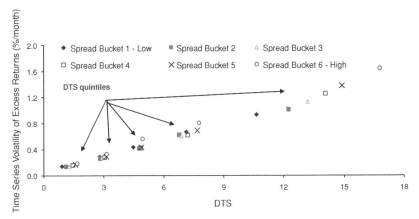

**FIGURE 1.12**   Excess Return Volatility vs. DTS
*Note:* Bonds in the U.S. Corporate Index are assigned monthly (September 1989–January 2005) to DTS quintiles and then further divided to six buckets by spread level.
*Source:* Barclays Capital.

This is indeed confirmed by a regression of the excess return volatility on average DTS, which finds a fit of 98% and an insignificant intercept. The slope estimate is 8.8%, which is in line with the estimated slope from the analysis of systematic spread volatility. Second, consistent with prediction 2, observations representing the same DTS quintile but with differing spread levels exhibit very similar excess return volatilities. The one exception to this is in the highest DTS quintile, where the subdivision by spread causes wide variations in DTS as well. As a result, the points no longer form a tight cluster; however, they continue to follow the same general relationship between DTS and volatility.

To fully appreciate the significance of the second result, Table 1.2 reports the average spread and spread duration for each of the 30 buckets. The table illustrates the extent of the differences among the spreads and corresponding spread durations of buckets with almost identical DTS. For example, the top and bottom spread buckets within the second DTS quintile (shown in bold) exhibit almost identical DTS values of 299 and 320, respectively. Yet they have very different spread and spread duration characteristics: bonds comprising the top bucket have average spread duration of 5.48 and trade at a spread of 54 bps, while bonds in the bottom cell have spread duration of 2.53 and a spread of 127 bps. Hence, a portfolio of high-spread bonds with short duration can be as risky as a portfolio comprised of low-spread bonds with high duration as long as they both have roughly the same DTS.[12]

**TABLE 1.2**   Summary Statistics by DTS and Spread Buckets

A. Spread

| | DTS Buckets | | | | |
|---|---|---|---|---|---|
| Spread Sub-Buckets | Low | 2 | 3 | 4 | High |
| Low | 41 | **54** | 64 | 77 | 97 |
| 2 | 52 | 68 | 79 | 94 | 116 |
| 3 | 60 | 78 | 88 | 106 | 135 |
| 4 | 69 | 87 | 98 | 118 | 156 |
| 5 | 79 | 99 | 112 | 135 | 184 |
| High | 100 | **127** | 143 | 172 | 246 |

B. Spread Duration

| | DTS Buckets | | | | |
|---|---|---|---|---|---|
| Spread Sub-Buckets | Low | 2 | 3 | 4 | High |
| Low | 2.38 | **5.48** | 7.20 | 9.53 | 11.15 |
| 2 | 2.19 | 4.24 | 6.12 | 7.17 | 10.62 |
| 3 | 2.17 | 3.80 | 5.50 | 6.51 | 9.78 |
| 4 | 2.17 | 3.54 | 4.96 | 6.09 | 9.09 |
| 5 | 2.09 | 3.25 | 4.43 | 5.72 | 8.23 |
| High | 1.65 | **2.53** | 3.52 | 4.53 | 6.91 |

*Source:* Barclays Capital.

## A Comparison of Excess Return Volatility Forecasts

A natural step to extend our analysis is to examine which approach provides a better forecast of the excess return volatility of a portfolio:

> Approach 1: Spread Duration × Historical volatility of absolute spread change.
>
> Approach 2: DTS × Historical volatility of relative spread change.

To directly compare the forecasting accuracy of the two measures, we compute the monthly realized excess return of each of the 24 buckets in the partition of the Corporate Index described earlier. The carry component (spread/12) is stripped from the realized excess return, and the random part is then divided by one of the two forecasts of excess return volatility.[13] If the projected excess return volatility is an unbiased estimate of the "true" volatility, then the time series volatility of these standardized excess return realizations should be very close to one.

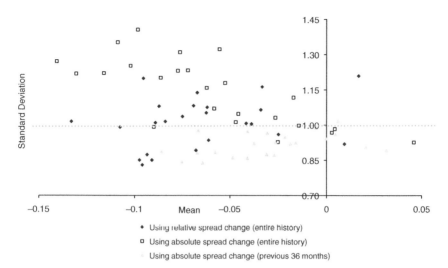

**FIGURE 1.13** Mean and Standard Deviation of Normalized Excess Return Realizations
*Note:* Conditional volatility estimates are computed monthly by sector and credit quality based on the entire available history or previous 36 months; using monthly spread change observations (September 1989–January 2005).
*Source:* Barclays Capital.

Our premise is that the approach based on relative spread change volatility should give a more timely risk projection since it can react almost instantaneously to a change in market conditions. Any spread widening will immediately flow through the DTS into the projection of excess return volatility. Hence, we expect the sample time series standard deviation of excess returns to be closer to one when using approach 2 than when using approach 1. A volatility measure that adjusts more quickly for changing market conditions should also generate less extreme realizations (i.e., realizations that fall above/below two or three standard deviations) relative to a measure that is slower to react.

Figure 1.13 displays the mean and standard deviation of the time series of normalized residuals separately for each volatility measure (each observation represents one of the 24 buckets). The volatilities used to calculate these normalized residuals are based on the entire history of returns that is available at the beginning of each month. For approach 1, Figure 1.13 also shows the results obtained if the absolute spread change volatility is calculated over only the previous 36 months. This corresponds to the approach taken by many investors in periods of exceptionally low or high volatility, namely to rely only on recent data.

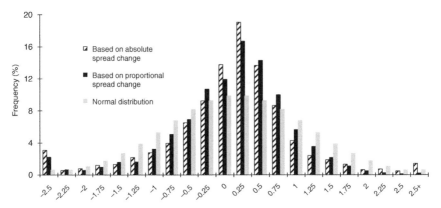

**FIGURE 1.14** Distribution of Standardized Excess Returns
*Note:* Based on observations (September 1992–January 2005) grouped across all sectors and credit ratings.
*Source:* Barclays Capital.

Comparing the three sets of observations reveals that using absolute spread changes produces downward (upward) biased estimates of volatility when using the entire available history (previous 36 months). As a result the average standard deviation of normalized excess returns using the entire and partial history is above and below one (1.14 and 0.92 respectively). In contrast, the observations generated using relative spread changes are evenly spread around one and the average standard deviation of standardized excess returns is 1.01. A close examination of the results does not suggest any relation between the deviation from one and the sector-quality bucket.

The findings in Figure 1.13 support our first empirical prediction. Excess return volatility estimates based on absolute spread changes are very sensitive to the length of the estimation period: They may overreact when using too few data points and can be slow to adjust when using a long history. What is the optimal estimation period is not clear ex ante when using absolute spread changes. In contrast, a longer estimation period is always desired when using proportional spread changes since it improves the accuracy of the proportionality factor, while at the same time the volatility estimate adjusts instantaneously because of the multiplication by the current spread level.[14]

The second empirical prediction states that the percentage of extreme realizations (positive or negative) should be lower when using relative rather than absolute spread change volatility. Figure 1.14 plots a histogram of the standardized excess return realizations for all sector-quality cells based on the two volatility measures. For comparison, the standard normal distribution is also displayed.

Not surprisingly, the histogram reveals that both volatility estimators generate distributions that are negatively skewed (–2.67 and –1.35 using the relative and absolute spread change based volatility measures). With respect to the percentage of outliers, 7.06% of the observations in the distribution based on absolute spread changes are located beyond two standard deviations from the mean. In the case of the distribution based on relative spread changes, the same figure is almost half, at 4.03%.

## REFINEMENTS AND FURTHER TESTS

### Spread Volatility as Spreads Approach Zero

What do our findings imply regarding the level of spread volatility as spreads approach zero? Taking our results at face value suggests that there is no lower bound for volatility and that spread volatility should decline to almost zero for very low-spread securities. Spread volatility, however, is not driven solely by changes in credit risk but also by non credit-risk based factors. Non credit-risk based spread changes can result from "noise" (e.g., pricing errors), technical demand/supply imbalances (for example, when securities enter/exit the Corporate Index), and other factors.

Spread volatility (systematic or idiosyncratic) can therefore be represented as the sum of two terms: one term that represents spread volatility due to changes in credit risk (which may be approximated by a linear function of spread) and a constant term that reflects spread volatility from all other sources, as follows:

$$\sigma(\Delta s) = \sqrt{\theta^2 \cdot s^2 + \sigma^2_{\text{noncreditrisk}}} \qquad (1.13)$$

Equation (1.13) makes it clear that for sufficiently high spreads, the first term dominates the second, and spread volatility can be well approximated by a linear function of spread, as we find for corporate bonds. As spreads tighten and approach zero, the second term dominates, and spread volatility should converge to some minimum "structural" level.

Agency debentures used to provide a natural framework to examine the behavior of spread volatility for very low spreads. Because market perception during the sample period saw the three main agencies as fully backed by the U.S. government, their debentures typically traded at very low spreads. Between September 1989 and April 2005, the median spread at which agencies traded ranged between 20 and 50 bps except for a few distinct months. We employ the same approach as we did for corporates: Each month, bonds are partitioned based on beginning-of-month spread level. Average spread

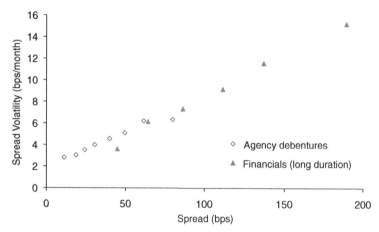

**FIGURE 1.15** Systematic Spread Volatility versus Spread Level of U.S. Agencies (September 1989–April 2005)
*Note:* Based on all Aaa-rated, non-callable debentures comprising the U.S. Agency Index.
*Source:* Barclays Capital.

change and median spread level are computed separately for each bucket. We then examine the relation between the time series volatility and average (median) spread level of each bucket.

The sample spans roughly the same time period as for corporates (September 1989 to April 2005) and includes all rated Aaa, non-callable debentures from the U.S. Agency Index.[15] As before, extreme observations (which reside in either the top or bottom percentile of the spread distribution) are discarded. Since the total number of observations (73,000) is about 17% of the corporate sample size, we use only eight spread buckets. The results are presented in Figure 1.15 alongside the results for long-duration financials computed earlier for comparison purposes. (We could as well compare the Agency results to any of the asset classes shown in Figure 1.7; the subjective choice of long-duration financials reflects the perceived similarity between Agencies and financials and the relatively long average maturity of non-callable Agency debentures.)

The plot in Figure 1.15 illustrates that spread volatility is roughly constant for spreads below 20 bps, and the level of "structural" systematic volatility is about 2.5 to 3.0 bps per month. Above 20 bps, the relation takes the usual linear shape and fits nicely with that of Long Financials. A regression of spread volatility against spread level reveals a flatter slope than we estimated for corporates (5.7% versus 9%), consistent with equation (1.13).[16] An analysis of idiosyncratic volatility indicates in a similar fashion

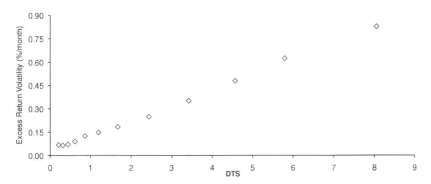

**FIGURE 1.16**   Excess Return Volatility vs. DTS
*Note:* Based on all Aaa-rated, non-callable debentures comprising the U.S.
Agency Index between September 1989 and April 2005. Bonds are assigned to
one of 12 buckets based on DTS.
*Source:* Barclays Capital.

that volatility increases moderately as spreads increase from 20 bps to 80 bps
and indicates a "structural" volatility level of 4.0 to 4.5 bps/month. The fact
that idiosyncratic "structural" volatility is higher than the corresponding systematic level is to be expected, as pricing noise should be more pronounced
for individual securities.

To complete the analysis, the sample is partitioned into 12 DTS buckets
and the excess return volatility of each bucket is plotted against its DTS
(Figure 1.16). Similar to corporate bonds, excess return volatility increases
linearly with DTS (the estimated slope from the regression is 9.8%, versus
8.8% for corporates). As the DTS approaches zero, however, there is a clear
flattening of the relation, and volatility does not decline further. Indeed, the
regression yields a significant intercept of 3 bps, which is consistent with our
previous estimate for the "structural" level of systemic volatility.

## DTS across Seniority Classes

Probably one of the most convincing pieces of evidence in support of the DTS
concept was the fact that portfolios that are remarkably different in terms of
their spread and spread duration, but where the product of the two (DTS)
is similar, exhibit the same excess return volatility. Underpinning this result
is the issue of whether credit risk is fully captured by spreads. If spreads
incorporate on average all publicly available information related to credit
risk, then all portfolios with similar DTS should have the same level of excess
return volatility. We re-examine this issue in the context of debt seniority
by looking at portfolios comprising bonds from different seniority classes

(e.g., senior notes, debentures, etc.), but with a very similar DTS. If spreads already incorporate the likelihood of default and the recovery value in such a case, then all portfolios should exhibit the same excess return volatility. Such a result would provide further support for our earlier findings.

Unlike credit rating, which naturally lends itself to cross-sectional comparisons, constructing portfolios based on debt seniority presents a challenge. The classification of a bond as senior or subordinated is based on its payment priority in case of a default. The recovery value of any bond will be affected by the existence of other claims issued by the same issuer that are more or less senior to that bond. Across issuers, however, the same seniority class does not necessarily imply a similar recovery value in case of a default. Furthermore, even for a given issuer it is not always clear if a certain claim is senior to another claim (e.g., a debenture versus a senior note).[17] As a result, simply grouping bonds into portfolios based on the seniority class is inappropriate.

To address these issues, we perform a detailed issuer-level analysis based on pairs of classifications for which the seniority relationship is clear. We label these two classifications as SENIOR and SUBORD, and identify issuers that have bonds outstanding in both of these categories. Each month, we construct two portfolios for each such issuer, titled SENIOR and SUBORD, which include all the securities (often just a single security) in each category. Months in which only one of the portfolios is populated are discarded. We first compute the market-weighted DTS and excess return for each portfolio and the DTS ratio of the SENIOR portfolio to the SUBORD portfolio. We then match the DTS of the SENIOR portfolio to that of the SUBORD portfolio (e.g., the DTS is scaled up or down) and adjust the excess return accordingly.[18] Therefore, for every issuer, we have a time series of excess returns for two portfolios with the same DTS each month.

Using this approach for portfolio construction has clear advantages over the cross-sectional technique. First, it controls for any issuer-specific effect. Second, it accurately captures the relative seniority of different claims. Third, the fact that by construction the two portfolios have the same DTS has testable implications: the ratio of excess-return volatility of the two portfolios should be one on average. In addition, any difference in excess return should be relatively small and reflect only idiosyncratic risk. For example, bonds in one portfolio may be less liquid than those in the second portfolio, reflecting differences in size and seasoning.

Table 1.3 presents the 25th percentile, 50th percentile, and 75th percentile of the ratio of excess return volatility for the SUBORD and SENIOR portfolios as well as the difference in average excess returns. These statistics are presented for different compositions of the SUBORD and SENIOR portfolios.

**TABLE 1.3** Summary Statistics for SENIOR and SUBORD Portfolios

| Portfolio Composition | | Number of Issuers | Ratio of Excess Return Volatility | | | Difference in Excess Returns (%/month) | | |
| --- | --- | --- | --- | --- | --- | --- | --- | --- |
| SENIOR | SUBORD | | $P_{25}$ | $P_{50}$ | $P_{75}$ | $P_{25}$ | $P_{50}$ | $P_{75}$ |
| Senior debt | Subordinated debt | 47 | 0.83 | 1.10 | 1.41 | –0.15 | –0.06 | –0.01 |
| Senior notes | Notes | 353 | 0.79 | 0.94 | 1.08 | –0.08 | –0.01 | 0.04 |
| Senior debentures + Debentures | Subordinated debentures | 46 | 0.80 | 0.94 | 1.04 | –0.05 | 0.02 | 0.05 |
| Senior debentures + Senior notes + Senior debt | Debentures + Subordinated debentures + Notes + Subordinated debt | 535 | 0.80 | 0.93 | 1.08 | –0.13 | –0.04 | 0.01 |

*Note:* Portfolios are constructed separately for each issuer; their composition is updated monthly based on the definition of senior and subordinated claims. The DTS of the SENIOR portfolio is scaled monthly to match that of the SUBORD portfolio and its excess return is adjusted accordingly.
*Source:* Barclays Capital.

For example, the second row reports the case in which the SUBORD and SENIOR portfolios include notes and senior notes, respectively. There were a total of 353 different issuers for which the two portfolios were populated over some time period. The median ratio of excess returns volatilities is 0.94, and does not indicate a significant difference between the two portfolios. One quarter of the issuers exhibited ratios below 0.79, and one quarter of the issuers had ratios above 1.08, with the remaining half falling between these values. The typical performance of the two portfolios is also very similar and the median difference is 1 bps/month (e.g., the SUBORD portfolio underperforms). The results reported for other portfolio compositions are similar (in particular the bottom row which represents the most inclusive case), and do not indicate that the two portfolios exhibit different risk characteristics.

To examine the relation between DTS and excess returns volatility across various seniority classes, the SENIOR and SUBORD portfolios constructed for each issuer are assigned each month to one of the DTS quintiles. We then calculate the weighted excess return and DTS for each quintile (separately by seniority class). The two aggregate portfolios in each

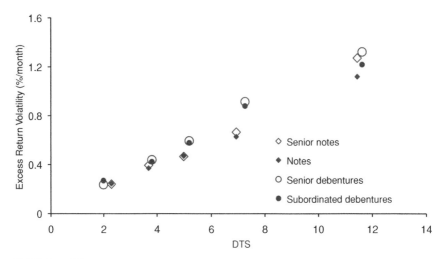

**FIGURE 1.17**    Excess Return Volatility versus DTS across Seniority Classes
*Note:* The SENIOR and SUBORD portfolios are divided into DTS quintiles and the weighted excess return and DTS is computed (separately by seniority class). The plot presents the time series volatility of excess returns and the average DTS of the 10 aggregate portfolios composed of senior notes and notes or senior debentures and debentures.
*Source:* Barclays Capital.

quintile have the exact same DTS since at the issuer-level the DTS of the SE-NIOR and SUBORD portfolios is equal by construction. As before, we compute the time series volatility of excess returns and the average DTS of the 10 portfolios.

Figure 1.17 presents the results of the analysis comparing senior notes to notes and senior debentures to subordinated debentures. The scatter plot shows that the linear relation between excess return volatility and DTS is preserved and that the slope does not depend on the seniority level. In both cases, there is an almost exact match between the volatilities of the SENIOR and SUBORD portfolios. We obtain similar results for other compositions of the two portfolios that are reported in Table 1.3.

## SUMMARY AND IMPLICATIONS FOR PORTFOLIO MANAGERS

This chapter presents a detailed analysis of the behavior of spread changes. Using our extensive corporate bond database, which spans 15 years and contains well over 560,000 observations, we demonstrate that spread changes are proportional to the level of spread. Systematic changes in spread across a sector tend to follow a pattern of relative spread change, in which bonds trading at wider spreads experience larger spread changes. The systematic spread volatility of a given sector (if viewed in terms of absolute spread changes) is proportional to the median spread in the sector; the nonsystematic spread volatility of a particular bond or issuer is proportional to its spread as well. Those findings hold irrespective of sector, duration, or time period.

In a sense, these results are not altogether surprising. The lognormal models typically used to represent changes in interest rates assume that changes in yield are proportional to current yield levels. Models for pricing credit derivatives such as Schönbucher (1999) have used a similar lognormal model to describe changes in credit spreads. An assumption of lognormal spread changes would imply two things: That spread changes are proportional to spreads, and that the relative spread changes are normally distributed. Our results can be seen as providing empirical evidence to support the first of these assumptions, but not necessarily the second.

There are several implications for a portfolio manager who wishes to act on these results. First, the best measure of exposure to a systematic change in spread within a given sector or industry is not the contribution to spread duration, but the contribution to DTS. At many asset management firms, the targeted active exposures for a portfolio relative to its benchmark are expressed as contribution-to-duration overweights and underweights along a sector by quality grid—and reports on the actual portfolio follow the same format. In the relative spread change paradigm, managers would express their targeted overweights and underweights in terms of contributions to DTS instead.

Second, our finding that the volatility of non-systematic return is proportional to DTS offers a simple mechanism for defining an issuer limit policy that enforces smaller positions in more risky credits. Many investors specify some ad hoc weight cap by credit quality to control issuer risk.[19] Alternatively, we can set a limit on the overall contribution to DTS for any single issuer. For example, say the product of Market value percentage × Spread × Duration must be 5 or less. Then, a position in issuer A, with a spread of 100 bps and a duration of five years, could be up to 1% of portfolio market value; while a position in issuer B, with a spread of 150 and an average duration of 10 years, would be limited to 0.33%.

Establishing issuer limits based on spreads has advantages and disadvantages relative to a ratings-based approach. One advantage, as described above, is the simplicity of specifying a single uniform limit that requires increasing diversification with increasing risk. The key difference between the two approaches, however, concerns the frequency with which issuer limits are adjusted. In a ratings-based framework, bond positions that are within policy on the date of purchase will tend to remain in policy unless they are downgraded. A spread-based constraint, by contrast, is by its very nature continuously adjusted as spreads change. One possible result is that as spreads widen, a position that was in policy when purchased can drift over the allowable DTS limit. Strict enforcement of this policy, requiring forced sales to keep all issuer exposures to stay within the limit, could become very distracting to managers, and incur excessive transaction costs as spreads trade up and down. One possible solution would be to specify one threshold for new purchases and a higher one at which forced sales would be triggered. This could provide a mechanism that adapts to market events more quickly than the rating agencies without introducing undue instability. Another possible disadvantage of the DTS-based issuer caps is that it allows for large positions in low spread issuers and exposes the portfolio to "credit torpedoes." This, too, would argue for using the DTS-based approach in conjunction with caps on market weights. We discuss these issues further in Chapter 11.

Third, there could be hedging implications. Say a hedge fund manager has a view on the relative performance of two issuers within the same industry, and would like to capitalize on this view by going long issuer A and short issuer B in a market-neutral manner. How do we define market neutrality? A typical approach might be to match the dollar durations of the two bonds, or to go long and short CDS of the same maturities with the same notional amounts. However, if issuer A trades at a wider spread than issuer B, our results would indicate that a better hedge against market-wide spread changes would be obtained by using more of issuer B, so as to match the contributions to DTS on the two sides of the trade. Chapter 8 examines this issue in detail.

Fourth, portfolio management tools such as risk and performance attribution models should represent sector exposures in terms of DTS contributions and sector spread changes in relative terms. A risk model for any asset class is essentially a set of factors that characterize the main risks that securities in that asset class are exposed to. The risk of an individual security or portfolio is computed based on its risk loadings or sensitivities to the various risk factors and the factor volatilities and correlations estimated from their past realizations. For credit-risky securities, traditional risk factors typically measure absolute spread changes based on a sector by quality partition that spans the universe of bonds. A risk factor specification based instead on relative spread changes has two important benefits. First, such factors would exhibit more stability over time and allow better forward-looking risk forecasts. Second, the partition by quality would no longer be necessary to control risk, and each sector can be represented by a single risk factor. This would allow managers to express more focused views, essentially trading off the elimination of the quality-based factors with a more finely grained partition by industry. Similarly, a key goal for attribution models is to match the allocation process as closely as possible. If and when a manager starts to state his allocation decisions in terms of DTS exposures, performance attribution should follow suit.

One practical difficulty that may arise in the implementation of DTS-based models is an increased vulnerability to pricing noise. For the most part, models of portfolio risk and reporting of active portfolio weights rely largely on structural information. Small discrepancies in asset pricing give rise to small discrepancies in market values, but potentially larger variations in spreads. Managers who rely heavily on contribution-to-DTS exposures will need to implement strict quality controls on pricing.

Indeed, we believe that perhaps one of the most useful applications of DTS is in the management of core-plus portfolios that combine both investment-grade and high-yield assets. Traditionally, investment-grade credit portfolios are managed based on contributions to duration, while high-yield portfolios are managed based on market value weights. Using contributions to DTS across both markets could help bring consistency to this portfolio construction process. Skeptics may point out that in high-yield markets, especially when moving towards the distressed segment, neither durations nor spreads are particularly meaningful, and the market tends to trade on price, based on an estimated recovery value. A useful property of DTS in that context is that in the case of distressed issuers, where shorter duration securities tend to have artificially high spreads, DTS is fairly constant across the maturity spectrum, so that managing issuer contributions to DTS becomes roughly equivalent to managing issuer market weights.

The introduction of the DTS paradigm in 2005 has had wide-ranging effects. It changed portfolio management practices across the industry and has been incorporated into some of the leading portfolio management analytics systems. We view it as a fundamental insight into the way credit markets behave; it is therefore not surprising that it is featured heavily throughout this book. The next two chapters explore empirical evidence from additional markets, and the theoretical underpinnings of DTS are explored in Chapter 4. In addition, Chapter 10 evaluates its performance during the 2007–2009 credit crisis. Even in chapters that focus on other topics, we use DTS to measure or control exposures to industries or issuers. Once one has become accustomed to the DTS approach, it is hard to approach any analysis of credit markets without taking DTS into account.

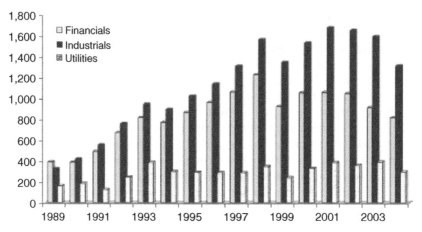

**FIGURE 1.18**   Sample Population by Sector and Year
*Note:* Investment grade bonds only; number of bonds is as of December of each year.
*Source:* Barclays Capital.

## APPENDIX: DATA DESCRIPTION

The data set used in the empirical analysis in Chapter 1 spans the period between September 1989 and January 2005, a total of 185 months. The sample includes all the bonds that comprise the U.S. Corporate Index excluding (1) zero-coupon bonds, (2) callable bonds, and (3) bonds with non-positive spreads. The final data set contains a total of 416,783 observations (see Figure 1.18 for a breakdown of the sample by sector and year). We also extend the analysis to include high-yield bonds rated Ba and B included in the U.S. High Yield Index (trading at a price above 80 to mitigate potential default effects) which increases the number of observations by roughly 35% (from 416,783 to 565,602).

Since spread figures are model-driven they can exhibit extreme values. To mitigate the effect of outliers, observations where changes in spread fall above the 99th percentile or below the 1st percentile are excluded. As a result, monthly spread changes included in our analysis range from −60 bps to +78 bps.

Table 1.4 outlines the exact breakdown into spread buckets by industry and maturity that we employ to analyze the relation between spread volatility and spread level. A careful look reveals that because of the general tendency of spread to rise with maturity, the population of the "short" maturity bucket is concentrated in the lowest spread bucket (denoted by 1) while

**TABLE 1.4** Sample Partition by Sector, Duration, and Spread

| Sector/ Maturity | Spread Bucket/Breakpoints | | | | | |
|---|---|---|---|---|---|---|
| | 1 | 2 | 3 | 4 | 5 | 6 |
| **Financials** | < 0.50 | 0.50–0.75 | 0.75–1.00 | 1.00–1.25 | 1.25–1.50 | > 1.5 |
| Short | 16,881 | 13,201 | 9,351 | 5,296 | 2,677 | 4,004 |
| | (50.8%) | (82.7%) | (64.9%) | (46.5%) | (30.8%) | (37.3%) |
| Medium | 5,839 | 14,838 | 11,156 | 8,173 | 5,133 | 6,904 |
| | (28.6%) | (65.4%) | (73.5%) | (61.6%) | (44.3%) | (48.1%) |
| Long | 2,183 | 12,875 | 10,743 | 8,174 | 6,130 | 11,993 |
| | (18.9%) | (54.6%) | (81.1%) | (73.0%) | (58.9%) | (55.1%) |
| **Industrials** | < 0.60 | 0.60–0.85 | 0.85–1.20 | 1.20–1.50 | 1.50–2.00 | > 2.00 |
| Short | 22,794 | 13,705 | 12,172 | 7,670 | 6,277 | 6,167 |
| | (84.9%) | (97.8%) | (78.9%) | (54.6%) | (48.6%) | (30.8%) |
| Medium | 12,814 | 14,621 | 14,424 | 9,109 | 9,300 | 9,131 |
| | (70.3%) | (85.4%) | (96.2%) | (65.4%) | (54.6%) | (43.2%) |
| Long | 9,212 | 13,961 | 16,248 | 10,088 | 11,010 | 8,940 |
| | (68.1%) | (81.6%) | (94.6%) | (69.7%) | (53.5%) | (40.5%) |
| **Utilities** | < 0.55 | 0.55–0.75 | 0.75–1.15 | 1.15–1.50 | > 1.50 | |
| Short | 5,017 | 3,233 | 4,443 | 2,388 | 2,350 | |
| | (46.5%) | (35.7%) | (48.6%) | (22.2%) | (16.8%) | |
| Medium | 3,430 | 3,552 | 4,484 | 2,699 | 3,889 | |
| | (41.1%) | (38.9%) | (41.1%) | (32.4%) | (23.2%) | |
| Long | 3,030 | 3,199 | 4,457 | 2,653 | 2,350 | |
| | (32.4%) | (40.5%) | (52.4%) | (25.4%) | (29.2%) | |

*Note:* Sample includes bonds with an investment grade rating between September 1989 and January 2005. The table reports the spread breakpoints, cell population, and the percentage of months where a bucket is populated by more than 20 bonds.
*Source:* Barclays Capital.

the opposite holds for the "long" maturity bucket. Table 1.4 also reports for each bucket the percentage of months during the sample period where the bond population exceeds 20. This statistic is of interest since months with less than 20 observations are filtered out from any volatility calculation. The percentage of months with a sufficient number of observations within a given spread range and market sector varies between 30% and 50% for Utilities and 50% to 80% for Financials and Industrials.

## NOTES

1. *Spread change return* is closely related to excess return, the return a corporate bond earns in excess of that of a duration-matched Treasury bond. *Excess return*

can be approximated by the sum of the spread change return and an additional component due to spread carry.

2. The studies reported in this chapter are based on data through 2005; Chapter 10 analyzes the model's out-of-sample performance through the events of the 2007–2009 financial crisis.

3. This practice leads to perennial questions about how much history should be used in such estimation. A longer time period leads to more stable estimates of volatility; a shorter time period (or a weighting scheme that gives more weight to recent observations) makes the estimate less stable, but better able to adapt to fundamental changes in the marketplace. In either case, the large swings in volatility that the market can experience mean that we are always trying to catch up to market events, and there will always be some amount of lag between the time of a volatility change and the time when it is first reflected in our estimates.

4. The sector breakdown is: banking, finance, basic industry, consumer cyclical, consumer non-cyclical, communications, energy, and utility. Bonds are assigned to one of three quality cells: Aaa/Aa, A, and Baa.

5. *Key issuers* refers to issuers that have outstanding issues with market value in excess of 1% of the sector aggregate market value. There are a total of 17 such issuers that represent 216 outstanding issues.

6. Since we compare models with and without an intercept, Table 1.1 reports uncentered $R^2$ values calculated using the total sum of squares (without subtracting the average spread change) rather than a centered $R^2$.

7. We find that the distribution of spread duration varies significantly across time and therefore does not allow for a partition based on constant spread duration values.

8. Despite our efforts to ensure uniform cell populations, some cells are very sparsely populated (or even empty) in some months. Months where a cell is populated by less than 20 bonds are not used in the analysis. As a robustness check, we repeat the analysis using the entire available time series of systematic spread changes and a weighted volatility estimate (where the weighting factor is the number of observations in each month). The results are essentially unchanged.

9. We have conducted statistical tests on the data shown in Figure 1.7, to see if a systematic difference is apparent between different industries and maturities. These tests did not detect a statistically significant difference in the slope due to either of these factors.

10. In order to be consistent with equation (1.6), the systematic spread effect that is subtracted in equation (1.12) should not be simply the average spread change in the cell. Rather, this amount should be scaled by the ratio of the bond's spread to the average spread of the cell. However, as we are carrying out this test over relatively narrow spread buckets, there is very little difference in practice between the two definitions.

11. Depending on the sample composition and population, this procedure produces between 38 and 66 observations yearly when examining systematic volatility, and 300 to 500 observations for idiosyncratic volatility. As before, only observations

that represent buckets populated by at least 20 bonds during the entire year are included in the analysis.

12. Our findings were unchanged when we repeated the analysis using other partitions.

13. Although the carry component is time varying, we analyze each month's excess return conditioned on the beginning-of-month spread. We can therefore treat the carry component as deterministic.

14. A longer estimation period is always desired as long as the proportionality factor is stable across periods.

15. Including publicly issued debt of U.S. government agencies, quasi-federal corporations, and corporate or foreign debt guaranteed by the U.S. government (such as USAID securities).

16. The results were unchanged when issues with a market value below $300 million were excluded or when non-U.S. agencies were excluded.

17. For example, when a bank is owned by a holding company, owners of a subordinated claim issued by the bank have priority in case of a default over owners of a senior claim issued by the holding company.

18. Excess returns can be adjusted by the same scaling factor (ratio of DTS of the two portfolios) since they are linearly related to DTS. Notice, also, that if this was to be implemented in practice, we would need to take into account financing costs. However, since we do not form a trading strategy but rather examine whether similar DTS portfolios exhibit similar excess return volatilities, borrowing costs can be ignored.

19. For example, an investment policy may specify that no more than 1% of the portfolio market value can be invested in securities of any single issuer rated Baa, no more than 2% in any issuer rated A, and no more than 4% in any issuer rated Aa.

### CHAPTER 2

# DTS for Credit Default Swaps

In this chapter, we extend the analysis of credit spread behavior beyond U.S. corporate bonds and look at *credit default swaps* (CDS). A priori, one would expect all the results in the previous chapter to hold for CDS as in theory, changes in their spreads and those of the underlying bonds should be closely related. In practice, however, this is not always the case. Blanco, Brennan, and Marsh (2005), for example, find that since CDS are often more liquid than cash bonds of the same issuers, CDS spreads incorporate new information quicker and exhibit higher volatility. This was especially the case during the 2007–2009 financial crisis when the CDS–cash bonds basis initially widened due to a decline in funding availability and limited arbitrage activity, and later mean-reverted as markets conditions improved. Furthermore, the two markets have a different investor base, which may also result in temporarily different dynamics for the same issuer. Finally, the spreads of corporate bonds are typically computed relative to the Treasury curve, whereas CDS spreads represent spreads over LIBOR.

In the process of examining whether the linear relation between spread volatility and spread level of U.S. corporate bonds is also evident for credit default swaps, we investigate the extent to which the results in Chapter 1 reflect the specific data, methodology, and geographical market used. First, the higher liquidity of CDS contracts (as compared to corporate bonds) allows us to conduct the analysis at a weekly rather than a monthly frequency. Second, we use the *quasi-maximum likelihood* (QML) approach to investigate the relation between spread volatility and spread level. This technique addresses the stochastic nature of conditional spread volatility and the fact that it is not directly observable (i.e., latent). Using QML enables us to assess the statistical validity of a prespecified explicit functional dependence between conditional volatility and spread level, and we discuss the relative merits of such an approach compared with the cell partition–based method used in Chapter 1. Third, we look beyond U.S. credit markets and also include European CDS and bond indexes in the analysis.

## ESTIMATION METHODOLOGY

In studying the relation between spread level and spread volatility, we face a problem: Volatility is ultimately unobservable. What is observed in practice are spread changes, which correspond to particular realizations of their distribution, which is in turn affected by the underlying and unobservable volatility. Sample estimates across multiple time periods can serve as a measure of the true underlying spread volatility only if the volatility is fairly stable over time. Yet, if spread volatility is related to the level of spread, then it would fluctuate over time in response to changes in the level of spread.

The approach we employed to address this issue in the previous chapter was to construct buckets that are populated monthly with corporate bonds trading within a certain spread range. While the composition of a bucket may change over time in response to changes in spreads of the underlying bonds, its (average) spread level remains fairly stable. This allows for an analysis of the behavior of spread volatility while holding the level of spread relatively constant.

The advantage of this approach is its flexibility: No assumption is needed regarding the exact nature of the relation between spread volatility and spread level. The observation that spread volatility of corporate bonds is linearly related to spread level relies on how the (buckets') spread volatility varies in response to changes in the level of spreads. However, the technique does not allow an analysis of spread volatility at the individual security or whole-sector level because of the stochastic nature of volatility, as explained above. It requires buckets with a homogenous population of bonds trading at similar spreads.

In this chapter, we employ a different technique based on *maximum likelihood*. In its purest form, maximum likelihood assumes that the true distribution of the sample data takes a known form with unknown parameters. In our analysis, we assume that spread changes are distributed normally with a mean of zero and volatility that is not constant over time but rather is a function of the level of spread.[1] The idea underlying this approach is to identify the shape of the relation between spread volatility and spread level that would maximize the probability (likelihood) of the observed data (e.g., spread changes).

We use the following specification to test the relation between spread volatility in month $t$ and spread level at the end of the previous month:

$$\sigma_t(\Delta s) = \alpha + \beta s_{t-1} + \gamma \hat{s}_{t-1}^2 \qquad (2.1)$$

where $\sigma_t(\Delta s)$ is the volatility of spread during period $t$ and $s_{t-1}$ is the beginning-of-period spread level. The last term in the specification $\hat{s}_{t-1}^2$ is meant to capture any potential non-linear relation between changes in spread level and spread volatility.[2] The maximum likelihood procedure determines the value of the parameters $\alpha$, $\beta$, and $\gamma$ such that the likelihood of observing the data in the sample under the assumed (normal) distribution is maximized.

For example, maximum likelihood estimates for $\alpha$ and $\gamma$ that are not significantly different from zero are consistent with spread volatility being linearly proportional to the level of spread. The proportionality factor is given by the $\beta$ estimate and can be compared with the 9% to 10% found in Chapter 1 for corporate bonds. However, if $\gamma$, the coefficient of the quadratic term, is positive (and significant) this would indicate that spread volatility increases with spread in a non-linear manner. In such a case, volatility would be lower than in the linear case for tight spreads and higher for wide spreads. Alternatively, if volatility is fairly unchanged over time (which forms the basis for using spread duration in the case of bonds and PV01 for CDS as a risk measure), this would result in a significant and positive $\alpha$ with the estimates of both $\beta$ and $\gamma$ not being significantly different from zero.

## EMPIRICAL ANALYSIS OF CDS SPREADS

The analysis of CDS spread behavior is based on weekly data collected by Markit. The list of individual credit default swaps is compiled from the constituents of the five-year CDX.IG and CDX.XO for the United States; and five-year iTraxx.IG and iTraxx.XO for Europe. This allows for a comparison of the results across different markets and a wide range of spread levels. The sample starting point varies by index to ensure spread changes are not affected by insufficient liquidity and ends in May 2006.

Table 2.1 displays details on the population of CDS contracts in our sample. In order to accurately capture systematic spread changes, only sectors that are represented by at least eight distinct issuers are included in the analysis.[3] In addition, several issuers are excluded due to multiple missing observations or because they experienced extreme issuer-specific spread widening events.

We complement the CDS data with monthly spread data of corporate bonds (computed relative to the local Treasury curve) to enable a direct comparison of the results using QML with those based on a cell partition. The data span the period from October 1990 to June 2006 for the U.S. Corporate Index and from June 2000 to June 2006 for the U.S. High Yield and Euro Corporate Indexes.

### Spread Volatility of Credit Default Swaps

Figure 2.1(A) displays volatilities and corresponding median spreads for all constituents of the CDX.IG and CDX.XO indexes between July 2004 and

**TABLE 2.1**  Description of CDS Dataset

| Index | Constituents | Starting Date | Initial | Universe after Exclusions |
|---|---|---|---|---|
| CDX.IG | Series 1–6 | 4/17/2003 | 104 | 92[a] |
| iTraxx.IG | Series 1–6 | 10/7/2003 | 107 | 99[b] |
| CDX.XO | Series 6 | 1/7/2004 | 35 | 30[c] |
| iTraxx.XO | Series 5 | 1/7/2004 | 45 | 32[d] |

[a]Three issuers with a substantial number of missing observations (over 30) and four issuers with weekly spread changes exceeding 100 bps are excluded. The Government and technology sectors are both excluded since they include only two issuers.
[b]Two issuers with weekly spread changes exceeding 100 bps and one issuer with an average spread level exceeding 100 bps are excluded. The Government and energy sectors, including only one issuer are excluded as well. Three issuers with substantial numbers of missing observations are excluded.
[c]One issuer from the utilities sector is excluded. We also exclude four issuers with substantial numbers of missing observations (more than 10 weeks).
[d]We exclude 11 issuers with multiple missing observations (more than 20 weeks) and one issuer with weekly spread changes exceeding 250 bps. The utilities sector is excluded since it includes only a single issuer.
*Sources:* Barclays Capital and Markit.

May 2006. It clearly shows that the standard deviation of spread changes increases with the median level of spread, and the plot for CDX.IG indicates a fairly smooth and linear relation. While the volatility of contracts comprising the CDX.XO is not as well behaved and observations are more scattered, the same general pattern is still evident. This is consistent with the findings that for corporate bonds, the linear relation extends well into spreads of 400 bps, when U.S. high-yield bonds rated Ba and B are included as well.

The results for European names included in the iTraxx.IG and iTraxx.XO, shown in Figure 2.1(B), are very similar. Investment grade names are clustered along a line passing through the origin, while contracts trading at higher spreads exhibit more dispersion due to a larger idiosyncratic risk component.[4] Another phenomenon that can be observed is that for very low spreads, the decline in volatility seems to decelerate and converge to a "lower bound," similar to what we documented for spreads of U.S. agencies.

**Systematic Volatility**   To analyze the time series of systematic spread changes of CDS, we first compute a weekly time series of average spreads

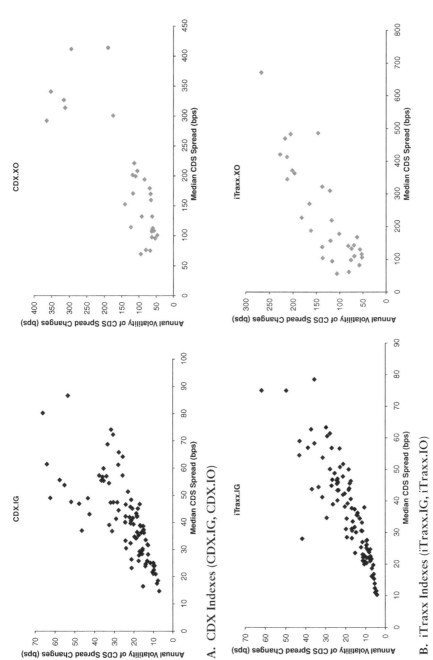

A. CDX Indexes (CDX.IG, CDX.IO)

B. iTraxx Indexes (iTraxx.IG, iTraxx.IO)

**FIGURE 2.1** Volatility of Spread Changes versus Median Spread Levels (weekly observations, July 2004–May 2006)
*Sources:* Barclays Capital and Markit.

and spread changes for each sector of the CDX.IG and iTraxx.IG indexes based on Markit sector classification. We then use QML to estimate the parameters in equation (2.1) separately for each sector with at least eight issuers. For the CDX.XO and iTraxx.XO Indexes, however, we calculate just a single aggregate time series because the idiosyncratic component of spread change for crossover names is relatively high. This in turn requires a greater degree of diversification (i.e., a larger number of contracts) in order to isolate systematic spread movements.

Table 2.2 reports the estimated values for $\alpha$ and $\beta$ and their associated $t$-statistics. For investment grade CDS, the estimates of the linear spread term $\beta$ are significant across all sectors except consumer cyclical and materials for CDX.IG, and consumer staple for iTraxx.IG. Comparing estimates for CDX sectors with those of equivalent sectors in iTraxx shows them to be fairly similar. In addition, most of the estimated coefficients range between 0.04 and 0.06, which is in line with the 0.09 to 0.10 estimated using corporate bond data over a monthly frequency.[5] The estimates of $\alpha$ are always insignificant, indicating once more that the relation between spread volatility and spread level is best described by a linear function that intersects the origin (i.e., $\alpha$ is equal to zero).

The last two columns in Table 2.2 show estimates of $\gamma$, which control for potential non-linear aspects of the relation between spread level and volatility and their $t$-statistics.[6] Such effects are evident in several sectors of the CDX.IG (communications, consumer cyclical, and consumer staple), as well as for the aggregate CDX index and are significant at a 10% confidence level. The positive values of the $\gamma$ estimates imply that conditional volatility becomes less sensitive to changes in spread at low spread levels. This is consistent with our earlier findings that spread volatility is roughly constant for spreads below 20 bps.

For crossover names, $\beta$ is found to be significant for CDX.XO at a 5% level. The magnitude of the estimate when converted to a monthly frequency (0.132) is generally higher than those for investment grade names and is quite similar to the results for U.S. high-yield bonds (11.5%). In contrast, $\beta$ is not significant for iTraxx.XO but $\gamma$ is significant at the 5% level.

The effect of the non-linear term on systematic volatility can be substantial. As an illustration, we examine the volatility of the CDX.IG communications sector where both the $\beta$ and $\gamma$ coefficients are significant. Figure 2.2 shows the predicted volatility with and without the non-linear term. As can be seen from the plot, the difference between the predicted volatilities, especially for high spread levels, is non-trivial.

**Idiosyncratic Volatility**     We also analyze the idiosyncratic spread volatility of constituents of the four CDS indexes. Idiosyncratic spread changes are

**TABLE 2.2** Estimation of the Conditional Relation between Systematic Spread Volatility and Spread Level Using QML

| | NO CDS | NO OBS | $\alpha$ | $t$-stat. | $\beta$ | $t$-stat. | $\gamma$ | $t$-stat. |
|---|---|---|---|---|---|---|---|---|
| **CDX** | | | | | | | | |
| CDX.IG (Index[a]) | 92 | 161 | 3.7E-05 | 0.8 | **3.4%** | **2.9** | 9.5 | 1.73 |
| Communications | 8 | 161 | 1.5E-05 | 0.2 | **5.1%** | **4.5** | **9.0** | **2.28** |
| Consumer cyclical | 17 | 161 | 6.5E-05 | 0.7 | **3.1%** | 1.4 | **31.0** | **2.38** |
| Consumer staple | 11 | 161 | 4.2E-05 | 0.7 | **3.6%** | **2.5** | **18.1** | **2.18** |
| Financial | 19 | 161 | −1.7E-06 | 0.0 | **6.1%** | **2.7** | −0.2 | −0.01 |
| Industrial | 14 | 161 | −2.3E-07 | 0.0 | **4.3%** | **4.0** | −1.4 | −0.31 |
| Materials | 9 | 161 | 1.1E-04 | 0.9 | **3.2%** | 1.2 | 35.0 | 1.54 |
| Utilities | 8 | 161 | −4.8E-05 | −0.7 | **5.8%** | **3.8** | 4.8 | 0.65 |
| CDX.XO (Index) | 30 | 103 | −1.2E-04 | −0.3 | **6.6%** | **2.6** | 6.7 | 1.1 |
| **iTraxx** | | | | | | | | |
| iTraxx.IG (Index[b]) | 99 | 149 | 1.1E-05 | 0.1 | **4.1%** | **2.0** | 22.5 | 1.0 |
| Communications | 14 | 149 | 1.0E-05 | 0.1 | **5.1%** | **2.1** | 26.9 | 1.6 |
| Consumer cyclical | 13 | 149 | −1.2E-04 | −0.7 | **7.9%** | **2.3** | 36.1 | 1.3 |
| Consumer staple | 14 | 149 | 1.3E-05 | 0.1 | 4.0% | 1.5 | 34.9 | 1.1 |
| Financial | 21 | 149 | −1.3E-05 | −0.5 | **5.3%** | **4.1** | 17.7 | 1.0 |
| Industrial | 9 | 149 | 1.9E-05 | 0.2 | **4.3%** | **2.1** | 12.9 | 0.7 |
| Utilities | 14 | 149 | 2.7E-05 | 0.8 | **3.2%** | **3.0** | 10.1 | 1.4 |
| iTraxx.XO (Index) | 32 | 103 | 3.4E-04 | 0.4 | 3.6% | 0.9 | **19.6** | **2.6** |

[a]Excluding the energy sector.
[b]Excluding the materials sector and unclassified contracts.
*Note:* Figures in bold are significant at the 5% level.
*Sources:* Barclays Capital and Markit.

calculated by subtracting the average sector or index spread change from that of the individual bond. As before, the specification of conditional volatility of idiosyncratic spread changes is based on equation (2.1) and maximum likelihood is used to estimate the parameters.

First, we calculate separate estimates of $\alpha$, $\beta$, and $\gamma$ for each constituent of CDX and iTraxx. Figure 2.3 shows the distribution of these $\beta$ estimates across each major market. The distributions are fairly similar, with estimates ranging between 0.034 and 0.064 for a majority of issuers. The estimates of $\beta$ are negative for only a few issuers (3 and 10 for CDX and iTraxx, respectively).

Table 2.3 reports the results of a *pooled estimation* where the time series of idiosyncratic spread changes of individual-issuer contracts are

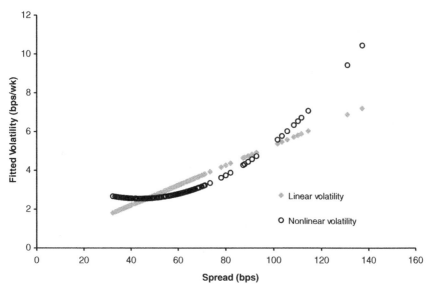

**FIGURE 2.2**  Predicted Spread Volatility of CDX.IG Communications Sector
Using a Linear and Nonlinear Specification of Spread Dependence
*Sources:* Barclays Capital and Markit.

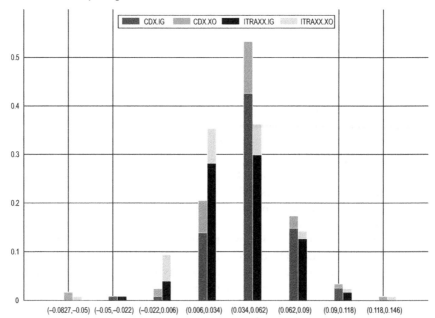

**FIGURE 2.3**  Distributions of the Linear Term Coefficient ($\beta$) for Idiosyncratic
Spread Changes
*Sources:* Barclays Capital and Markit.

**TABLE 2.3**  Pooled Estimation of the Conditional Relation between Idiosyncratic Spread Volatility and Spread Level Using QML

| | NO CDS | NO OBS | $\alpha$ | *t*-stat. | $\beta$ | *t*-stat. | $\gamma$ | *t*-stat. |
|---|---|---|---|---|---|---|---|---|
| **CDX** | | | | | | | | |
| CDX.IG (Index[a]) | 92 | 14,652 | **3.1E-05** | **2.0** | **5.1%** | **16.8** | 0.9 | 1.1 |
| Communications | 8 | 1,288 | **9.4E-05** | **2.4** | **3.8%** | **6.9** | 2.3 | 1.6 |
| Consumer cyclical | 17 | 2,737 | 3.6E-05 | 1.6 | **4.3%** | **7.1** | 0.7 | 0.4 |
| Consumer staple | 11 | 1,771 | −3.6E-06 | −0.2 | **6.2%** | **11.9** | 0.6 | 0.5 |
| Financial | 6 | 3,059 | 5.4E-05 | 1.7 | **5.1%** | **8.8** | 1.2 | 0.9 |
| Industrial | 19 | 2,254 | **4.5E-05** | **2.7** | **3.5%** | **8.2** | 0.6 | 0.7 |
| Materials | 14 | 1,449 | **6.6E-05** | **2.5** | **3.4%** | **5.6** | 0.8 | 0.4 |
| Utilities | 8 | 1,288 | 2.9E-05 | 0.6 | **4.0%** | **4.1** | 1.7 | 0.8 |
| CDX.XO (Index) | 30 | 3,058 | **3.6E-04** | **4.0** | **4.8%** | **10.9** | 0.3 | 1.0 |
| **iTraxx** | | | | | | | | |
| iTraxx.IG (Index[b]) | 99 | 14,759 | 2.6E-06 | 0.2 | **4.7%** | **17.5** | 0.5 | 0.5 |
| Communications | 14 | 2,128 | −8.9E-06 | −0.4 | **4.4%** | **10.0** | 1.4 | 1.2 |
| Consumer cyclical | 13 | 1,976 | −5.3E-05 | −1.9 | **5.9%** | **9.8** | 0.0 | 0.0 |
| Consumer staple | 14 | 2,128 | −1.0E-05 | −0.6 | **5.2%** | **11.1** | 1.1 | 0.8 |
| Financial | 21 | 3,192 | 9.9E-06 | 1.0 | **3.6%** | **9.0** | 2.5 | 1.3 |
| Industrial | 9 | 1,368 | 4.8E-05 | 1.3 | **3.4%** | **6.5** | 3.7 | 0.6 |
| Utilities | 14 | 2,128 | 1.1E-05 | 1.0 | **2.9%** | **8.2** | **2.4** | **2.6** |
| iTraxx.XO (Index) | 32 | 3,230 | **7.7E-04** | **5.7** | **2.4%** | **5.4** | 0.0 | 0.2 |

*Note:* Figures in bold are significant at the 5% level.
[a]Excluding the energy sector.
[b]Excluding the materials sector and unclassified contracts.
*Sources:* Barclays Capital and Markit.

combined within a sector (for investment-grade names) or the entire index (for crossover names) and the three parameters are estimated as before. The result is a single set of parameter estimates that are representative of the relation between idiosyncratic spread volatility and spread level in each sector (or aggregate index for crossover contracts).

Overall, the results in Table 2.3 lend further support to a linear specification of the relation between spread volatility and spread level. The estimates for the linear term are always significant at the 1% significance level. In addition, the magnitudes of the estimates are quite similar and consistent with the estimates for corporate bonds when converted to a monthly frequency. The figures in the last column indicate that a non-linear effect is detected only in a single sector (utilities in iTraxx.IG), similar to the case of systematic spread volatility shown in Table 2.2.

## Spread Volatility of Corporate Bonds

To complement our analysis of CDS spread volatility, we apply the QML procedure to the monthly corporate bond data that we used in Chapter 1. Rather than using individual bonds, however, the analysis is based on the aggregated spread changes of several indexes (U.S. and Euro Corporate Indexes and the U.S. High Yield Index). We report results for the three major sectors (financials, industrials, and utilities) as well as for various underlying industries, between October 1990 and January 2006. To ensure proper measurement of systematic spread changes, we examine only sectors that are populated monthly by at least 10 issuers for investment grade bonds and 20 issuers for high-yield bonds. Furthermore, we analyze the index data in a way designed to minimize the effect of issuer-specific events.[7]

For each selected index, the time series of spread changes is lined up against the beginning-of-month spreads and the regression of equation (2.1) is carried out to determine the dependence of spread volatility on spread. To ensure that our results are not an artifact of a specific time period, we also report separately the results for two subperiods: October 1990 to June 1998 and October 1998 to January 2006.[8] The partition into these periods corresponds to the belief by many investors that credit markets changed fundamentally in 1998 following the "Russian Crisis" and the downfall of Long-Term Capital Management.

For U.S. investment-grade corporates, our results strongly support the DTS paradigm. We do not find statistically significant results for $\alpha$ or $\gamma$ in any of the industry groups or time periods tested, whereas $\beta$ is found to be highly significant in almost every case. That is, the relation between spread and spread volatility is best described by a linear specification. Table 2.4 presents the estimates of $\beta$ and the associated $t$-statistics at the sector and industry level for the U.S. Corporate Index, for the full-time period and the two sub-periods. We find that while the estimates of the $\beta$ parameter can vary across industry groups and time periods, the numbers seem to be in overall agreement with our prior results (notice that the index results, unlike the CDS results, are based on monthly data, and are therefore consistent with the data from Chapter 1 without rescaling). Over the entire period, the estimates of $\beta$ for the broader financials (12.7%) and industrials (12.5%) sectors are in agreement with the earlier results of about 10% despite the different statistical techniques used. Comparing the results for the two sub-periods reveals a general pattern of stability similar to that observed in

**TABLE 2.4** Estimation of Systematic Spread Volatility Using QML for the U.S. Corporate Index

| | Average Number of Bonds | October 1990– June 2006 | | October 1990– June 1998 | | October 1998– June 2006 | |
|---|---|---|---|---|---|---|---|
| | | $\beta$ | *t*-stat. | $\beta$ | *t*-stat. | $\beta$ | *t*-stat. |
| Financials | 886 | **12.7%** | **5.4** | **9.5%** | **4.1** | **13.9%** | **5.6** |
| Banking | 359 | **12.6%** | **4.7** | **11.8%** | **4.9** | **11.8%** | **3.4** |
| Brokerage | 105 | **15.2%** | **2.6** | **16.1%** | **3.4** | **12.6%** | **3.6** |
| Finance comp. | 277 | **16.8%** | **7.5** | **11.5%** | **4.6** | **19.3%** | **7.0** |
| Insurance | 54 | **16.2%** | **3.4** | NA | NA | **16.2%** | **3.4** |
| REITS | 41 | **5.4%** | **3.0** | NA | NA | **5.4%** | **3.0** |
| Industrials | 1,166 | **12.5%** | **5.2** | **10.3%** | **2.7** | **11.8%** | **3.7** |
| Basic industrials | 144 | **8.8%** | **5.8** | **8.0%** | **2.8** | **5.9%** | **2.2** |
| Capital goods | 146 | **11.5%** | **5.8** | **11.3%** | **4.4** | **9.9%** | **3.0** |
| Communications | 124 | **18.8%** | **4.7** | NA | NA | **18.8%** | **4.7** |
| Consumer cyclical | 216 | **20.1%** | **5.4** | **15.5%** | **3.4** | 17.2% | 1.8 |
| Energy | 137 | **10.9%** | **2.1** | **13.5%** | **2.2** | 6.8% | 1.7 |
| Consumer non-cyclical | 228 | **10.5%** | **2.7** | **11.4%** | **2.0** | **8.3%** | **2.3** |
| Technology | 49 | **17.2%** | **3.0** | **16.8%** | **3.6** | **17.8%** | **3.4** |
| Transportation | 99 | **10.2%** | **4.2** | **8.8%** | **3.5** | **15.5%** | **3.8** |
| Utilities | 359 | **13.6%** | **3.7** | **8.3%** | **2.3** | **16.3%** | **3.2** |
| Electric | 229 | **15.4%** | **2.9** | **11.8%** | **2.9** | **17.8%** | **2.4** |
| Natural gas | 80 | **13.5%** | **5.5** | **5.4%** | **3.4** | **17.3%** | **4.9** |

*Note:* Figures in bold are significant at the 5% level.
*Source:* Barclays Capital.

Figure 1.11, with industries containing fewer issuers typically exhibiting a higher degree of variation.[9]

Table 2.5 repeats the analysis of corporate bonds using QML for the U.S. High Yield Index and the (investment grade) Euro Corporate Index, from June 2000 through June 2006. The estimates of the intercept $\alpha$ are always statistically insignificant and are omitted from the table for brevity. Results for U.S. High Yield in Table 2.5(A) once again provide clear evidence that the linear factor $\beta$ is the only significant factor, and that its value once again is shown to vary around 10%. The data in Table 2.5(B), for the Euro Corporate Index, support our hypothesis as well, but not as strongly. In most sectors, $\beta$ is statistically significant, with parameter values around 10%, and

**TABLE 2.5** Estimation of Systematic Spread Volatility Using QML for the U.S. High Yield and Euro Corporate Indexes

| | Average Number | June 2000–June 2006 | | | |
|---|---|---|---|---|---|
| A. U.S. High Yield | of Bonds | $\beta$ | $t$-stat. | $\gamma$ | $t$-stat. |
| Financials | 27 | **14.1%** | **2.1** | −2.5 | −0.9 |
| Industrials | 418 | **10.3%** | **3.2** | 0.8 | 0.5 |
| Capital goods | 41 | **16.6%** | **2.7** | −0.2 | −0.1 |
| Communications | 54 | **18.3%** | **2.8** | 0.1 | 0.1 |
| Consumer cyclical | 126 | **8.7%** | **2.1** | 1.2 | 0.6 |
| Consumer non-cyclical | 64 | **7.2%** | **2.2** | −0.3 | −0.1 |
| **B. Euro Investment Grade** | | | | | |
| Financials | 515 | **12.8%** | **6.0** | 5.4 | 0.5 |
| Banking | 385 | **6.7%** | **2.7** | 15.1 | 0.5 |
| Finance companies | 56 | **23.6%** | **5.4** | 0.1 | 0.0 |
| Insurance | 34 | 14.4% | 1.6 | −5.5 | −0.2 |
| Industrials | 353 | 11.4% | 1.4 | −2.3 | −0.1 |
| Basic industrials | 29 | **14.2%** | **3.5** | 4.3 | 0.4 |
| Capital goods | 38 | **20.0%** | **4.3** | 1.0 | 0.1 |
| Communications | 91 | **18.5%** | **2.1** | 0.5 | 0.0 |
| Consumer cyclical | 74 | 25.1% | 1.5 | 44.9 | 0.7 |
| Consumer non-cyclical | 62 | 10.2% | 1.4 | −3.1 | −0.1 |
| Utilities | 78 | **9.8%** | **2.2** | 26.1 | 1.8 |
| Electric | 58 | **6.2%** | **2.5** | **24.0** | **2.0** |

*Note:* Figures in bold are significant at the 5% level.
*Sources:* Barclays Capital and Markit.

$\gamma$ does not play a meaningful role. However, some sectors (e.g., consumer cyclical) show reduced significance for $\beta$, while the utility sector shows a significant estimate for $\gamma$, indicating some degree of non-linearity is present in the relation between spread level and the volatility of spread.

## CONCLUSION

The results of the analysis in this chapter lend further support to the DTS concept and illustrate that it is not confined to the realm of U.S. corporate bonds. Both systematic and idiosyncratic spread volatility of investment-grade and crossover CDS contracts are found to be linearly proportional to the level of spreads, with only a few instances of significant systematic second-order effects, at both the aggregate index and sector levels, in European and U.S. markets. Despite the use of a different estimation technique and higher frequency data, the estimated sensitivity of volatility to changes in spreads—the parameter $\beta$ in equation (2.1)—is generally consistent with those documented for corporate bonds when converted to a monthly frequency.

These findings have important implications for managing the risk of credit default swaps. For example, in Chapter 8, we illustrate that for hedging market risk in CDS trades, the DTS paradigm is far more effective than other traditional approaches.

## APPENDIX: QUASI-MAXIMUM LIKELIHOOD APPROACH

*Maximum likelihood estimation* (MLE) begins with an assumption about the true distribution of the sample data. This probability density function is assumed to be known up to the value of certain parameters that need to be estimated from an available sample of observations. An optimal specification is sought for the distribution of those variables by searching for parameters that maximize an objective function, which is the likelihood. The MLE procedure chooses parameters in such a way that maximizes the likelihood of drawing the sample under consideration from the calibrated distribution. This likelihood optimization is carried out by means of maximization, with respect to the parameters, of the so-called (log-) likelihood function of the observed data under the parameterized probability density function.

Specifically, let $f(y|x, \theta)$ denote the probability density function of a random variable $y$ conditional on a random variable $x$ and a set of parameters $\bar{\theta}$. In the context of our analysis, $y$ represents the spread change, $x$ the level of spread and $\bar{\theta}$ the set of parameters defining the dependence of spread change volatility on spread level. Given a sample of independent observations $y_1 \dots y_n$ we can write their joint probability density function $L(\bar{\theta}|\bar{x}, \bar{y})$, in the following way:

$$L\left(\bar{\theta}|\bar{x}, \bar{y}\right) \equiv f\left(y_1 \dots y_n|x_1 \dots x_n, \bar{\theta}\right) = \prod_{i=1}^{n} f\left(y_i|x_i, \bar{\theta}\right) \qquad (2.2)$$

This joint density function, when defined as a function of the unknown parameter vector $\bar{\theta}$, is called the likelihood function, where $\bar{y}$ and $\bar{x}$ indicate the collection of observations in the sample. The logarithm of the likelihood function is called the *log-likelihood function:*

$$\ln L\left(\bar{\theta}|\bar{x}, \bar{y}\right) = \sum_{i=1}^{n} \ln f\left(y_i|x_i, \bar{\theta}\right) \tag{2.3}$$

Parameter estimates $\hat{\theta}$ can be obtained by maximizing the log-likelihood function with respect to the parameter set:

$$\hat{\theta} = \arg\max_{\bar{\theta}} \left[\ln L\left(\bar{\theta}|\bar{x}, \bar{y}\right)\right] \tag{2.4}$$

It can be shown that the estimates obtained by MLE procedure are asymptotically consistent and efficient. Namely, that as the number of sample observations increases, the MLE parameter estimates converge to their true values and that the asymptotic variance of MLE estimates is the smallest possible in the class of consistent estimates.

One shortcoming of the MLE procedure is that it assumes a particular form for the probability density function of the sample observations. It is usually the case that this distribution is not known a priori. Nevertheless, even assuming normal probability distribution for the data will, under certain conditions, lead to consistent results.[10,11]

### Estimation Methodology

In our analysis, we assume that the conditional volatility of spread change is a function of spread level, that is,

$$\sigma_t = \alpha + \beta s_{t-1} + \gamma \hat{P} s_{t-1}^2 \tag{2.5}$$

in which $\hat{P} s_{t-1}^2$ is the in-sample projection of $s^2$ to the linear space orthogonal to $L(1, s)$. In terms of an OLS regression, $\hat{P} s_{t-1}^2$ is the residual term from regressing $s_t^2$ on $s_t$ and a constant. The idea is that the estimate of the parameter $\gamma$ would represent the potential non-linear relation between conditional variance of spread changes and the level of spread. The reason for using the orthogonal projection of $s_t^2$ rather than simply $s_t^2$ is that the latter is highly correlated with the level of spread. Introducing such a high level of multicollinearity into the model would severely reduce the significance level of the estimates of $\hat{\alpha}$ and $\hat{\beta}$. As a result, the linear coefficient becomes non-informative as we cannot see whether the linear model per se explains the data well. To avoid this effect, we split the contribution of the quadratic term into linear and non-linear components. Eventually, we would include only the non-linear component of the quadratic term into the specification leaving out the linear component. To achieve this we use the in-sample projection of the quadratic term into the orthogonal space. The result is that estimates $\hat{\alpha}$ and $\hat{\beta}$ do not depend on the inclusion of the non-linear term. This construct is purely artificial and, in fact, does not affect the conclusion regarding the quadratic term in the specification of the model. Whether we include the quadratic term or its orthogonal projection does not affect parameter estimate $\hat{\gamma}$ and its *t*-statistic.

Using the Gaussian conditional probability density function we can write the log-likelihood function in the form:

$$\ln L\left(\alpha, \beta, \gamma \,|\, \Delta\tilde{s}, \tilde{s}\right) = -\frac{T}{2}\ln\left(2\pi\right) - \sum_{t=1}^{T}\ln\sigma_t - \frac{1}{2}\sum_{t=1}^{T}\frac{\Delta s_t^2}{\sigma_t^2} \qquad (2.6)$$

The parameter estimates can be obtained by maximizing this likelihood function of the observed data with respect to parameters $\alpha$, $\beta$, and $\gamma$.

We estimate the parameters in two steps hoping to achieve a better robustness. First, we estimate parameters of the linear specification only. Then, we fix the linear coefficients and rerun the estimation with the non-linear term included. This procedure is justified since inclusion of the orthogonal projection, as mentioned earlier, does not change the previously estimated linear coefficients $\hat{\alpha}$ and $\hat{\beta}$.

## NOTES

1. Notice that our results do not rely on spread changes being normally distributed. This result and its application is known as *quasi-*, or *pseudo-*, *maximum likelihood* (QML). Lee and Hansen (1994) prove consistency of the quasi-maximum likelihood estimation for the GARCH(1,1) specification of conditional volatility, which is methodologically similar to our specification.
2. The value of $\hat{s}_{t-1}^2$ is determined from a regression of squared spreads on spread levels and a constant. See this chapter's appendix for a detailed explanation.
3. The requirement of eight issuers per sector was imposed to ensure that our study remains focused on systematic effects and is not overly influenced by issuer-specific events.
4. The one outlier is BAA plc, which had a low median spread of 28 bps and a relatively high volatility of 41 bps per year. The spreads on BAA plc widened almost 60 bps after a hostile takeover bid from Ferrovia and subsequently recovered when the company agreed to include a new clause into issued debt

that allowed bondholders to sell bonds at their face value in case of rating downgrade resulting from merger or acquisition.

5. Volatilities based on weekly observations can be converted to a monthly frequency (assuming spread changes are distributed independently over time) by multiplying them by $\sqrt{4}$.

6. See this chapter's appendix for details of the exact estimation procedure.

7. Rather than capturing the month-over-month spread change averaged over the set of index bonds in a given sector as of the beginning of the month, we simply take the difference in the average spread from month to month. The key difference between the two approaches is that bonds that drop out of the index during the course of a month (e.g., due to defaults or to downgrades below investment grade) will not be included in our month-end average of index spreads. This helps keep our study focused on systematic effects and can be viewed as a crude equivalent to the filtering out of contracts with large spread changes in the study of CDS data. This technique helps avoid large anomalies from the Enron and NRG events in the U.S. energy sector, and the Ahold and Parmalat events in our study of European investment-grade bonds.

8. The results for the entire sample reflect the effect of July 1998–September 1998, which are excluded from the subperiods.

9. Recall that in Chapter 1, we examined the year-over-year stability of the proportionality factor without controlling for sector classification. These two studies, taken together, show stability of the slope both over time and across industry groups.

10. The formal conditions under which consistency is assured are given, for example, in Huber (1967) and White (1982).

11. The reason is that the estimators can be alternatively interpreted as *extremum estimators* with the resulting parameters converging in probability to some (pseudo-true) values. These parameters approximate the imposed model using the normal log-likelihood as a criteria function with a normal distribution. These pseudo-true parameters often turn out to coincide with the true parameters of the model.

### CHAPTER 3

# DTS for Sovereign Bonds

The 2007–2009 financial crisis led to deteriorating economic conditions in several of the Eurozone economies as high deficits and debt ratios raised solvency concerns. As a result, Euro sovereign spreads widened significantly in 2010, to the point where treasuries contributed a larger share of spread risk in the Euro Aggregate Index than corporate bonds. The recognition that even sovereign debt of developed countries may exhibit credit-like characteristics has forced market participants to closely examine their assumptions, exposures, and risk management practices relating to sovereign bonds. It also prompted many investors to question whether the DTS framework is applicable to sovereign bonds in addition to corporates.

To examine to what extent sovereign bonds are similar to corporate debt, we first analyze the spread dynamics of dollar-denominated bonds issued by emerging market countries. Historically, the pricing of this asset class has resembled that of corporate bonds in that it has been driven mainly by spreads rather than rates. We then proceed with a short overview of the behavior of spread levels and volatilities in the Euro-area countries since 1999, and demonstrate that the sovereign spread risk of developed countries can indeed resemble that of corporate issuers in many respects. Consequently, we find that DTS was very effective in quantifying the spread risk of Euro sovereigns in 2010, and generated volatility forecasts that quickly adjusted to changes in market conditions. We conclude with an illustration of a DTS-based risk framework to characterize changes in the risk profile of the Euro Aggregate Index, and demonstrate that in 2010 Euro treasuries contributed a larger part of the overall spread risk of the index than did Euro corporates.

## SPREAD DYNAMICS OF EMERGING MARKETS DEBT

To examine the behavior of emerging market spreads, we use monthly data from the Emerging Markets Dollar Denominated Index between January

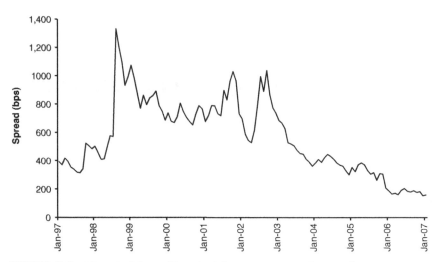

**FIGURE 3.1**   Historical Spread Level of the Emerging Markets Dollar
Denominated Index
*Source:* Barclays Capital.

1997 and January 2007.[1] The nature of the emerging markets data set
presents several challenges. First, spreads have changed by an order of magnitude during the course of the 10-year period, as illustrated in Figure 3.1.
In addition, the composition of the index is far from homogeneous. Bonds
from different issuer countries have varying credit qualities, and the country
composition of the index changes over time as various countries are included
or excluded. Therefore, we partition the data on the basis of issuer country,
and we examine only 13 countries that have been selected for their weight
in the index, diverse geographical location (thus spanning major emerging
market areas), and population of securities in the index throughout the
period of study.

A simple approach to examine the dynamics of spread behavior is to
estimate a general model as given in equation (3.1):

$$|\Delta s_{i,t}| = \alpha_i + \beta_i s_{i,t-1} + \varepsilon_{i,t} \tag{3.1}$$

where $|\Delta s_{i,t}|$ is the absolute change in spreads of country $i$ in month $t$ and
$s_{i,t-1}$ is the spread level as of the end of the previous month. Assuming a zero-
mean distribution for spread changes, $|\Delta s|$ in this model can serve as a proxy
for the spread volatility. Equation (3.1) therefore allows us to use month-
to-month changes in spreads to examine the relationship between spread
volatility and spread level. The advantage of using a regression rather than a

**TABLE 3.1** Regression Estimates for Spread Level Dependent Model of Spread Change

| | January 1999–January 2007 | | | | |
| | Coefficients | | t–stats | | |
| Country | Shift (bps) | Slope (%) | Shift | Slope | $R^2$ |
|---------|-------------|-----------|-------|-------|-------|
| Argentina | −138 | 37% | −2.64 | 4.59 | 0.35 |
| Brazil | −3 | 10% | −0.24 | 5.49 | 0.29 |
| Colombia | 14 | 7% | 1.15 | 2.93 | 0.08 |
| Mexico | −1 | 10% | −0.12 | 6.26 | 0.32 |
| Panama | 3 | 7% | 0.42 | 3.06 | 0.09 |
| Peru | 8 | 9% | 0.80 | 4.75 | 0.19 |
| Venezuela | 1 | 8% | 0.11 | 3.98 | 0.18 |
| Lebanon | −1 | 9% | −0.11 | 3.17 | 0.10 |
| Russia | −9 | 12% | −1.43 | 8.44 | 0.53 |
| Turkey | 0 | 12% | −0.01 | 4.19 | 0.17 |
| Indonesia | 6 | 5% | 0.61 | 2.01 | 0.06 |
| Kazakhstan | −17 | 17% | −1.65 | 5.86 | 0.27 |
| Philippines | −22 | 12% | −1.95 | 5.42 | 0.24 |

*Source:* Barclays Capital.

bucketing approach is that there is no need for time aggregation, which may be problematic when spreads experience large variations over the period as was the case for several EM countries.

Table 3.1 reports the coefficients for the set of countries in our data set estimated over the period January 1999 to January 2007. Observations with a spread greater than 1,000 bps (indicative of situations in which bonds are trading on price rather than spread) are excluded. Consistent with the DTS framework the estimated intercepts are insignificant for all but one of the countries (Argentina). In addition, the slope coefficients are positive and significant for all countries, ranging from 7% to 12% (with the exception of Argentina). The results are unchanged if the sample start date is set to January 1998 in order to capture the dynamics of the financial crisis in that year.

Figure 3.2 displays spread levels separately for each country over the January 1999–January 2007 period. While the first half of the period (January 1999–January 2003) was characterized by wide spreads, the second half is characterized by spread tightening. Thus, partitioning the entire sample on the basis of spread is not possible since certain buckets, especially low- and high-spread buckets, would be sparsely populated.

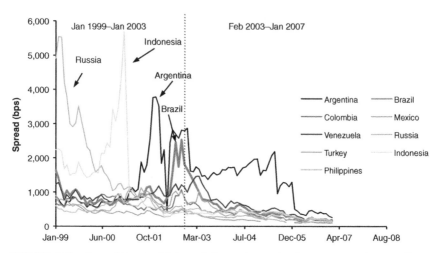

**FIGURE 3.2**   Spread Level of Selected Countries in the Emerging Markets Dollar
Denominated Index
*Source:* Barclays Capital.

Instead, we examine the relationship between spread volatility and spread
level separately in these two spread regimes.

Figure 3.3(A) shows the spread volatilities and corresponding average
spreads for each of the countries separately for the two periods.[2] The chart
indicates that most of the observations lie on the same diagonal line passing
through the origin, suggesting that the linear relationship held with the
same proportionality factor. Excluding observations with spreads greater
than 1,000 bps, a regression of spread volatility against spread level reveals
a slope of 13.2% with an insignificant intercept ($R^2 = 0.78$). This estimate
is in line with the 9.4% for U.S. corporate bonds reported in Chapter 1.

The pattern is distorted noticeably by only three countries: Indonesia,
Argentina, and Brazil (in this order). The behavior of these countries during the January 1999–January 2003 period can be explained by looking at
Figure 3.2, which reveals a rapid widening of spreads caused by financial
crises in these respective countries (Indonesia in early 2001, Argentina in
2001–2002, and Brazil in June 2002). Spikes in spreads have a dispropor-
tionate impact on the volatility of spread changes, relative to the average
spread level measured over a four-year period.[3] This distorts the results for
these countries.

Figure 3.3(B) plots the corresponding relation between DTS and excess
return volatility.[4] As was the case for corporate bonds, excess return volatility changes linearly with DTS and a straight line through the origin provides
an excellent fit ($R^2 = 0.96$), with a regression yielding a slope estimate of
12% and an insignificant intercept.

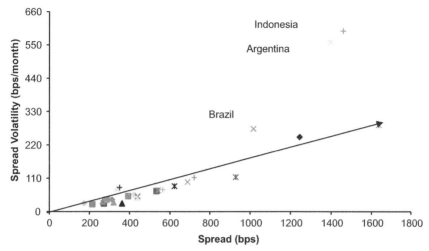

A. Spread Volatility versus Spread Level

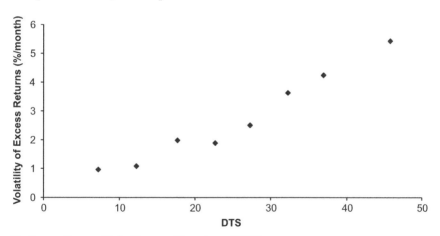

B. Excess Return Volatility as a Function of DTS

**FIGURE 3.3** Evidence of DTS Relation for Emerging Markets Sovereign Debt
*Note:* Monthly observations in Panel A: solids from February 2003 to January 2007; non-solids from January 1999 to January 2003.
*Source:* Barclays Capital.

## DTS FOR DEVELOPED MARKETS SOVEREIGNS: THE CASE OF EURO TREASURIES

Figure 3.4 depicts the historical spreads for several Euro sovereign issuers as well as the average spread of the Euro Treasury Index from January

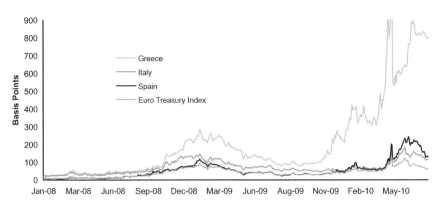

**FIGURE 3.4** Spreads of Selected European Treasury Indexes
*Source:* Barclays Capital.

2008 to July 2010.[5] The chart shows that, while Greece was in a category by itself—hitting a peak of 1,207 bps on May 7, 2010, before rallying back to less than 600 bps when the European Union (EU) announced a rescue package—spreads of other European sovereign countries increased simultaneously as the Greek crisis progressed and concerns about sovereign debt load propagated across the region.[6]

To better appreciate the fundamental shift in the market perception of Euro sovereign issuers, Figure 3.5 plots the spread over LIBOR for the Euro Treasury ex-Germany Index alongside that of the German Treasury Index since the introduction of the Euro in January 1999. The chart suggests that Euro sovereign spreads relative to the swaps curve were negative and very

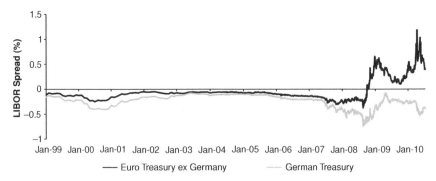

**FIGURE 3.5** Spread to LIBOR of German Treasury and Euro-Treasury excluding Germany Indexes
*Source:* Barclays Capital.

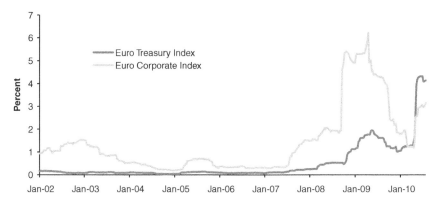

**FIGURE 3.6** Annualized Excess Return Volatilities of the Euro Corporate and Treasury Indexes
*Note:* Based on weekly excess returns, January 2002 to July 2010. Return volatilities are estimated over a 30-week rolling window and then annualized.
*Source*: Barclays Capital.

stable until early 2008, but then started to increase in the second half of 2008. As the sovereign crisis developed, a significant divergence emerged between the German Treasury curve and that of other issuers as Germany, and to a lesser extent other core countries, benefited from a flight to quality.

This increase in sovereign spreads has been accompanied by an increase in spread volatility and a resulting spike in the volatility of excess returns (computed over duration-matched German Treasury bonds). In fact, the volatility of excess returns for the Euro Treasury Index even surpassed that of the Euro Corporate Index in the middle of 2010, as shown in Figure 3.6. Collectively, the message from Figures 3.4, 3.5, and 3.6 is that, at least for part of the Euro Treasury Index, the rise of solvency concerns has given rise to a risk-return profile that mirrors that of a credit asset class.

Although the Merton (1974) structural model (see Chapter 4) suggesting a DTS-like behavior for the spread of corporate issuers is not directly applicable to sovereign issuers, the results earlier in this chapter and in Chapter 2 indicate that DTS is not limited in scope to corporate bonds. We therefore investigate the extent to which spreads of Euro sovereign issuers exhibit similar behavior.

Figure 3.7 shows the relation between the level of spread and spread volatility for the five countries at the center of the Euro sovereign crisis (Greece, Portugal, Ireland, Italy, and Spain). The analysis is conducted using a pooled data set of daily country-level spreads from May 2007 to May 2010. Each observation is first assigned to one of 12 predefined spread buckets, which are determined such that all buckets are reasonably populated.[7] The

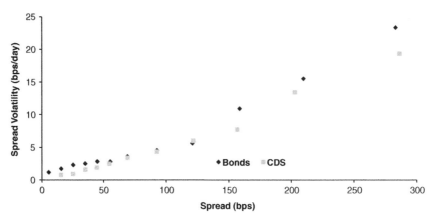

**FIGURE 3.7**   Spread Volatility versus Spread Level for High-Spread Euro Countries
*Note:* Based on daily spread levels for Greece, Portugal, Ireland, Italy, and Spain between May 15, 2007, and May 15, 2010. Each observation is first assigned to one of 12 predefined spread buckets. The spread volatility of each bucket is then calculated as the standard deviation of all daily spread changes assigned to a given bucket.
*Source:* Barclays Capital.

spread volatility of each bucket is then calculated as the standard deviation of all daily spread changes assigned to that bucket.

Four key points are evident from Figure 3.7. First, Euro sovereign bond spread volatility exhibits a near-linear relation with spread level, consistent with our expectations. Second, when we repeat the analysis for these countries using spreads of credit default swaps instead of bonds, we obtain a very similar pattern despite the differences in liquidity and pricing for the two sets of instruments. (Swaps are priced off the LIBOR curve, whereas bond spreads are quoted off the German Treasury curve.) Third, for spreads below 20 bps, there is a flattening of the linear relation, with spread volatility converging to a lower bound of about 1.5 bps/day, similar to the findings in Chapter 1 for roughly the same spread level.[8]

Fourth, regressing spread volatility against spread level yields an $R^2$ of 95% for bonds and 97% for CDS, with very similar slopes, 8.2% and 7% respectively. We can scale these figures up to monthly terms by a factor of $\sqrt{20}$ (based on an average of 20 business days per month). The resulting monthly slopes of 31% to 35% are much higher than both the 10% long-term estimate for corporate issuers we found in our original study (Chapter 1) and the 15% figure reached during the height of the 2007–2009 financial crisis (Chapter 10).[9] There are two reasons for the large discrepancy between the previous estimates for corporates and these results. First, the slope estimates of relative spread volatility in Figure 3.7 are based on sovereign issuers' total spread volatility. In contrast, the analysis of corporate bonds measured the systematic and idiosyncratic components of spread volatility separately, and found they have approximately the same magnitude. This implies in turn that monthly total spread volatility of a corporate bond would range between 14.1% and 21.2%. Furthermore, the simple conversion of daily to monthly estimates assumes independence of consecutive spread changes. A detailed analysis of the autocorrelation of daily spread changes reveals long periods where this assumption is not valid. As a result, monthly volatilities may be lower than those obtained by scaling up the daily estimates since the impact of large spread change realizations may be reversed intra-month. Indeed, estimates of relative spread volatility for sovereign issuers based on monthly data (reported in Table 3.3 in the column titled Factor Volatility) correspond closely to the total monthly volatility estimates of corporate bonds, ranging from 13% for France to 21% for Ireland and 24% for Portugal.

The results in Figure 3.7 suggest that spread volatility of Euro sovereigns should be measured in relative terms rather than in absolute terms. Using relative spreads should result in enhanced stability of the volatility estimates over time and, hence, a better ability to project risk.

Figure 3.8 compares the spread volatility of several Euro countries over two distinct time periods. Volatility between August 2008 and July

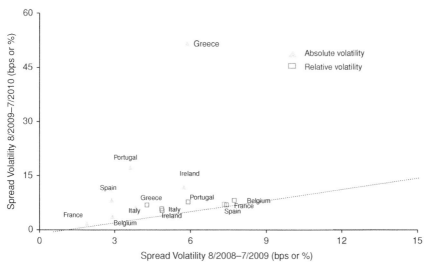

**FIGURE 3.8** Absolute and Relative Volatility of Daily Spread Change by Sovereign Issuer
*Source:* Barclays Capital.

2009 is represented on the $x$-axis, whereas the $y$-axis shows the volatility from August 2009 to July 2010. This partition was selected to highlight two periods with roughly the same length but which experienced very different spread dynamics. Each observation represents either the absolute or relative spread volatility of a particular country. Observations along the diagonal line indicate that the volatilities are the same over the two time periods.

Two clear patterns can be observed in the plot. First, most of the observations representing absolute spread volatilities are located quite far above the line, pointing to an increase in volatility in the second period of the sample. In contrast, relative spread volatilities are quite stable with almost all observations located on the straight line crossing the origin. This is because the pickup in volatility in the second period was accompanied by a similar increase in spreads. In particular, the absolute spread volatility of Greece has increased by a factor of almost 10 (from 5.9 bps to 51.6 bps) where in relative terms it only increased from 4.3% to 6.8%.

Second, relative spread volatilities of various countries are quite tightly clustered, ranging from 4.5% to a bit over 8%, whereas the range of absolute volatilities is much wider, ranging from 1.6 bps/month to more than 17 bps/month for Portugal and even higher for Greece. Furthermore, spread proportionality seems to capture well not only the spread dynamics of the countries that were in the center of the 2010 crisis (Greece, Portugal, Spain, Ireland, and Italy), but also countries that were less affected by it, such as Belgium and France. Belgium (rated Aa1) is a relatively small issuer that traded at an average spread of 30 bps and peaked just above 100 bps during the period studied, whereas France is a large issuer (rated Aaa) whose spread averaged 14 bps and peaked at around 50 bps. While the chart suggests that volatility remained essentially unchanged for the two countries whether measured in absolute or relative terms, the absolute spread volatility for Belgium is about double that of France, while their relative spread volatilities are quite similar. Using relative spreads thus offers the advantage of similar volatilities across all sovereign issuers.

Figure 3.9 presents the daily spread change of the Euro Treasury Index, normalized by two estimates of future spread volatility. The DTS-based forecast is the product of daily spread level and the estimate of relative spread proportionality using all available past relative spread realizations.[10] Forecasts using realized volatility are based on a trailing 90-day window. The plot illustrates that the DTS volatility estimates were consistently superior to those generated using realized volatilities over the past two years. Although the realized forecast relied on very recent history, it was unable to adjust properly to the speed at which market dynamics have changed, as evidenced by the 6.1 and −12.2 standard deviation realizations in May 2010.

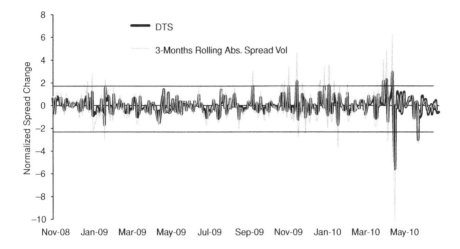

| Estimator | DTS | Realized Historical Vol. |
|---|---|---|
| Standard deviation | 0.96 | 1.27 |
| Max | 3.93 | 6.14 |
| Min | -7.56 | -12.15 |
| Skewness | -0.82 | -1.4 |
| Excess Kurtosis | 10.54 | 22.25 |

**FIGURE 3.9**   A Test of Spread Volatility Projections for the Euro Treasury Index Based on DTS and Historical Volatility

*Note:* Normalized spread changes are daily changes in spreads divided by a volatility projection based on an 8% (daily) spread proportionality slope or the realized spread volatility computed over the trailing 90 days between November 2008 and July 2010.

*Source:* Barclays Capital.

In addition, extreme outliers can be seen in the last quarter of 2009, before the Euro sovereign crisis went into full swing.[11]

The DTS-based forecasts quickly (albeit not perfectly) reflected the increased level of risk throughout the crisis, with almost all spread realizations corresponding to less than two standard deviations. A notable exception was May 10, 2010, when the EU approved a rescue package, causing spreads to tighten by almost 50 bps (−7.56 standard deviations). However, as discussed earlier, the forecasts using realized spread volatility often under- or overestimated the risk by a factor of two to three times more than the DTS-based forecast.

Indeed, the statistical properties of the distribution of normalized spread changes reported in the note at the bottom of Figure 3.9 suggest that DTS generates better estimates than historical realized volatility. A standard deviation of normalized spreads equal to one implies that the risk projections are on average accurate and do not exhibit any systematic bias. The standard deviation of the DTS-based normalized spread changes of 0.96 implies strong predictive power. By contrast, the value of 1.27 for the method based on realized volatility indicates a bias towards underestimating risk. In addition, the DTS estimator seems to have better tail properties: the largest absolute daily spread change in the period analyzed corresponds to a 7.56-standard deviation event, versus 12.15 for the realized volatility estimator; and excess kurtosis, which measures the "fatness" of the tails of a distribution, is 10.54 versus 22.25 respectively.

Figure 3.9 illustrates the advantage of the DTS approach over the risk projections based on absolute spread changes. The incorporation of spread information allows DTS-based estimates to adjust quickly to changing market conditions. In contrast, estimates based solely on historical data rely on a pre-specified time period, the selection of which requires subjective judgment. In addition, the time period selected should ideally reflect a market state that is similar to the current one, which may not exist. Indeed, as Figures 3.4 to 3.6 illustrate, there was no recent precedent to the Euro sovereign crisis. The rapid incorporation of market conditions as reflected in the level of spreads proved especially valuable in the current crisis in light of the abrupt and unprecedented deterioration in the credit markets' perception of sovereign issuers.

## MANAGING SOVEREIGN RISK USING DTS

To illustrate how DTS can be used in practice to manage sovereign risk, we construct a simple pro forma risk model. The model combines exposures to interest rate changes and relative changes in spreads of key treasury (by country) and non-treasury issuers (by sector). By maintaining a covariance matrix of changes in rates and relative spread changes, and measuring the exposures to each factor in terms of contributions to *key rate durations* (KRDs) and contributions to DTS (by country for Euro sovereigns or by sector for non-sovereigns), we can estimate the overall risk of a portfolio or benchmark, or the relative risk between the two, resulting from a set of active exposures. Table 3.2 shows the set of factors used in this pro forma risk model.

One can estimate return volatility by multiplying analytical measures of exposure such as KRD and DTS contributions by their factor volatilities and correlations. Table 3.3 provides an example of this risk calculation

**TABLE 3.2** Description of Risk Factors and Exposures in a Pro Forma DTS Risk Model

| Category | Systematic Risk Factor | Sensitivity |
|---|---|---|
| Yield curve | Yield changes for six tenors of the treasury curve 6 mo, 2 yr, 5 yr, 10 yr, 20 yr, 30 yr | Key rate duration |
| Non-Sovereign spreads | Proportional spread changes for five spread sectors Government-related, securitized, financial, industrial, and utility | Spread duration × Spread (DTS) |
| Sovereign spreads | Proportional spread changes for nine individual countries BE, FR, GR, IE, IT, NL, PT, ES, DE, and others | Spread duration × Spread (DTS) |

*Source:* Barclays Capital.

**TABLE 3.3** Estimated Return Volatility (bps/month) of the Euro Aggregate Index (as of July 30, 2010)

| Factor | Units | Exposure | Factor Volatility | Isolated Volatility | Total Volatility |
|---|---|---|---|---|---|
| KR 6 mo | KRD | 0.07 | 22 bps/mo | | |
| KR 2 yr | KRD | 0.74 | 24 | | |
| KR 5 yr | KRD | 1.65 | 22 | | |
| KR 10 yr | KRD | 1.68 | 19 | 103 bps/mo | |
| KR 20 yr | KRD | 0.87 | 16 | | |
| KR 30 yr | KRD | 0.58 | 17 | | |
| Government-related | DTS | 0.62 | 12%/mo | | |
| Securitized | DTS | 0.82 | 13 | | |
| Finance | DTS | 0.90 | 13 | 33 bps/mo | |
| Industrial | DTS | 0.43 | 14 | | 98 bps/mo |
| Utility | DTS | 0.11 | 11 | | |
| Treasury Belgium | DTS | 0.11 | 17 | | |
| Treasury France | DTS | 0.19 | 13 | | |
| Treasury Greece | DTS | 0.00 | 22 | | |
| Treasury Ireland | DTS | 0.15 | 21 | | |
| Treasury Italy | DTS | 1.12 | 15 | 35 bps/mo | |
| Treasury Netherlands | DTS | 0.04 | 15 | | |
| Treasury Portugal | DTS | 0.17 | 24 | | |
| Treasury Spain | DTS | 0.48 | 19 | | |
| Treasury Others | DTS | 0.09 | 17 | | |

*Note:* Covariances estimated from equally weighted monthly data since 2001.
*Source:* Barclays Capital.

for the Euro Aggregate Index as of July 30, 2010. Note that in this case, risk estimates are based on monthly data, corresponding to a one-month portfolio risk horizon. The isolated return volatilities associated with rates, all non-sovereign spreads and all sovereign spreads are 103 bps, 33 bps, and 35 bps a month respectively. Taking correlations into account, the return volatility is estimated at 98 bps/month for the entire index, less than the isolated rates risk since correlations between spread and rates factors are typically negative.

Interestingly, the return volatility embedded in sovereign spreads appears to be larger than all other sources of spread risk put together. This observation is consistent with the direct analysis of excess return volatility shown in Figure 3.6, albeit with a different time scale. If we repeat the exercise of calculating the isolated risks of the Euro Aggregate Index due to rates and spreads (sovereign and non-sovereign) over time (Figure 3.10), we find that sovereign spread risk had overtaken other sources of spread risk by the second quarter of 2010.

Figure 3.11 displays the increase in spread exposure of the Euro Aggregate Index, as measured by DTS, both overall and by sector. As spreads rose from 2007 to mid-2010—for both corporates and sovereigns, in turn—the DTS exposure in the Euro Aggregate Index increased dramatically, as seen in Figure 3.11(A). Figure 3.11(B) shows that as the sovereign crisis progressed, the proportion of DTS from sovereigns continued to rise, eventually exceeding the contribution of corporate issuers. Figure 3.11(C) demonstrates

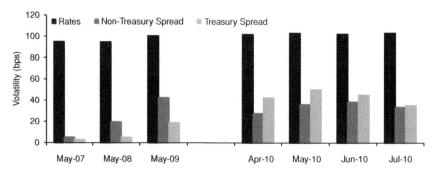

**FIGURE 3.10**   Isolated Return Volatilities in the Euro Aggregate Index (as of July 30, 2010)

*Note:* Covariances are estimated from equally weighted monthly data since 2001. Greece was excluded from the Euro Aggregate Index at the end of June 2010 following its downgrade below investment grade and so the June and July 2010 bars in this figure exclude Greece.

*Source:* Barclays Capital.

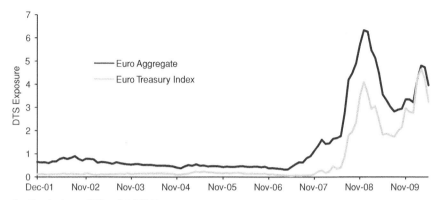

A. Evolution of Total DTS Exposure

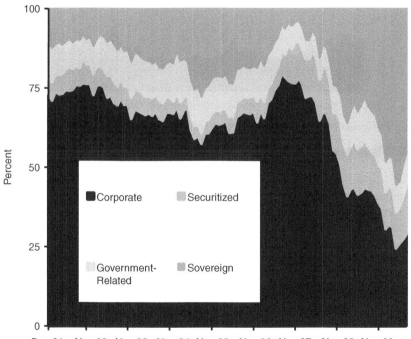

B. Evolution of DTS Exposure in the Euro Aggregate Index by Sector

**FIGURE 3.11** Evolution and Attribution of DTS exposure in the Euro Treasury and Euro Aggregate Indexes

*Note:* Greece was excluded from the Euro Aggregate Index at the end of June 2010 following its downgrade below investment grade.

*Source:* Barclays Capital.

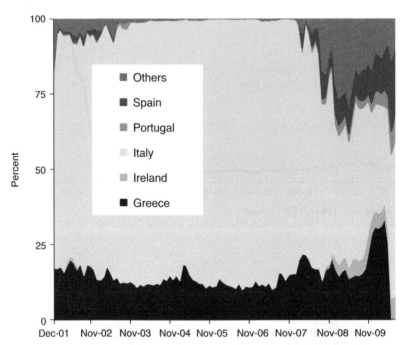

**C. Evolution of DTS Exposure in the Euro Treasury Index by Country**

**FIGURE 3.11**   (*Continued*)

a similar progression for the Euro Treasury Index, though the increase in DTS exposure was much more sudden. The spread widening of corporates in 2007 and early 2008 had little or no effect; concerns in the sovereign market struck towards the end of 2008.[12] Whereas prior to the sovereign crisis, the spread exposure in the Euro Treasury Index was dominated by Italy, the 2010 experience was characterized by a growing portion of DTS coming from other European sovereigns, notably Greece (up to the end of June 2010, when it was excluded from investment-grade indexes).

## CONCLUSION

The Euro sovereign crisis of 2010 forced investors to revisit the risk management practices and portfolio management processes for their Euro fixed income portfolios (and global treasuries more generally). While many investors in the Euro Treasury Index had viewed this as an asset class containing little or no credit risk, this was certainly no longer the case. Not only had the total amount of spread risk increased, but the magnitude of the spread risk coming from sovereigns had grown larger than that coming from the corporate sector!

To help manage these exposures, it is important to put in place the right framework for measuring and monitoring risk. Investors can no longer disregard the spread risk (and implicit default risk) of many developed countries and focus only on interest rate risk. Instead, they should adopt a DTS approach, similar to that used to manage the risk of corporate issuers. This can help managers measure and control sovereign spread risk in a more timely and accurate manner.

## NOTES

1. Since the index includes Brady bonds that are collateralized by U.S. treasuries, we use stripped spread over treasuries, which reflects true sovereign risk as opposed to spread measures, such as blended spread as our measure of spread. (Blended spread is the spread measure for all the cash flows, computed without distinguishing between sovereign and guaranteed cash flows. Stripped analytics, on the other hand, values only the non-collateralized cash flows and is therefore a better measure of sovereign risk.)
2. Spread data for Mexico is missing for January 2005–November 2005 period. Spreads of Mexican bonds tightened considerably during this period culminating in an exit from the EM index. The sovereign rating ceiling for emerging market index eligibility was raised in January 2006 to include countries rated Baa1/BBB+ from Baa3/BBB–. This resulted in Mexico coming back into the Emerging Market Dollar–Denominated Index.
3. For this reason, we use average spread level rather than the median spread. Due to spikes in spreads, the median spread measure will not capture the true relationship with spread volatility. The average spread measure, though not perfect, does a better job in this respect.
4. The country level data are partitioned monthly into buckets based on DTS values. Each country is assigned to one of the eight DTS buckets every month if its spread is less than 1,000 bps (observations with spread over 1,000 bps are excluded). We then calculate the median beginning-of-month DTS and the average excess return within each bucket each month. The volatility of excess returns and the average DTS for each bucket are then computed over the entire time period.
5. Spreads and excess returns of all European countries are computed relative to the German Treasury curve.
6. This pattern of contagion was subsequently followed repeatedly. Each time a new cause for concern surfaced in a Euro sovereign (e.g., Greece, Ireland, and Portugal), spreads would tend to widen for all vulnerable issuers in the region.

7. We use the following spread buckets: $\leq$ 10 bps, 11–20, 21–30, 31–40, 41–50, 51–60, 61–80, 81–105, 106–140, 141–180, 181–230, and 231–382 bps. Each bucket contains at least 110 observations.

8. Spread volatility at very low spreads is driven primarily by technical reasons, such as supply and demand imbalances and the pricing model used, rather than by changes in the perceived default risk.

9. This assumes independence of the daily spread changes and 20 trading days per month.

10. This approach prevents "look-ahead" bias. Following Ben Dor, Dynkin, and Hyman (2005b) spread changes are normalized by the larger of the spread level or 20 bps.

11. A "long-term" forecast (using all available history) performed even worse since there was no precedent to the crisis and a longer window results in a slower incorporation of new information.

12. The financial crisis and the ensuing sovereign crisis may in fact be closely related. Schuknecht, von Hagen, and Wolswijk (2010) demonstrate that the penalty for fiscal imbalances imposed by the government bond market increased sharply after the Lehman default in September 2008.

### CHAPTER 4

# A Theoretical Basis for DTS

In the previous three chapters, we presented the DTS approach to credit risk measurement, with empirical evidence from the corporate bond, CDS, and sovereign debt markets. Fundamental to this approach is the empirical observation that the dependence of spread volatility on spread level tends to be very nearly linear. We have found this result to have strong intuitive appeal: It makes sense, for example, that a typical "flight-to-quality" scenario is more likely to follow a relative spread change than a parallel shift in spreads. Issuers and sectors that were already trading at higher spreads will widen by more than their less risky counterparts. However, we have not yet demonstrated any reason this should be the case according to theoretical models of credit spreads. If this linear relationship between spreads and spread volatilities is so fundamental to the way our markets behave, why was this not already a well-established result in the theoretical literature? Can we find support for it in fundamental models? In this chapter, we investigate the relationship between credit spreads and their volatilities according to the simple structural credit model introduced in Merton (1974).

The usefulness of DTS as a primary measure of credit exposures hinges on the two main conclusions of our empirical studies:

1. Spread volatility grows linearly with spread.
2. This relationship remains consistent across a wide range of other bond characteristics—notably, maturity and credit rating.

We turn to theory in an effort to corroborate these qualitative findings, as well as the numeric values we have found for the slope of this relationship. Over the long term, as illustrated in Figure 1.8, the monthly volatility of systematic changes in sector spreads was found to be about 10% of the spread (so that a sector with an average spread of 100 bps would be expected to be exposed to a spread volatility of 10 bps/month). Similarly, the monthly volatility of idiosyncratic spread changes was found to be about 10% of bond spread, as shown in Figure 1.10. Putting these two sources of spread volatility together, assuming their independence, leads us to expect the total monthly spread volatility for any bond to be about 14% to 15% of its spread.

The model we explore in this chapter belongs to the class of structural models, in which the main state variable is the value of a firm's assets. Given a specified set of assumptions for the capital structure of the firm, changes in firm asset value determine the likelihood of default and the valuations of the firm's debt and equity. We focus on the original formulation of the Merton (1974) model, which assumes a simple capital structure in which all of the firm's debt is concentrated in a single zero-coupon bond of maturity $T$.

Subject to the assumptions of the model, we obtain approximate formulas for both credit spreads and their volatilities. We do not get an analytical result that indicates a perfectly linear relationship; the formulas that emerge from these models are highly non-linear by their nature. However, when we evaluate the results numerically, we find strong support for the DTS approach; the relationship between spread and spread volatilities can be shown to be nearly linear over a range of parameter values that is most relevant to credit markets.

## THE MERTON MODEL: A ZERO-COUPON BOND

Merton (1974) presents a fairly general framework for pricing debt securities based on a structural model of the issuing firm. He then details a specific solution for a special case in which the firm's debt is modeled as a single zero-coupon bond. We will focus on this case, which allows for a particularly tractable solution.

The key source of uncertainty in the model is expressed in the evolution over time of the asset value of the firm $v_t$, whose dynamics are modeled as a lognormal stochastic process with drift $\mu$ and volatility $\sigma$.[1] The asset value follows a geometric Brownian motion given by

$$dv = \mu \cdot v \, dt + \sigma \cdot v \, dz \tag{4.1}$$

where $dz$ is a standard Gauss-Wiener process. We also assume that the risk-free term structure of interest rates is flat at a given rate $r$ and does not vary over time.

The firm has a simple capital structure in which its entire debt consists of a single zero-coupon bond of face value $F$ maturing at time $T$. We further assume that the firm will be dissolved at time $T$, with its assets distributed between the owners of the bond and the equity. If, at maturity, the firm has sufficient assets to repay its debt ($v_t \geq F$), then the firm is solvent, the bondholders receive $F$, and the equity holders receive $v_t - F$. If not, then the bondholders receive all of the firm's assets $v_t$, and the equity holders get nothing. The key insight provided by Merton is that, in this setup, the firm's equity is equivalent to a European option on the firm's asset value and can be valued using the Black-Scholes option pricing equation.

To simplify the notation, we introduce the normalized firm value, $x_t = v_t/F$, expressed relative to the amount of the debt. Because of the geometric nature of the process, $x$ follows the same dynamics as $v$, as described earlier. At time $T$, the firm is solvent if the firm value is greater than the face value of the debt, that is, if $x \geq 1$. In this case, the bondholders get back the face value of the bond and equity holders get $x - 1$. Otherwise, the firm is bankrupt, and stockholders get nothing while bondholders get $x$.

To discuss the pricing of the bond, we introduce the following additional notation. Let

$B =$ the price of a zero-coupon bond of maturity $T$, per unit of face value

$s =$ the spread of the corporate bond over the risk-free rate (continuous compounding)

$\sigma_{\text{spread}} =$ absolute volatility of spreads = volatility of change in $s$

We would like to establish the theoretical relationship between $s$ and $\sigma_{\text{spread}}$. We will do this implicitly, by expressing each of these quantities as a function of $x$, the normalized asset value of the firm. If we find the sensitivities of each of these quantities to $x$, we can then use these to implicitly establish the sensitivity of $\sigma_{\text{spread}}$ to changes in $s$.

Given the assumption that the risk-free interest rate $r$ is constant and independent of the time to maturity $T$, the price and the spread of the bond are just two equivalent ways of quoting its value and are related to each other by simple discounting, $B = e^{-(r+s)T}$.

To obtain the price of the bond, we express the present value of the firm as the sum of the present value of the bond and that of the equity, which is modeled as a European call option:

$$x = \text{Bond} + \text{Equity} = B + C(x)$$
$$B = x - C(x) \tag{4.2}$$

where the call option $C(x)$ is valued according to the Black-Scholes-Merton formulas, which give us its sensitivity to $x$ as well, in the form of the option delta. We can then find the sensitivity of $s$ to $x$ using the chain rule as follows:

$$\frac{\partial s}{\partial x} = \frac{\partial s}{\partial B}\frac{\partial B}{\partial x} = -\frac{1}{T}\frac{1}{B}\frac{\partial B}{\partial x} \qquad (4.3)$$

Assuming that changes in $x$ are the only cause of change in $s$, this can be manipulated to express a differential change in $s$ in terms of a relative differential change in $x$:

$$ds = -\frac{1}{T}\frac{x}{B}\frac{\partial B}{\partial x}\frac{dx}{x} \qquad (4.4)$$

While a rigorous mathematical proof is beyond the scope of this chapter, we can then equate the volatilities of these two differential changes:

$$\text{volatility}\,(ds) = \frac{1}{T}\frac{x}{B}\frac{\partial B}{\partial x}\,\text{volatility}\left(\frac{dx}{x}\right)$$

$$\sigma_{\text{spread}} = \frac{1}{T}\frac{x}{B}\frac{\partial B}{\partial x}\sigma \qquad (4.5)$$

We have now expressed both $s$ and $\sigma_{\text{spread}}$ as functions of $x$. We are now in position to calculate both of these quantities numerically for various values of $x$ and plot one versus the other to observe the relationship.

The relationship between spread and spread volatility derived from this model is shown in Figure 4.1, assuming an asset return volatility of 15% and a debt maturity of five years. Over the range of spreads from 0 to 200 bps that typically characterizes investment-grade corporate bonds, the model

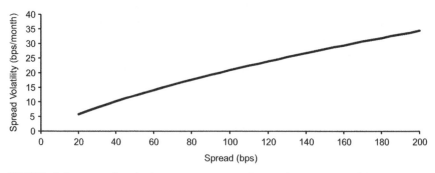

**FIGURE 4.1** Spread Volatility as a Function of Spread, Merton Model ($\sigma = 15\%$, $T = 5$ years)

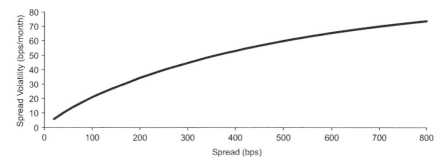

**FIGURE 4.2** Spread Volatility as Function of Spread, Merton Model, Extended Scale ($\sigma = 15\%$, $T = 5$ years)

yields a nearly linear relationship. The slope of the observed relationship shown in Figure 4.1 is 15.6%, consistent with the results of our empirical studies.

However, if we look a little more closely at the results obtained here, we begin to run into difficulties. First of all, when we extend the range of spreads to higher spread levels, we find that the nonlinearities in the option pricing formula become much more apparent. Figure 4.2, which simply extends the relationship shown in Figure 4.1 out to spreads of 800 bps, can hardly be described as linear. This model shows spread volatility to be a concave function of spreads that levels off as spreads rise beyond a certain point. While the analysis in the previous chapters found some minor evidence of such a phenomenon, the linear relationship was found to hold up for high-yield spreads as well, out to spreads of at least 500 bps.

## DEPENDENCE OF SLOPE ON MATURITY

The empirical results shown in Chapter 1 indicate that spread volatility is proportional to spread, and excess return volatility is proportional to DTS, with no further information being offered by maturity. Ben Dor, Dynkin, and Hyman (2005b) conducted additional empirical tests to test explicitly for dependence on sector and maturity. Ben Dor et al. (2005b) report regression results using dummy variables showing that longer-maturity bonds exhibit a somewhat lower slope than shorter-maturity bonds. However, the reported slope differences between the longest and shortest duration cells were only 1.2% for systematic volatility and 2.3% for idiosyncratic volatility. These would give slope estimates for overall volatility of 15.6% for long-duration bonds compared to 18.2% for short-duration bonds.

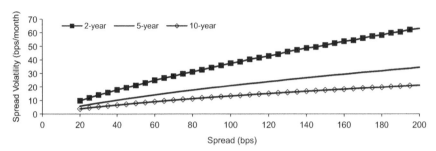

**FIGURE 4.3** Maturity Dependence of the Relation between Spread Volatility and Level Implied by the Merton Model

However, the theoretical model discussed in this chapter indicates a strong dependence on maturity. Figure 4.3 (and equation 4.5) shows that for any given level of spread, the expected spread volatility should be much higher for the 2-year maturity than it is for the 10-year maturity; the slope of the dependence of volatility on spread, based on the data shown in Figure 4.3, is 29.1% for $T = 2$ years and 9.5% for $T = 10$ years.

In order to explain this apparent discrepancy, we must carefully review the assumptions underlying our theoretical model as well as the statistical techniques used in the empirical studies of Chapter 1. First, we should make sure to not misrepresent the results shown in Figure 4.3. This figure does not compare the spreads and volatilities of three bonds of different maturities from the same issuer. Rather, it should be viewed as comparing three firms with very different capital structures. Each firm is financed by a zero-coupon bond maturing at a specific point in time, which then becomes the only point in time at which a default event may occur. For the firm just two years from this date to deserve a spread of 50 bps, its net asset value must be much closer to zero than the firm with 10 years to go; it will therefore be much more sensitive to further changes in firm value, leading to increased spread volatility.

In reality however, firms are not typically financed by a single zero-coupon bond. An issuer will borrow at a range of maturities, such that any given bond represents but a small part of its capital structure. The holders of a 2-year bond and 10-year bond from the same issuer should not have different models for how likely that issuer is to default in the coming year. To accurately assess the differences in risk characteristics for corporate bonds of different maturities, we need to decouple our modeling of a corporate default event from the description of a particular bond. We also need to consider the differences between zero-coupon debt and the more prevalent coupon-bearing bonds. The net result of these adjustments would likely be to reduce the maturity dependence of the volatility-to-spread slope.

At the same time, we should not entirely discount the theoretical evidence shown in Figure 4.3 that short-dated spreads should exhibit greater volatilities. The empirical studies reported in Chapter 1, while they do not indicate such a trend, were also not designed to test for it explicitly. They were formed from long-term statistical averages over many bonds and across many different types of market environments. More recently, we have undertaken studies that focus on relative spread volatility, and have found that shorter-dated bonds do indeed tend to have greater relative spread volatilities, as predicted by the theory. The magnitude of this effect is such that it should not be material in most typical portfolio management situations, but could be significant for portfolios that leverage up their exposures to the short end of the curve. Further research is underway to resolve these issues.

## CONCLUSION

In this chapter, we have developed a theoretical basis for DTS, based on a simple variant of the Merton model. Using a single zero-coupon bond to model the debt portion of the corporate structure, we can express both the spread of the bond and the volatility of this spread in terms of a common set of variables that determine the creditworthiness of the issuing firm. This model allows us to develop an analytical relationship between spread and spread volatility, and confirms that this relationship is very close to linear within the investment-grade range of spreads. For a reasonable set of input parameters, we also obtain a slope estimate that is consistent with our observed empirical results. The many simplifying assumptions underlying this model mean that we cannot blindly rely on it as an accurate depiction of market behavior. Nevertheless, the model indicates that the slope of the spread–volatility relationship should exhibit dependence on both the maturity of a bond and on equity market volatility. This provides a theoretical starting reference for evaluation of additional empirical evidence.

## NOTE

1. Merton (1974) also provides for the firm to pay out dividends at a fixed rate; we have chosen to set the dividend yield to zero for simplicity. Allowing for non-zero dividend yields did not have a material effect on our results.

### CHAPTER 5

# Quantifying the Liquidity of Corporate Bonds

## Liquidity Cost Scores

Liquidity can mean different things depending on the market environment, the nature of the underlying asset, and the portfolio objective. In a broad sense, however, liquidity refers to how efficiently a portfolio's dynamism can be managed. While all portfolio managers, traders, and risk managers acknowledge the importance of "liquidity," they struggle to quantify it. Our goal is to offer investors an objective measure of bond-level liquidity while acknowledging that it captures only one aspect of liquidity.

Liquidity has long been studied and measured in the equity market, but data limitations have prevented similar progress in measuring liquidity in the fixed income market. While bond-level trading volume data have become available in recent years, bonds that do not trade are not necessarily illiquid; conversely, bonds that trade are not necessarily liquid, such as *fallen angels*, which experience forced selling upon their downgrade. (See Chapter 13 for more details.)

We have chosen to define liquidity as the cost of a roundtrip institutional-size transaction in a bond. For each bond in our database we compute a Liquidity Cost Score (LCS)™ based on bid-ask spread data and other bond attributes.[1] We selected this definition of fixed income liquidity from the multitude of possibilities for two reasons. First, we have access to good quality, synchronized bond-level bid-ask spread indications for institutional-size trades. Second, other measures of liquidity, such as market impact, require trade volume data combined with trade prices. While these data are becoming increasingly available, they are still sparse at the bond level. In addition, although measuring market impact would be useful, many market participants believe that bid-ask spreads are likely to be highly correlated with other liquidity measures.

Portfolio managers, plan sponsors, and researchers can use LCS in a number of ways:

- *Construction of "liquid" tracking portfolios.* A manager who wants a high level of transactional flexibility can use LCS as a filter to identify bonds for a portfolio. Such a portfolio can be used either to capitalize on views of changes in market liquidity or to improve the ability to liquidate the portfolio during illiquid times.
- *Identify liquidity cost embedded in credit spreads.* A portfolio manager might use LCS to disentangle the portions of a bond's expected excess return due to liquidity risk and credit risk. This would facilitate hedging, as the two risks can be hedged using different instruments, such as VIX futures for liquidity and CDS for credit risk. (See Chapter 6.)
- *Execution strategies.* LCS allows investors to monitor the relative liquidity behavior of bonds over time. During times of illiquidity, do bonds with high LCS perform much worse than bonds with low LCS? If so, then a strategy of selling illiquid bonds at the beginning of a liquidity crisis may be more productive than selling liquid bonds first.
- *Liquid credit benchmarks.* LCS gives plan sponsors the ability to define custom liquid credit benchmarks for their credit managers.

## LIQUIDITY COST SCORES (LCS) FOR U.S. CREDIT BONDS[2]

A bond's LCS uses trader bid-ask indications to estimate a bid-ask market spread (i.e., the difference between the spread [to treasuries] that the trader is willing to sell the bond and the spread at which the trader is willing to buy the bond). We define LCS as the bond's OASD multiplied by this spread. Consequently, a bond's LCS can be interpreted as the cost, in percentage points, of immediately executing a roundtrip transaction.

Before discussing the specific details of the LCS calculation, we first show how to use LCS to quantify macro changes in market liquidity over time. Figure 5.1 shows the aggregated LCS time series (using market value weights) for the U.S. IG Credit and High Yield Indexes (hereafter referred to as the IG Index and the HY Index) from January 2007 through June 2009.

Over this time period, the LCS for the IG Index ranged from 0.59% to 3.40%. Although the spike in illiquidity that occurred in October 2008 is painfully clear, the index's LCS values had already *doubled* between June 2007 and September 2007, in the very early stages of the credit crisis.

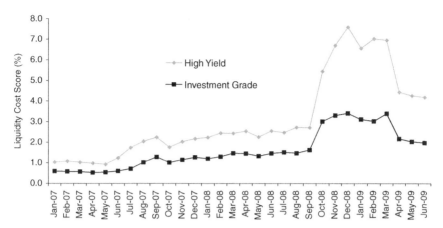

**FIGURE 5.1**   Liquidity Cost Score for the U.S. IG and HY Credit Indexes (January 2007–June 2009)
*Source:* Barclays Capital.

Because LCS is measured in price percentage terms, the absolute difference in LCS is what is relevant to portfolio managers when comparing two asset classes. As seen in Figure 5.1, at the beginning of 2007 the LCS for the HY Index was approximately 40 bps greater than that for the IG Index. By the end of 2008, however, the gap had widened to more than 400 bps.

Although the increase in illiquidity over that two-year period is widely known, what is perhaps less appreciated is the extent of the change in the distribution of liquidity across bonds. Figure 5.2(A) shows the frequency distribution of LCS scores for all bonds in the IG Index as of January 2007, November 2008, and June 2009. Figure 5.2(B) shows the cumulative distribution.

The LCS distribution for IG bonds in January 2007 is very concentrated around the mean of 0.59%. However, note what happened to the distribution by November 2008: Not only did the mean LCS score increase to 3.40%, but the standard deviation of the distribution increased sharply. Interestingly, despite the improvement in LCS by June 2009 (mean LCS = 1.97%) and claims of normalcy returning to the credit markets, the distribution remained widely dispersed, suggesting that the credit markets still had some distance to go to return to the January 2007 environment. LCS distribution for the HY Index (not shown) displayed similar properties.

We can also calculate a sector-level LCS. Figure 5.3 shows the LCS time series for various IG and HY sectors. Although all sectors experienced reduced liquidity in the two years after 2007, some sectors (e.g., financial IG

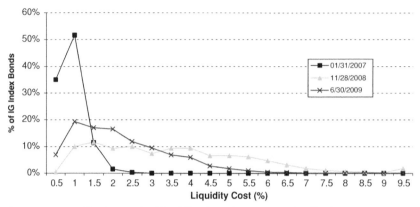

**A.** Investment-Grade Bonds: Liquidity Cost Frequency Distribution

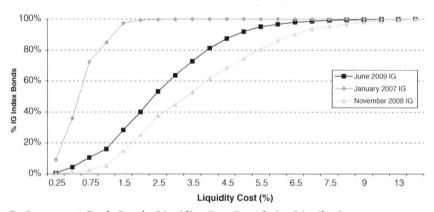

**B.** Investment-Grade Bonds: Liquidity Cost Cumulative Distribution

**FIGURE 5.2**   Distribution of LCS Values: IG Index (January 2007, November 2008, and June 2009)
*Source:* Barclays Capital.

subordinate bonds and financial HY seniors) experienced a greater deterioration in liquidity than others (e.g., IG industrial seniors and HY energy).

It is also instructive to sort the IG Index into LCS quintiles. Each month bonds are assigned to quintiles based on their LCS values. Quintile 1 includes the 20% of index bonds with the lowest LCS while Quintile 5 contains the 20% of bonds with the highest LCS. Consequently, as time passes, the specific bonds in each quintile can change. Figure 5.4 shows the average LCS by quintile since January 2007. We see that the deterioration in liquidity was not even; the higher the quintile, the greater the deterioration in LCS as overall market liquidity deteriorated.

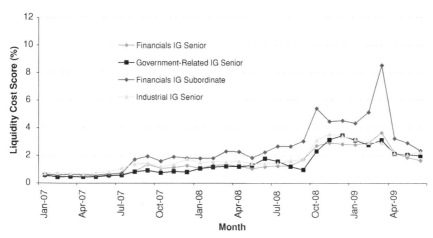

A. Liquidity Cost Scores by Sector: IG

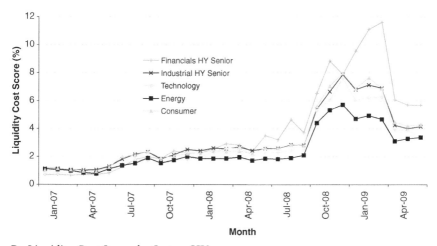

B. Liquidity Cost Scores by Sector: HY

**FIGURE 5.3** Distribution of LCS Values by Sector for the IG and HY Indexes
(January 2007–June 2009)
*Source:* Barclays Capital.

There is likely to be a relationship between a bond's LCS and its excess returns (versus U.S. Treasuries), depending on the market environment. During times of good market liquidity, potential buyers of a bond with a high LCS would likely demand a lower price (higher yield), all else equal, to cover future transactions costs. The higher yield, in turn, should lead to a greater excess return for buy-and-hold investors (as represented by the

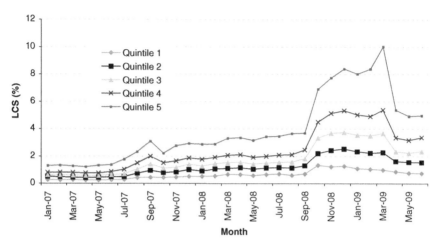

**FIGURE 5.4**   Average LCS by Quintile: IG Index (January 2007–June 2009)
*Source:* Barclays Capital.

index). In addition, if there is a relationship between a bond's LCS and the risk that its LCS can change sharply over time (i.e., liquidity risk), then we might also expect that investors will demand even lower prices (higher yields)—a so-called "liquidity premium"—to invest in relatively high LCS bonds. However, during times of a market liquidity crisis, when liquidity risk is realized, the severe mark-to-market impact of holding illiquid bonds can produce large negative excess returns.

We examine the excess return performance of the various quintiles as the credit liquidity crisis unfolded. Figure 5.5 shows the relative excess return performance of Quintile 4 versus Quintile 1, as well as the net LCS difference between the two quintiles. Although the results are more dramatic comparing Quintile 5 with Quintile 1, we chose Quintile 4 to avoid any possible idiosyncratic issues associated with the bonds in Quintile 5.

As Quintile 4's LCS deteriorated relative to Quintile 1, it also suffered worse excess returns. From January 2007 to December 2008, as the LCS gap between Quintile 4 and Quintile 1 increased by 3.50% points, Quintile 4 experienced a cumulative excess return almost 14% points lower than Quintile 1. The deterioration in relative excess return performance for Quintile 4 began in mid-2007 as market liquidity began to decline. Since March 2009, Quintile 4's performance improved significantly relative to Quintile 1, coinciding with the relative improvement in Quintile 4's LCS versus Quintile 1.

At this point, we cannot conclude that Quintile 4's relative performance was tied directly to its relative LCS as the market became more or less liquid. This is because a bond's LCS is closely related to its credit risk (DTS

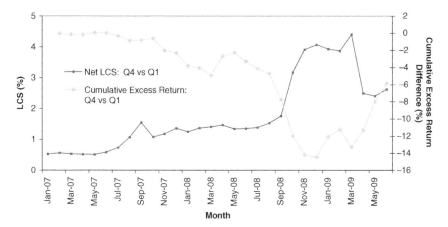

**FIGURE 5.5**   Difference in LCS and Cumulative Excess Return between Quintile 4 and Quintile 1 of IG Credit Index (January 2007–June 2009)
*Source:* Barclays Capital.

or OAS). As the market's liquidity deteriorated, so did the perception of creditworthiness. How much of Quintile 4's 2008 underperformance was due to liquidity and how much was due to heightened credit risk? With bond-level LCS, we can attempt to disentangle credit risk and liquidity risk as contributors to spreads (see Chapter 6).

Finally, we examine how LCS at an aggregate level is related to other indicators of market-wide liquidity used by portfolio managers. For example, the TED spread (short-term Eurodollar deposit rates minus Treasury bill rates) and VIX (volatility index) are common indirect measures of market liquidity. Figure 5.6 shows the relationship between the LCS for the IG Credit Index and the TED spread and VIX.

The VIX shows a close relationship with LCS (correlation = 0.90), confirming the intuition of many portfolio managers and traders that VIX futures, despite being a measure of implied volatility in equity markets, might be a good hedging tool for market illiquidity. In contrast, the TED spread, which *a priori* might be considered a more direct measure of illiquidity in fixed income markets, seems less highly correlated (correlation = 0.45). However, the clear breakdown in the TED spread correlation during October 2008–January 2009 may be related to the widely reported problems in the LIBOR value calculation. It is alleged that during this time, some participants did not accurately report their borrowing cost levels so as not to highlight any funding problems they might have been experiencing.

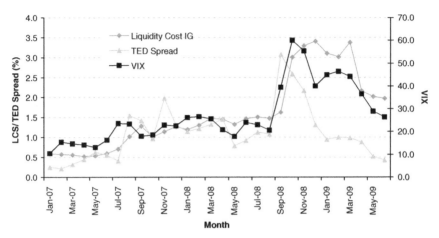

**FIGURE 5.6**   Relationship between LCS of the IG Index, TED Spread, and VIX
(January 2007–June 2009)
*Source:* Barclays Capital.


## LIQUIDITY COST SCORES: METHODOLOGY

We define a bond's liquidity as its bid-ask market spread multiplied by the
bond's spread duration (for spread-quoted bonds) or as its bid-ask price
spread as a fraction of its bid price (for price-quoted bonds):

$$LCS = \begin{cases} (\text{Bid-Ask spread}) \times \text{Option-adjusted spread duration} \\ \text{if bond is spread quoted} \\[2ex] \dfrac{\text{Ask price} - \text{Bid price}}{\text{Bid price}} \\ \text{if bond is price quoted} \end{cases}$$

   A bond's LCS, therefore, represents the *roundtrip cost*, as a percent of
the bond's value, of immediately executing a standard institutional transaction. According to this definition, a higher LCS value represents less liquidity.
For example, an LCS value of 2.00% indicates that it would cost the manager 2% of the bond's value to execute a roundtrip transaction (e.g., buy,
then sell, the bond) for a "normal-sized" transaction amount (e.g., $3 to
$5 million par). (*Note:* Although LCS values are measured in percentage
points, we sometimes drop the % symbol.)

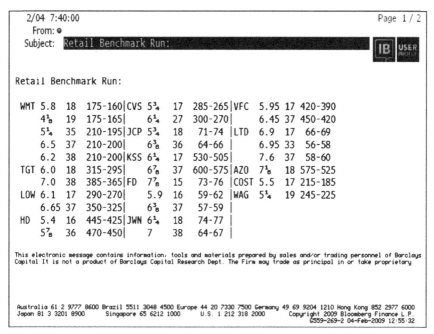

**FIGURE 5.7** Sample Bloomberg Message Screen Used by Traders to Communicate Bid-Ask Indications

*Note:* Bloomberg is not responsible for any aspect of LCS.

*Source:* Bloomberg.

We obtain bond-level bid-ask spread indications (or bid-ask price indications if the bond is quoted on price) from messages that Barclays Capital traders regularly send to clients. A sample message is presented in Figure 5.7.

Barclays Capital, a major and longstanding participant in U.S. cash credit markets, is a trading counterparty to the world's largest institutional credit market investors. As a result, Barclays Capital's messages are followed closely by a wide audience, boosting the quality of the LCS values. In addition, these messages have been collected, parsed, and stored by the Barclays Capital Index Production Team as part of its normal index price verification processes. Given the close scrutiny of the Barclays Capital indexes, Index Production has developed procedures to capture trader bid-ask indications and rigorous parsing algorithms to match a trader's shorthand bond indication to the right CUSIP (Committee on Uniform Security Identification Procedures) number. Each year Index Production collects millions of bid-ask spread quotes.

LCS starts with Index Production's CUSIP-level indications and passes them through additional filtering processes to produce a database of bond-level bid and ask spread (or, price) indications, along with other bond-level indicative information. Some bonds may have multiple quotes per day while others may have only one or two quotes a month. For each CUSIP, we first average any multiple LCS values in a day to generate a daily value, which, in turn, is averaged across all days in a month to produce a monthly average LCS.

There are pros and cons to using trader data. First, a nice feature of trader indications is their simultaneity. Although it is possible to capture transaction spread data *via* TRACE,[3] for most bonds the time between a broker-dealer buy and sell transaction for a given CUSIP can be very long, so it is difficult to calculate an accurate bid-ask spread using TRACE.

However, a drawback of trader indications is that a bond's bid-ask spread may not be the "market's best" bid-ask spread. For example, while a Barclays Capital trader may indicate a +180/+160 spread market for a bond, another broker-dealer may indicate +170/+150. Consequently, if there is a search across broker-dealers, the investor would face a +170/+160 effective market, indicating better liquidity than that suggested by the Barclays Capital indication by itself. This may result in LCS overstating bond liquidity costs.

Another limitation of bid-ask trader indications is the potential that they could be influenced by a trader's outlook or inventory. If a trader were temporarily long inventory of a particular bond, then the trader might quote the bond with a tighter spread (i.e., a higher offered spread) to entice a bid, and vice versa. Unfortunately for our purposes, this tighter bid-ask spread reflects a trader's position, not necessarily better inherent liquidity in the bond. To mitigate the effect of temporary trader positions on the quoted bid-ask spread, we average a bond's bid-ask spread indications over an entire month to produce a single monthly bid-ask indication.

A more fundamental weakness in the trader quote data is that trader messages provide recipients with bid-ask *indications*, rather than live, transactable, two-way *markets*. While live two-way transactable markets would be more desirable in measuring LCS, such data are scarce in the cash credit market unlike in the equity and foreign exchange markets. Since the goal of LCS is to measure the round-trip transaction cost that a portfolio manager would face, the LCS method needs to check that a bid-ask indication is a realistic bid-ask market. If not, we need to adjust the bid-ask indication to make it more representative of a bid-ask market.

To see how such a situation can arise, consider a bond issued long ago, with little or no current trading volume, and a recently issued bond from the same issuer. Compared to the new issue, the seasoned bond will likely have lower trading activity. Given the low trading activity, a trader would be reticent to make a market on the seasoned bond. While he might be willing to buy such a bond at a slightly wider bid spread than the new issue bond, he very likely would offer the bond only at a significantly tighter offer spread. This is because if the trader does not have the bond in inventory, he would need to go to the market with a high enough bid to entice holders to release bonds with which to quickly close out his position. However, the trader may *indicate* that this bond should trade with only a modestly wider bid-ask spread than the new issue. This indication is more of a theoretical representation of where the bond should trade. This indicative quote is usually tighter than a market quote because a trader can use an attractive indication to generate inquiries (which provide the trader with information). In reality, the bid-ask market for the seasoned bond will be considerably wider than the bid-ask indication.

Some trader bid-ask indications are likely to be closer to a bond's bid-ask market than others. For example, a trader's indication for an actively traded bond is likely to be close to the bond's market. In contrast, the indication for a less actively traded bond is likely to be a theoretical indication of where the bond might trade, but not where the trader is willing to buy and sell at the moment. In practice, the trader would bid and offer the bond only at a much wider spread.

## LCS Credit Market Segmentation

To estimate bid-ask markets from traders' indications, we take the following approach. First, we distinguish between trader-quoted and non-quoted bonds. Trader-quoted bonds are those for which there are at least two bid-ask spread indications during a month. Non-quoted bonds have one or no indications during a month. For quoted bonds, the bid-ask market is estimated based on the trader's indication. The bid-ask market for non-quoted bonds is imputed based on a model for LCS described in the next section. Figure 5.8, for example, shows that in June 2009 traders provided quotes for 1,177 of the approximately 3,600 total issues in the U.S. IG Credit Index, while 2,456 issues were non-quoted.

The next step in estimating a bid-ask market is to determine if a bond, either quoted or non-quoted, is a benchmark bond. A *benchmark bond* is defined as an *on-the-run* and/or *high-volume bond*. An on-the-run bond is the most recent issue of an issuer at key points on the yield curve (e.g., the issuer's most recent 10-year bond would be an *on-the-run issue* for the issuer). A high-volume bond is a bond that may or may not be an on-the-run issue, but has relatively high trading volume (i.e., greater than the 80th percentile across all bonds) compared with other credit bonds. Referring to

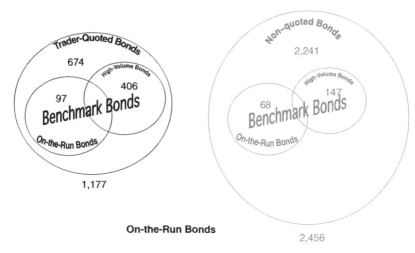

**FIGURE 5.8**   LCS Segmentation of the U.S. IG Credit Index (June 2009)
*Note*: Figure is not drawn to scale.
*Source*: Barclays Capital.

Figure 5.8, in June 2009 traders provided quotes for 503 benchmark bonds and 674 non-benchmark bonds in the Credit Index.

## LCS FOR TRADER-QUOTED BONDS

A trader's bid-ask indication for a benchmark bond is likely to be close to the bid-ask market because such bonds are *high-profile bonds* that experience active two-way flow and are closely monitored by broker-dealers and investors. A trader is unlikely to quote a benchmark bond poorly as it would signal inattention to the market or weak market-making capability. If a quoted benchmark bond with an OASD of 5 has a trader bid-ask spread indication of 20 bps, then the LCS for the bond (in percentage points) will be 5 × 20 bps = 1.00%.

By definition, a *non-benchmark bond* is an *off-the-run issue* with relatively low trading volume. As discussed above, while traders do provide bid-ask quotes for non-benchmark bonds, these indications are often simply a signal that the trader is willing to consider trading the bond and that potential counterparties should contact the trader to discuss further. In other words, the bid-ask indication is unlikely to be a bid-ask market, but rather just an advertisement that interested parties should call the broker-dealer.

For non-benchmark bonds, traders will often say: "In theory, this is where the bond should trade...," "I have not seen this bond in a long time . . . ," or "I will not offer the bond at that spread, but would work an order." In time, the bond might trade at the trader's indicative bid-ask spread, but it is clear that the trader is not making a bid-ask market for immediate execution. Since the bond is quoted, however, the trader is interested in the bond. When pressed, the trader is generally able to offer a tradable bid-ask spread for the bond, but usually at wider levels than the indication.

While we use trader bid-ask indications to compute an LCS for non-benchmark quoted bonds, we "adjust" the indication to reflect that the bid-ask market for the bond will be wider. This *adjustment factor* (AdjF) is related to the current dispersion of liquidity in the market, as inferred from the bid-ask indications provided by the traders across benchmark and non-benchmark bonds. The adjustment factor is estimated each month and reflects how much higher transaction costs are for "non-benchmark" bonds than "benchmark" bonds. The adjustment factor is used to "correct" the quotes for non-benchmark bonds. Since January 2007, the adjustment factor has fluctuated between 1.50 (an exogenous lower bound) and 1.83.

For example, consider a non-benchmark quoted bond with an OASD of 5.0 and a trader bid-ask indication of 25 bps. Assume that the current adjustment factor is 1.60. To estimate this bond's bid-ask market, LCS multiplies the bond's indication by 1.60 to produce an estimated bid-ask market of 40 bps. The bond's final LCS is then calculated to be $5 \times 40$ bps = 2.000%.

As a specific example, Lowe's Corp. (LOW) had 10 bonds in the IG Index as of December 31, 2008 (see Table 5.1). Five of the bonds were trader quoted (see "Quoted?" column). Of the five, we consider one bond (the 6.65s of 9/37–548661CP) to be a benchmark bond because of either its on-the-run status or high volume. Consequently, the LCS for this bond (3.762%) was computed directly from the trader's average bid-ask indication over the month.

The other four quoted bonds were non-benchmark bonds. As a result, their initial LCS, computed from the trader's bid-ask indications, were multiplied by the adjustment factor (1.563) to determine each bond's final LCS. Table 5.1 shows the December 2008 LCS values for the trader-quoted LOW bonds. Table 5.1 also provides a number of characteristics for all LOW bonds (e.g., age, DTS, and amount outstanding). This information will be useful below when we discuss the relationship between a non-trader-quoted bond's attributes and its modeled LCS value.

## Relationship of LCS to Bond-Level Indicatives

The LCS for quoted bonds is typically related to the bond's attributes in a way that is intuitive to portfolio managers. For quoted bonds in the June

**TABLE 5.1** LCS Results for Quoted LOW Bonds (December 2008)

| Monthly TRACE Volume | CUSIP | Amount Out | OAS | OASD | DTS | Index_P | Age in yrs | Yrs to mat | Bid_P | Bid_Sp | Ask_Sp | Bid_Ask | Orig mat | Quoted? | Benchmark? | LCS | Implied B-A |
|---|---|---|---|---|---|---|---|---|---|---|---|---|---|---|---|---|---|
| 9,888,000 | 548661CA | 500,000 | 4.73 | 1.4 | 6.4 | 104 | 8.6 | 1.5 | 102.89 | 530 | 480 | 50 | 10 | YES | NO | 1.059 | 78 |
| 14,664,000 | 548661CM | 550,000 | 4.34 | 3.3 | 14.5 | 100.12 | 1.3 | 3.8 | 99.37 | 440 | 390 | 50 | 5 | YES | NO | 2.589 | 77 |
| 12,980,000 | 548661CH | 500,000 | 3.45 | 5.8 | 20 | 98.58 | 3.2 | 6.9 | 93.6 | 380 | 330 | 37 | 10 | YES | NO | 3.31 | 58 |
| 7,305,000 | 548661CK | 550,000 | 3.5 | 6.3 | 22.2 | 98.74 | 2.2 | 7.9 | | | | | 10 | NO | NO | 4.67 | |
| 17,505,000 | 548661CN | 250,000 | 4.14 | 6.7 | 27.6 | 97.36 | 1.3 | 8.8 | | | | | 10 | NO | NO | 3.88 | |
| 1,000,000 | 548661AH | 300,000 | 3.85 | 10.3 | 39.6 | 99.34 | 10.9 | 19.2 | | | | | 30 | NO | NO | 6.80 | |
| 3,659,000 | 548661AK | 397,740 | 3.98 | 10.7 | 42.6 | 94.25 | 9.9 | 20.3 | | | | | 30.1 | NO | NO | 7.15 | |
| 5,450,000 | 548661CJ | 500,000 | 4.14 | 12.7 | 52 | 82.09 | 3.2 | 26.9 | | | | | 30 | NO | NO | 5.99 | |
| 10,461,000 | 548661CL | 450,000 | 4.16 | 12.7 | 52.2 | 85.52 | 2.2 | 27.9 | 77.53 | 490 | 465 | 22 | 30 | YES | NO | 4.446 | 35 |
| 115,469,000 | 548661CP | 500,000 | 4.22 | 12.4 | 51.7 | 95.25 | 1.3 | 28.8 | 89.1 | 470 | 439 | 30 | 30 | YES | YES | 3.762 | 30 |

*Source:* Barclays Capital.

**TABLE 5.2** Relationship between Quoted Bonds' LCS and Issue Size and Age (June 2009)

| Issue Size | Investment Grade | | | High Yield | | |
|---|---|---|---|---|---|---|
| Category | No. of Bonds | Avg. LCS | Std. Dev. | No. of Bonds | Avg. LCS | Std. Dev. |
| 1 (small) | 558 | 3.42 | 1.59 | 639 | 5.72 | 3.41 |
| 2 | 1,036 | 3.13 | 1.52 | 440 | 4.77 | 3.11 |
| 3 | 798 | 2.53 | 1.49 | 276 | 4.25 | 2.9 |
| 4 | 335 | 2.12 | 1.43 | 98 | 4.02 | 2.92 |
| 5 | 474 | 1.85 | 1.31 | 64 | 3.64 | 2.64 |
| 6 | 160 | 1.43 | 0.96 | 22 | 3.29 | 2.5 |
| 7 (big) | 272 | 1.13 | 0.93 | 19 | 3.37 | 2.63 |

| Age | Investment Grade | | | High Yield | | |
|---|---|---|---|---|---|---|
| Category | No. of Bonds | Avg. LCS | Std. Dev. | No. of Bonds | Avg. LCS | Std. Dev. |
| 1 (young) | 608 | 1.33 | 0.97 | 166 | 3.73 | 2.27 |
| 2 | 1,125 | 1.86 | 1.36 | 437 | 4.58 | 3.23 |
| 3 | 630 | 2.37 | 1.61 | 442 | 4.61 | 3.14 |
| 4 | 520 | 2.36 | 1.38 | 255 | 4.55 | 3 |
| 5 | 426 | 1.86 | 1.45 | 149 | 3.66 | 2.6 |
| 6 | 316 | 3.98 | 1.72 | 106 | 6.58 | 3.95 |
| 7 (old) | 8 | 3.07 | 0.64 | 3 | 11.31 | 4.7 |

*Source:* Barclays Capital.

2009 IG Index, Table 5.2 groups bonds into buckets depending on issue size and age (since issuance). The table shows that as a bond's issue size increases, its LCS tends to decrease. In contrast, the relationship between LCS and age is not so clear-cut. As some bonds age, their LCS tends to improve, not deteriorate. Upon closer examination, we found relatively tight bid-ask markets (i.e., relatively low LCS) for original issue long-maturity bonds whose remaining term has fallen below two years. These tend to be bonds initially purchased for buy-and-hold portfolios (e.g., insurance companies) that are replaced by new issue longer-duration bonds and sold to willing buyers (e.g., short-duration mutual funds).

The intuitive relationship between a bond's LCS and risk (either DTS or OAS) is apparent, as indicated in Table 5.3. For a market maker, it is particularly risky to make a two-way market for a bond with a relatively high DTS. If a trader's bid (offer) is hit (lifted), the trader now has a position in a relatively high-risk bond. To protect himself, a trader is inclined to quote wider bid-ask spreads for riskier bonds.

What is the relationship between a bond's LCS and its trading volume? At first glance (Figure 5.9), LCS seems to be negatively related to trading volume. In other words, a bond with greater volume is likely to have a lower LCS. However, this figure is somewhat distorted by very high-volume bonds. In fact, more than 80% of all bonds have monthly trading volume of $50 million or less. As shown in Figure 5.10, if we look only at these 80% of the bonds in the IG and HY indexes, we find a much weaker (although still negative) relationship between LCS and trading volume. In fact, we see that bonds with relatively high trading volume can have a relatively high LCS; conversely, bonds with relatively low trading volume can have relatively low LCS. Volume alone is not always a strong proxy for liquidity as measured by a bond's bid-ask spread. For instance, in November 2008, heavy selling by investors in an illiquid market led to both very high volumes and high LCS.

## LCS FOR NON-QUOTED BONDS: THE LCS MODEL

By definition, non-quoted bonds do not have trader-reported bid-ask indications. In a given month, traders may provide indications for only about a third of the bonds in the indexes. To generate an LCS value for the remaining bonds (i.e., the non-quoted bonds), we use the LCS values for quoted bonds to estimate an LCS model. Attributes (e.g., volume, risk, and time since last quoted) of non-quoted bonds are then used as inputs to the model to impute their LCS values.

**TABLE 5.3** Relationship between Quoted Bonds' LCS and OAS and DTS (June 2009)

| OAS Category | Investment Grade No. of Bonds | Avg. LCS | Std. Dev. | High Yield No. of Bonds | Avg. LCS | Std. Dev. |
|---|---|---|---|---|---|---|
| 1 (low) | 519 | 1.33 | 0.72 | 0 | | |
| 2 | 777 | 1.77 | 1.08 | 1 | 1.46 | 0 |
| 3 | 1,293 | 2.01 | 1.37 | 5 | 2.55 | 1.89 |
| 4 | 843 | 2.48 | 1.83 | 455 | 3.01 | 1.54 |
| 5 | 155 | 4.52 | 2.19 | 623 | 4.17 | 2.21 |
| 6 (high) | 46 | 5.15 | 1.86 | 474 | 7.3 | 4.27 |

| DTS Category | Investment Grade No. of Bonds | Avg. LCS | Std. Dev. | High Yield No. of Bonds | Avg. LCS | Std. Dev. |
|---|---|---|---|---|---|---|
| 1 (low) | 508 | 1.12 | 0.54 | 11 | 1.45 | 0.49 |
| 2 | 749 | 1.35 | 0.8 | 29 | 2.17 | 0.62 |
| 3 | 1,138 | 1.97 | 1.09 | 160 | 2.69 | 1.16 |
| 4 | 788 | 2.82 | 1.65 | 510 | 3.33 | 1.53 |
| 5 | 378 | 3.62 | 2.03 | 400 | 4.31 | 1.93 |
| 6 (high) | 72 | 5.79 | 2.27 | 448 | 8.19 | 4.26 |

*Source:* Barclays Capital.

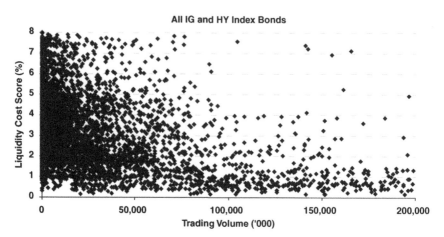

**FIGURE 5.9**  Relationship between LCS and TRACE Trading Volume: IG and HY Sectors (June 2009)
*Source:* Barclays Capital.


## LCS Model Specification

To assign an LCS value to every bond in the IG and HY indexes, we use a model that relates LCS to those bond characteristics that a portfolio manager would intuitively consider closely related to liquidity. As we show, the following bond attributes are significant in explaining a bond's LCS:

- *Trading volume.* While a high level of trading volume is not necessarily a guarantee of low trading cost, LCS is negatively related to a bond's trading volume. In general, more volume is associated with lower liquidity

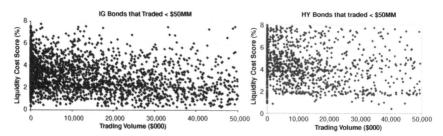

**FIGURE 5.10**  Relationship between TRACE Volume and LCS Excluding the Most Actively Traded Bonds: IG and HY Sectors
*Source:* Barclays Capital.

costs. Traders are comfortable making tight bid-ask markets for bonds with large trading volume because there are many other market participants on which to offload any undesired risk.

■ *Amount outstanding.* LCS is lower for larger-sized issues. Traders are likely to be more willing, all else equal, to make a tighter bid-ask market for issues with large amounts outstanding. Traders are likely to be able to find more buyers and sellers as a bond's issue size increases.

■ *Age.* Many credit bonds are acquired by buy-and-hold investors. These investors manage portfolios with trading constraints and low turnover. They are reluctant to sell bonds (i.e., book gain/loss constraints), selling only if there is a compelling price. As a result, the LCS for seasoned bonds will typically be higher, all else constant, compared with newly issued bonds.

■ *DTS or OAS.* As discussed earlier, making a bid-ask market exposes traders to mark-to-market risk. Bonds with greater excess return volatility are likely to have a higher LCS, all else equal, because of the risk the market maker must bear until the trade can be covered. As discussed extensively in Chapters 1 through 4, bonds with higher DTS tend to be more volatile.

We summarize the relationship between a quoted bond's LCS and its attributes[4] by running a multiple regression of bonds' LCS on various bond attributes: age, time to redemption, issue size, trading volume, and DTS. Table 5.4 shows the results for the period from January 2007 to June 2009:

**TABLE 5.4** Regression of LCS on Bond Attributes: Quoted IG and HY Bonds (January 2007–June 2009)

**Dependent Variable: LCS (%)**
**Sample Period: January 2007 to June 2009**

| Explanatory Variables | Coefficient | *t*-stat |
|---|---|---|
| Intercept | 0.247 | 5.8 |
| Age (years) | 0.049 | 16.9 |
| Time to redemption (years) | −0.0539 | −55.4 |
| Issue size ($bn) | −0.2575 | −20.3 |
| Monthly trading volume ($mn) | −0.0016 | −18.4 |
| DTS (year %) | 0.1232 | 182.2 |
| Monthly dummies? | Yes | |
| Number of observations | 25,379 | |
| Adjusted $R^2$ | 0.69 | |

*Source:* Barclays Capital.

The regression results show that bond attributes can explain a high percentage of the variability in LCS, both across bonds and across time. All the coefficients have the expected sign. For example, the riskier the bond (i.e., higher DTS), the greater the LCS; the larger the issue size, the smaller the LCS; and the greater the volume, the smaller the LCS. We rely on these findings to help specify a fuller econometric LCS model for non-quoted bonds.

For non-quoted bonds, we also make an adjustment to estimated LCS values. A quoted bond has an inherent liquidity advantage in that the trader is advertising an interest to trade. A non-quoted bond, on the other hand, has a diminished level of trader interest. In addition, non-quoted bonds are generally smaller and have lower volume than their quoted counterparts (Table 5.5). While some of this will no doubt be captured by the bond's attributes, using LCS from quoted bonds is likely to bias downward the estimated LCS for non-quoted bonds. Consequently, we use an adjustment factor to account for the incremental illiquidity.

We adjust the estimated LCS for a non-quoted bond by multiplying its regression-estimated LCS value by a *non-quoted adjustment factor* (NQAdjF) to compute a final LCS value. Like the AdjF, the NQAdjF depends on the dispersion of liquidity in the market. However, the NQAdjF is modulated depending on whether the bond has been quoted in recent months. In other words, if the bond was recently quoted, just not in the current month, then its NQAdjF is close to 1.0.

We can now complete the Lowe's bond example. Returning to Table 5.1 we see the computed LCS for the five non-quoted bonds as of December 2008. (*Note:* None of the non-quoted bonds was a benchmark bond.) For example, the "double-old" 30-year bond, 548661CJ, had an estimated LCS of 5.990%, compared with 4.446% for the off-the-run 30-year bond and 3.762% for the on-the-run 30-year bond. The "triple-old" and "quadruple-old" bonds (548661AK and 548661AH, respectively) had final LCS values of 7.150% and 6.800%, respectively. The quadruple-old bond, despite lower volume and issue size than the triple-old bond, benefits from its lower spread risk (i.e., DTS), which is a major driver of liquidity cost.

The two non-quoted off-the-run 10-year issues for LOW are treated similarly. The most recent 10-year 548661CN, not given benchmark status because of its small issue size, was non-quoted in December 2008 and had a final LCS of 3.884%. The old 10-year 548661CK, also non-quoted, had a higher final LCS of 4.670% because of the bond's lower trading volume and higher age, although its liquidity score benefitted from the bond's larger issue size and lower DTS. The double-old 10-year (548661CH), however, was, oddly enough, a quoted bond. Consequently, its LCS, at 3.310%, was the lowest of the three recent 10-year bonds. Finally, note that the oldest 10-year

**TABLE 5.5** Comparison of Quoted and Non-Quoted Universes (June 2009)

Average Characteristics of Bonds with and without Trader Quotes for June 2009

| | Quoted? | Number of Bonds | Age | Years to Redemption | DTS | Volume ($) | Size ($000) | Price | Not Traded during Month | Number of Bonds with Trades |
|---|---|---|---|---|---|---|---|---|---|---|
| HY | No | 958 | 4.7 | 7 | 46.02 | 14,824,653 | 412,779 | 78.47 | 250 | 708 |
| | Yes | 604 | 3.76 | 7.08 | 40.63 | 22,753,755 | 511,527 | 82.8 | 129 | 475 |
| IG | No | 2,456 | 4.94 | 9.78 | 16.47 | 22,383,059 | 635,897 | 100.01 | 621 | 1,835 |
| | Yes | 1,177 | 3.03 | 11.47 | 20.37 | 91,630,141 | 1,025,035 | 98.68 | 51 | 1,126 |

*Source:* Barclays Capital.

**TABLE 5.6**  LCS Approach to Estimating Bid-Ask Markets from
Bid-Ask Indications

| Quote Status | Benchmark Status | Estimation of Bid-Ask Market |
|---|---|---|
| Trader-quoted | Benchmark bond (on-the-run and/or high volume) | Bid-ask market = Bid-ask indication |
| | Non-benchmark bond | Bid-ask market = AdjF × Bid-ask indication |
| Non-quoted | Benchmark bond (on-the-run and/or high volume) Non-benchmark bond | Bid-ask market = NQAdjF × Estimated bid-ask indication (Estimated bid-ask indications based on data from trader-quoted bonds. Estimation includes a "benchmark dummy" to reflect better liquidity for non-quoted benchmark bonds.) |

*Source:* Barclays Capital.

bond, 548661CA, issued 8.6 years earlier, had the lowest LCS. This bond
was a quoted bond. While its implied bid-ask spread was relatively high
at 78 bps, its very low spread duration produced an LCS of only 1.059%.
The likely reason for this bond being quoted is that insurance companies
that originally bought this long-maturity bond were now selling out of this
position to replace it with new-issue, longer-duration bonds. This dynamic
is explicitly considered by the LCS model.

Table 5.6 provides a schematic summarizing how LCS is calculated for
all bonds in the IG and HY indexes.

## TESTING THE LCS MODEL: OUT-OF-SAMPLE TESTS

Testing the LCS model is difficult as the market bid-ask spread is not observable for non-quoted bonds. However, we conduct three out-of-sample
LCS model tests. First, we randomly eliminate approximately 10% of our
quoted benchmark bond sample. We then estimate the LCS model assuming that these bonds are not quoted, compute the model implied LCS for
these bonds, and compare them with the actual LCS based on trader bid-
ask quotes. We only consider benchmark bonds for this exercise, since here
we are primarily interested in the model's estimates, rather than the subsequent adjustments. This is repeated for several months. The results for

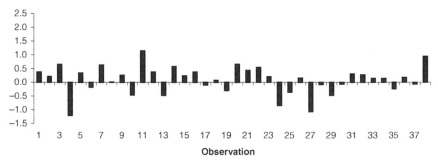

A. November 2008

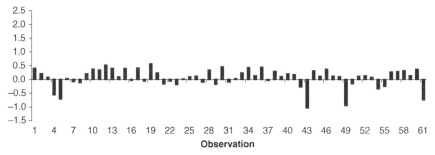

B. June 2009

**FIGURE 5.11**   Out-of-Sample Test for IG Sector (November 2008 and June 2009)
*Source:* Barclays Capital.

November 2008 (a volatile, very illiquid month) and June 2009 are reported in Figure 5.11. The absolute value of the prediction error as a proportion of true LCS is between 30% and 35% in both cases. So, the large errors in Figure 5.11 refer to bonds with very high LCS, which the model matches closely in a relative sense.

The second out-of-sample test involves first identifying a non-quoted bond with a modeled LCS similar to that of a trader-quoted bond from the same issuer. Then we observe these two bonds in a subsequent month when both are quoted (or both are modeled). If the LCS model provides a reasonably consistent liquidity score, then the LCS of similar bonds by the same issuer should move in tandem across different months, irrespective of whether one of the bonds changes from being trader quoted or modeled.

Table 5.7 shows the validation of the LCS model using LOW as an example by comparing LCS data for December 2008 from Table 5.1 with LOW's LCS scores for June 2009. For example, consider two off-the-run 10-year bonds in December 2008: 548861CH and 548661CK. The former

**TABLE 5.7** Out-of-Sample Test Comparing LCS for LOW's Bonds (December 2008 and June 2009)

December 2008

| Monthly TRACE Volume | CUSIP | OAS | OASD | DTS | Index_P | Bid_P | Bid_Sp | Ask_Sp | Bid_Ask | Quoted? | Benchmark? | LCS | Implied B-A |
|---|---|---|---|---|---|---|---|---|---|---|---|---|---|
| 9,888,000 | 548661CA | 4.73 | 1.4 | 6.4 | 104 | 102.89 | 530 | 480 | 50 | YES | NO | 1.059 | 78 |
| 14,664,000 | 548661CM | 4.34 | 3.3 | 14.5 | 100.12 | 99.37 | 440 | 390 | 50 | YES | NO | 2.589 | 77 |
| 12,980,000 | 548661CH | 3.45 | 5.8 | 20 | 98.58 | 93.6 | 380 | 330 | 37 | YES | NO | 3.310 | 58 |
| 7,305,000 | 548661CK | 3.5 | 6.3 | 22.2 | 98.74 | | | | | NO | NO | 4.670 | 74 |
| 17,505,000 | 548661CN | 4.14 | 6.7 | 27.6 | 97.36 | | | | | NO | NO | 3.884 | 58 |
| 1,000,000 | 548661AH | 3.85 | 10.3 | 39.6 | 99.34 | | | | | NO | NO | 6.800 | 66 |
| 3,659,000 | 548661AK | 3.98 | 10.7 | 42.6 | 94.25 | | | | | NO | NO | 7.150 | 67 |
| 5,450,000 | 548661CJ | 4.14 | 12.7 | 52 | 82.09 | | | | | NO | NO | 5.990 | 47 |
| 10,461,000 | 548661CL | 4.16 | 12.7 | 52.2 | 85.52 | 77.53 | 490 | 465 | 22 | YES | NO | 4.446 | 35 |
| 115,469,000 | 548661CP | 4.22 | 12.4 | 51.7 | 95.25 | 89.1 | 470 | 439 | 30 | YES | YES | 3.762 | 30 |

June 2009

| Monthly TRACE Volume | CUSIP | OAS | OASD | DTS | Index_P | Bid_P | Bid_Sp | Ask_Sp | Bid_Ask | Quoted? | Benchmark? | LCS | Implied B-A |
|---|---|---|---|---|---|---|---|---|---|---|---|---|---|
| | 548661CA | | | | Out index | | | | | | | | |
| 13,880,000 | 548661CM | 1.68 | 2.9 | 4.9 | 106.57 | 104.74 | 150 | 130 | 20 | YES | NO | 0.988 | 34 |
| 24,610,000 | 548661CH | 1.29 | 5.4 | 7 | 104.05 | | | | | NO | NO | 2.390 | 44 |
| 19,260,000 | 548661CK | 1.46 | 6 | 8.8 | 104.12 | | | | | NO | NO | 2.558 | 42 |
| 6,800,000 | 548661CN | 1.35 | 6.5 | 8.8 | 108.55 | 108.4303 | 135 | 120 | 16 | YES | NO | 1.738 | 27 |
| 220,000 | 548661AH | 1.86 | 10.5 | 19.5 | 108.38 | | | | | NO | NO | 4.363 | 42 |
| 10,999,000 | 548661AK | 1.9 | 11 | 20.8 | 103.79 | | | | | NO | NO | 4.418 | 40 |
| 3,977,000 | 548661CJ | 1.78 | 13.1 | 23.4 | 92.62 | | | | | NO | NO | 4.242 | 32 |
| 13,100,000 | 548661CL | 1.79 | 13.1 | 23.5 | 96.49 | | | | | NO | NO | 4.139 | 31 |
| 17,686,000 | 548661CP | 1.85 | 12.8 | 23.7 | 107.15 | 107.26 | 180 | 165 | 20 | YES | YES | 2.507 | 20 |

*Source*: Barclays Capital.

bond is quoted with an LCS of 3.310%, while the other bond is non-quoted (i.e., modeled LCS) with a higher LCS value of 4.670%. In June 2009, both bonds are non-quoted (so, both have modeled LCS). While both LCS values in June are lower than their December 2008 values, reflecting the sharp improvement in market liquidity since December, the LCS for the non-quoted bond in both months maintains its LCS proximity and ranking relative to the bond that was first quoted and then non-quoted. In other words, the fact that a bond's LCS is modeled in one month, and then is not modeled, does not cause its relative LCS (to other bonds of the same issuer) to suddenly change. While the bond that became non-quoted suffered some increase in LCS relative to the bond that was non-quoted in both months, reflecting its new non-quoted status, the LCS model still produced consistent values.

Similarly, compare the LCS for the two old 10-year bonds (548661CJ and 548661CL). In December 2008, the first bond was non-quoted while the latter was quoted and had a lower LCS given its quoted status. In June 2009, both bonds were non-quoted, and the LCS model produced comparable values for both bonds. If the LCS model were not consistent, we would not observe the LCS for both bonds moving in a similar fashion across the two months as bonds move in and out of quoted status.

In summary, Table 5.7 highlights that the LCS ranking of all of LOW's bonds remains relatively unchanged from December 2008 to June 2009 despite the large change in overall market liquidity and the fact that some bonds changed from quoted to non-quoted (i.e., modeled LCS) or from non-quoted to quoted status during the period.

The final out-of-sample test occurred serendipitously. Independent of the LCS effort, in June 2009, Barclays Capital polled its cash corporate bond traders for their opinions regarding the liquidity of various bonds. These bonds belonged to a set of approximately 200 relatively large, moderately seasoned to newly issued 10-year bonds that were under consideration for inclusion in a liquid basket of cash bonds. This basket would be a small set of bonds containing only one bond per issuer. For the bonds selected for the basket, traders were told that they would have to be prepared to make two-way markets *for the next six months.*

Traders were asked to provide a subjective 1-2-3 liquidity ranking (1 means highly liquid and should be in basket; 2 means liquid enough to be in basket; and 3 means illiquid, do not include in basket) for each of the 200 issues (henceforth, 1-2-3 rankings). Traders knew that bonds rated a 1 (or, perhaps a 2) would be selected for the basket whereas bonds rated a 3 would not be selected.

The 1-2-3 rankings provide a valuable out-of-sample test of the LCS method. Assuming that the 1-2-3 rankings are an accurate, albeit subjective, measure of liquidity, a comparison of the LCS with the trader 1-2-3 rankings gives an indication of how much liquidity information is embedded in bid-ask quotes. If the LCS values are consistent with traders' views on liquidity as expressed by their 1-2-3 rankings, then one would generally expect the following correspondence relationship:

LCS (bonds ranked a 1) < LCS (bonds ranked a 2) < LCS (bonds ranked a 3)

However, there are some important differences between LCS and the 1-2-3 rankings that disrupt the above relationship:

- LCS represents the current month's roundtrip execution cost whereas the 1-2-3 rankings represent a trader's willingness to select a bond for the liquid basket and assume the obligation to make two-way markets *for the next six months.* Since the 1-2-3 ranking involves a measure of liquidity forecasting, as opposed to LCS's measurement of current liquidity, these two measures can differ. For example, suppose that a company issues a 10-year bond that becomes the on-the-run issue. The issuer's other 10-year bond, issued three months earlier, is now an off-the-run issue. Although the older issue may currently have decent liquidity (and a fairly low LCS value), the trader may give that bond a 3 ranking and the new issue a 1 because the trader knows that over the next six months, the off-the-run issue will become increasingly illiquid.
- 1-2-3 rankings may reflect the trader's ability to execute transactions outside the $3–5 million range, something that LCS does not capture.
- LCS is an objective measure, while the 1-2-3 rankings are subjective, which may prevent direct comparison across traders and, potentially, across issuers. (As shown in Table 5.8, liquidity varies substantially across traders.)

To allow a better comparison between LCS and the 1-2-3 rankings, we examine the correspondence between the two liquidity measures at the individual trader level. We expect to see a close correspondence between LCS and the 1-2-3 rankings for a given trader. However, even this comparison is not totally precise. The same trader can rank an off-the-run (but fairly liquid and with low LCS) bond for one issuer as a 3 (since more liquid alternatives from the same issuer exist), but may rank another issuer's less liquid bond as a 1 if this is the most liquid bond from that issuer available for inclusion in the liquid basket.

Table 5.8 presents, by trader, the average LCS for the set of bonds given a particular 1-2-3 ranking. Generally, we would expect the average

**TABLE 5.8** Comparison of LCS and 1-2-3 Ranks by Trader (June 2009)

| Trader | Number of Ranked Bonds | Average LCS (%) | Average LCS by Ranking Category | | |
|---|---|---|---|---|---|
| | | | Rank = 1 (%) | Rank = 2 (%) | Rank = 3 (%) |
| Trader #1 | 6 | 1.314 | 0.717 | 1.493 | 1.343 |
| Trader #2 | 40 | 1.737 | 1.247 | 0.987 | 3.295 |
| Trader #3 | 26 | 1.159 | 0.634 | 0.605 | 1.389 |
| Trader #4 | 10 | 1.992 | | 0.927 | 2.702 |
| Trader #5 | 31 | 1.570 | 1.422 | 1.307 | 1.734 |
| Trader #6 | 36 | 1.320 | 0.803 | 1.209 | 1.448 |
| Trader #7 | 41 | 1.309 | 0.800 | 1.232 | 1.407 |
| Trader #8 | 4 | 4.274 | | 4.773 | 3.775 |
| Trader #9 | 1 | 4.000 | | | 4.000 |

*Source:* Barclays Capital.

LCS value for a trader's ranked bonds to increase with the 1-2-3 ranking. (Some subgroups have very few bonds, so the results are heavily influenced by outliers.) The table also presents the average LCS for all bonds ranked by the trader. For example, the average LCS for bonds ranked by Trader #3 (1.159%) is 74% that of Trader #5 (1.570%). As discussed earlier, a bond ranked 3 by Trader #3 may, in fact, be more liquid than a bond ranked 1 by Trader #5, as subjective liquidity rankings depend on the trader and market segment and, therefore, cannot be objectively compared.

If LCS corresponds well with subjective measures of liquidity, we should see average LCS increase, for a given trader, as the rank category increases (ignoring issuer-level complications, discussed below). For example, for Trader #6, the average LCS for bonds ranked 1 is 0.803%, less than the average LCS for the bonds ranked 2 (1.209%), which is, in turn, less than the LCS for the bonds ranked 3 (1.448%). While this relationship does not always hold, the deviations are generally small in magnitude (a few basis points in roundtrip costs) relative to average LCS levels.

While the average LCS generally corresponds to trader's 1-2-3 rankings, it is important to see the dispersion of LCS by ranking. Assuming that a trader assigns a 2 to a bond that has worse liquidity than all of the bonds he ranks as a 1, then all of a trader's 1s should have a lower LCS than any of the trader's 2s, and all of the trader's 2s should have a lower LCS than any of the trader's 3s. Figure 5.12 plots bonds' LCS versus their 1-2-3 ranking for two traders, #3 and #6. Ideally, these graphs should resemble a staircase

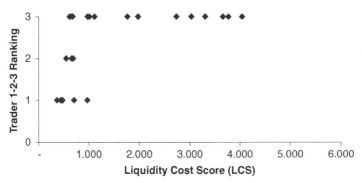

A. Trader #3

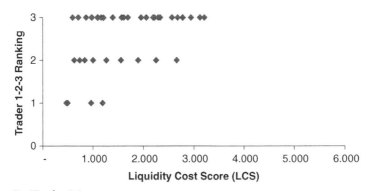

B. Trader #6

**FIGURE 5.12** Distribution of LCS across Different Rank Categories for Two Traders (June 2009)
*Source:* Barclays Capital.

function. However, given the subjective nature of the 1-2-3 rankings and the fact that only three subjective scores are possible, it is extremely unlikely that the LCS and 1-2-3 rankings will match up that precisely. In addition, it is likely that this correspondence will hold only across bonds by a single issuer but not across all bonds that a trader ranks, because of liquidity differences across names (which we observe, but do not report here) and the trader's desire to get broad issuer representation in the liquid basket. Nevertheless, we see a fairly close correspondence between LCS and a trader's 1-2-3 rankings.

Finally, we note that some of the bonds ranked by traders do not have bid-ask quotes (i.e., were not quoted in published messages during June

**TABLE 5.9** Comparison of LCS and 1-2-3 Ranks: Trader-Quoted versus Non-Quoted, i.e., LCS Modeled (June 2009)

| | Number of Bonds | Average LCS | | |
|---|---|---|---|---|
| | | Rank = 1 | Rank = 2 | Rank = 3 |
| Non-quoted | 62 | 1.652 | 1.695 | 1.757 |
| Quoted | 138 | 0.825 | 1.213 | 1.866 |

*Source:* Barclays Capital.

2009). As discussed earlier, the model estimates the LCS value for a non-quoted bond based on the bond's attributes. Does the LCS method work well only when trader quotes are available for a bond, or can the model do a fairly good job of estimating liquidity costs for non-quoted bonds? This can be answered by comparing the modeled LCS value for non-quoted bonds with the subjective 1-2-3 rankings. Do non-quoted bonds with a ranking of a 1 have lower modeled LCS than non-quoted bonds with higher rankings?

As shown in Table 5.9, the correspondence of the LCS and the 1-2-3 rankings has been preserved for both the quoted and the non-quoted bond universe (i.e., LCS increases as rank increases).

Overall, all three out-of-sample tests support our LCS model for non-quoted bonds. Investors with access to bid-ask markets for non-quoted bonds can, of course, perform their own tests.

## LCS Persistence

How likely will a bond maintain its liquidity position relative to other bonds? In other words, is a relatively liquid bond likely to remain this way, as the market's overall liquidity changes?

To examine the persistence of a bond's LCS, we assign bonds to six equally populated LCS buckets based on their LCS values as of June 2008. A bucket's population does not change over time, so LCS bucket 1 has the same bonds in June 2008 and November 2008. In addition, the set of bonds is limited only to bonds with LCS values for all months between January 2007 and June 2009 (e.g., bonds that were issued after January 2007 or matured before June 2009 are excluded).

Table 5.10 shows the average LCS for the six LCS buckets as of June 2008. For example, the lowest LCS bucket had a June 2008 average value of 1.082% and a within-bucket standard deviation of 0.20%, while

**TABLE 5.10** LCS Persistence: LCS Summary Statistics of LCS-Sorted Portfolios (June 2008) over Time

| Liquidity Score Averages (standard deviation in italics) in Various Months | | | | |
|---|---|---|---|---|
| June 2008 LS Category | June 2007 | June 2008 | November 2008 | June 2009 |
| 1 (lowest LCS bucket) | 0.576% | 1.082% | 2.525% | 2.049% |
| | *0.24%* | *0.20%* | *1.50%* | *0.96%* |
| 2 | 0.790 | 1.490 | 3.768 | 2.926 |
| | *0.33* | *0.09* | *1.85* | *1.26* |
| 3 | 0.918 | 1.770 | 4.654 | 3.655 |
| | *0.37* | *0.11* | *2.02* | *1.60* |
| 4 | 1.013 | 2.207 | 5.383 | 4.208 |
| | *0.33* | *0.15* | *1.84* | *1.63* |
| 5 | 1.199 | 2.797 | 6.125 | 5.088 |
| | *0.38* | *0.21* | *2.04* | *1.74* |
| 6 (highest LCS bucket) | 1.464 | 4.819 | 7.198 | 6.702 |
| | *0.62* | *2.17* | *3.36* | *4.14* |

*Source:* Barclays Capital.

the highest LCS bucket had an average LCS of 4.819% and a standard deviation of 2.17%.

As market liquidity deteriorated over the latter half of 2008, Table 5.10 shows that the relative ordering of the six LCS buckets remained unchanged. Bucket 1 had the lowest average LCS in November 2008, and Bucket 6 still had the highest LCS. As the market recovered into 2009, the relative ranking was still unchanged. This persistence offers investors the opportunity to construct portfolios with *relatively* low (or high) LCS with some confidence that the portfolio will continue to have a relatively low (or high) LCS.

Although relative LCS values seem to persist in aggregate, there is potential for LCS migration at the bond level. While Bucket 1 remained the lowest LCS bucket, note that the standard deviation of LCS within the bucket increased sharply by November 2008 (from 0.20% to 1.50%). This is also true for the other LCS buckets. For example, many financial bonds had low LCS values in June 2008, but experienced large increases by November 2008. This implies that maintaining a target LCS (either absolute or relative) for a portfolio comprising a small set of bonds may involve significant rebalancing.

Another way to measure bond-level persistence is to examine transition matrices. For each month we again sort bonds into six buckets according to

**TABLE 5.11** Transition Matrices for LCS-Sorted Portfolios across Various Horizons

| | | | June 2008 | | | | | |
|---|---|---|---|---|---|---|---|---|
| | | | 1 | 2 | 3 | 4 | 5 | 6 |
| Transition from | June | 1 | 50.3% | 20.8% | 11.1% | 6.1% | 5.8% | 5.3% |
| June 2007 to | 2007 | 2 | 31.9% | 29.7% | 17.5% | 13.1% | 5.0% | 2.5% |
| June 2008 | | 3 | 11.9% | 25.6% | 26.9% | 16.4% | 9.7% | 9.4% |
| | | 4 | 3.1% | 10.3% | 25.0% | 28.9% | 16.7% | 16.1% |
| | | 5 | 1.4% | 7.2% | 9.7% | 27.0% | 38.9% | 15.3% |
| | | 6 | 1.4% | 6.4% | 9.2% | 8.1% | 21.9% | 51.4% |

| | | | November 2008 | | | | | |
|---|---|---|---|---|---|---|---|---|
| | | | 1 | 2 | 3 | 4 | 5 | 6 |
| Transition from | June | 1 | 60.6% | 22.8% | 7.5% | 6.1% | 1.9% | 1.1% |
| June 2008 to | 2008 | 2 | 18.9% | 40.6% | 20.8% | 10.8% | 3.6% | 5.3% |
| November | | 3 | 8.9% | 21.7% | 31.7% | 15.6% | 12.8% | 9.4% |
| 2008 | | 4 | 4.2% | 8.4% | 22.6% | 28.7% | 23.7% | 12.5% |
| | | 5 | 2.5% | 4.4% | 11.9% | 25.3% | 33.6% | 22.2% |
| | | 6 | 5.0% | 2.2% | 5.6% | 13.3% | 24.4% | 49.4% |

| | | | June 2009 | | | | | |
|---|---|---|---|---|---|---|---|---|
| | | | 1 | 2 | 3 | 4 | 5 | 6 |
| Transition from | June | 1 | 54.2% | 31.1% | 9.7% | 3.1% | 1.4% | 0.6% |
| June 2008 to | 2008 | 2 | 17.2% | 38.9% | 21.4% | 9.7% | 3.9% | 2.8% |
| June 2009 | | 3 | 11.7% | 12.2% | 30.8% | 18.3% | 13.9% | 6.9% |
| | | 4 | 7.0% | 7.8% | 15.3% | 30.6% | 22.6% | 10.6% |
| | | 5 | 2.2% | 2.5% | 8.9% | 16.7% | 38.3% | 25.3% |
| | | 6 | 2.2% | 3.3% | 7.8% | 14.4% | 14.7% | 51.4% |

*Source:* Barclays Capital.

their current LCS (but, we are not keeping the composition of the buckets fixed). Table 5.11 shows how individual bonds migrate across LCS buckets over time. For example, of the bonds in LCS Bucket 1 in June 2008, by November 2008 only 60.6% remained in LCS Bucket 1 and the rest migrated to higher buckets. While the 60% value suggests persistence, especially considering the change in market environment, it is important to highlight that almost 16% of the bonds in Bucket 1 migrated to Bucket 3 or worse by November 2008.

## LCS FOR PAN-EUROPEAN CREDIT BONDS

Although European LCS was developed after U.S. LCS, the two are very similar, allowing for direct comparisons of their values. Both use bid-ask quotes supplied by traders, and explicitly recognize that some trader quotes are "indicative only" and likely do not reflect bid and ask market levels. The models penalize such indicative bid-ask quotes (using an adjustment factor) to make the LCS more representative of market conditions. For index bonds without trader bids and offers, we use cross-sectional regression models (separate models for the United States and Pan-Europe) to estimate their LCS values.

However, the different trading conventions that govern U.S. and European credit markets, as well as differences in data availability, give rise to some interesting distinctions between our LCS methodology for these two regions. In particular, the quotes we obtained from our London-based traders are accompanied by bid and offer quote sizes; and the quotes are considered live for a trade up to the specified size. As a result, model-based adjustments are required for a smaller percentage of quoted European bonds compared to quoted U.S. bonds.

Table 5.12 provides some comparative information for the U.S. and Pan-European Credit Indexes as of August 2010. The table shows significantly more bonds in the U.S. indexes than in the Pan-European indexes. U.S. IG bonds also have a longer duration, on average, than Pan-European bonds. While the Pan-European IG bonds appear to be of slightly higher quality, as indicated by the distribution of index ratings, their average OAS is slightly higher than that of U.S. bonds, reflecting summer 2010's credit strains in Europe.

Before presenting LCS values for the Pan-European credit indexes, it is important to note that LCS data are only available since May 2010, coinciding with the start of a turbulent period in European credit markets. Consequently, the Pan-European LCS values, and their relationship to U.S. LCS values, may not reflect normal market conditions. To provide some perspective, Figure 5.13 shows the time series of OAS for the European and U.S. indexes beginning in January 2007. The OAS for the Pan-European IG index was well below that of the U.S. IG index for much of this time, but exceeded the U.S. IG OAS beginning in March 2010 as the European sovereign crisis worsened.

We gather bid-ask data from London-based Barclays Capital traders who provide simultaneous bid and offer quotes. Unlike in the United States, these trader quotes feed vendor quote and trading systems that display Barclays Capital's bids and offers, and are accessible to clients for comparison with similar information from competing broker-dealers. In addition to

**TABLE 5.12** Characteristics of Pan-European and U.S. Credit Indexes (August 31, 2010)

| | Number of Bonds | OAS (bps) | OASD | Average Price | Average Issue Size (millions) | Average Age (yrs) | Distribution of Index Ratings | | | | |
| --- | --- | --- | --- | --- | --- | --- | --- | --- | --- | --- | --- |
| | | | | | | | Aaa or Aa (%) | A (%) | Baa (%) | Ba or B (%) | C or Lower, NR (%) |
| PE IG Credit | 2,388 | 175 | 5.1 | 107.1 | €836 | 3.4 | 37 | 41 | 21 | | |
| US IG Credit | 4,069 | 170 | 6.4 | 111.2 | $770 | 3.8 | 26 | 40 | 34 | | |
| PE HY Credit | 326 | 660 | 4 | 92.5 | €430 | 3.3 | | | | 88 | 12 |
| US HY Credit | 1,747 | 680 | 4.2 | 98.2 | $484 | 3.3 | | | | 80 | 20 |
| PE FRN Credit | 643 | 278 | 1.9 | 97.4 | €805 | 3.3 | 38 | 53 | 9 | | |

*Source:* Barclays Capital.

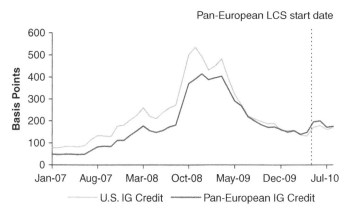

**FIGURE 5.13** Time Series of OAS for U.S. and Pan-European IG Credit Indexes
*Source:* Barclays Capital.

bid-ask quotes, this database also contains the traders' bid and offer quote sizes. For example, a trader may report that for a particular ISIN he is bidding 102.25 for €2 million bonds and offering 102.45 for €1 million bonds. These bid-ask quote size data provide us with a mechanism to decide which Pan-European quotes reflect actual market bid-ask spreads and which are indicative only and possibly need to be adjusted. (Quote size data are not available for U.S. bonds.) We gather bond-level bid-ask data (prices and quote sizes) each day and aggregate over a calendar month.

Unlike the U.S. markets, where many quotes are indicative only, trader quotes in London tend to be more binding. Traders in London are expected to make markets at the levels and sizes they quote. If a trader is unenthusiastic about making a market for a bond, then the trader may indicate either a wide bid-ask spread, a very small quote size on one or both sides of the market, or not provide any quote for the bond at all. Because London-based traders need to be more realistic about levels at which they are willing to trade, raw bid-ask spreads for Pan-European bonds are generally wider than for U.S. bonds and vary more with bond characteristics. And, with the bid-ask spreads being more realistic, not "indicative only," there is less need to adjust European trader quotes to convert them to realistic market levels than with U.S. trader quotes.

As shown in Table 5.13, traders quote a larger proportion of the bonds in the Pan-European (PE) IG index (73%) than of the U.S. IG index (42%). Hence, compared with the U.S., relatively fewer bonds in the Pan-European index need to have their LCS estimated via a regression model.

**TABLE 5.13** Pan-European and U.S. Credit Indexes: Liquidity Characteristics (August 31, 2010)

| | Average LCS (%) | Average Monthly Trading Volume (millions) | Median Monthly Trading Volume (millions) | 70th Percentile Monthly Trading Volume (millions) | Quoted (%) | Benchmark (%) | Quoted & Benchmark (%) |
|---|---|---|---|---|---|---|---|
| PE IG Credit | 0.854 | €38 | €18 | €35 | 73 | 54 | 51 |
| US IG Credit | 0.976 | $54 | $13 | $40 | 42 | 19 | 13 |
| PE HY Credit | 1.591 | €40 | €23 | €43 | 48 | 35 | 32 |
| US HY Credit | 1.777 | $51 | $17 | $44 | 51 | 17 | 10 |
| PE FRN Credit | 0.949 | €29 | €6 | €23 | 32 | 38 | 30 |

*Sources:* Barclays Capital, Xtrakter, and TRACE.

We also measure bond-level trading volume using data from Xtrakter, a subsidiary of Euroclear, a major clearer of Pan-European credit bond trades.

For the Pan-European LCS, we apply similar benchmark status criteria as for the United States. In addition, given the availability of the data, we also incorporate the magnitude of the trader's bid-ask quote sizes. All bonds with bid-ask quote sizes of at least €1 million on each side of the market are also given "benchmark" status. All remaining trader-quoted bonds are considered non-benchmark bonds, and their quotes considered "indicative only."

We compute a quoted bond's *raw LCS* by calculating the difference between its bid and ask prices as a percentage of the bid price. As with U.S. LCS, for non-benchmark bonds, we then adjust this raw LCS by an adjustment factor.

## Pan-European Non-Quoted LCS Model

We estimate the LCS for non-quoted bonds using regression to determine the relationship between LCS values and bond characteristics. The Pan-European model (equation 5.1) is very similar to the U.S. LCS model. However, we now control for currency-level effects as well as liquidity differences between fixed rate and floating rate markets.

$$\text{LCS}_i = f(\text{age, trading volume, issue size, DTS, benchmark, currency,}$$

$$\text{FRN indicator, sector}) \tag{5.1}$$

Also, as for the U.S. LCS model, we estimate the Pan-European model by running separate regressions for high-yield bonds (and some high-spread investment-grade bonds) and investment-grade bonds.

The left side of Table 5.14 shows the results of a panel regression for the Pan-European market of bond-level LCS against various bond attributes for the May 2010–August 2010 period. The right side of Table 5.14 shows a similarly specified regression for the U.S. market for the same time period. These attributes are core explanatory variables for the LCS model. For both markets, the regression explains a high percentage of the variability in LCS across bonds over time.

The estimated coefficients for the Pan-European bonds are larger in absolute value compared with their U.S. counterparts. What would explain this? For much of the May–August 2010 period the Pan-European credit market was experiencing a European sovereign crisis that began in late April, reached its worst point in mid-June, and recovered somewhat by August. The larger coefficients probably reflect a more stressed liquidity environment. During this period, there was a larger liquidity penalty for older and riskier

**TABLE 5.14** Regression of LCS on Bond Attributes: Pan-European and U.S. Fixed Rate IG and HY Bonds (May 2010–August 2010)

| Dependent Variable: LCS (%) Sample: May 2010 to August 2010, Quoted Pan-European Bonds Only | | | Dependent Variable: LCS (%) Sample: May 2010 to August 2010, Quoted U.S. Bonds Only | | |
| --- | --- | --- | --- | --- | --- |
| Explanatory Variables | Coefficient | $t$-stat | Explanatory Variables | Coefficient | $t$-stat |
| Intercept | 0.34 | 8.14 | Intercept | 0.42 | 23.5 |
| Age (years) | 0.057 | 12.88 | Age (years) | 0.026 | 14.18 |
| Issue Size ($billion) | −0.392 | −15.07 | Issue Size ($billion) | −0.155 | −18.6 |
| Monthly trading volume ($million) | −0.0007 | −5.83 | Monthly trading volume ($million) | −0.0006 | −20.45 |
| DTS (year %) | 0.071 | 65.29 | DTS (year %) | 0.049 | 109.83 |
| Monthly dummies? | Yes | | Monthly dummies? | Yes | |
| Number of observations | 8,372 | | Number of observations | 10,373 | |
| Adjusted $R^2$ | 0.41 | | Adjusted $R^2$ | 0.59 | |

*Source:* Barclays Capital.

bonds, while larger issues enjoyed a relative liquidity benefit, all else equal. In addition, the monthly dummy (not shown) for May in the Pan-European regression is large and positive, whereas the May dummy for the U.S. market is small, suggesting different liquidity regimes in the two markets for the month. This is consistent with the onset of the European sovereign crisis in May.

Is liquidity cost higher in the United States or Pan-Europe? We pool the U.S. and Pan-European trader-quoted benchmark bonds for May 2010 through August 2010, and run a similar regression. In the regression, we include a dummy variable indicating the U.S. market. This dummy variable's coefficient will help indicate which market was more liquid, adjusting for differences in bond attributes, over this time period. Table 5.15 shows the results. The U.S. dummy is negative and significant, suggesting that a roundtrip transaction cost for the average bond, after adjusting for bond attributes, is about 26 bps lower in United States than in Europe for this time period.

## Comparing Pan-European and U.S. LCS

We examine the distribution of LCS values across all index bonds. Figure 5.14 shows the LCS frequency distribution in May 2010 for both the Pan-European and U.S. fixed rate IG markets. For Pan-European credit we

**TABLE 5.15** Common Regression of U.S. and Pan-European LCS on Bond Attributes (May 2010–August 2010)

Dependent Variable: LCS (%)
Sample: May 2010 to August 2010, U.S. and Pan-European–quoted Benchmark Bonds

| Explanatory Variables | Coefficient | *t*-stat |
| --- | --- | --- |
| Intercept | 0.245 | 11.76 |
| Age (years) | 0.04 | 14.59 |
| Issue size ($billion) | −0.127 | −12.38 |
| Monthly trading volume ($ million) | −0.0002 | −5.91 |
| DTS (year %) | 0.046 | 85.84 |
| U.S. dummy | -0.264 | −15.07 |
| Monthly dummies? | Yes | |
| Number of observations | 8,057 | |
| Adjusted $R^2$ | 0.534 | |

*Source:* Barclays Capital.

see a peak in the distribution centered at an LCS of 0.5%, indicating that there are more bonds (compared with the United States) with relatively low LCS values. However, the fat right tail in the distribution for Pan-European bonds (Figure 5.14(A)) indicates that there were a sizeable number of bonds with very high LCS. These high-LCS bonds include financial sector subordinate bonds, which were traded nervously by investors and dealers in May because of regulatory changes and headlines of European sovereign difficulties. If we exclude financial bonds from the distribution (Figure 5.14(B)), we find that the fat tail has disappeared.

We estimate U.S. LCS and Pan-European LCS independently using data from their respective geographies. However, there are many companies that issue in both markets. While local market liquidity conditions are definitely important in deciding LCS levels for a particular bond, we would likely expect some comparability in the LCS of similar duration bonds of the same ticker in both markets.

To examine this, Table 5.16 shows duration-based groups of Pan-European and U.S. bonds from Kraft Foods (KFT), Vodafone (VOD), and General Electric (GE), respectively. We identify four duration groups of KFT bonds, five groups of GE bonds, and four groups of VOD bonds that have at least one bond in each market.

For example, we identify five relatively short-duration Pan-European GE bonds (as of July 2010) that we group together in the first GE row of the

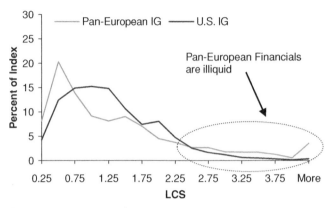

A. May 2010: IG Bonds

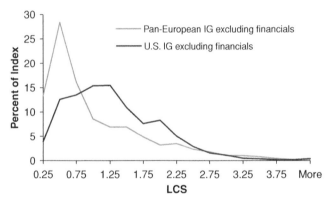

B. May 2010: IG Bonds excluding Financials

**FIGURE 5.14**  LCS Distribution; Pan-European and U.S. Fixed Rate IG Bonds (May 2010)
*Source:* Barclays Capital.

top panel. This group of five bonds has an average OASD of 1.39, DTS of 1.76, and price of 102.91. We then construct a group of similar duration of U.S. GE bonds, shown in the first GE row of the bottom panel. This group of 11 bonds has an average OASD of 1.37, DTS of 1.40, and price of 104.45. We can now more directly compare the LCS for these two rows. We can also do other row-by-row LCS comparisons.[5]

For the GE bonds, the average LCS for all duration buckets is lower in the United States than in Europe. This difference is largely due to relative trading volume and issue size. Trading volume for GE in the United States

**TABLE 5.16** Fixed Rate IG Bonds: Comparison between U.S. and Pan-European Bonds by Issuer (July 2010)*

Pan-European IG

| Ticker | Number of Observations | Average Trading Volume (€) | Average Issue Size (€) | Average Price | Average OASD | Average DTS | Average Age | B/M Status (%) | Trader Quoted? (%) | Average LCS (%) |
|---|---|---|---|---|---|---|---|---|---|---|
| KFT | 1 | 108,380,000 | 2,000,000 | 105.7 | 1.6 | 2.3 | 2.3 | 100 | 100 | 0.229 |
| KFT | 1 | 46,069,402 | 360,631 | 107.9 | 3.9 | 5.7 | 1.3 | 0 | 100 | 0.956 |
| KFT | 1 | 15,820,000 | 850,000 | 114.3 | 4.1 | 5.4 | 2.3 | 100 | 100 | 0.466 |
| KFT | 1 | 29,105,322 | 420,736 | 118.4 | 6.3 | 9.5 | 2 | 0 | 100 | 1.066 |
| VOD | 3 | 46,336,800 | 1,100,613 | 107.3 | 3 | 4 | 3.7 | 67 | 100 | 0.384 |
| VOD | 3 | 26,074,333 | 750,000 | 111.2 | 4.7 | 5.8 | 4.3 | 33 | 100 | 0.684 |
| VOD | 3 | 27,815,482 | 670,736 | 113.1 | 6.3 | 8.8 | 3.3 | 33 | 100 | 0.928 |
| VOD | 2 | 25,246,571 | 420,736 | 104.4 | 11.2 | 14.1 | 7.1 | 0 | 100 | 2.25 |
| GE | 5 | 15,763,989 | 886,636 | 102.9 | 1.4 | 1.8 | 5 | 40 | 60 | 0.693 |
| GE | 15 | 16,566,653 | 986,057 | 105.9 | 2.8 | 4.2 | 4.1 | 62 | 87 | 0.578 |
| GE | 12 | 24,689,200 | 876,551 | 97.8 | 5.2 | 17.5 | 3.9 | 33 | 92 | 1.457 |
| GE | 7 | 24,422,024 | 784,721 | 108.9 | 6.9 | 11.7 | 2.9 | 57 | 100 | 0.944 |
| GE | 9 | 19,134,447 | 699,724 | 99.4 | 12.8 | 22.1 | 4.4 | 44 | 100 | 2.416 |

(*Continued*)

**TABLE 5.16** (Continued)

U.S. IG

| Ticker | Number of Observations | Average Trading Volume (€) | Average Issue Size (€) | Average Price | Average OASD | Average DTS | Average Age | B/M Status (%) | Trader Quoted? (%) | Average LCS (%) |
|---|---|---|---|---|---|---|---|---|---|---|
| KFT | 2 | 95,285,000 | 1,750,000 | 106.9 | 1.5 | 1.4 | 8.5 | 60 | 100 | 0.173 |
| KFT | 4 | 93,987,750 | 762,500 | 109.4 | 2.8 | 2.9 | 3 | 25 | 75 | 0.541 |
| KFT | 3 | 81,895,667 | 1,216,667 | 113.8 | 4.9 | 6.6 | 6.2 | 50 | 67 | 0.73 |
| KFT | 3 | 509,697,333 | 2,333,333 | 112.4 | 6.6 | 8.8 | 1.8 | 73 | 100 | 0.633 |
| VOD | 3 | 63,104,667 | 1,050,000 | 108 | 3.6 | 4.9 | 5.2 | 27 | 100 | 0.461 |
| VOD | 4 | 152,857,000 | 825,000 | 108.2 | 4.9 | 6.8 | 3.4 | 38 | 50 | 0.81 |
| VOD | 2 | 65,167,000 | 875,000 | 105.8 | 6.9 | 10 | 4.1 | 50 | 50 | 1.063 |
| VOD | 3 | 84,966,667 | 979,800 | 110.6 | 11.7 | 23.4 | 7 | 33 | 33 | 1.952 |
| GE | 11 | 126,144,727 | 1,364,617 | 104.4 | 1.4 | 1.4 | 4.8 | 41 | 36 | 0.391 |
| GE | 11 | 107,792,909 | 1,768,182 | 107.3 | 3.1 | 4.8 | 3.3 | 50 | 45 | 0.566 |
| GE | 10 | 217,571,200 | 1,245,000 | 104.7 | 5.1 | 12.3 | 3.7 | 24 | 20 | 1.109 |
| GE | 4 | 504,147,750 | 2,275,000 | 108.6 | 7.1 | 11.3 | 1.8 | 75 | 75 | 0.623 |
| GE | 6 | 164,244,833 | 3,025,000 | 107.5 | 12 | 24.2 | 5.8 | 63 | 67 | 1.061 |

*All averages in this table are equal-weighted averages.
*Sources:* Xtrakter, TRACE, and Barclays Capital.

places it in the 95th percentile, while its trading volume in Europe is in the 60th percentile. In addition, the U.S. GE bonds have an average issue size of approximately twice that of the Pan-European GE bonds. For example, the low duration GE bonds in the United States have an average LCS of 0.391% compared with the average LCS of 0.693% for Pan-European GE bonds. The average trading volume in the United States is about six times that in Europe and the average issue size is considerably larger as well. Somewhat offsetting the tendency for U.S. GE bonds to have lower LCS is that a higher percentage of the GE bonds in Europe are trader-quoted. Comparing similar duration bonds in different markets for the same issuer, we see that the LCS values are very comparable between the two geographies, reflecting the similarity in bond attributes.

## USING LCS IN PORTFOLIO CONSTRUCTION

Investors can use LCS when constructing portfolios. For example, suppose that a portfolio manager in early 2007 was worried about increased liquidity risk but still wanted to track the U.S. IG Index as closely as possible. In other words, the manager wanted to construct a tracking portfolio but with a tilt to a portfolio with better liquidity than the index. How could the manager construct such a portfolio? Traditionally, many managers would construct the portfolio using recent, large-sized issues. With LCS, managers can either select from a set of bonds with an LCS below a set target or constrain their portfolios to meet an overall LCS target.

To investigate the use of LCS in portfolio construction, we use a linear risk model and optimizer to construct three index-tracking portfolios. Portfolios are constructed at month-end January 2007 and rebalanced monthly subject to a turnover constraint to make the exercise realistic. In addition, each portfolio contains about 200 bonds to minimize the effect of idiosyncratic risk on the result.

- *Portfolio A.* No liquidity constraints are used.
- *Portfolio B.* We use traditional liquidity criteria to select only bonds with issue size greater than $500 million and time since issuance (i.e., age) of less than two years.
- *Portfolio C.* Portfolio *must* be rebalanced each month so that its LCS is less than or equal to 70% of the index's LCS.

At each month-end, any cash is reinvested and the optimizer will execute a handful of trades to improve expected TEV. Although all three portfolios will try to keep turnover to a minimum (we allow the optimizer to trade

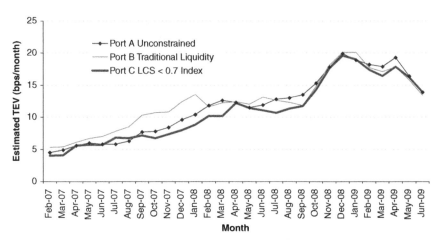

**FIGURE 5.15** Monthly Estimated TEV versus IG Index: Portfolios A, B, and C (January 2007–June 2009)
*Source:* Barclays Capital.

off turnover versus improved TEV), Portfolio C must meet its liquidity target each month irrespective of the degree of turnover. We track each of the portfolios through June 2009 and report their performance, LCS, and turnover.

Figure 5.15 shows that the three portfolios have similar ex ante TEVs at the beginning of the period (approximately 5 bps/month). All three portfolios also have low LCS (Figure 5.16). In addition, Portfolio C's LCS equals 0.7 times the index LCS as required. Recalling the concentrated frequency distribution of LCS in the index as of January 2007 (Figure 5.2), it is relatively easy for the optimizer to construct a tracking portfolio with a constrained LCS with a TEV similar to the other two portfolios. However, as liquidity deteriorates in the second half of 2007 and into 2008, the 70% LCS constraint has the potential to become problematic. Recall (Figure 5.2A) the very spread-out LCS frequency distribution for November 2008.

Over time, the three portfolios are rebalanced to keep the projected TEV to a minimum. To try to mimic actual portfolio management behavior, we restrict the amount of monthly turnover in the pursuit of TEV minimization using an objective function that is a weighted average of TEV and a penalty for every dollar of rebalancing. TEV increases steadily over time through the end of 2008 for all three portfolios, but for different reasons. Portfolios A and B are constrained primarily by the desire to minimize turnover, while for Portfolio C the liquidity constraint dominates. As the aggregate market LCS increases, the 70% LCS constraint for Portfolio C results in significantly greater turnover and more skewed credit sector exposures (i.e.,

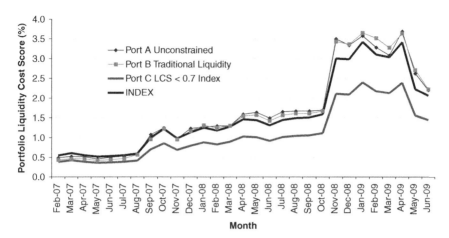

**FIGURE 5.16** Portfolio and Index-Level LCS (January 2007–June 2009)
*Source:* Barclays Capital.

bigger overweights to bonds and sectors with better than average LCS and underweights to bonds and sectors with worse than average LCS) than the other two portfolios. Although higher turnover is undesirable because of the cost and portfolio performance drag, the higher turnover does give the portfolio an opportunity to rebalance to help keep overall estimated TEV low. In contrast, Portfolios A and B trade off some increase in estimated TEV with a reasonably low level of turnover. This is why the estimated TEV for Portfolio C remains generally lower than the TEV for the other two portfolios.

To illustrate this effect, Figure 5.17 shows the TEV breakdown, in terms of risk factor exposures, for each of the three portfolios as of April 2008. Compared to Portfolios A and B, Portfolio C has a greater contribution to TEV from mismatches in credit sector exposures, forced by the LCS constraint. However, we also see that the additional turnover forced on Portfolio C allows it to keep hedged with respect to curve risk, while Portfolios A and B develop more TEV due to term structure mismatches.

As the market became increasingly illiquid, Portfolio C's cumulative excess return began to surpass the other two portfolios. Interestingly, the traditional way to construct liquid portfolios performed the worst. Large, recent issues were typically financial issues that suffered greatly during the liquidity crisis in 2008. By the time market illiquidity peaked in December 2008 (based on LCS), Portfolio C had outperformed Portfolio A (unconstrained) by approximately 200 bps and Portfolio B (issue size and age) by almost 350 bps. Figure 5.18 shows the cumulative excess returns of each of these portfolios versus the IG Index.

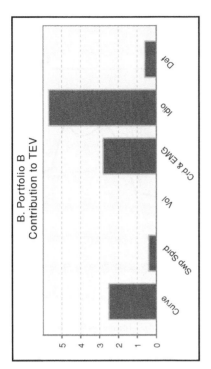

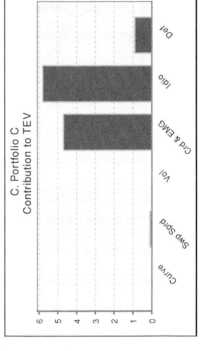

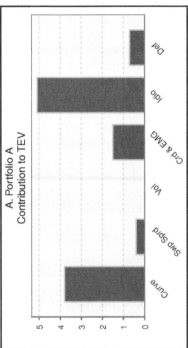

**FIGURE 5.17** TEV Details: Portfolios A, B, and C (April 2008)
*Source:* Barclays Capital.

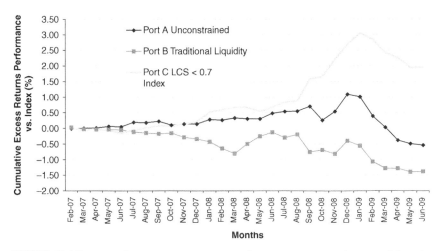

**FIGURE 5.18** Cumulative Excess Return Performance versus Index: Portfolios A, B, and C (February 2007–June 2009)
*Source:* Barclays Capital.

Figure 5.19 highlights the sharp cumulative outperformance of Portfolio C versus Portfolio B. This relative performance closely tracks the aggregate LCS level of the IG index. Although Portfolios B and C are both tracking portfolios, as per the risk model, they have very different LCS profiles. As liquidity deteriorated, the lower LCS portfolio outperformed. While LCS may serve as a proxy for other risk factors not captured by the risk model, these

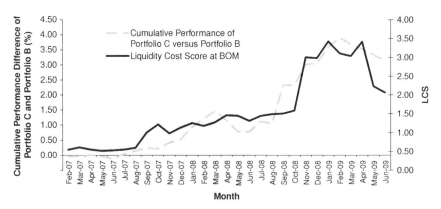

**FIGURE 5.19** Cumulative Excess Return Difference: Portfolio C (70% LCS) versus Portfolio B (issue size and age), LCS of IG Index (February 2007–June 2009)
*Source:* Barclays Capital.

results indicate that a portfolio manager with a view on market liquidity can use LCS to structure portfolios to capitalize on that view.

Maintaining a highly liquid tracking portfolio is an idea many portfolio managers would readily embrace. LCS enables investors to *objectively* construct such a portfolio (see Chapter 14). However, maintaining a relatively liquid portfolio is difficult, and could involve high turnover, which may offset the liquidity benefits. A bond's LCS generally increases with age, holding all else constant. This will cause a portfolio's overall LCS to drift higher. We see this effect in Figure 5.16, as the LCS for Portfolios A and B, which have some turnover constraints, begin to exceed that of the index. Consequently, a portfolio manager trying to keep the portfolio's LCS close to that of the index will need some turnover to add lower LCS bonds to the portfolio from time to time.

However, maintaining a *targeted* portfolio LCS value less than the index is likely to require considerable turnover. For Portfolio C to keep its LCS at 70% of the index, a challenge considering the distribution of LCS across bonds, it needed a high degree of turnover. Figure 5.20 presents monthly turnover (as a percent of portfolio MV) for the three tracking portfolios. Turnover for Portfolio C averages almost 7% per month, compared with about 2% per month for Portfolios A and B. Portfolio C has high turnover because bonds it had initially purchased with low LCS subsequently became higher LCS bonds (e.g., financials). During the liquidity crisis, Portfolio C had to turn over approximately 33% of its portfolio in October 2008. As the

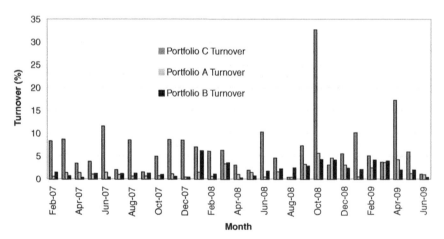

**FIGURE 5.20** Turnover of Portfolios A, B, and C: [($Buys + $Sells)/$Portfolio] (February 2007–June 2009)
*Source:* Barclays Capital.

credit markets improved, Portfolio C took advantage and added back some bonds whose LCS returned to better-than-average values. Again, this produced relatively high turnover: 10% in January 2009 and 17% in April 2009.

Figures 5.18 and 5.19 show that Portfolio C outperformed Portfolios A and B, but those numbers did not account for Portfolio C's much higher turnover. Using the LCS values as estimates of turnover costs, the cumulative outperformance of Portfolio C versus Portfolio B as of December 2008 falls from 350 bps to 312 bps.

The large difference in turnover between the two portfolios does not translate into a large difference in net cumulative returns. This is because the bonds in Portfolio C, which are churned, are cheaper to trade than the bonds in Portfolios A or B. Over the time period under study, the relative outperformance of Portfolio C dwarfs its incremental transaction cost of 70 bps with respect to Portfolio A and 40 bps with respect to Portfolio B.

## Creating Highly Liquid and Tradable Cash Basket Proxies

Many investors have an interest in replicating a cash index using a small portfolio of cash bonds. However, it is sometimes hard to determine which bonds are liquid and, then, how to weight them in a portfolio to get good tracking performance to the index. In Chapter 14, we present a transparent proxy construction methodology that uses LCS, along with other constraints, to identify objectively a liquid universe of cash bonds, and then uses stratified sampling to construct a cash bond proxy portfolio.

## TRADE EFFICIENCY SCORES (TES)

The *Trade Efficiency Score* (TES)[TM] is a bond-level liquidity ranking from 1 (best) to 10 (worst). TES blends information from relative LCS levels and trading volume data. The idea behind TES is to provide a liquidity ranking that allows an investor to quickly judge a bond's relative liquidity, both currently and over time. While a bond's LCS measures its liquidity cost at a particular moment, its LCS value will fluctuate over time as both the overall market liquidity, and the bond's relative liquidity, ebb and flow. For example, a bond may have an LCS of 2.200% in December 2008, 1.563% in May 2009 and 1.235% in December 2009. Compared with its peers, did this bond have a relatively good or bad LCS in each of these months? The purpose of TES is to give each bond a monthly liquidity ranking so an investor can quickly determine a bond's relative liquidity. Since the TES is a ranking, a bond's TES is unlikely to change as much as LCS over time as general market liquidity conditions fluctuate.

When creating the TES ranking based on LCS values, it is important to take into account that a bond's LCS is heavily influenced by its spread duration, as LCS tends to increase with duration (all else equal). Since investors generally select bonds for a given duration exposure, we compute a bond's TES using the ratio of its LCS to OASD. Having rankings based on LCS adjusted by OASD allows a portfolio manager to construct a liquid portfolio by simply filtering on bonds ranked, say, a 1, 2, or 3, knowing that these will be the most liquid bonds for a given spread duration at the time the analysis is done.

While LCS captures liquidity cost, it does not directly measure the level of trading in a bond. Many bonds in broad credit indexes rarely trade. A bond with low trading volume generally has a higher LCS to reflect a higher cost of execution. However, LCS may not adequately reflect the ease of implementing large or numerous trades. Investors interested in immediate execution, or traders who may need to commit to making a market in a bond for a time going forward, may prefer a bond with higher current trading volume over another bond, with a similar LCS, but with lower volume. TES combines both LCS (adjusted by spread duration) and trading volume into a single score that reflects a bond's relative trade efficiency (i.e., trading cost and trading flow) over time and across bonds. In this way, TES may come closer to a trader's intuitive idea of measuring the potential market impact of trading a bond.

To compute TES, each bond in the corporate universe is first assigned to a (spread duration–adjusted) LCS quintile and a monthly trading volume decile. The quintile and decile rankings are added, and the sum (which can range from 2 to 15) is then mapped to a TES ranking from 1 to 10. Table 5.17 provides the details of this mapping as well as the average liquidity characteristics of each TES ranking as of August 31, 2010.

Portfolio managers can also use the TES liquidity ranking as a filter when constructing portfolios or strategies. TES can be used to construct a portfolio, or as a tool for back-testing strategies. For example, a portfolio manager interested in building liquid and easily transactable proxy portfolios can specify a TES filter to restrict the eligible universe of bonds. Or, a manager interested in back-testing an alpha strategy can limit his or her analysis only to bonds with very low TES rankings to see if the strategy could have been realistically implemented.

## CONCLUSION

This chapter introduces LCS, an objective measure of bond-level liquidity. We detail the LCS methodology and discuss the cross-sectional and time

**TABLE 5.17** TES Mapping Scheme: TES Breakdown of Euro and U.S. Fixed Rate IG Corporate Indexes (August 31, 2010)

| Sum of Trading Volume Decile and LCS Quintile | Trade Efficiency Score (TES) | Euro Fixed Rate IG Corporate Index | | | | U.S. Fixed Rate IG Corporate Index | | | |
|---|---|---|---|---|---|---|---|---|---|
| | | % Count of Euro Corporate Index | MV of Euro Corporate Index (%) | Average Adjusted LCS | Average Trading Volume (€000s) | % Count of U.S. IG Corporate Index | MV of U.S. IG Corporate Index (%) | Average Adjusted LCS | Average Trading Volume ($000s) |
| 2 3 | 1 | 8.90 | 14.00 | 0.072 | 179,911 | 14.40 | 31.60 | 0.08 | 305,466 |
| 4 5 | 2 | 15.50 | 21.70 | 0.11 | 71,587 | 10.00 | 14.30 | 0.136 | 108,585 |
| 6 | 3 | 9.50 | 11.10 | 0.153 | 45,720 | 6.40 | 7.00 | 0.185 | 74,812 |
| 7 | 4 | 9.20 | 9.90 | 0.189 | 34,014 | 7.90 | 8.00 | 0.225 | 46,898 |
| 8 | 5 | 10.20 | 9.60 | 0.165 | 23,847 | 9.30 | 8.00 | 0.231 | 29,859 |
| 9 | 6 | 8.30 | 7.80 | 0.172 | 17,452 | 8.10 | 6.00 | 0.243 | 19,196 |
| 10 | 7 | 5.60 | 4.50 | 0.25 | 14,385 | 9.00 | 6.00 | 0.28 | 12,442 |
| 11 | 8 | 7.00 | 5.40 | 0.24 | 10,563 | 9.00 | 5.60 | 0.262 | 6,101 |
| 12 13 | 9 | 6.10 | 4.40 | 0.345 | 7,574 | 9.00 | 4.90 | 0.301 | 3,693 |
| 14 15 | 10 | 19.60 | 11.50 | 0.566 | 791 | 17.00 | 8.40 | 0.357 | 1,047 |

*Source:* Barclays Capital.

series properties of LCS, which fit closely with ex post market perceptions of liquidity.

LCS also provides managers with a straightforward indication of the cost of liquidating a portfolio, thereby serving as a measure of liquidity risk management. LCS can be used in a variety of portfolio management applications: constructing portfolios with various target levels of liquidity to take views on changes in market liquidity; designing optimal execution strategies for portfolio transitions; and designing custom credit benchmarks.

## NOTES

1. Copyright Barclays Bank PLC (2010). All rights reserved. Liquidity Cost Scores (LCS) is a trademark of Barclays Capital, and the Liquidity Cost Scores (LCS)™ methodologies are patent pending.
2. Monthly LCS values are now available for many more markets: U.S. treasuries, Treasury Inflation-Protected Securities (TIPS), mortgage-backed securities (MBS), Pan-European Sovereigns, and Linkers.
3. Trade Reporting and Compliance Engine (TRACE), introduced by the Financial Industry Regulatory Authority (FINRA)—when it was still the National Association of Securities Dealers (NASD)—disseminates trade-by-trade corporate bond execution information within 15 minutes to all market participants. At this time, TRACE data are censored at $5 million for investment grade and $1 million for high-yield securities.
4. Some other important explanatory variables are: non-par priced status, benchmark status, sector, and subordination type.
5. We see that an issuer's LCS generally increases along with the duration bucket because higher duration (or DTS) bonds will tend to have higher liquidity costs. There is a break in this pattern, however, either when there is a big change in trading volume or amount outstanding.

### CHAPTER 6

# Joint Dynamics of Default and Liquidity Risk

Credit bonds are issued at a positive yield spread (i.e., a credit spread) over comparable maturity Treasury bonds to compensate investors for the chance that a bond may default with a recovery value less than par. However, many studies have documented that credit bond spreads are generally much larger than is justified by their subsequent default and recovery experience.[1]

A portion of the credit spread may reflect an expected liquidity cost to execute a roundtrip trade in a credit bond as measured by the bond's bid-ask spread. This cost is typically greater for a credit bond than for a comparable-maturity Treasury bond. A credit investor who anticipates selling the bond at some point wants compensation for this cost in the form of a wider spread at the time of purchase. Another portion of the credit spread may reflect a risk premium demanded by risk-averse investors because of the uncertainty associated with the timing, magnitude, and recovery of defaults and liquidity costs.[2] Consequently, the greater the degree of uncertainty, or the more risk averse the marginal investor, the more the credit spread will diverge from the expected default and recovery rates. In this chapter, we illustrate how a bond's spread can be decomposed into components due to risk premium, expected default loss, and expected liquidity cost. A cornerstone of this research is the Liquidity Cost Score (LCS) model presented in Chapter 5.

Credit spread decomposition can serve several purposes. For example, an insurance company may be holding a large portfolio of credit bonds currently at wide spreads. The company's portfolio strategy will likely depend on whether the wide spreads are due to large expected default losses, high liquidity costs, or a high risk premium. Presumably, the company can ride out periods of high liquidity cost and risk aversion, as the firm is generally a buy-and-hold investor. However, if the wide spreads reflect an increase in expected default losses, the company may need to reposition or hedge its portfolio. Active portfolio managers can also use spread decomposition to

**133**

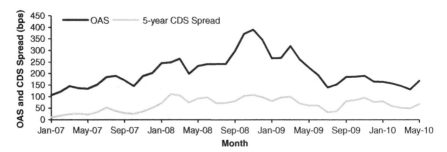

**FIGURE 6.1** OAS and CDS for KFT 6.5s of 11/31
*Source:* Barclays Capital.

take specific exposures to bonds that have large liquidity or default components, depending on their views about how compensation for default or liquidity costs is likely to evolve. Finally, regulators can use spread decomposition to monitor separately the liquidity and credit risk of the institutions they supervise.

As a simple example of the value of spread decomposition, consider the spread behavior of the Kraft (KFT) 6.5s of 11/31 from January 2007 to May 2010. As shown in Figure 6.1, the bond's *option-adjusted spread* (OAS) varied substantially over the period. The figure also shows the level of KFT's five-year CDS spread—a measure of the expected default losses from the issuer. Movements in the bond's OAS loosely track changes in the issuer's CDS. However, there is a wide, and variable, gap between the two spreads. The magnitude of the gap has ranged from a low of 82 bps in April 2010 to a maximum of 282 bps in November 2008. Presumably, this gap reflects risk premium and expected liquidity costs. To measure the expected liquidity costs, Figure 6.2 plots the bond's LCS over the same period. The chart illustrates that much of the variability in the OAS-CDS spread gap reflects movements in the bond's LCS.

These figures suggest that the rise in KFT's OAS in July 2007 was driven by both default and liquidity concerns (all three lines moved up), whereas the spike in September 2008 was mainly a liquidity event (the line plotting the LCS moves much more than the CDS line). Understanding the sources of OAS movements allows investors to better protect their portfolio from particular sources of OAS changes, or take advantage of them.

Alternatively, investors may have a situation in which a bond's OAS has been very stable or declining—suggesting improved creditworthiness. However, the declining OAS may simply reflect improved liquidity and a lower market-wide risk premium, while the CDS may be widening, reflecting

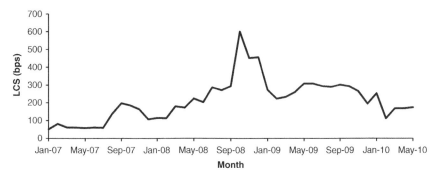

**FIGURE 6.2** LCS for KFT 6.5s of 11/31
*Source:* Barclays Capital.

a deteriorating credit profile. For instance, from July 2009 to October 2009, the OAS of the TWX 6.75s of 4/11 declined to 157 bps from 199 bps. Did this spread tightening reflect improved credit quality, or improved liquidity and/or a lower market risk premium? Over this period, TWX's CDS spread increased to 57 bps from 45 bps, suggesting higher expected default losses. So why the reduction in OAS? The LCS for this bond fell to 21 bps from 49 bps. In addition, as we will show, there was a reduction in market-wide risk premium. In other words, despite an increase in expected default losses, the OAS for the bond declined because of lower liquidity costs and risk premium.

These two examples illustrate that to properly interpret OAS changes we need to measure the components of OAS. We have only shown how other variables (CDS and LCS) move in relation to OAS. Our goal, however, is to decompose a bond's OAS into the three components, and measure their relative contributions. Although researchers[3] were able to explain a large part of the spread time series using a broad market measure of liquidity cost, such as the spread between on- and off-the-run Treasury bonds, the lack of a bond-level liquidity cost measure has hindered cross-sectional spread decomposition analysis.

Figure 6.3 previews the results of our spread decomposition model using the earlier KFT bond as an example. As we will discuss, we assume that the part of the OAS not attributed to default or liquidity captures the effects of market-wide risk premium that is not specific to KFT's liquidity and default characteristics. The figure shows that the effects of both default and liquidity on the bond's OAS were low in 2007. Throughout 2008, however, as the OAS widened, most of the increase in OAS was liquidity and market risk related, with the default component remaining relatively stable. In other

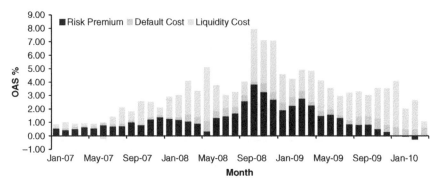

**FIGURE 6.3**    Spread Decomposition for KFT 6.5s of 11/31: Risk Premium,
Expected Default Losses, and Liquidity Costs
*Source:* Barclays Capital.

words, at the peak of the crisis with the KFT bond's OAS at extremely wide
levels, investors didn't really believe that it was likely to default.

This bond-level information can be invaluable to portfolio managers as
they choose which bonds to hold, or which hedging instruments to employ
for protection from certain market movements. For example, suppose spread
decomposition indicates that a bond has relatively low default risk, but large
spread components due to liquidity and risk premium. Long-term investors,
with reduced mark-to-market constraints, can choose to provide liquidity
to the market and buy the bond, comfortable with the low default risk. For
tactical mark-to-market investors, this distinction is perhaps less critical;
they would worry about short-term dislocations arising from any source of
risk. For them, the key benefit of understanding the source of spreads would
be as an aid to hedging. To hedge default-related risks at the issuer level,
investors may use the issuer's CDS. For hedging systemic liquidity risks,
VIX futures might be a more appropriate instrument. The close relationship
between LCS and VIX was discussed in the previous chapter (see Figure 5.6).
For example, the correlation between LCS and VIX from January 2007 to
April 2009 was 0.90.

We can also aggregate the bond-level spread decomposition results to
examine any differences at the sector level. For example, in Figures 6.4 and
6.5, we apply the spread decomposition methodology to investment-grade
bonds in two sectors—consumer goods and financials—and examine the
relative differences. In early 2007, in terms of both liquidity and default
contributions, there appears to be no difference between these two sectors.
The rise in default contribution for financials in August 2007 was related

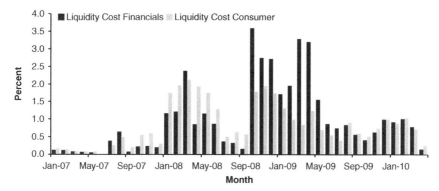

**FIGURE 6.4** Liquidity Contribution: Consumer and Financial Sectors
*Source:* Barclays Capital.

to the first wave of financial sector difficulties (e.g., mortgage companies), and the liquidity contribution went up for both sectors. Clear differences in liquidity across the two sectors appeared after the Bear Stearns takeover in March 2008. Default contributions for financials increased in the form of wider CDS spreads, but financials were still pretty liquid until the Lehman Brothers bankruptcy in September 2008. Thereafter, liquidity contributions to spreads for financials shot up and remained elevated until the second quarter of 2009. While the liquidity differences between the two sectors abated, the default contribution differences that began during the crisis persisted.

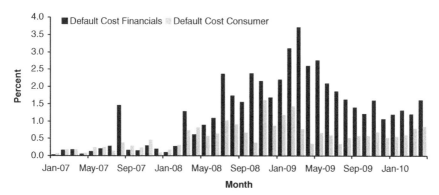

**FIGURE 6.5** Default Contribution: Consumer and Financial Sectors
*Source:* Barclays Capital.

## SPREAD DECOMPOSITION METHODOLOGY

We model a bond's OAS (to Treasuries) with three variables: a variable reflecting expected default cost, a variable reflecting expected liquidity cost, and a market-wide variable unrelated to the bond's attributes representing the market-wide risk premium demanded by investors. Specifically, for every month $t$, we run the following cross-sectional OLS regression:

$$OAS_{it} = \alpha_t + \beta \, \text{ExpectedDefaultCost}_{it} + \gamma \, \text{ExpectedLiquidityCost}_{it} + \eta_{it}$$

$$(6.1)$$

The risk premium captured by $\alpha$ (the intercept term) represents a market-level risk premium, not a risk premium specific to each bond. We argue that any bond-level risk premium will likely be highly correlated with the bond's default cost or liquidity cost variable. In other words, a bond with a high LCS will also likely be a bond for which an investor will demand a higher spread premium as compensation for liquidity cost uncertainty. This would make it difficult to separate a bond's spread into a portion from expected liquidity cost and liquidity risk premium. If default risk or liquidity risk premia are highly correlated with default or liquidity costs, then the regression coefficient ($\beta$ and $\gamma$) will be larger and/or more significant. Any part of risk premia that is unrelated to bond-level default and liquidity cost—in other words, a market-level risk premium—will show up in the intercept.[4]

To measure bond-level expected default cost, we have a choice of variables. First, we use an issuer's market-quoted five-year CDS as a measure of its expected default cost (i.e., default probability and loss given default). CDS markets, however, are not necessarily liquid and therefore cannot always be considered as a pure default proxy. To use CDS as a default loss variable, we confine ourselves to bonds close to the five-year point on the curve, since five-year CDSs are usually the most liquid. To identify issuers with liquid CDS, we restrict our analysis to names that are part of the CDX Index.

We also use another measure of expected default cost—the *corporate default probability* (CDP) multiplied by one minus the *conditional recovery rate* (CRR).[5] CDP and CRR are not market variables. Instead, they are output from a quantitative model that uses firm-specific fundamental information, equity prices, and macroeconomic data to estimate a one-year default probability and recovery rate for the issuer. Importantly, CDP and CRR are both computed independently of a bond's OAS.[6] Having two independent measures of expected default losses helps to assess the stability of the spread decomposition results.

We measure a bond's expected liquidity cost using its LCS value. We use bonds whose LCS are computed directly from traders' bid-ask quotes rather than bonds whose LCS are estimated from our LCS model.[7]

We thus have two spread decomposition models depending on the variable chosen to represent expected default losses:

$$OAS_{it} = \alpha_t + \beta_t \, CDS_{it} + \gamma_t \, LCS_{it} + \eta_{it} \qquad (6.2a)$$

$$OAS_{it} = \alpha_t + \beta_t \, CDP_{it}(1 - CRR_{it}) + \gamma_t \, LCS_{it} + \eta_{it} \qquad (6.2b)$$

We refer to model (6.2a) as the *CDS model* and to model (6.2b) as the *CDP/CRR model*. To get a sense of the value of incorporating a bond-level liquidity variable (LCS) to explain the cross-sectional distribution of spreads, we examine two versions of each model. First, we estimate each model without LCS as an explanatory variable. Then, we re-estimate each model with LCS added and compare the results with the first version to see if adding LCS improves the fit of the regression. In addition, we check to see if including LCS detracts from CDS (or CDP/CRR) as an explanatory variable. If LCS is a useful explanatory variable, we would expect to see an improvement in the adjusted $R^2$ and a significant (and positive) LCS coefficient, with little disturbance to the significance and magnitude of the CDS coefficient.

We use monthly data from January 2007 to April 2010.[8] For a bond to be included in the sample set, it must satisfy the criteria discussed above (i.e., trader-quoted LCS and [for the CDS model] the issuer's CDS must be a member of the CDX universe for the month the regression is estimated). The number of bonds in our sample also varies depending on the regression model, as we have more bonds with CDP/CRR data than with liquid CDS. We also analyze both investment-grade and high-yield bonds, but report them in separate regressions. One drawback of our parsimonious spread decomposition modeling is that liquidity and default are unlikely to be completely independent of each other, so multicollinearity may be a concern. Nevertheless, as we will show, the improvement in adjusted $R^2$ and the robustness of the CDS coefficients to the inclusion of LCS in the specification suggest that the model is well specified.

## WHAT DRIVES OAS DIFFERENCES ACROSS BONDS?

Table 6.1 presents the April 2010 investment-grade regression results. The regression for the first version of the CDS model (i.e., without LCS) produced an $R^2$ of 0.54 with a significant CDS coefficient and an intercept that was

**TABLE 6.1** Investment-Grade Bonds: Regression of OAS on CDS and LCS (April 2010)

| Same in Both Regressions | | Specification 1: Only CDS | | | | Specification 2: Both CDS and LCS | | | |
|---|---|---|---|---|---|---|---|---|---|
| Month | Number of Observations | | Intercept | CDS | $R^2$ | | Intercept | CDS | LCS | $R^2$ |
| April-10 | 123 | Coefficients | 0.16 | 1.23 | 0.54 | Coefficients | 0.05 | 1.17 | 0.28 | 0.60 |
| | | $t$-stats | 1.31 | 12.02 | | $t$-stats | 0.40 | 12.05 | 4.27 | |

*Source:* Barclays Capital.

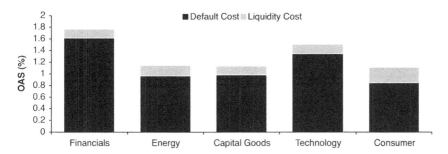

**FIGURE 6.6** Sector-Wise Spread Decomposition: Default and Liquidity
Contributions (April 2010)
*Source:* Barclays Capital.

not significantly different from zero. When we estimated the second version
by including LCS, the $R^2$ increased to 0.60. More importantly, the LCS
coefficient is both positive and significant. In addition, the CDS coefficient
is largely unchanged. In other words, in April 2010, bonds with higher
LCS were characterized by higher OAS, holding expected loss from default
constant. Hence, bond-level LCS is important in explaining relative OAS
levels across bonds, after accounting for default risk.

We can use these results to look at the contribution of default and
liquidity effects on OAS for various sectors, as shown in Figure 6.6. This
figure uses the regression coefficients in the right column of Table 6.1 and
multiplies them by the respective average values of CDS and LCS for each
sector. We find that, in April 2010, liquidity effects were relatively small
and uniform across sectors. In contrast, the extent of variation in the default
component across sectors was larger.

## HOW HAS THE COMPOSITION OF OAS CHANGED?

We repeat the spread decomposition exercise for every month in the sample
period January 2007–April 2010 to show fluctuations in the relative contributions to OAS of the three components. Table 6.2 presents the monthly
regression results for investment-grade bonds for both versions of the CDS
spread decomposition model for all 40 months. (The CDP/CRR model results are shown in this chapter's appendix.)

In the first half of 2007, when liquidity was abundant, LCS might not
have played an important role in explaining spread differences across bonds.
In fact, we see that adding LCS to the regression did not meaningfully
improve the $R^2$.[9] In contrast, when liquidity conditions began to deteriorate

**TABLE 6.2** Investment-Grade Bonds–Only Regression of OAS on CDS and LCS (January 2007–April 2010)

| Same in Both Regressions | | Specification 1: Only CDS | | | Specification 2: Both CDS and LCS | | | |
|---|---|---|---|---|---|---|---|---|
| Month | Number of Observations | Intercept | CDS | $R^2$ | Intercept | CDS | LCS | $R^2$ |
| Jan-07 | 116 | **0.67** | **0.36** | 0.25 | **0.54** | **0.27** | **0.57** | 0.31 |
| Feb-07 | 103 | **0.55** | **0.81** | 0.70 | **0.42** | **0.77** | **0.58** | 0.77 |
| Mar-07 | 115 | **0.59** | **0.74** | 0.76 | **0.50** | **0.70** | **0.39** | 0.79 |
| Apr-07 | 116 | **0.72** | **0.30** | 0.32 | **0.64** | **0.27** | 0.36 | 0.33 |
| May-07 | 109 | **0.62** | **0.78** | 0.66 | 0.55 | 0.73 | **0.31** | 0.67 |
| Jun-07 | 99 | **0.70** | **0.56** | 0.62 | **0.77** | **0.66** | −0.37 | 0.64 |
| Jul-07 | 74 | **0.83** | **0.63** | 0.68 | **0.69** | **0.36** | **0.92** | 0.77 |
| Aug-07 | 59 | **1.08** | **0.70** | 0.87 | **0.71** | **0.53** | **0.88** | 0.90 |
| Sep-07 | 78 | **1.17** | **0.52** | 0.54 | **1.00** | **0.48** | **0.34** | 0.57 |
| Oct-07 | 77 | **1.13** | **0.57** | 0.51 | **0.79** | **0.35** | **0.92** | 0.65 |
| Nov-07 | 46 | **1.43** | **0.79** | 0.54 | **1.23** | **0.45** | **0.69** | 0.59 |
| Dec-07 | 36 | **1.51** | **0.57** | 0.34 | **1.38** | 0.32 | **0.51** | 0.39 |
| Jan-08 | 68 | **1.63** | **0.93** | 0.32 | **1.27** | 0.14 | **1.34** | 0.67 |
| Feb-08 | 75 | **1.64** | **0.72** | 0.27 | **1.18** | 0.19 | **1.46** | 0.68 |
| Mar-08 | 71 | **1.76** | **1.03** | 0.54 | **1.08** | **0.49** | **1.41** | 0.83 |
| Apr-08 | 71 | **1.41** | **1.31** | 0.55 | **0.91** | **0.69** | **1.12** | 0.77 |
| May-08 | 80 | **1.35** | **1.19** | 0.42 | 0.33 | **0.83** | **1.80** | 0.66 |
| Jun-08 | 81 | **1.71** | **0.86** | 0.47 | **1.33** | **0.53** | **0.95** | 0.65 |
| Jul-08 | 78 | **1.64** | **0.97** | 0.93 | **1.46** | **0.86** | **0.34** | 0.94 |
| Aug-08 | 81 | **1.84** | **0.80** | 0.86 | **1.67** | **0.68** | **0.40** | 0.89 |
| Sep-08 | 75 | **2.87** | **0.56** | 0.44 | **2.57** | **0.55** | **0.35** | 0.49 |
| Oct-08 | 135 | **5.32** | **0.35** | 0.65 | **3.83** | **0.20** | **0.65** | 0.86 |
| Nov-08 | 148 | **3.54** | **1.23** | 0.51 | **3.26** | **0.60** | **0.71** | 0.82 |
| Dec-08 | 151 | **3.22** | **1.33** | 0.41 | **2.69** | **0.58** | **0.84** | 0.76 |
| Jan-09 | 147 | **2.59** | **1.08** | 0.49 | **1.91** | **0.69** | **0.78** | 0.72 |
| Feb-09 | 170 | **2.56** | **1.04** | 0.65 | **2.22** | **0.69** | **0.61** | 0.79 |
| Mar-09 | 157 | **3.45** | **0.97** | 0.65 | **2.76** | **0.59** | **0.68** | 0.82 |
| Apr-09 | 120 | **4.04** | **0.56** | 0.63 | **2.26** | **0.35** | **0.90** | 0.80 |
| May-09 | 92 | **2.32** | **0.78** | 0.75 | **1.48** | **0.60** | **0.74** | 0.85 |
| Jun-09 | 103 | **2.09** | **0.76** | 0.59 | **1.59** | **0.61** | **0.53** | 0.69 |
| Jul-09 | 86 | **1.82** | **0.81** | 0.68 | **1.32** | **0.66** | **0.50** | 0.76 |
| Aug-09 | 117 | **1.42** | **0.94** | 0.54 | **0.87** | **0.75** | **0.72** | 0.67 |
| Sep-09 | 150 | **1.28** | **0.92** | 0.57 | **0.81** | **0.79** | **0.62** | 0.68 |
| Oct-09 | 153 | **1.19** | **0.83** | 0.54 | **0.83** | **0.74** | **0.54** | 0.64 |
| Nov-09 | 152 | **1.02** | **0.98** | 0.56 | **0.50** | **0.85** | **0.86** | 0.69 |
| Dec-09 | 103 | **1.10** | **0.87** | 0.44 | **0.30** | **0.67** | **1.41** | 0.68 |
| Jan-10 | 167 | **0.78** | **0.91** | 0.46 | −0.02 | **0.80** | **1.38** | 0.65 |
| Feb-10 | 129 | **0.68** | **0.99** | 0.51 | −0.05 | **0.79** | **1.39** | 0.69 |
| Mar-10 | 108 | **0.41** | **1.12** | 0.43 | −0.24 | **0.97** | **1.30** | 0.68 |
| Apr-10 | 123 | 0.16 | **1.23** | 0.54 | 0.05 | **1.17** | **0.28** | 0.60 |

*Note:* Coefficients in bold significant at the 95% level.
*Source:* Barclays Capital.

in 2008, the $R^2$ increased significantly after adding LCS to the regression. For most months, the inclusion of LCS in the regression did not affect the size and significance of the CDS coefficient. This confirms that LCS is providing new information.

The regression intercept captures the portion of (average) spread that is independent of CDS and LCS. As discussed earlier, the market risk premium is likely to be an important contributor to the level of OAS, and we use the time series of the intercept as an indicator of the variation of the market risk premium that is not already embedded in the bond-level default and liquidity variables.

For example, for the CDS model with LCS, the intercept increases to 2.76 in March 2009 from about 0.5 in early 2007, before decreasing to near zero towards the end of the sample. The general movement in the intercept over time aligns well with investors' perception of fluctuations in the level of the market risk premium.

The regression coefficients for CDS and LCS are statistically significant for most months (except CDS from December 2007 to February 2008 and May 2008, and LCS in May 2007). LCS has a consistently large effect on the distribution of OAS values across bonds. Since default risk for high-grade bonds has been very low over time (see Chapter 12), a relatively large proportion of the OAS is potentially liquidity related. As shown in Table 6.2, the relationship of CDS with OAS is naturally tight, but may not be as close as one might have thought.

The magnitudes of the CDS and LCS coefficients generally change in a similar fashion with the intercept value. This is not surprising as the CDS and LCS coefficients can be interpreted as the compensation (in spread terms) demanded by investors per unit of the corresponding cost. The prices of default and liquidity risk are likely to move similarly to the market risk premium.

When the intercept explains a relatively high proportion of OAS, this suggests that systematic market factors rather than bond-specific factors are driving spreads. This may occur because of very high levels of aggregate risk aversion (e.g., late 2008 and early 2009) or because the market was pricing bonds with little concern for issuer-specific information (e.g., most of 2007). When the intercept explains a relatively low proportion of OAS, this suggests that bond-specific factors are driving spreads. For example, the OAS level in September 2007 was similar to its level in April 2010. However, the intercept was a large component of total spreads in the first period, but a negligible component in the second. This suggests that the market was possibly less discriminating across bonds in the first period, and much more discriminating in the second.

We can take the results in Table 6.2 and break down the OAS value into the three components in terms of basis points. In December 2009,

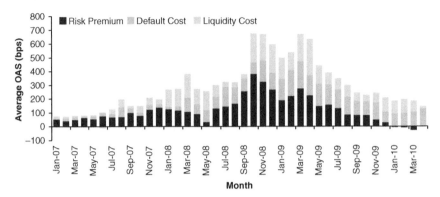

**FIGURE 6.7** Contributions of Risk Premium, Default, and Liquidity Components to Market OAS Level (January 2007–April 2010)
*Source:* Barclays Capital.

for example, the average OAS, LCS, and CDS were 2.09%, 0.73%, and 1.14%, respectively. The coefficients of LCS and CDS were 1.41 and 0.67, respectively, and the intercept value was 0.30%. As expected, 0.30% + 0.67 × 1.14% + 1.41 × 0.73% = 2.09%, which is the average OAS. We refer to the product of the average value of the variable and its coefficient (i.e., 0.67 × 1.14% and 1.41 × 0.73%) as the contribution of average CDS and LCS, respectively, to average OAS in December 2009.[10]

Figure 6.7 presents the contributions, in basis points, of the market risk premium, default cost, and liquidity cost to the market OAS every month since January 2007. The contribution pattern in Figure 6.7 diverges from the time series of coefficient values in Table 6.2 during periods in which the mean values of the variables and the OAS varied a lot. For example, from September 2008 to October 2008, the average CDS spread jumped to 413 bps from 166 bps, but the coefficient of the CDS spread fell to 0.2 from 0.5, leading to a decline in the amount of OAS explained by CDS. This is because aggregate risk aversion, as measured by the intercept, shot up during this period. In October 2008, 383 bps of the 6.76% OAS was explained by the intercept, 82 bps by CDS, and 211 bps by LCS.

Figure 6.8 shows the same information as Figure 6.7, but expresses the contributions of the three spread components as percentages of the average OAS value. This makes some earlier observations clearer. For instance, although the average OAS levels in April 2010 are similar to those in September 2007, the breakdown is very different. The market in early 2007 was attributing OAS levels to overall market uncertainties, whereas in early

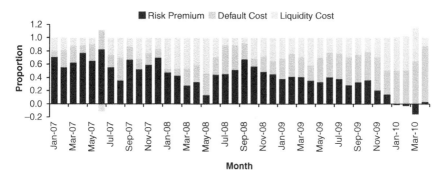

**FIGURE 6.8** Risk Premium, Default, and Liquidity Components as Percentage of OAS (January 2007–April 2010)
*Source:* Barclays Capital.

2010, much more of the OAS could be explained by the variation in CDS spreads across bonds.

If an investor seeks to hedge the default or liquidity components separately, then the contribution to OAS in basis points is the appropriate measure. If an investor is analyzing current market compensation for taking on additional amounts of the expected default or liquidity cost, the coefficient provides that information. Nevertheless, a view on liquidity or default should be based not just on the coefficients, but also on the expected future levels of these variables.

Figure 6.9 compares data from March 2009 and April 2010 to provide a sense of how contributions to a sector's OAS can change over time. We observe that for every sector, a large proportion of the spread in March 2009 consisted of market risk aversion and liquidity components. However, these factors play a far smaller role in April 2010. Most of the OAS in April 2010 is attributed to CDS. Of course, the OAS went down to 1.64% in April 2010 from 6.70% in March 2009, so the total contribution of CDS did not change nearly as much. Also, while there is a significant difference in cross-sectional contributions to spreads in March 2009, the market appears to be more homogeneous in April 2010.

## SPREAD DECOMPOSITION USING AN ALTERNATIVE MEASURE OF EXPECTED DEFAULT LOSSES

So far, we have used an issuer's CDS to measure the expected default loss of its bonds. However, since both OAS and CDS are market spreads, part of the

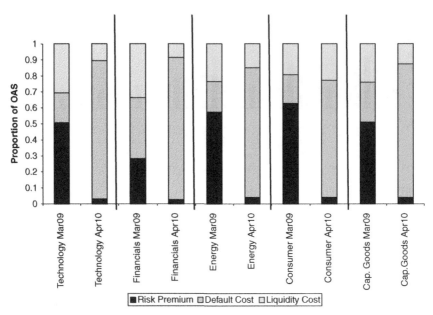

**FIGURE 6.9**  Sector-Wise Spread Decomposition: Default Contribution and Liquidity Contribution (March 2009 and April 2010)
*Source:* Barclays Capital.

explanatory power of CDS may be the result of both spreads being quoted in relationship to each other. In addition, even though LCS is measured directly from trader quotes, a bond's liquidity cost is heavily influenced by the bond's spread volatility. To test the model's fit, we would ideally like the expected default loss variable to be independent of market spreads. Fortunately, we have such expected default probability and loss-given-default measures: *conditional default probability* (CDP) and *conditional recovery rate* (CRR). Using CDP and CRR also provides us with a larger sample, because we have more tickers with CDP and CRR data than tickers with CDS in the CDX.

We estimate month-by-month regressions using $CDP_{i,t} \times (1 - CRR_{i,t})$ as the expected default loss variable (model 6.2b). Results for investment-grade bonds are reported in Table 6.7 of this chapter's appendix. The regressions use a larger sample size and confirm the results presented earlier. The $R^2$ using $CDP \times (1 - CRR)$ is lower than the $R^2$ using CDS spreads in many months, especially in 2007. This is not surprising, because market CDS spreads are likely to be more closely related to OAS than to a modeled default probability estimator. The intercept is of a similar magnitude. The one notable difference is that the $CDP \times (1 - CRR)$ coefficient changes more when LCS is included as an additional variable than did the CDS spread coefficients in Table 6.2.

## HIGH-YIELD SPREAD DECOMPOSITION

We perform the same analysis for high-yield bonds, with CDS spreads and $CDP \times (1 - CRR)$ as alternative default measures. For brevity, we present the results only using CDS in Table 6.8 of this chapter's appendix. (Because high-yield bonds have higher expected default losses, it is only natural that their default loss will be more important than for investment-grade bonds.) Until October 2008, LCS is insignificant in explaining cross-sectional high-yield OAS. However, from October 2008 to November 2009, LCS consistently and significantly improves the regression fit. These results suggest that liquidity cost provides additional explanatory power for the cross-sectional variation in high-yield spreads only during periods of market stress. This may be because CDS spreads of high-yield issuers may be less liquid and contaminated with liquidity effects, weakening the effect of LCS inclusion in the regression.

Overall, the CDS coefficient is similar in magnitude for both investment-grade and high-yield bonds, but the LCS coefficient is smaller for the high-yield sector early in the sample period. The intercept is larger for high yield, suggesting that risk aversion, unrelated to the bond's default or liquidity characteristics, may drive a large proportion of high-yield spreads. Despite the low importance of liquidity in the earlier part of the sample period, the adjusted $R^2$ is uniformly high, again pointing to the greater importance of default.

## APPLICATIONS OF SPREAD DECOMPOSITION

### Identifying Relative Value

So far, our analysis has used contemporaneous monthly data to attribute levels and changes in OAS to levels and changes in default and liquidity cost components, ex post. We now consider whether we can apply spread decomposition analysis to ex ante investment decisions.

In principle, spread decomposition should help to identify relative value opportunities. To the extent that a bond's OAS is compensation for expected default and liquidity cost, a bond's market OAS can be compared with the estimated OAS using the parameters from the spread decomposition model.

If the actual OAS is wider than the estimated OAS, it suggests that the bond is trading too wide, and vice versa. This may be a trading signal that the bond's OAS may change in the direction of reducing this "mispricing."

We examine whether the regression residuals, $\hat{\eta}_{i,t}$, of model (6.2a) can help predict future OAS changes. Specifically, if the residual (observed OAS minus estimated OAS) is large and positive in a given month, is it likely that the bond's OAS will tighten in the near future? We conduct this test for OAS changes for various horizons, ranging from one month to six months. In other words, we take the residual from the spread decomposition model for any bond this month and examine whether the bond's future OAS changes are of opposite sign to the sign of the residual. If so, in which future month does this reversal occur? We run the following regression, where we expect $\theta$ to be negative:

$$\Delta OAS_{it,t+j} = \alpha + \theta\,\hat{\eta}_{it} + \delta\,\text{MonthDummy}_t + e_{it} \qquad (6.3)$$

Because we employ six out-of-sample months for each in-sample monthly prediction error dataset, we can estimate this regression only through October 2009. Figure 6.10 shows that results for investment-grade bonds are significant and strong across all horizons from one to six months, suggesting that even this simple approach has some predictive power, on average. The values of the month dummy variables (not shown) are also

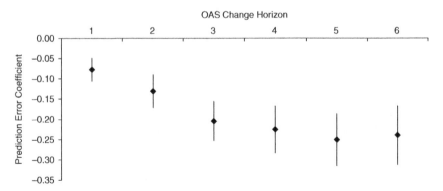

**FIGURE 6.10**  Investment-Grade Bonds: Coefficient ($\theta$) of Residual and Confidence Intervals for Various OAS Change Horizons, (predictions from February 2007–October 2009)
*Note:* The chart shows the estimated coefficient ($\theta$) and the 95% confidence interval based on equation (6.3), estimated using various horizons of one to six months.
*Source:* Barclays Capital.

as expected: they are large and positive in the second half of 2008 and consistently negative since Q2 2009.

## Hedging a Credit Bond Portfolio

Credit spread decomposition might be considered when hedging a credit portfolio. Because a hedge is employed to help neutralize spread *changes*, we begin by repeating our month-by-month spread decomposition exercise using *changes* in OAS, CDS, and LCS. We estimate this cross-sectional regression every month. We use the regression coefficients at the end of each month to determine hedges for the next month for an equally weighted portfolio of all the bonds in our regression. The five-year CDS for each bond and the one-month VIX futures are the hedging instruments. VIX and LCS are highly correlated (see Chapter 5), even in changes, so we can consider using VIX futures to get exposure to LCS changes.

Figure 6.11 shows the actual out-of-sample excess returns of the unhedged portfolio and the excess returns of the hedged portfolio over time. This is also compared with only a CDS hedge, using cross-sectional univariate regression hedge ratios.[11] The summary statistics of the return time series are presented in Table 6.3. The standard deviation is lowest for the portfolio hedged with CDS and VIX futures. The extreme values are also lower, because the short VIX position usually moves in a direction opposite to the OAS. Despite the improvement in hedged results, significant portfolio volatility unfortunately remains even after hedging with CDS and

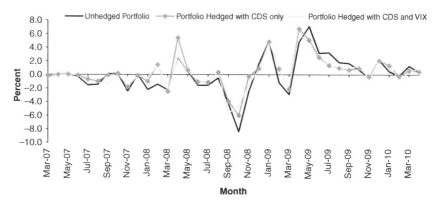

**FIGURE 6.11** Excess Returns of Hedged and Unhedged Portfolios
*Source:* Barclays Capital.

**TABLE 6.3**   Monthly Portfolio Excess Returns

|  | Portfolio | | |
| --- | --- | --- | --- |
|  | Unhedged Portfolio | Hedged with CDS Only | Hedged with CDS and VIX Futures |
| Average | 0.04 | 0.40 | 0.21 |
| Standard deviation | 2.72 | 2.39 | 2.25 |
| MIN | −8.38 | −6.01 | −5.68 |
| MAX | 7.10 | 6.74 | 6.00 |

*Source:* Barclays Capital.

VIX—reflecting the difficulty of hedging cash credit bonds with derivatives during much of this period (see Chapter 14).

## ALTERNATIVE SPREAD DECOMPOSITION MODELS

In this section, we explore several alternative formulations of our spread decomposition model, each of which helps shed light on our subject from a slightly different angle. To simplify the evaluation of the results, we do not report results of separate month-by-month regressions as in Table 6.2. Instead, we pool the data and run a single regression in each case, using monthly dummy variables to adjust for time-varying effects that run across the market.

As discussed earlier, the analysis so far has ignored explicit bond-level risk premium variables. Instead, we have assumed that the risk premium would be highly related to either the expected liquidity cost or the expect default cost. We now consider an alternative model that includes a term to represent a bond-level liquidity risk premium. This is the additional spread investors demand as compensation for the risk that the actual liquidity cost may be different than the expected liquidity cost as measured by LCS. As a measure of liquidity risk, we calculate each bond's LCS volatility over the prior 12 months. Two bonds may have the same LCS today, but bond A may have had a much more volatile LCS history than bond B. An investor may then view bond A as having a riskier liquidity cost and demand an OAS premium versus bond B, all else equal.

Equation (6.4) shows the spread decomposition model incorporating a bond-level liquidity risk factor, $LCSVol_{i,t}$. The results, shown in Table 6.4, indicate that $LCSVol_{i,t}$ is highly significant, but absorbs part of the effect of LCS (the coefficient of LCS declines by more than 20%, from 0.98 to 0.80),

**TABLE 6.4** Regression of OAS on CDS Spread, LCS and LCS Volatility (January 2008[a]–April 2010)

|  | Intercept | CDS | LCS | LCS Volatility | Month Dummies | Number of Observations | Adjusted $R^2$ |
|---|---|---|---|---|---|---|---|
| Coefficients | 1.31 | 0.371 | 0.980 |  | Yes | 5,715 | 0.77 |
| *t*-statistics | 9.3 | 71.65 | 57.57 |  |  |  |  |
| Coefficients | 1.016 | 0.333 | 0.803 | 0.789 | Yes | 5,546 | 0.80 |
| *t*-statistics | 7.51 | 64.11 | 44.54 | 23.3 |  |  |  |

[a]Twelve months of data are lost because they are used to estimate LCS volatility.
*Source:* Barclays Capital.

thereby not improving the regression's adjusted $R^2$ substantially, despite the high significance.

$$OAS_{it} = \alpha + \beta\, CDS_{it} + \gamma\, LCS_{it} + \phi\, LCS\,Vol_{it} + \delta\, \text{MonthDummy}_t + \eta_{it}$$

$$(6.4)$$

We also estimate a regression in differences to check if the changes in OAS are explained by changes in LCS and CDS spreads. The results hold in differences, too, suggesting that changes in liquidity and default proxies affect contemporaneous returns. The regression model in equation (6.5) details the specification, where $\Delta OAS_{it}$, $\Delta CDS_{it}$, and $\Delta LCS_{it}$ refer to changes in a bond's characteristics in consecutive months. The results are shown in Table 6.5, in which we can observe the significant coefficients of the explanatory variables.

$$\Delta OAS_{it} = \alpha + \beta\, \Delta CDS_{it} + \gamma\, \Delta LCS_{it} + \delta\, \text{MonthDummy}_t + \eta_{it} \qquad (6.5)$$

One might suspect that the spread decomposition results were driven by outliers, especially since default and liquidity are arguably more important

**TABLE 6.5** Regression of $\Delta OAS$ on $\Delta CDS$ Spread and $\Delta LCS$ (January 2007–April 2010)

|  | Intercept | $\Delta CDS$ | $\Delta LCS$ | Month Dummies | Number of Observations | Adjusted $R^2$ |
|---|---|---|---|---|---|---|
| Coefficients | −0.184 | 0.097 | 0.406 | Yes | 7,304 | 0.48 |
| *t*-statistics | −2.59 | 29.97 | 35.44 |  |  |  |

*Source:* Barclays Capital.

**TABLE 6.6** Outlier-Robust Regression of Spread Decomposition (January 2007–April 2010)

|  | Intercept | ln(CDS) | ln(LCS) | Month Dummies | Number of Observations | Adjusted $R^2$ |
|---|---|---|---|---|---|---|
| Coefficients | −1.3 | 0.425 | 0.26 | Yes | 7,578 | 0.89 |
| t-statistics | −45.56 | 107.33 | 44.67 |  |  |  |

*Source:* Barclays Capital.

considerations for higher spread bonds. To check this, we run log regressions (e.g., the dependent variable is log($OAS$) instead of $OAS$, similarly for the independent variables), as shown in equation (6.6). The conclusions from Table 6.6 are similar to those of model (6.2a), indicating that outliers are not driving the results.

$$\ln(OAS_{it}) = \alpha + \beta \ln(CDS_{it}) + \gamma \ln(LCS_{it}) + \eta_{it} \tag{6.6}$$

## CONCLUSION

We illustrate how credit bond spreads (OAS) can be decomposed into risk premium, default cost, and liquidity cost components. We find strong explanatory power for both investment-grade and high-yield bonds, using LCS as a liquidity proxy and either CDS spreads or CDP and CRR as default proxies. Liquidity is incrementally important (after accounting for default effects) throughout the sample period for investment-grade bonds. However liquidity is generally important for high-yield bonds only during stressful times. The results hold in a variety of specifications and datasets, including differences, logs, and additional controls. Spread decomposition can help portfolio managers understand spread movements better. Investors can use spread decomposition for hedging, forecasting future OAS changes, and developing alpha strategies.

## APPENDIX

This appendix includes month-by-month regression results for the spread decomposition model using CDP as a default proxy for IG bonds (Table 6.7) and results for the HY bonds using CDS spreads as the default proxy (Table 6.8).

**TABLE 6.7** Investment-Grade Bonds: Regression of OAS on $CDP \times (1 - CRR)$ and LCS (January 2007–April 2010)

| | Same in Both Regressions | | Specification 1: Only $CDP \times$ $(1 - CRR)$ | | | Specification 2: Both $CDP \times$ $(1 - CRR)$ and LCS | | | |
|---|---|---|---|---|---|---|---|---|---|
| Month | Number of Observations | Intercept | $CDP \times$ $(1 - CRR)$ | $R^2$ | Intercept | $CDP \times$ $(1 - CRR)$ | LCS | $R^2$ |
| Jan-07 | 132 | **0.80** | −0.18 | 0.00 | **0.65** | −0.18 | **0.47** | 0.18 |
| Feb-07 | 107 | **0.79** | −0.04 | −0.01 | **0.66** | −0.03 | **0.40** | 0.25 |
| Mar-07 | 120 | **0.82** | 0.23 | 0.00 | **0.69** | 0.21 | **0.42** | 0.16 |
| Apr-07 | 129 | **0.85** | 0.45 | 0.02 | **0.70** | 0.35 | **0.55** | 0.12 |
| May-07 | 123 | **0.84** | 0.17 | 0.00 | **0.58** | 0.14 | **0.94** | 0.17 |
| Jun-07 | 112 | **0.90** | **0.64** | 0.05 | **0.76** | **0.58** | **0.45** | 0.18 |
| Jul-07 | 80 | **1.13** | **1.14** | 0.17 | **0.32** | **1.06** | **2.59** | 0.41 |
| Aug-07 | 66 | **1.40** | **2.96** | 0.33 | **0.92** | **1.11** | **0.95** | 0.59 |
| Sep-07 | 93 | **1.31** | **1.88** | 0.66 | **1.12** | **1.77** | **0.30** | 0.72 |
| Oct-07 | 85 | **1.28** | **1.83** | 0.59 | **0.76** | **1.28** | **0.98** | 0.76 |
| Nov-07 | 59 | **1.79** | **2.52** | 0.51 | **1.04** | **1.50** | **1.14** | 0.72 |
| Dec-07 | 57 | **1.50** | **2.92** | 0.48 | **1.11** | **2.21** | **0.70** | 0.53 |
| Jan-08 | 87 | *2.04* | **2.20** | 0.44 | **1.45** | **0.81** | **0.85** | 0.66 |
| Feb-08 | 99 | **2.25** | **1.76** | 0.48 | **1.51** | **0.78** | **0.89** | 0.73 |
| Mar-08 | 91 | **2.47** | **3.95** | 0.44 | **1.57** | **1.45** | **1.21** | 0.72 |
| Apr-08 | 101 | **2.32** | **2.05** | 0.33 | **1.35** | **0.50** | **1.17** | 0.71 |
| May-08 | 114 | **2.21** | **1.83** | 0.31 | **1.38** | **0.59** | **1.14** | 0.58 |
| Jun-08 | 120 | **2.71** | **1.30** | 0.30 | **1.74** | **0.42** | **1.09** | 0.73 |
| Jul-08 | 114 | **2.98** | **1.55** | 0.30 | **2.03** | **0.77** | **0.78** | 0.78 |
| Aug-08 | 115 | *2.85* | **2.15** | 0.38 | **2.17** | **1.18** | **0.70** | 0.79 |
| Sep-08 | 97 | **3.58** | **1.73** | 0.41 | **3.30** | **1.48** | **0.30** | 0.43 |
| Oct-08 | 220 | **5.30** | **5.30** | 0.41 | **3.27** | **2.44** | **0.70** | 0.87 |
| Nov-08 | 231 | **5.77** | **5.07** | 0.32 | **3.56** | **2.31** | **0.84** | 0.82 |
| Dec-08 | 220 | **5.81** | **4.68** | 0.22 | **2.86** | **2.04** | **0.98** | 0.85 |
| Jan-09 | 137 | **4.10** | **2.12** | 0.31 | **2.48** | **1.25** | **0.80** | 0.69 |
| Feb-09 | 166 | **4.07** | **1.86** | 0.40 | **2.81** | **1.17** | **0.72** | 0.66 |
| Mar-09 | 210 | *5.10* | **4.20** | 0.43 | **3.45** | **2.23** | **0.72** | 0.78 |
| Apr-09 | 127 | **3.93** | **1.21** | 0.21 | **2.30** | **0.70** | **0.79** | 0.62 |
| May-09 | 176 | **4.08** | **1.20** | 0.16 | **1.83** | **0.51** | **1.24** | 0.62 |
| Jun-09 | 185 | **3.66** | **1.37** | 0.17 | **1.84** | **0.75** | **1.11** | 0.62 |
| Jul-09 | 147 | **3.19** | **1.64** | 0.31 | **1.61** | **0.91** | **1.04** | 0.61 |
| Aug-09 | 194 | **2.88** | **1.15** | 0.13 | **1.13** | **0.51** | **1.43** | 0.60 |
| Sep-09 | 236 | **2.24** | **1.37** | 0.20 | **0.98** | **0.79** | **1.24** | 0.57 |
| Oct-09 | 237 | **2.06** | **1.05** | 0.21 | **1.17** | **0.70** | **0.98** | 0.52 |
| Nov-09 | 246 | **2.07** | **1.27** | 0.27 | **0.93** | **0.87** | **1.36** | 0.62 |
| Dec-09 | 200 | **1.86** | **1.22** | 0.20 | **0.67** | **0.72** | **1.47** | 0.70 |
| Jan-10 | 295 | **1.70** | **1.12** | 0.20 | **0.51** | **0.70** | **1.62** | 0.60 |
| Feb-10 | 270 | **1.74** | **1.43** | 0.23 | **0.52** | **0.92** | **1.56** | 0.68 |
| Mar-10 | 211 | **1.53** | **1.24** | 0.20 | **0.51** | **0.70** | **1.50** | 0.61 |
| Apr-10 | 223 | **1.45** | **1.18** | 0.18 | **0.93** | **0.92** | **0.79** | 0.39 |

*Note:* Coefficients in bold significant at the 95% level.
*Source:* Barclays Capital.

**TABLE 6.8** High-Yield Bonds—Regression of OAS on CDS Spreads and LCS, January 2007–April 2010

| Same in Both Regressions | | Specification 1: Only CDS | | | Specification 2: Both CDS and LCS | | | |
|---|---|---|---|---|---|---|---|---|
| Month | Number of Observations | Intercept | CDS | $R^2$ | Intercept | CDS | LCS | $R^2$ |
| Jan-07 | 45 | 1.21 | 0.51 | 0.58 | 1.18 | 0.50 | 0.04 | 0.57 |
| Feb-07 | 50 | 1.37 | 0.50 | 0.51 | 1.24 | 0.48 | 0.17 | 0.51 |
| Mar-07 | 42 | 1.37 | 0.44 | 0.45 | 1.46 | 0.45 | −0.12 | 0.44 |
| Apr-07 | 97 | 1.17 | 0.59 | 0.55 | 1.27 | 0.60 | −0.13 | 0.55 |
| May-07 | 99 | 1.05 | 0.56 | 0.51 | 1.11 | 0.56 | −0.08 | 0.50 |
| Jun-07 | 87 | 1.48 | 0.48 | 0.41 | 1.74 | 0.49 | −0.34 | 0.42 |
| Jul-07 | 63 | 1.17 | 0.63 | 0.65 | 0.67 | 0.55 | 0.69 | 0.69 |
| Aug-07 | 57 | 1.66 | 0.60 | 0.80 | 1.28 | 0.54 | 0.31 | 0.81 |
| Sep-07 | 64 | 1.25 | 0.69 | 0.78 | 1.29 | 0.69 | −0.04 | 0.77 |
| Oct-07 | 72 | 1.40 | 0.65 | 0.79 | 1.58 | 0.68 | −0.22 | 0.80 |
| Nov-07 | 95 | 2.39 | 0.55 | 0.78 | 2.48 | 0.56 | −0.11 | 0.78 |
| Dec-07 | 108 | 2.60 | 0.52 | 0.78 | 2.72 | 0.54 | −0.12 | 0.78 |
| Jan-08 | 103 | 2.72 | 0.58 | 0.73 | 1.94 | 0.52 | 0.73 | 0.75 |
| Feb-08 | 96 | 2.40 | 0.66 | 0.80 | 1.84 | 0.62 | 0.52 | 0.81 |
| Mar-08 | 96 | 3.56 | 0.53 | 0.81 | 3.26 | 0.51 | 0.27 | 0.81 |
| Apr-08 | 83 | 2.85 | 0.50 | 0.58 | 2.29 | 0.47 | 0.49 | 0.59 |
| May-08 | 97 | 3.01 | 0.46 | 0.69 | 2.62 | 0.45 | 0.28 | 0.69 |
| Jun-08 | 82 | 4.27 | 0.33 | 0.48 | 4.29 | 0.33 | −0.01 | 0.47 |
| Jul-08 | 89 | 3.48 | 0.51 | 0.72 | 3.10 | 0.49 | 0.28 | 0.73 |
| Aug-08 | 85 | 3.67 | 0.52 | 0.66 | 2.81 | 0.44 | 0.73 | 0.70 |
| Sep-08 | 50 | 3.13 | 0.71 | 0.83 | 3.49 | 0.81 | −0.47 | 0.84 |
| Oct-08 | 60 | 6.21 | 0.57 | 0.59 | 4.46 | 0.48 | 0.76 | 0.64 |
| Nov-08 | 59 | 8.94 | 0.40 | 0.67 | 7.24 | 0.19 | 1.15 | 0.81 |
| Dec-08 | 48 | 7.56 | 0.54 | 0.71 | 6.18 | 0.32 | 0.89 | 0.79 |
| Jan-09 | 84 | 7.26 | 0.50 | 0.54 | 4.67 | 0.33 | 1.05 | 0.76 |
| Feb-09 | 67 | 7.70 | 0.28 | 0.44 | 5.94 | 0.19 | 0.88 | 0.59 |
| Mar-09 | 65 | 8.32 | 0.29 | 0.50 | 5.21 | 0.23 | 0.93 | 0.83 |
| Apr-09 | 59 | 3.88 | 0.65 | 0.69 | 2.50 | 0.47 | 0.78 | 0.84 |
| May-09 | 73 | 4.18 | 0.53 | 0.66 | 3.35 | 0.34 | 0.80 | 0.85 |
| Jun-09 | 79 | 4.13 | 0.49 | 0.54 | 3.34 | 0.40 | 0.72 | 0.62 |
| Jul-09 | 75 | 5.88 | 0.21 | 0.32 | 3.14 | 0.13 | 1.39 | 0.77 |
| Aug-09 | 88 | 4.23 | 0.47 | 0.48 | 2.69 | 0.36 | 1.05 | 0.65 |
| Sep-09 | 96 | 2.33 | 0.72 | 0.58 | 1.19 | 0.64 | 0.80 | 0.66 |
| Oct-09 | 94 | 2.70 | 0.65 | 0.55 | 1.26 | 0.51 | 1.29 | 0.71 |
| Nov-09 | 94 | 2.93 | 0.69 | 0.57 | 1.62 | 0.53 | 1.28 | 0.73 |
| Dec-09 | 89 | 1.66 | 0.85 | 0.73 | 1.23 | 0.76 | 0.53 | 0.75 |
| Jan-10 | 88 | 5.67 | 0.03 | 0.04 | 4.05 | 0.03 | 1.03 | 0.20 |
| Feb-10 | 99 | 2.28 | 0.68 | 0.60 | 1.76 | 0.56 | 0.75 | 0.66 |
| Mar-10 | 96 | 2.30 | 0.59 | 0.60 | 1.74 | 0.56 | 0.51 | 0.61 |
| Apr-10 | 107 | 2.29 | 0.61 | 0.60 | 1.64 | 0.58 | 0.58 | 0.63 |

*Source:* Barclays Capital.

# NOTES

1. In Chapter 12, we investigate this excess credit spread; see also Elton, Gruber, Agrawal, and Mann (2001).
2. Our work on Liquidity Cost Scores (LCS)$^{TM}$ indicates that a bond's liquidity cost can be highly variable. See Chapter 5.
3. See Collin-Dufresne, Goldstein, and Martin (2001).
4. Our spread decomposition model assumes that any default or liquidity risk premium either does not vary across bonds in a given month or are highly correlated with expected default and liquidity costs. However, to try and capture any effect of risk aversion on cross-sectional OAS, we analyzed an alternative model in which we included the volatility of LCS over the past 12 months (i.e., a measure of liquidity risk) as an additional regressor. The results remain qualitatively the same.
5. See Asvanunt and Staal (2009a) and Asvanunt and Staal (2009b).
6. Both CDP and CDS (independent variables) vary at the ticker level, while LCS (another independent variable) and OAS (the dependent variable) vary at the bond level. Consequently, two five-year bonds from the same issuer will have the same CDP (and CRR) and corresponding five-year CDS values while having potentially different LCS. We have kept all bonds for each ticker (i.e., issuer) in the sample since the variation in OAS across bonds of similar duration by the same issuer can only be because of liquidity considerations. We have also done a robustness test using only one bond per ticker to avoid a situation in which the bond-level variability (rather than the incremental information in LCS) may be responsible for significant LCS coefficients. As discussed in the methodology section, to make sure that issue-level variation in OAS and LCS for a given issuer (along with the ticker-level variation in CDS and CDP) is not driving our results, we rerun model (6.2) using only one bond per ticker. We use this version of model (6.2) in the "Applications" section of this chapter to avoid issuer concentration.
7. Since our LCS model uses a bond's OAS as an explanatory variable, regressing a bond's OAS on its LCS for spread decomposition could produce an artificial relationship between the two. To avoid this, we use only LCS values that are computed directly from trader quotes. See Chapter 5.
8. LCS data begin in January 2007. See Chapter 5.
9. This is also related to our LCS research, in which we show the very low dispersion of LCS across bonds in early 2007. See Chapter 5.
10. We used the results in Table 6.2 to present the contributions of CDS and LCS to OAS for KFT in Figure 6.3 and the contributions for all sectors in Figure 6.6.
11. A time series analysis based on hedge ratios computed using rolling regressions has not been presented, since we have only 40 months of observations for both in-sample and out-of-sample analysis. However, it did not perform better than the cross-sectional hedge using VIX futures and CDS, for the few out-of-sample months we have data for, based on 18-month rolling window regressions. Also, this short time series does not provide an insight into the crisis and pre-crisis months.

### CHAPTER 7

# Empirical versus Nominal Durations of Corporate Bonds

**M**any portfolio managers with investment-grade benchmarks are allowed out-of-benchmark ("core-plus") allocations to high-yield debt. As with any other asset class, they need to understand the effect such allocations have on the overall duration of their portfolio. It is widely acknowledged that the interest rate sensitivity of high-yield securities is not necessarily what their stated cash flows imply. Yet there is a wide range of opinions on this issue among portfolio managers. At one extreme, there are those who account for the full analytical duration (i.e., assuming all cash flows are paid as promised) of the high-yield component. At the other extreme are managers who ignore the duration contribution of high-yield debt, claiming that it exhibits equity-like behavior. The majority of portfolio managers consider the actual durations to be between these extremes, typically employing a heuristic rule of thumb such as assigning high-yield bonds 25% of their analytical duration.

Uncertainty about the interest rate sensitivity of high-yield bonds can severely affect the ability of portfolio managers to accurately express their views on rates. Assume, for example, that a portfolio and its benchmark both have durations of 5 and that the manager shifts 10% of the portfolio into high-yield bonds which also have an analytical duration of 5. Depending on one's opinion, the "true" duration of the portfolio is anywhere between 4.5 and 5.0—a wide range for many managers used to tweaking duration in much smaller increments when expressing their rate views. If the portfolio target duration is 4.80 and the manager is prepared to adjust the Treasury component of the portfolio to hit this target, does he need to add or subtract duration?

In response to investors' inquiries, we investigated this topic in 2005, and found both theoretical and empirical evidence establishing a relation between empirical duration and spread levels (Ben Dor, Dynkin, and

Hyman 2005a and 2005c) . The findings showed that interest rate sensitivity decreases as spreads widen. While this is most pronounced when looking at bonds with different credit ratings, we found this to be true even across bonds with the same credit quality. Similar patterns were evident for emerging markets bonds.

The main focus of our initial research was high-yield bonds. The key concern was that high-yield managers tended to ignore the yield curve sensitivity of their portfolios. As we explored the dependence of empirical duration on spread levels, the operative conclusion was that as spreads continued to tighten, the effective duration of high-yield debt was likely to increase towards its analytical value. Continuing to ignore the curve duration seemed inappropriate in a low-spread environment.

In late 2008 and early 2009, as spreads widened to unprecedented levels, many investors began to ask the reverse question: have investment-grade empirical durations declined to levels typical of high-yield bonds? Certainly, the spread-dependent relation we documented would lead us to expect empirical durations that are significantly lower than the analytical ones, even for investment-grade bonds.

The extreme conditions in the credit market during that period also serve as a true "out-of-sample" test of the earlier results and the framework we suggested for estimating empirical duration. We find that our pre-crisis qualitative and quantitative conclusions largely hold, although the slope of the spread dependence of empirical duration is flatter than what could have been expected. Despite the historically abnormal spread levels that characterized the crisis period beginning in 2007, investment-grade bonds seemed reluctant to give up their interest rate sensitivity, while high-yield bonds continued to demonstrate equity-like behavior, with zero or even negative empirical durations. This clear difference between investment-grade and high-yield debt was quite prominent and consistent. Furthermore, default and recovery considerations could not account for the observed gap.

The first part of this chapter provides a unified and coherent treatment of the relation between the analytical and empirical duration of corporate bonds. In the second part, we investigate two alternative explanations for the different interest-rate sensitivities exhibited by investment and non-investment-grade debt.

The first explanation we examine is that the difference in rate sensitivity is a result of "stale" pricing. Specifically, we test whether differences in pricing conventions and liquidity levels mechanically cause high-yield bonds to *appear* to have lower interest rate sensitivity than investment-grade bonds. We conduct several tests including using the TRACE volume database to examine whether our results may be driven by stale pricing, a more prevalent phenomenon in the high-yield market. While we do find a relationship between trading volume and pricing dynamics, our results are robust to the existence of stale pricing. There is no indication that the sharp observed decline in interest rate sensitivity for bonds crossing from investment-grade to high-yield territory is merely an artifact of the data.

A second possibility is that the findings may at least partially reflect differences in bond characteristics across rating categories, which in turn affect the observed hedge ratios. To explore this, we analyze changes in the empirical duration of individual bonds downgraded from investment-grade to high-yield as well as those upgraded from high-yield to investment-grade. This type of "event study" approach, in which the same population of bonds is examined before and after the downgrade/upgrade, controls for bond-specific characteristics.

We find that downgraded bonds experience a large decline in their interest-rate sensitivity as they approach the downgrade. Furthermore, the magnitude of the change in empirical duration is very similar to that of the general population of bonds. The reverse patterns are observed for high-yield bonds upgraded to investment grade.

What then can account for the apparent credit market segmentation between investment-grade and non-investment-grade bonds? We hypothesize that investors in the two markets use different performance metrics. Investment-grade credit managers are typically evaluated in terms of excess returns earned over treasuries or swaps, whereas high-yield managers tend to think in terms of total return and default risk. These different approaches to performance, and the hedging practices that result from them, may lead to the reduced effect of interest rate movements on high-yield valuations. We provide some indirect evidence supporting this theory. The chapter concludes with a discussion of several practical applications using empirical duration to hedge interest rate exposure in credit portfolios.

## EMPIRICAL DURATION: THEORY AND EVIDENCE

One of the main characteristics of a bond portfolio is its sensitivity to interest rates, as measured by its Treasury duration. While any portfolio analytics system will dutifully compute bond duration numbers based on projected cash flows, the typically negative correlation between rates and spreads can dampen the actual response of corporate bonds to changes in rates. Investors have long been aware of this phenomenon and, therefore, distinguish between analytical duration and empirical duration—the amount by which a bond's absolute return will actually change, given a particular yield change.

Despite the importance of understanding the relation between analytical and empirical duration and being able to quantify their difference over time, there is no commonly accepted approach for doing so. Some portfolio managers regress price returns against changes in Treasury yield over "rolling" windows of various length. Others use a heuristic rule of thumb such as defining the duration of high-yield bonds as a fixed proportion of their analytical duration or simply ignore the issue altogether.

To understand under what conditions empirical and analytical duration differ, we first derive an explicit theoretical linkage between the two. We then describe the estimation methodology and the empirical findings across different rating categories and periods.

## The Relation between Analytical and Empirical Duration

Let us assume that, in a macro sense, the returns of credit securities can be broadly described by a simple two-factor model, where the factors are a parallel shift in Treasury yield $\Delta y$ and a relative change in spreads $\Delta s_{rel} = \Delta s/s$ reflecting the findings in Chapter 1 regarding the behavior of corporate spreads. If we assume further that security $i$'s Treasury duration and spread duration are approximately the same, given by $D_i$, the return to this security can be approximated as follows:

$$R_i \cong -D_i \times \Delta y - (D_i \times s_i) \times \Delta s_{rel} \qquad (7.1)$$

To measure the sensitivity of the overall return to a change in Treasury yields, we use a simple approximation for the relationship between spreads and yields, based on the sample variances and covariance of the two:[1]

$$\frac{\partial s_{rel}}{\partial y} \cong \frac{\mathrm{cov}(\Delta y, \Delta s_{rel})}{\mathrm{var}(\Delta y)} = \frac{\rho_{y,s}\sigma_y\sigma_s}{\sigma_y^2} = \rho_{y,s}\frac{\sigma_s}{\sigma_y} \qquad (7.2)$$

Using the above relationship to obtain the sensitivity of return to a shift in Treasury yield, $\Delta y$, we have

$$\frac{\partial R_i}{\partial y} \cong -D_i - D_i \times s_i \times \frac{\mathrm{cov}(\Delta y, \Delta s_{rel})}{\mathrm{var}(\Delta y)} = -D_i\left(1 + s_i\rho_{y,s}\frac{\sigma_s}{\sigma_y}\right) \qquad (7.3)$$

The expression in equation (7.3) is the theoretical value for what we term empirical duration—the amount by which the absolute return will actually change given a particular yield change. Since volatilities and spread levels are non-negative, the magnitude of the empirical duration relative to the analytical figure depends on $\rho_{y,s}$, the correlation between yield and relative spread changes. If this correlation is negative, the empirical duration would be lower than the analytical one and may even end up being negative.

## Estimation Methodology and Empirical Analysis

The expression derived in equation (7.3) can easily be tested by estimating the following regression:

$$R_i = \beta_i \cdot D_i \cdot \Delta y + \gamma_i \cdot D_i \cdot s_i \cdot \Delta y + \varepsilon_i \qquad (7.4)$$

The regression provides a linear approximation for the empirical hedge ratio $H_i^{emp}$ (the ratio of the empirical duration and the analytical duration) as a function of spread $s_i$, as follows:

$$H_i^{emp}(S) = \beta_i + \gamma_i \cdot s_i \qquad (7.5)$$

where $\beta$ is the upper limit of the empirical hedge ratio that might be expected for a bond $i$ as spreads approach zero; the second coefficient, $\gamma_i$, which is negative in general, reflects the reduction in hedge ratio as spreads widen.[2]

While the estimation of equation (7.4) is straightforward in principle, the results may be sensitive to the choice of a sample frequency, period, and level of bond return aggregation. We choose to conduct most of the analysis using daily data, for two reasons: The use of daily data allows us to match the hedging frequency employed in practice by portfolio managers and to achieve a larger sample and, consequently, higher statistical power.

Daily data for individual bonds, however, are unavailable to us prior to 2006, limiting our ability to evaluate the results across different market regimes. We can extend our sample period back to August 1998 by instead using aggregated daily return data of six credit rating categories spanning the Corporate and High Yield indexes (Aaa–Aa, A, Baa, Ba, B, and Caa).[3] The regressions are estimated using the price returns for each rating category and the contemporaneous yield changes of the 10-year on-the-run Treasury note. The spread $s_i$ is represented by the option-adjusted spread of all securities (market value-weighted) comprising each rating category and is measured with a one-day lag (i.e., based on the previous day's closing mark).

Table 7.1(A) displays the regression coefficients estimated over the entire sample period from August 1998 through November 2009, by rating category. The results confirm a strong relationship between hedge ratios and the level of spreads, consistent with equation (7.5). The spread slope coefficient is negative and significant (at the 1% confidence level) for all credit ratings, and the sensitivity at the limit (beta) for high-grade bonds is close to one as implied from equation (7.3). Substituting, for example, the

**TABLE 7.1**  Treasury Hedge Ratio of Corporate Bonds by Credit Rating

**A. Regression-Based Hedge Ratios**

| Coefficients | Aaa–Aa | A | Baa | Ba | B | Caa |
|---|---|---|---|---|---|---|
| $\beta$: Hedge ratio limit | 0.94 | 0.92 | 0.85 | 0.41 | 0.15 | 0.07 |
| $t$-statistic | 70.69 | 58.36 | 50.66 | 11.94 | 2.80 | 0.79 |
| $\gamma$: Spread slope | −0.05 | −0.05 | −0.02 | −0.05 | −0.03 | −0.02 |
| $t$-statistic | −8.19 | −7.60 | −4.55 | −7.85 | −4.51 | −3.12 |
| $R^2$ | 0.79 | 0.75 | 0.74 | 0.06 | 0.01 | 0.01 |

| OAS | | | | | | |
|---|---|---|---|---|---|---|
| Minimum | 0.37 | 0.56 | 1.05 | 1.46 | 2.21 | 3.68 |
| Average | 1.04 | 1.50 | 2.16 | 3.92 | 5.77 | 10.75 |
| Maximum | 4.71 | 5.95 | 7.70 | 13.75 | 18.58 | 28.33 |

| Hedge Ratios at: | | | | | | |
|---|---|---|---|---|---|---|
| Minimum OAS | 0.92 | 0.89 | 0.83 | 0.34 | 0.08 | −0.01 |
| Average OAS | 0.88 | 0.85 | 0.80 | 0.22 | −0.03 | −0.15 |
| Maximum OAS | 0.68 | 0.64 | 0.67 | −0.26 | −0.42 | −0.52 |

**B. Model-Based Hedge Ratios**

| | Aaa–Aa | A | Baa | Ba | B | Caa |
|---|---|---|---|---|---|---|
| $\sigma_s$: Volatility of relative spread changes | 2.3% | 1.8% | 1.6% | 2.5% | 2.0% | 1.8% |
| $\rho_{y,s}$: Correlation with 10-year Treasury yield change | −0.14 | −0.17 | −0.23 | −0.50 | −0.56 | −0.40 |
| $\sigma_y$: Volatility of Treasury yield changes (bps) | 6.4 | 6.4 | 6.4 | 6.4 | 6.4 | 6.4 |
| $\rho_{y,s}(\sigma_s/\sigma_y)$: Linkage factor | −4.9% | −5.0% | −5.7% | −19.4% | −18.1% | −11.5% |
| Theoretical hedge ratio at average spread level, based on equation (7.3) | 0.95 | 0.93 | 0.88 | 0.24 | −0.04 | −0.23 |

*Note:* All calculations are based on daily data between August 1, 1998, and November 30, 2009. The results in panel A are based on estimating equation (7.4) separately for each rating category using the daily (market value–weighted) price returns of all bonds comprising each category.
*Source:* Barclays Capital.

estimated beta and gamma for Baa rated bonds (0.85 and −0.02, respectively) in equation (7.5) yields an empirical hedge ratio of 0.83 for spreads of 1%, which declines to 0.75 when spreads rise to 5%.

Table 7.1(B) presents an evaluation of the expression in equation (7.3) based on direct observation of daily changes in credit spreads and Treasury yields. For each of the six quality groups, we measure the standard deviation of relative spread changes, as well as the correlation with changes in Treasury yield. We then use these to calculate the linkage factor shown in equation (7.2), which gives approximately the amount of relative spread widening expected if yields were to drop by a certain amount. The linkage factor, along with the average spread level for each quality group over the period, is used to calculate the theoretical hedge ratio—the quantity in parentheses at the end of equation (7.3). The theoretical hedge ratio, in turn, can be compared with the average hedge ratio estimated for each quality group using the regression coefficients reported in Table 7.1(A).

The results in Table 7.1(B) corroborate the regression-based results, in three ways. First, relative spread volatility is fairly similar across the various quality groups, consistent with the DTS paradigm and the formulation in equation (7.1). Second, both sets of hedge ratios are similar in magnitude. Third, the model-based results display the same steep drop in hedge ratios as bonds move from IG to HY.

Table 7.1(B) also shows a negative correlation between interest rates and credit spreads, confirming the findings in Hyman (2007). It is this negative correlation that makes the total return volatility of investment-grade credit indexes lower than that of treasuries. In our context, the negative correlation manifests itself as a decrease in empirical duration as the exposure to credit spread risk grows. As spreads increase, the effect of this negative correlation is magnified, as per equation (7.3), making the effect more pronounced for high-yield bonds than for investment-grade bonds. In the extreme, exposure to credit spreads may become high enough to even result in negative durations.

## Variation in Hedge Ratios across Credit Ratings

Figure 7.1 displays the regression-based hedge ratios from Table 7.1(A) as a function of spread, over the range of spreads at which bonds from each rating category were trading during the sample period. The plot illustrates that the interest-rate sensitivities of the three investment-grade rating categories form a coherent pattern. While the hedge ratios of investment grade bonds decline with widening spreads, they maintain strong sensitivity to interest rates at all relevant spread levels. In contrast, high-yield bonds seem almost completely disconnected from interest rates, even at spread levels that overlap with

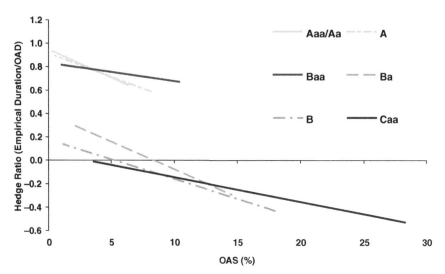

**FIGURE 7.1**    Hedge Ratios as a Function of Spread by Credit Rating
*Note:* The plot is based on substituting the regression coefficients from Table 7.1(A) and the minimum and maximum spread level during the sample period (August 1, 1998–November 30, 2009) separately for each credit rating in equation (7.5).
*Source:* Barclays Capital.

those of investment-grade bonds. With hedge ratios near or below zero across most spread levels, high-yield securities more closely resemble equities than bonds.

One possible explanation for this sharp difference is that high-yield bonds trade mostly on default or recovery expectations and are, thus, less sensitive to Treasury yields. When the likelihood of default is perceived as high, the primary determinant of a bond's value is the assumed rate of recovery upon default. In extreme cases, this may cause all bonds of a given issuer (at the same seniority level) to be marked at the same dollar price, regardless of maturity. The observed negative correlation between Treasury yields and spreads in such situations may be just an artifact of a misspecified model, in which the bond's price is related to the discounted value of cash flows that the market assumes will never arrive.[4] It can also be due to a view that promised cash flows are positively correlated with yield changes (i.e., increase in Treasury yields signals a higher probability of a recovery and, therefore, the likelihood of receiving future cash flows).

We examine the possible effect of perceived credit risk on empirical duration by repeating the analysis after excluding from the data set all bonds with a price below 80. This threshold was intended to separate securities "trading on price," that is, on estimates of recovery value, from those priced by discounting cash flows to redemption at a spread to treasuries. However, the results are essentially unchanged and the discontinuity in hedge ratios is still evident, suggesting that the difference in interest rate sensitivities between the two markets is not solely due to considerations of default and recovery. Furthermore, to the extent that credit risk is broadly captured by the level of spread, one would expect bonds with the same spread level to exhibit similar hedge ratios (as is also implied from equation (7.3)). While this is generally the case when all bonds are rated either investment-grade or high-yield, it does not hold across the two markets.

Figure 7.2 plots the hedge ratios as a function of spread level for Baa bonds during July 2007–November 2009 and for Ba bonds from August 1998 until December 2005.[5] While the spreads of Baa bonds during the crisis period almost exactly overlapped with those of Ba bonds in the earlier period, their observed hedge ratios were very different, as were their sensitivities to spread (i.e., the slope, or gamma). It seems that there is a clear

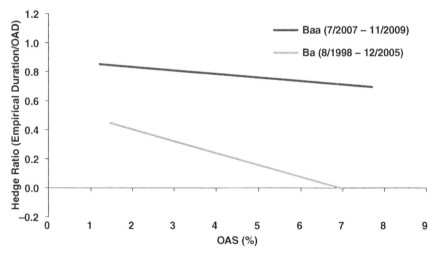

**FIGURE 7.2** Discontinuity in Hedge Ratios between Investment-Grade and High-Yield Markets

*Note:* The plot is based on estimating equation (7.4) separately for bonds rated Baa and Ba using the daily (market value–weighted) price returns of all bonds over different time periods during which they had similar spreads. We use Baa data from July 2007 to November 2009 and Ba data from August 1998 to December 2005.

*Source:* Barclays Capital.

separation between the two markets irrespective of spread levels that cannot be accounted for by default and recovery considerations.

We investigate several alternative explanations to the apparent discontinuity in hedge ratios between high-grade and high-yield bonds. First, however, we examine how stable our results are over time, as market conditions vary.

## Stability and Predictability of Hedge Ratios

The time that elapsed since our initial analysis of empirical durations in 2005 has been anything but uneventful. For example, the average OAS for the A-rated portion of the U.S. Corporate Index has widened from 57 bps at the end of February 2005 to 188 bps at the end of November 2009, after reaching a record high of 578 bps in early December 2008. As the widest observed spread in our earlier data set was 230 bps (in October 2002), the recent experience serves as a powerful "out-of-sample" test for past results.

If we were to project empirical hedge ratios as a function of spread using our original regression estimates in Ben Dor, Dynkin and Hyman (2005a), how closely would these projections match the empirical hedge ratios that were actually observed during the following several years? Figure 7.3 compares the extrapolated hedge ratios based on the original set of regression coefficients shown in Table 7.2(A) to the trailing 90-day empirical hedge ratios observed in practice, over June 2005 to November 2009.[6] This test is somewhat unfair, though, as a straight-line approximation for a spread-dependent quantity should be applied only for interpolation within the range of spreads used in the fitting procedure. As spreads during the 2007–2009 financial crisis widened well beyond the limits of the original data set, caution should be applied when a linear model is used for extrapolation. Despite these reservations, we found the outcome quite impressive.

Despite volatile markets that led the empirical hedge ratios to exhibit some unstable behavior, the results in Figure 7.3 suggest that the projected hedge ratios provided a fairly good fit overall. As spreads began to widen after June 2007, both sets of hedge ratios declined.[7] However, the empirical hedge ratios tended to decline less quickly than their projected counterparts, especially for investment-grade bonds. Apparently, no matter how much spreads widened, investment-grade investors did not stop paying attention to interest rates, continuing to trade these securities as bonds rather than equity. Sensitivity to interest rates disappeared only below a certain credit-rating threshold.

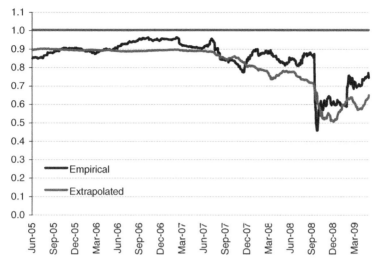

A. U.S. Investment Grade Corporate Index: Rated A

B. U.S. Investment Grade Corporate Index: Rated Baa

**FIGURE 7.3** Comparison of Empirical and Projected Hedge Ratios
*Note:* The empirical hedge ratios are based on regressing price returns against the product of Treasury duration and yield changes of the 10-year on-the-run note using a trailing 90-day window between June 2005 and November 2009. The projected hedge ratios are extrapolated using the coefficients reported in Table 7.2(A).
*Source:* Barclays Capital.

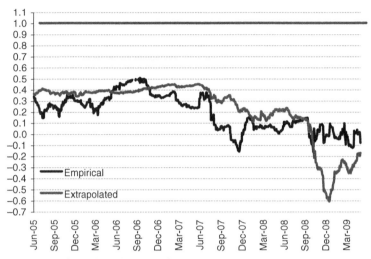

**C. U.S. High Yield Index: Rated Ba**

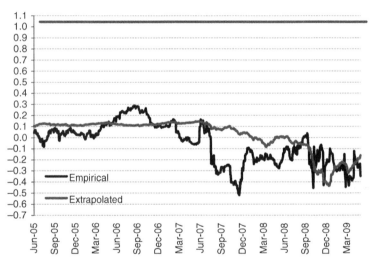

**D. U.S. High Yield Index: Rated B**

**FIGURE 7.3**    (*Continued*)

**TABLE 7.2** Empirical Hedge Ratios by Credit Rating and Period

|  | Aaa–Aa | A | Baa | Ba | B | Caa |
|---|---|---|---|---|---|---|
| **A. August 1998 to February 2005** | | | | | | |
| $\beta$: Hedge ratio limit | 0.90 | 0.95 | 0.99 | 0.60 | 0.22 | 0.17 |
| *t*-statistics | 34.67 | 32.72 | 27.44 | 9.83 | 2.74 | 1.25 |
| $\gamma$: Spread slope | −0.02 | −0.08 | −0.11 | −0.09 | −0.04 | −0.02 |
| *t*-statistics | −0.46 | −3.48 | −6.14 | −5.72 | −2.80 | −1.81 |
| **OAS** | | | | | | |
| Minimum | 0.37 | 0.56 | 1.05 | 1.46 | 2.21 | 3.68 |
| Average | 1.04 | 1.50 | 2.16 | 3.92 | 5.77 | 10.75 |
| Maximum | 4.71 | 5.95 | 7.70 | 13.75 | 18.58 | 28.33 |
| **Hedge Ratio at:** | | | | | | |
| Minimum OAS | 0.89 | 0.91 | 0.88 | 0.47 | 0.14 | 0.10 |
| Average OAS | 0.88 | 0.84 | 0.76 | 0.25 | 0.02 | −0.04 |
| Maximum OAS | 0.83 | 0.49 | 0.17 | −0.61 | −0.44 | −0.38 |
| **B. July 2007 to November 2009** | | | | | | |
| $\beta$: Hedge ratio limit | 1.02 | 0.90 | 0.88 | 0.05 | −0.17 | −0.32 |
| *t*-statistics | 16.19 | 13.18 | 15.68 | 0.41 | −0.91 | −1.43 |
| $\gamma$: Spread slope | −0.08 | −0.04 | −0.02 | −0.01 | −0.01 | −0.01 |
| *t*-statistics | −3.69 | −2.28 | −2.00 | −0.52 | −0.38 | −0.55 |
| **OAS** | | | | | | |
| Minimum | 0.70 | 0.90 | 1.21 | 2.05 | 2.70 | 4.30 |
| Average | 2.26 | 2.92 | 3.73 | 6.35 | 8.44 | 13.00 |
| Maximum | 4.71 | 5.95 | 7.70 | 13.75 | 18.58 | 28.33 |
| **Hedge Ratio at:** | | | | | | |
| Minimum OAS | 0.97 | 0.86 | 0.85 | 0.03 | −0.19 | −0.36 |
| Average OAS | 0.84 | 0.78 | 0.79 | 0.00 | −0.23 | −0.43 |
| Maximum OAS | 0.65 | 0.65 | 0.70 | −0.06 | −0.30 | −0.55 |

*Note:* The estimated coefficients are based on equation (7.4). The regressions are estimated separately for each rating category using the daily market-value price returns of all bonds comprising each category, between August 1998 and February 2005 (panel A) or July 2007 and November 2009 (panel B).
*Source:* Barclays Capital.

To investigate this issue more closely, Figure 7.4 plots the time series of 90-day trailing average spread and empirical duration from December 1998 until November 2009. The plots confirm the negative relationship between empirical durations and spread levels. As spreads have risen since the second half of 2007, empirical durations have declined across the board, even for higher-quality bonds such as A and Baa. This should not be surprising, given that spreads for A-rated bonds during this period were multiples of Ba spreads in February 2005.

However, extrapolating from prior historical experience would have suggested lower empirical durations than those observed in practice. In spite of investment-grade spreads going into traditionally high-yield territory, their empirical durations have not reached the low levels observed in high yield. Indeed, as the decomposition of credit spreads in Chapter 6 illustrated, the massive spread widening during the 2007–2009 crisis reflected mostly a lack of liquidity and not a rise in default expectations. As a result, using the absolute level of investment-grade credit spreads to project empirical duration during the crisis led to estimates that were lower than those observed in practice.

The rise in spreads due to worsening liquidity conditions in the market may also explain the weakening of the spread dependence in the high-yield segment. As spreads widened to record levels since mid-2007, empirical durations showed resilience, refusing to fall as low as the historical negative correlation would imply. For example, when Ba spreads topped 600 bps in 2002, the corresponding empirical duration was as low as $-2$; we might have expected it to be even more negative as spreads climbed above 1,000 bps in early 2009. Yet it never dipped too far below zero.

The evidence in Figures 7.3 and 7.4 not only clearly supports the notion that the relation between empirical and analytical duration is a function of spread level, but also indicates that behavior during the crisis period has deviated, to a certain extent, from what one may have expected. Therefore, it is instructive to compare the results from re-estimating equation (7.4) over the crisis period (June 2007–November 2009) with the original results (August 1998–February 2005).

The results in Table 7.2 indicate that some of the patterns discussed earlier seem to slide up the quality scale. During the tumultuous period of the 2007–2009 credit crisis, there seemed to be a pronounced relation between empirical durations and spreads even for bonds rated Aaa or Aa. The regression coefficients are remarkably close to those in the earlier period for A-rated bonds. In contrast, at the lower end of the spectrum, it is the independence between empirical durations and spreads that crept up to higher quality securities. Now, we do not see any spread dependence even for bonds rated Ba.

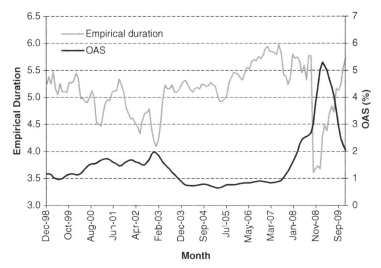

A. U.S. Investment-Grade Corporate Index: Rated A

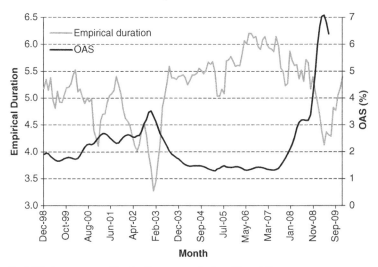

B. U.S. Investment-Grade Corporate Index: Rated Baa

**FIGURE 7.4** Relation between Empirical Duration and Spread Level
*Note:* The empirical durations are based on regressing price returns against changes in the yield of the 10-year on-the-run note using a trailing 90-days window between December 1998 and November 2009.
*Source:* Barclays Capital.

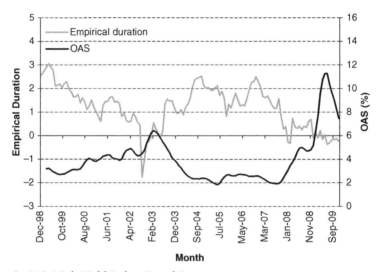

C. U.S. High Yield Index: Rated Ba

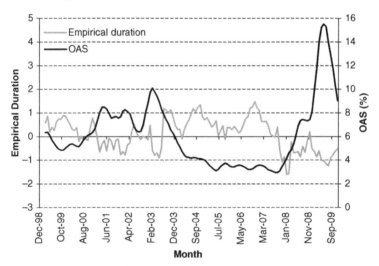

D. U.S. High Yield Index: Rated B

**FIGURE 7.4**  (*Continued*)

## SEGMENTATION IN CREDIT MARKETS

The evidence in the previous section suggests that there is a clear separation between the hedge ratios of investment-grade and high-yield bonds. The sharp drop in hedge ratios when crossing to high-yield territory could not be fully explained by considerations of default and recovery and persisted through the entire sample period despite the unstable behavior of hedge ratios at times. What can account for this phenomenon?

One possibility is that the discontinuous behavior of hedge ratios simply reflects different market pricing conventions for investment-grade and high-yield bonds. Investment-grade bonds are typically quoted as a spread to a Treasury security with similar maturity ("parent"), whereas high-yield bonds are quoted on price. Therefore, even when daily quotes for an investment-grade bond are unchanged, it would still exhibit interest rate sensitivity in our analysis as long as the Treasury curve has changed. In contrast, for a high-yield bond, the price return would be zero, suggesting no sensitivity to Treasury rates.

In liquid markets, securities are transacted frequently and prices are likely to closely reflect the valuations of market participants. However, corporate bonds as an asset class are fairly illiquid, and most bonds do not trade on any given day. For example, trading volume data for September 2009 reported in TRACE indicate that about half of the bonds in the Corporate and High Yield indexes traded less than 15 times during that month and 25% to 30% did not trade even once. Furthermore, the average monthly turnover was only about 5% for investment-grade bonds and roughly 4% for high-yield bonds.[8] As a result, daily corporate bond pricing data mostly reflect traders' quotes, rather than actual transactions. If these quotes are stale, the different pricing conventions between the two markets can create the apparent segmentation we observe. To investigate this hypothesis, we construct several proxies for liquidity and test whether our results are sensitive to the existence of stale pricing.

## POTENTIAL STALE PRICING AND ITS EFFECT ON HEDGE RATIOS

Traders' quotes are more likely to accurately reflect the aggregate demand and supply dynamics when markets are liquid. To the extent that stale quotes are less of a concern for more liquid bonds, we examine the variation in interest rate sensitivity across credit ratings conditional on trading volume as a proxy for liquidity. Each month, bonds in our sample are assigned into quintiles based on their total dollar trading volume as reported in TRACE. Quintile breakpoints are determined separately for investment and non-investment-grade bonds. We then compute aggregate market value–weighted statistics (price return, spread, and spread duration) separately for each investment-grade and high-yield quintile.

Table 7.3 reports the average traded volume and number of bonds in each quintile by credit rating from January 2007 through November 2009.[9] Table 7.3 clearly illustrates the relative illiquidity of the corporate bond market. For example, bonds in the top quintile with an A-rating have an average monthly trading volume of $167.8 million, whereas those in the second most liquid quintile have roughly one-fifth of that volume. Furthermore, A-rated bonds in the bottom quintile were essentially not traded at all, and a similar pattern is evident across all credit qualities. Notice also that since the typical amount outstanding of an investment-grade bond is two to three times larger than that of a high-yield bond, investment-grade, and high-yield bonds in the same quintile exhibit fairly similar turnover rates despite large differences in absolute volume.

Is higher liquidity (as measured by trading volume) associated with more timely and efficient pricing? While it is difficult to address this question directly, Table 7.4 presents some indirect results. Table 7.4(A) reports the standard deviation of the daily aggregate price returns for all quintile-rating combinations and their durations, whereas Table 7.4(B) reports the average correlation of price return across volume quintiles, $\rho_{q_i,q_j}$.[10] If liquid bonds experience more frequent price adjustments than less liquid bonds (within the same credit rating), then the standard deviation of their price returns should be higher. Similarly, return correlations should decline the further apart two quintiles are from each other.

The results from Table 7.4 are consistent with both predictions. First, the volatility of price returns for the second quintile is uniformly lower than that of the top quintile for each of the credit rating groups. Furthermore, the magnitude of decline between the top and bottom quintiles (despite the generally higher duration of bonds in the bottom quintile) increases as credit quality deteriorates, consistent with a potentially larger degree of stale pricing for lower credit qualities. Second, the correlation of price returns between any two quintiles declines the further apart they are in terms of their liquidity profiles. For example, for $\rho_{q_1,q_2}$, the correlation between the highest and second-highest liquidity quintile is 0.85, whereas it is only 0.75 for $\rho_{q_1,q_5}$. These results suggest that trading volume as a proxy for liquidity is able to capture some cross-sectional variation in bonds' price adjustment dynamic. Hence, more liquid (e.g., traded) bonds, particularly those comprising the top liquidity quintile, are less likely to have stale prices.

**TABLE 7.3** Liquidity Quintiles: Bond Composition and Volume

### Investment Grade

| | Bond Composition (average number of issues per month) | | | | | |
|---|---|---|---|---|---|---|
| | Q1 (most liquid) | Q2 | Q3 | Q4 | Q5 (least liquid) | |
| Aaa–Aa | 142 | 89 | 63 | 57 | 72 |
| A | 254 | 257 | 256 | 266 | 235 |
| Baa | 213 | 262 | 289 | 286 | 303 |
| Total | 609 | 609 | 609 | 610 | 611 |

| | Trading Volume ($millions/month) | | | | |
|---|---|---|---|---|---|
| Aaa–Aa | 188.5 | 37.3 | 15.7 | 5.3 | 0.3 |
| A | 167.8 | 36.4 | 15.5 | 5.1 | 0.4 |
| Baa | 154.8 | 35.9 | 15.2 | 5.1 | 0.4 |

### High Yield

| | Bond Composition (average number of issues per month) | | | | | |
|---|---|---|---|---|---|---|
| | Q1 (most liquid) | Q2 | Q3 | Q4 | Q5 (least liquid) | |
| Ba | 94 | 106 | 110 | 117 | 106 |
| B | 113 | 119 | 123 | 106 | 125 |
| Caa | 84 | 69 | 63 | 56 | 77 |
| Total | 291 | 294 | 296 | 279 | 308 |

| | Trading Volume ($millions/month) | | | | |
|---|---|---|---|---|---|
| Ba | 79.8 | 17.9 | 7.8 | 2.2 | 0.0 |
| B | 84.9 | 18.0 | 7.9 | 2.4 | 0.0 |
| Caa | 93.7 | 18.2 | 7.9 | 2.4 | 0.0 |

*Note:* Based on daily transaction data from TRACE between January 2007 and November 2009. Quintile breakpoints are determined separately for investment- and non-investment-grade bonds each month based on the total trading volume per bond. The aggregate trading volumes are market value–weighted across all bonds in each quintile-rating bucket.
*Source:* Barclays Capital.

**TABLE 7.4** Price Return Volatilities and Correlations across Liquidity Quintiles

**A. Standard Deviation**

| | Standard Deviation of Price Returns (bps/day) | | | | | |
|---|---|---|---|---|---|---|
| | Aaa–Aa | A | Baa | Ba | B | Caa |
| Q1 (most liquid) | 47 | 59 | 52 | 67 | 86 | 122 |
| Q2 | 38 | 44 | 46 | 38 | 44 | 77 |
| Q3 | 40 | 47 | 46 | 35 | 38 | 61 |
| Q4 | 47 | 50 | 48 | 30 | 33 | 54 |
| Q5 (least liquid) | 52 | 56 | 48 | 39 | 54 | 72 |
| | Option-Adjusted Durations (years) | | | | | |
| Q1 (most liquid) | 5.51 | 6.39 | 6.92 | 4.84 | 4.22 | 4.21 |
| Q2 | 4.67 | 5.85 | 6.09 | 4.69 | 4.04 | 4.06 |
| Q3 | 5.19 | 6.29 | 6.07 | 4.56 | 4.12 | 4.02 |
| Q4 | 5.88 | 6.75 | 6.14 | 4.83 | 4.24 | 4.23 |
| Q5 (least liquid) | 6.58 | 7.38 | 6.44 | 5.01 | 4.60 | 4.41 |

**B. Average Correlation**

| | Daily Price Return Correlation | | | | |
|---|---|---|---|---|---|
| | Q1 (most liquid) | Q2 | Q3 | Q4 | Q5 (least liquid) |
| Q1 (most liquid) | 1.00 | 0.85 | 0.77 | 0.73 | 0.75 |
| Q2 | | 1.00 | 0.92 | 0.87 | 0.85 |
| Q3 | | | 1.00 | 0.90 | 0.84 |
| Q4 | | | | 1.00 | 0.82 |
| Q5 (least liquid) | | | | | 1.00 |

*Note:* Based on daily transaction data from TRACE between January 2007 and November 2009. Quintile breakpoints are determined separately for investment and non-investment-grade bonds each month based on the total trading volume per bond. Panel A reports price returns standard deviations computed using the daily market value–weighted price returns of all bonds in each quintile-rating combination. Panel B reports price return correlations computed between daily price returns of every quintile-rating combination over the sample period and then averaged across all credit ratings groups.
*Source:* Barclays Capital.

Figure 7.5 displays the results of re-estimating equation (7.4) separately for each credit rating group using only the most liquid bonds—those comprising quintile 1. The large drop in empirical hedge ratios when crossing from investment-grade to non-investment-grade territory documented

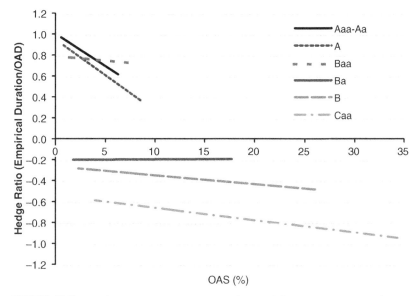

**FIGURE 7.5**  Hedge Ratios as a Function of Spread for Liquidity Quintile 1 (most liquid)
*Note:* The plot is based on estimating equation (7.4) separately for each rating category using daily data of all bonds comprising liquidity quintile 1, between January 1, 2007, and November 30, 2009. The resulting coefficients and the minimum and maximum spread level during the sample period are then substituted separately for each credit rating in equation (7.5).
*Source:* Barclays Capital.

earlier is still evident. For example, despite the extreme market dynamics during the sample period (January 2007–November 2009), Baa bonds maintained a hedge ratio of 0.71, even at spreads of 700 bps, whereas high-yield bonds exhibited zero or even negative hedge ratios for the same level of spreads. Furthermore, the results are very similar to those reported in Table 7.2, despite the difference in populations.

While Figure 7.5 nicely illustrates the large difference in interest rate sensitivity for the most liquid subset of investment-grade and high-yield bonds, note that the same pattern is observed for less liquid bonds. Figure 7.6 plots hedge ratios as function of spread level for bonds rated Baa and Ba separately for all liquidity quintiles. Figure 7.6 indicates that the gap in hedge ratios between the lowest quality investment-grade bonds (Baa) and the highest quality high-yield bonds (Ba) is largely independent of their underlying liquidity profile and can be observed even for bonds in quintile 5, where the potential for stale pricing is likely to be the largest.

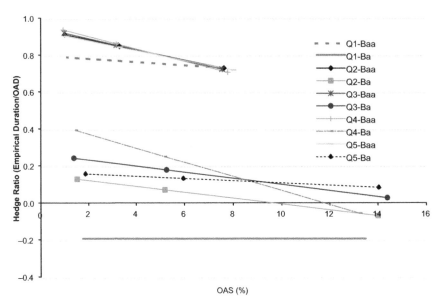

**FIGURE 7.6** Hedge Ratios for Bonds Rated Baa and Ba by Liquidity Quintile
*Note:* The reported coefficients are based on estimating equation (7.4). The
regressions are estimated separately for each liquidity-rating combination using
daily price return between January 2007 and November 2009.
*Source:* Barclays Capital.

In addition to controlling for trading volume, we conduct two more ex-
periments to ensure that the lack of rate sensitivity in high-yield bonds is not
an artifact of stale pricing. First, we repeat the analysis using biweekly rather
than daily price returns over the same period as in Table 7.1 (August 1998
and November 2009). Using a biweekly frequency reduces the likelihood of
having unchanged prices, while still keeping the sample size large enough
to ensure sufficient statistical power. Second, we attempt to directly identify
and exclude observations that possibly reflect stale prices. Specifically, all
bonds comprising the Corporate and High Yield indexes with a sequence of
five or more unchanged quotes in any month are excluded from the eligible
population of bonds for that month.[11] Equation (7.4) is then re-estimated
separately for the six ratings groups using only the eligible population of
bonds from January 2007 through November 2009.

The results from filtering out consecutive unchanged prices and using
biweekly price returns (not reported for brevity) are almost identical to those
using daily data and the entire population of bonds. Once again, they reject

the notion that the difference in pricing conventions and relative illiquidity of corporate bonds are responsible for our results.

## HEDGE RATIOS FOLLOWING RATING CHANGES: AN EVENT STUDY APPROACH

Our analysis of the relation between analytical and empirical duration has thus far relied upon aggregated statistics of various bond portfolios constructed based on credit ratings. This approach was taken, in part, to examine the relation between hedge ratios and credit qualities but mainly to achieve a sufficiently long sample period that reflects diverse credit market conditions.

One disadvantage of using aggregated data is that our findings may reflect, at least partially, differences in bond characteristics across rating categories, which can affect the observed hedge ratios. For example, many of the bonds rated as high-yield at issuance are callable. If market perception about the likelihood of a bond being called is materially different than that implied by the option-adjusted duration (OAD) model, it can lead to a large discrepancy between the analytical and empirical duration. If the proportion of callable bonds in the high-yield universe is higher than in investment-grade, this may cause the empirical durations of the two groups to diverge. The same would be true for any other systematic differences that exist between investment-grade and high-yield bonds.

To account for systematic differences between the markets, we repeat the analysis using daily data on individual bonds that were downgraded from investment-grade to high-yield or were conversely upgraded from high-yield to investment-grade since 2006. For each bond, we estimate the change in hedge ratio before and after the "rating event" (upgrade or downgrade). This "event study" approach controls for all bond-specific characteristics and allows us to conduct a direct test of the difference in hedge ratios between investment-grade and high-yield bonds.

### Data and Methodology

The analysis was carried out for all bonds that were part of the Corporate and High Yield indexes and experienced a "rating event" between January 2006 and November 2009. A *rating event* is defined as a downgrade from any investment-grade rating to high-yield status or, conversely, an upgrade from any high-yield rating to investment-grade status.[12] Credit ratings were based on the index rating methodology, which used the middle rating of Moody's, S&P, and Fitch. We require each bond to have at least 50 data

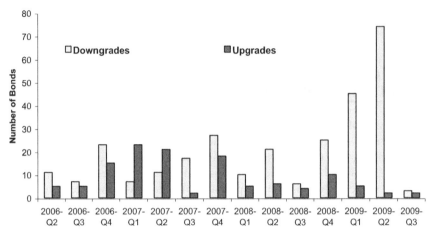

**FIGURE 7.7**   Frequency of Bonds Experiencing Rating Events by Quarter
*Note:* Based on all bonds that were part of the Corporate and High Yield indexes and experienced a "rating event" between January 1, 2006, and November 30, 2009. A *rating event* is defined as a downgrade from any investment-grade rating to high-yield status or conversely an upgrade from any high-yield rating to investment-grade status.
*Source:* Barclays Capital.

points (after excluding all zero price returns to mitigate potentially stale pricing) before and after the event (i.e., a minimum of 100 observations per bond).

The resulting sample includes 410 rating events of which 123 are up-grades and 287 are downgrades. They represent 402 bonds from 137 individual issuers. Figure 7.7 displays the total number of rating events by type in each quarter during the sample period. Not surprisingly, the rating events are not uniformly distributed over time. Most of the downgrades occurred during the third quarter of 2008 and onward, whereas the upgrades mostly concentrated around the beginning and middle of the period.

Before reporting the results of the analysis for the entire sample, it is instructive to look at one specific example. Figure 7.8 displays the 90-day trailing hedge ratio, average spread (over the same period), and credit rating (shown at the bottom of the chart) for a 30-year Alltel bond with a 7.875% coupon issued in July 2001. The bond experienced several rating changes since 2006, making it an interesting test case for the relation between hedge ratio and credit quality.

The bond was issued at an investment-grade rating of A2 and exhibited a hedge ratio close to 1 for the first couple of years. As the bond's spread

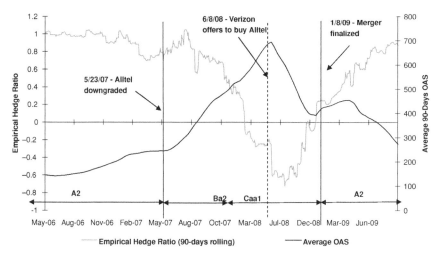

**FIGURE 7.8** Variation in Alltel 30-Year Bond Hedge Ratio Following Rating Changes
*Note:* The plot displays the 90-day trailing hedge ratio, average spread (over the same period) and credit rating for a 30-year bond with a 7.875% coupon issued by Alltel in July 2001 (CUSIP 020039DC).
*Source:* Barclays Capital.

widened to over 200 bps, its hedge ratio declined to 0.75, consistent with the estimates for A-rated bonds in Table 7.1. Following the downgrade to high-yield status (A2 to Ba2) on May 23, 2007, the hedge ratio declined steadily to about 0.4 as spreads widened to 450 bps. When the bond was further downgraded to Caa1 on November 21, 2007, the hedge ratio dropped even further to negative territory (as a low as −0.6).

The hedge ratio (and spread) reversed course soon after Verizon's offer to acquire Alltel was announced in June 2008, in spite of an unchanged credit rating. Once the acquisition was completed on January 8, 2009, the bond was upgraded to investment-grade and regained its initial rating (A2). Similarly, the hedge ratio gradually increased (and spread level decreased) from about 0.25 to roughly 0.95 at the end of August 2009, similar to its value at the beginning of 2006.

## Empirical Analysis

To study the behavior of hedge ratios for the sample of bonds that experienced a rating event, we estimate equation (7.4) for each bond separately

**TABLE 7.5**  Summary Statistics for Bonds Experiencing a Rating Event

| | Downgrades | | | Upgrades | | |
|---|---|---|---|---|---|---|
| | Before | After | p-value for Difference | Before | After | p-value for Difference |
| Beta | 1.00 | 0.45 | < 0.0001 | 0.43 | 0.88 | < 0.0001 |
| Gamma | −0.04 | −0.05 | 0.021 | −0.07 | −0.02 | 0.153 |
| Mean OAS (bps) | 255 | 749 | | 180 | 360 | |
| Hedge ratio at mean OAS | 0.86 | 0.08 | < 0.0001 | 0.20 | 0.80 | < 0.0001 |
| Bonds with hedge ratio change as expected | 86% | | | 80% | | |
| $R^2$ | 0.16 | 0.01 | < 0.0001 | 0.02 | 0.14 | < 0.0001 |
| Sample size | 287 | 287 | | 123 | 123 | |

*Note:* The figures are based on estimating equation (7.4) for each bond separately before and after the rating event using all available data except the month during which the rating event occurred, which is excluded. If a bond experienced more than one rating change, we estimate the regression using data up to three months before the next event or starting three months after the previous event. Values for beta, gamma, mean OAS, hedge ratio, and $R^2$ are based on the sample median. The p-value reflects the probability that the median values before and after the rating event are drawn from the same distribution using the Wilcoxon-Mann-Whitney test. The percentage of hedge ratio change as expected is the proportion of bonds where hedge ratios decreased after a downgrade or increased after an upgrade.
*Source:* Barclays Capital.

before and after the rating change using all available data excluding the month during which the rating event occurred. If a bond experienced more than one rating change, we estimate the regression using data up to three months before the next event or starting three months after the previous event to avoid any spillover effects.

   Table 7.5 reports summary statistics for the pre- and post-rating event regressions, separately for upgraded and downgraded bonds. The values in Table 7.5 represent sample medians rather than means to mitigate the potential effect of outliers. The p-values for the null hypothesis of equal medians before and after the rating event are computed based on the Wilcoxon-Mann-Whitney test.[13]

   The results are generally consistent with our previous findings for upgraded and downgraded bonds. For bonds initially rated investment grade, the typical limit hedge ratio (beta) decreased from 1.00 to 0.45 after the rating change, compared with 0.85 and 0.41 reported in Table 7.1 (for bonds rated Baa and Ba, respectively). The results for upgraded bonds are similar but with the opposite directionality with beta increasing from 0.43 to 0.88. The spread slope coefficient (gamma) is always negative and fairly stable, although for downgraded bonds, the 0.01 difference (from −0.04 to −0.05) is significant at the 5% level. The changes in explanatory power are also in accordance with previous results and highly significant. The regressions' $R^2$ dramatically decline for downgraded bonds (from 0.16 to 0.01) and rise for upgraded bonds (from 0.02 to 0.14).

Not surprisingly, the average spread level of downgraded bonds increased from 255 bps before the rating event to 750 bps after it. While the similar rise in spread level for bonds that were upgraded may look unreasonable at first, it reflects the general timing of upgrades (Figure 7.7) and the sharp rise in spreads following the credit crisis.

Hedge ratios (computed using estimates of beta and gamma, and the average spread of each bond during the estimation window) for downgraded bonds declined from 0.86 to 0.08, very similar to the results generated if we were to employ the coefficients from Table 7.1 for the respective spread levels (0.79 and 0.05 before and after the rating event, respectively). In addition, the hedge ratios for downgraded bonds before the rating change are very similar to those of upgraded bonds after the rating change (0.80), despite the fact that these are two distinct bond populations. Table 7.5 also reports the percentage of bonds where the hedge ratio changed "as expected"—that is, consistent with our null hypothesis of a decrease after a downgrade and an increase after an upgrade. In both cases, this "hit ratio" is very high—86% in the case of downgraded bonds and 80% for upgraded bonds.

These results are also illustrated in Figure 7.9. Each observation represents a single bond where the x- and y-axis measure the hedge ratio before and after the rating event, respectively. The scatter plot reveals the sharp contrast in hedge ratios before and after the rating event. Hedge ratios for downgraded bonds mostly ranged between 0.8 and 1.0 while they were investment-grade, but hovered around zero after the downgrade. Many bonds even exhibited negative hedge ratios, consistent with what was documented in Figure 7.1 for the high-yield market. In contrast, for upgraded bonds, almost all observations are located above the 45-degree line, implying that the hedge ratios have increased, mostly ranging between 0.6 and 0.8.

## Performance Evaluation and Hedge Ratios

The analysis of individual bonds that experienced a rating event suggests that data aggregation did not affect our findings, thereby confirming all prior results (both qualitatively and quantitatively). In particular, the sharp

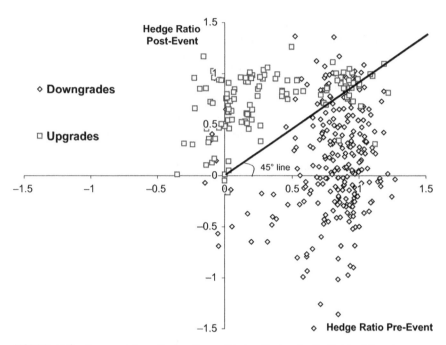

**FIGURE 7.9**   Pre- and Post-Rating Event Hedge Ratios for Individual Bonds
*Note:* Hedge ratios are computed using the estimates of beta, gamma, and the
average spread of each bond during the estimation window. Each observation
represents a single bond where the x- and y-axis measure the hedge ratio before and
after the rating event, respectively.
*Source:* Barclays Capital.

drop in hedge ratios when crossing to high-yield territory, which we termed
*market segmentation,* cannot be explained by security-specific attributes
characterizing high-yield bonds. The considerations of credit risk (default
and recovery) and differences in pricing conventions between the markets
also do not fully account for this phenomenon.

Another possible explanation is based on the difference in performance
metrics used by investors in the two markets. Despite the fact that seemingly
similar securities (corporate bonds) are traded in both, investment-grade
credit managers are typically evaluated in terms of excess returns over treasuries (or swaps). High-yield managers, on the other hand, tend to think
in terms of total return and default risk. This difference, and the hedging
practices (or lack thereof) that result from it, may result in the observed
reduced sensitivity of high-yield bonds to interest rate changes.

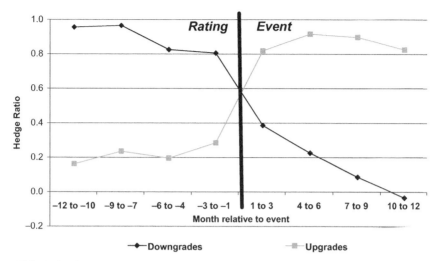

**FIGURE 7.10**   Variation in Hedge Ratio over Time by Rating Event
*Note:* Each observation represents the median hedge ratio over one of eight
three-month, non-overlapping periods spanning the two-year window around the
rating event date. Hedge ratios are computed by using the estimates of beta,
gamma, and the average spread of each bond during the estimation window. The
coefficients are based on estimating equation (7.4) separately for each bond with at
least 50 data points in a given three-month period.
*Source:* Barclays Capital.

   While the hypothesis is simple and intuitive, it is difficult to test directly
as we are unable to observe the hedging activity employed by portfolio managers. Still, the rating event analysis may provide some important, albeit indirect, evidence to support this theory. Figure 7.10 plots the median hedge ratio
as a function of time relative to the rating event (separately for downgraded
and upgraded bonds). Hedge ratios are estimated over one of eight three-
month, non-overlapping periods spanning the two-year window around the
rating event date.[14] The population of bonds varies across time and declines
the further the period is from the event date (either before or after).
   The results in Figure 7.10 illustrate the strong discontinuity in hedge
ratios around the rating event date. For downgraded bonds, the hedge ratio
drops from 0.80 in the three months just before the downgrade to 0.38 in
the three months following it. Similarly, the hedge ratio for upgraded bonds
rises from 0.28 to 0.81 over the same time frame. In contrast, the degree of
variation in the prior and subsequent nine months ($-12$ to $-3$ and 3 to 12)
is limited. For example, for upgraded bonds, the hedge ratio ranged from
0.16 to 0.23 before the rating change, similar to the level just before the

rating change. Similarly, the hedge ratio after the upgrade initially increased further from 0.81 to 0.91 but then declined back to 0.82.

One exception is the continued decline of the hedge ratio for investment-grade bonds after they were downgraded (from 0.38 to −0.04). This reflects the relative clustering of the downgrade events in our sample around the height of the credit crisis. As Figure 7.7 shows, a total of 144 downgrades occurred between the last quarter of 2008 and the second quarter of 2009. This clustering, coupled with the extreme widening of spreads, resulted in the seemingly continued deterioration of hedge ratios up to a year after the downgrade.

Overall, the pattern of fairly stable hedge ratios up to three months before the rating change, a sharp change around the rating event, and then stabilization at a new level is fully consistent with our hypothesis. Notice also that this argument implies that such behavior should be observed, even if market participants are able to anticipate the rating changes well in advance. Despite the fact that rating agencies are often slow to incorporate new information and adjust credit ratings accordingly, investment-grade bonds pending a downgrade should still exhibit high interest rate sensitivity and vice versa for high-yield bonds.

## USING EMPIRICAL DURATION IN PORTFOLIO MANAGEMENT APPLICATIONS

What are the practical implications of our findings to a portfolio manager? If one is passively managing the duration exposures of a corporate bond portfolio relative to a corporate index, the issue is largely irrelevant. As long as the two sets of duration exposures are systematically matched, and the bonds in the portfolio are qualitatively similar to the benchmark, we would expect them to react similarly to changes in the yield curve. The empirical relationship is more important when a large corporate exposure is hedged purely with treasuries or swaps. In such cases, if an adjustment is not made, the portfolio might end up over-hedged with respect to rates. Let us examine several such examples in greater detail.

### Index Replication with Derivatives

Investors often prefer to replicate a target index with only liquid instruments such as Treasury futures, interest rate swaps, and credit default swaps. Barclays Capital publishes returns on several baskets (known as RBI®—Replicating Bond Index baskets—see Chapter 14), designed to replicate the returns of several of its indexes using combinations of derivatives. The baskets are reconstituted monthly, based on the analytical sensitivities to

a set of market risk factors (such as yield curve sensitivities, spread durations, and currency exposures) of the replicated index. The weight of each
derivative instrument is determined using a predefined algorithm.

One series of these baskets (RBI-2) is designed to track the U.S. Credit
Index with only interest rate swaps. (RBI-1 uses CDX to add explicit spread
exposure, and its performance is closely linked to the cash-CDS basis.) While
the rates exposure of the credit component of the index (based on a six-
point key rate duration [KRD] profile) is matched, the spread exposure is
left unhedged. However, our results suggest that a better tracking should
be achieved with a hedge ratio somewhat lower than 1. In other words,
the KRDs of the swaps in the basket should be less than the corresponding
analytical KRDs used in the standard product. Would such an adjustment
lead to an appreciable reduction in TEV?

We conducted an experiment in which we reweighted the swaps in
RBI-2 baskets monthly from March 2004 (the product launch date) through
November 2009. Each month, we estimated equation (7.4), separately for
each credit quality group, using an expanding window of daily data (from
August 1998). Then, using the market weights and average OAS of each
quality group, we calculated a single hedge ratio for the index, applied it to
the six KRDs (and, therefore, the weights) of the swaps in the basket, and
computed the basket's return. The resulting time series of these empirical
RBI returns was compared with that of the standard published product to
determine whether the tracking error volatility versus the Credit Index was
improved by switching to empirical hedging.

The TEV for the overall period of 69 months declined by 13 bps, from
209 to 196 bps/month. While the reduction in realized TEV is not very
large, this should not come as a surprise. Clearly, the tracking errors reflect
first and foremost the mismatch in spread exposure between credit bonds
and swaps. It is important to note, however, that improvement in TEV has
been consistent through the entire period. Figure 7.11 displays the TEV on
an expanding window, starting at 12 months and working its way to the
full 68-month period. Figure 7.11(A) compares the TEV of the standard
and empirical RBI. Figure 7.11(B) plots just the difference to highlight the
improvement. The plot suggests that the TEV of the empirical RBI has
always stayed below that of the standard product and the improvement has
actually increased during the crisis of 2007–2009.

## Hedging an Active Credit Exposure

Should a portfolio manager looking to hedge the rates exposure in a credit
portfolio (with Treasury futures or swaps) use analytical or empirical durations? The answer to this question is more complex than it might seem
at first glance. Different types of hedges may be appropriate to express

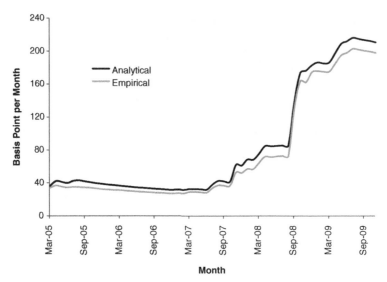

**A. TEV, Empirical vs. Analytical**

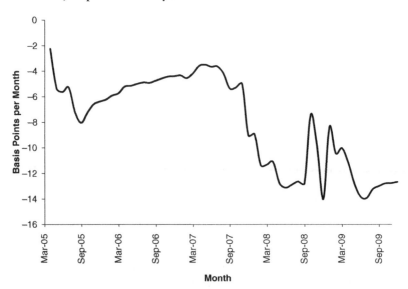

**B. TEV Differential (empirical minus analytical)**

**FIGURE 7.11** Credit Index RBI-2 Based on Empirical and Analytical Durations and the Effect on Tracking Error Volatility (TEV)
*Source:* Barclays Capital.

different views; it is important to understand the precise implications and consequences of each approach.

The decision to maintain an active credit position may express the view that current spread levels are high relative to the investor's estimate of credit risk. As such, long-horizon credit exposure should generate a steady stream of positive carry returns. If the investor has no view on the near-term direction of spread movements, he may wish to hedge this position against mark-to-market volatility stemming from fluctuations in both rates and spreads. If the hedge consists of only Treasury futures and swaps, the overall volatility of the position may be minimized when the hedge ratio to the rates exposure is less than one, as our empirical research suggests.

However, an active credit exposure may also be motivated by a view that spreads will tighten. In this case, an empirical adjustment to hedge ratios may be counterproductive. Imagine a scenario in which interest rates rise and spreads tighten exactly as implied by the historical relationship between the two. An empirical hedge, reduced to reflect this known correlation, would exactly offset both of these market effects. Is this what the investor intended? In this example, the view that spreads would tighten may prove correct, but would not result in any net profit, as the gain from the spread tightening would be offset by the under-hedged losses from the rise in rates. If, however, the credit overweight were implemented by a full analytical rates hedge, then the position would profit on spread tightening and lose on widening, regardless of what happened to interest rates.

These two approaches can perhaps be expressed most concisely in the context of a simple two-factor risk model. A long credit position has exposure to a yield factor and a spread factor, with a negative correlation between them. Suppose two investors wish to hedge the interest-rate risk of this position with a rates-only hedge, but with different goals in mind. The first investor wants to earn the carry of the position, while putting in place the minimum-risk hedge. He will end up with less than complete hedging of the rates exposure, reflecting the negative correlation with the remaining spread exposure. The second investor wants to maintain the exposure to the spread factor, while fully hedging the exposure to rates. She may end up with a greater overall TEV, but a smaller TEV component due to rates, on which she had no view and, therefore, sought neutrality.

## Core-Plus Investment in High-Yield Bonds

Consider a credit portfolio manager with a core-plus mandate that allows him to make an allocation to high-yield bonds. Because of the much lower interest rate sensitivity of high-yield bonds, replacing part of his investment-grade allocation with an otherwise similar allocation to non-investment-grade bonds would shorten the empirical duration of his portfolio. This may carry a practical implication for credit managers who would like to shorten their portfolios' duration in expectation of a rise in interest rates in the near future.

We examine a strategy that purchases bonds with the highest high-yield rating (Ba) and sells short bonds with the lowest investment-grade rating (Baa). Since the strategy is not designed to express a view on the direction of credit spreads, it has an additional (long) investment in bonds rated A to achieve perfect hedging of analytical duration and DTS. In practice, the manager could implement such a strategy as an overlay to his existing portfolio, shifting some of his Baa-rated assets to bonds rated A and Ba.

To implement the strategy, we use all bonds rated A and Baa in the U.S. Corporate Index and bonds rated Ba in the U.S. High Yield Index from January 1992 to November 2009. The analysis is conducted within industry sectors to mitigate any sector-specific risk.[15] The strategy is rebalanced monthly so that the analytical duration and DTS of the long and short positions match. Since the long and short positions may not be dollar equivalent, the strategy also invests (or borrows) cash at one-month USD LIBOR rate. The sector-level returns are aggregated to obtain the overall strategy return, weighing each sector by the market value of the bonds rated Baa in that sector.

Figure 7.12 plots the strategy monthly returns versus the contemporaneous average change in 2-, 5-, and 10-year rates. If this strategy is short empirical duration as a consequence of the credit market segmentation, the strategy should generate positive returns when rates rally and negative returns in months when rates decline (assuming that credit exposure is perfectly hedged using DTS). The plot indicates some positive relation between the performance of the strategy and the change in interest rates. However, there are many months in which the strategy does not perform according to expectation. For example, the strategy gained 2.3% in December 2008 when rates, on average, declined by 43 bps, and lost 1.5% in May 2009 when rates increased by 23 bps. A simple performance attribution for the strategy based on regressing the strategy returns against changes in interest rates and credit spreads (measured by changes in AA spread) finds a significant positive loading on change in rates (coefficient of 0.39, $t$-statistic = 3.86), with an insignificant loading on change in credit spreads (coefficient of $-0.17$, $t$-statistic $= -1.09$) and a zero intercept. However, the low explanatory power ($R^2 = 8\%$) suggests that there are other factors that influence the performance of the strategy.

The relationship between the strategy performance and the change in rates may be more ambiguous in months with small changes in rates, when any effect of the short empirical duration position may be overshadowed by credit shocks or defaults. Table 7.6, therefore, tabulates the performance

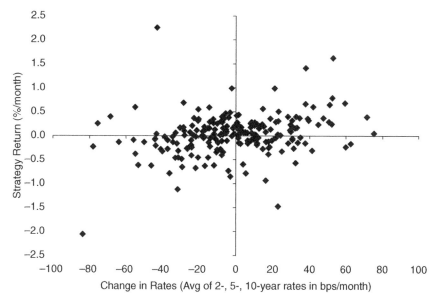

**FIGURE 7.12**   Changes in Rates and the Performance of a "Short" Empirical Duration Strategy
*Source:* Barclays Capital.


**TABLE 7.6**   Summary Statistics for "Short" Empirical Duration Strategy

|  | Positive/Negative Monthly Change in Rates | | Monthly Change in Rates > 1 Standard Deviation | |
|---|---|---|---|---|
|  | Rising Rates | Declining Rates | Rising Rates | Declining Rates |
| Average return (%/mo) | 0.10 | −0.04 | 0.25 | −0.14 |
| Volatility (%/mo) | 0.40 | 0.45 | 0.44 | 0.63 |
| Number of months | 101 | 112 | 36 | 37 |
| *t*-statistics | 2.49 | −0.89 | 3.39 | −1.37 |
| Best month | 1.62 | 2.26 | 1.62 | 2.26 |
| Worst month | −1.47 | −2.06 | −0.57 | −2.06 |
| Up months (%) | 61 | 48 | 69 | 30 |

*Source:* Barclays Capital.

statistics for the strategy in months when the change in rates is positive or negative, as well as when the change in rates is larger than one standard deviation.[16] The results suggest that the strategy earns positive average returns when rates rise and negative average returns when rates decline. Moreover, the pattern is stronger when changes in rates exceed one standard deviation with positive (negative) returns in 70% of months with rising (declining) rates.

The performance of the strategy further supports the segmentation between the investment-grade and high-yield markets and highlights the importance of considering empirical durations when investing in high-yield.

## NOTES

1. Notice that the expression in equation (7.2) is the estimated coefficient from a univariate regression of changes in relative spread against changes in yields.
2. If $\rho_{y,s} \frac{\sigma_s}{\sigma_y}$ represented by the coefficient $\gamma_i$ varies over time, it may cause $\beta$ to be different than the value implied from equation (7.3), which is one.
3. We report results based on biweekly data, using individual bonds and after applying different liquidity filters in the next section.
4. Even in less extreme situations, the pricing of credit-risky securities is influenced by the probabilities that the issuer will default at different times and the assumptions investors make about what the recovery rate would be should this occur. Including the possibility of a recovery event in which we receive a principal payment smaller than the full amount, but earlier in time, lessens the sensitivity of the pricing model to changes in Treasury rates. Berd, Mashal, and Wang (2004) present a survival-based valuation framework that offers an analytical approach to the calculation of interest rate sensitivity, as opposed to the empirical approach explored here.
5. The estimation for each rating category was done separately over the respective period.
6. The analysis starting date in June 2005 reflects the 90-day window beginning in March 2005, when the initial study was published. The results for the two credit rating categories not plotted in Figure 7.3 (Aaa–Aa and Caa) are similar.
7. For example, A-rated bonds experienced a sharp decline in their empirical duration, which was later reversed, as a result of the market turmoil that followed the September 2008 bankruptcy of Lehman Brothers, rated A at the time.
8. Hotchkiss and Jostova (2007) report similar results based on a comprehensive data set of insurance companies transactions from the National Association of Insurance Commissioners (NAIC)
9. We chose January 2007 as the starting date of our analysis since TRACE market coverage before that date is incomplete.

10. Values for $\rho_{q_i,q_j}$ in panel B represent the correlation between daily price returns of quintiles $i$ and $j$ over the sample period averaged across all credit ratings groups.

11. For investment-grade bonds, unchanged quotes are in spread terms whereas for high-yield bonds, they are in price terms. On average, about 50% and 4% of the bonds comprising the High Yield and Corporate indexes respectively are excluded in each month.

12. For example, a downgrade from a rating of A to Baa would not qualify as a rating event.

13. A $p$-value $< 0.0001$ implies that, with a 99.99% confidence, these parameters have different values before and after the ratings event, and that our results are not simply the results of random noise.

14. Hedge ratios are computed by using the estimates of beta, gamma, and the average spread of each bond during the estimation window. As before, bonds with less than 50 data points (in any three-month period) are excluded from the median calculation.

15. Bonds are classified into one of the following 18 sectors: finance (banking, brokerage, finance companies, insurance, REITs, other), industrials (basic industry, capital goods, consumer cyclical, consumer non-cyclical, energy, technology, transportation, communications, other), and utility (electric, natural gas, other). To mitigate idiosyncratic risk, the strategy is implemented for a given sector only on months when the sector is populated by at least 20 bonds.

16. We calculate the volatility of interest rates as the standard deviation of the average change in 2-, 5-, and 10-year rates, over the January 1992 to November 2009 period, which comes out as 28 bps/month.

# Managing Corporate Bond Portfolios

### CHAPTER 8

# Hedging the Market Risk in Pairs Trades

Consider the case of an investor whose goal is to construct trades that express a view favoring certain issuers relative to others while taking as little directional market risk as possible. The investor may be a portfolio manager working in a long–short market-neutral hedge fund, or in a traditional fund seeking to overlay issuer-specific alpha strategies onto his or her set of active exposures versus the benchmark.

The primary driver of the performance of such trades should be the investor's skill at forming views on issuers. However, to achieve the best possible risk-adjusted results, it is equally important to control the risk of the portfolio and to minimize any unintended systematic risk. The focus of this chapter is not on how to best form such views, but instead on the relative sizing of the long and short positions, and the net risk profile resulting from the use of different hedging mechanisms.

To compare different hedging approaches, we use weekly CDS data and employ the following simple simulation framework. A pair of securities from within the same industry is selected, and randomly assigned a directional view. A long–short trade corresponding to this view is then implemented at the start of each month in our data sample according to the selected hedging mechanism, and its performance is recorded. This is repeated for all available same-industry pairs and for all hedging strategies considered.

How might we construct the hedged position? The most basic method would be to match spread duration exposures—that is, to hedge against a parallel shift in the spreads of the two securities. As our data set consists of five-year CDS from different issuers, durations are quite uniform. Hence, this is essentially equivalent to matching the notional amounts of the positions, which in the extreme scenario of both issuers defaulting, would also be the ideal hedge. Another possibility would be to match DTS exposures, thereby hedging against a common relative change in spreads of the two issuers. With similar spread durations, matching DTS exposures means that the ratio of position sizes should be the reciprocal of the ratio of spreads. This means the trades will also be zero-carry trades. Yet another alternative for hedging is the use of empirical betas—hedge ratios formed based on the extent to which each issuer's spread has tracked the market over some trailing historical window. Some investors use this approach, based on the belief that the best measure of an issuer's market exposure over the near term is its sensitivity to market returns over the recent past.

What is the definition of the "market risk" against which each trade should be hedged? One approach would be to ensure that all trades are hedged against changes in a single broad corporate index. When spreads tighten or widen across the board, our paired trades should be unaffected. However, any paired trade that expresses a pure issuer-specific view should involve two securities from the same industry; otherwise, it will embed an industry view as well. Accordingly, to most efficiently shield such a trade from market risk, we hedge it with respect to an index formed from all the issuers within its industry.[1]

Which metric should be used to determine the most successful hedge is also not obvious. Ideally, one would like to maximize the information ratio: the return per unit of risk. However, due to the lack of ability to measure alpha in our framework, this is not feasible.[2] Another possible approach may be to minimize the total risk of the hedged position; that is, given a unit long position in security $L$, find the size of the short position in security $S$ that minimizes the overall risk. However, while this may be easy to quantify, it does not necessary align with the goals of our investor. After all, the goal is not to minimize all risks; the investor is trying to get exposure to both of these securities in order to translate his or her issuer-specific views into alpha. A third alternative is to seek a trade whose returns have the lowest possible correlation with the market. This metric, presumably, should tend to select hedging strategies that take more issuer risk and less market risk. A fourth and final possibility is to attempt to quantify this distinction directly by attributing the risk of the hedged position to systematic and issuer-specific components. We can then seek the hedge that derives the lowest percentage of its variance from systematic risk.

We find that the DTS hedge performs far better than the simple duration hedge, according to any of these performance metrics. The case is a little less clear when comparing DTS with empirical betas. While the DTS hedge produces lower-risk trades, the empirical-beta hedge produces returns that are less correlated with the market. A closer examination however, reveals that the low correlations are a result of unstable hedge ratios; the percentage of systematic risk is lowest for the DTS-hedged trades.

Essentially, the crux of the matter boils down to how to form the best ex ante estimate of market sensitivity for each security. Therefore, we supplement our study of the performance of hedged trades with an additional investigation into estimating market betas. Here, too, we find clear evidence that the DTS approach performs better than empirical betas; the difficulty we encounter when using historical betas as forward-looking estimates is consistent with extant research on measuring betas for equity portfolios.

## DATA AND HEDGING SIMULATION METHODOLOGY

We conduct the analysis using weekly spread data on constituents of the five-year CDX.NA.IG Index between November 2003 and December 2006, a total of 161 weekly samples. Out of the 84 issuers that have been in the CDX index throughout the study period, we identify five industry groups with sufficient representation throughout: consumer cyclical, consumer stable, industrials, financials, and utilities. From among these groups, comprising 63 issuers, we are able to form 392 distinct pairs of issuers from within the same industry.

We use the following procedure to evaluate the different hedging strategies for each traded pair. Given that we have selected to go long issuer $L$ and short issuer $S$, we size the positions such that each side of the trade is long one unit of market risk. In the first strategy, this equivalence is established in terms of exposure to parallel shifts in spread, or contributions to spread duration. Since we are trading CDS and not bonds, the appropriate measure is risky PV01, the sensitivity of the position to a 1 bp move in spread. The positions on the two sides of the trade are therefore given by

$$h_L^{RPV} = \frac{RPV01_M}{RPV01_L} \quad h_S^{RPV} = -\frac{RPV01_M}{RPV01_S} \tag{8.1}$$

where $M$ represents the market, which we take to be an equally weighted portfolio of all the issuers from the relevant industry group. Given that all of the swaps have maturities of about five years, and fairly low default probabilities, the risky PV01s are all very similar to each other. Thus, this method is essentially equivalent to hedging the notional amounts: long one unit of $L$ and short the same notional amount of $S$.

The second strategy, based on DTS, scales the position to be hedged with respect to market moves that take the form of relative changes in spread:

$$h_L^{DTS} = \frac{RPV01_M \cdot s_M}{RPV01_L \cdot s_L} \quad h_S^{DTS} = -\frac{RPV01_M \cdot s_M}{RPV01_S \cdot s_S} \tag{8.2}$$

The third hedging approach uses empirical betas. We measure the beta of each security relative to the market, taken as the slope coefficient in a regression of the weekly issuer spread change on the market spread change, over a trailing window initially set at 24 weeks. We then use these betas to size each side of the trade to a single unit of market exposure:

$$h_L^{beta} = \frac{RPV01_M}{RPV01_L} \cdot \frac{1}{\beta_L} \quad h_S^{beta} = -\frac{RPV01_M}{RPV01_S} \cdot \frac{1}{\beta_S} \tag{8.3}$$

As we assume that the views driving these trades are focused on the relative widening or tightening of the spreads over the near term, we ignore the carry portion of the return, and measure the performance of the trade strictly in terms of the impact of the weekly spread changes:

$$r_{L,S} = -h_L RPV01_L \Delta s_L - h_S RPV01_S \Delta s_S \tag{8.4}$$

Technically, $r$ represents the P&L per unit of market; as the positions are unfunded, the notion of return is not relevant. However, as we normalize these P&Ls with respect to a standard trade size, they can be considered analogous to returns.

## ANALYSIS OF HEDGING RESULTS

We track the performance of all trades over time, rebalancing monthly as described above. For each pair, we calculate various time series statistics including its P&L volatility, return correlation with the industry, market beta, systematic percentage of variance, hedge ratio, and the standard deviation of the hedge ratio over time. Each of these statistics is then averaged across all pairs. For the P&L volatility, correlation, and hedge ratio we also compute the dispersion across pairs. The results are summarized in Table 8.1.

Let us first compare the DTS hedge with the RPV, or notional-matched trade. The average P&L volatility produced by the DTS-weighted trade is 11.2 bps/week, versus 13.3 bps/week for the RPV-weighted trade. The P&L volatility of the DTS-weighted trade is also much more uniform across different pairs, as indicated by a dispersion of 2.7 bps/week, as opposed to 5.6 bps/week for the RPV-weighted trade. In addition, the DTS hedge was consistently more successful at removing market risk from the trade P&L, as indicated by both the absolute correlations and the standard deviation of the correlation with the market beta.

Next, we turn our attention to the beta-weighted hedge. If we use correlations as our guide, the beta hedging approach seems to achieve even better

**TABLE 8.1** Performance Statistics by Hedging Mechanism for Intra-Industry Pairwise CDS Trades

|  | RPV | DTS | Empirical Beta | DTS/2 |
|---|---|---|---|---|
| Average P&L volatility (bps/week) | 13.3 | 11.2 | 18.0 | 9.7 |
| Std. deviation of P&L volatility (over pairs) | 5.6 | 2.7 | 6.9 | 2.2 |
| Average absolute market correlation | 0.37 | 0.23 | 0.11 | 0.43 |
| Mean market correlation | 0.01 | 0.04 | 0.01 | 0.41 |
| Standard deviation of market correlation | 0.43 | 0.28 | 0.14 | 0.24 |
| Mean hedge ratio | 1.0 | 1.2 | 1.9 | 0.6 |
| Standard deviation of hedge ratio | 0.0 | 0.3 | 1.3 | 0.1 |
| Systematic percentage of variance | 18.6% | 12.6% | 18.9% | 27.0% |
| Market beta of trade P&L | 0.01 | 0.05 | 0.00 | 0.51 |

*Note:* Based on weekly data between April 2004 and December 2006. Empirical betas are computed using a trailing time window of 24 weeks. The results in the last column, labeled "DTS/2" are discussed in the section titled "The Minimum Variance Hedge."
*Sources:* Barclays Capital and Markit.

performance. The correlations of the trade P&L with that of the market are significantly closer to zero, whether we measure this by the average of their absolute values or by the cross-sectional standard deviation of these correlations across all pairs.

However, the performance of the beta-hedged strategy raises some red flags. First, it has a relatively large P&L volatility of 18.0 bps/week. Second, the dispersion of this volatility across pairs is very large indicating that many pairs produced a trade volatility of 25 bps/week or more. Should we be concerned about this? Or should we consider the increased return volatility of the strategy as an increased opportunity for generating alpha by making the right directional calls on issuers?

Let us first consider the expected volatility of the trade. The P&L volatility on a unit position in the market over this time period was about 7 bps/week. This is consistent with the 10% estimate of the long-term monthly volatility of systematic relative spread changes documented in Chapter 1. Given that the median market spread over this time period was about 30 bps, a weekly relative spread volatility of 5% would imply a spread volatility of about 1.5 bps/week, which when multiplied by the median market RPV01 of 4.7 would bring us to about 7 bps/week. Furthermore, the results in Chapters 1 and 2 suggest that the volatility of idiosyncratic spread changes is roughly similar in magnitude to that of systematic spread changes. Therefore, a position in a bond with a systematic P&L volatility of 7 bps/week should carry with it a non-systematic P&L volatility of similar magnitude. If, in the ideal hedge, we can get the systematic exposures of the long and short legs to offset each other, we should be left with two independent exposures of similar magnitude, giving us a net trade volatility that is roughly $\sqrt{2}$ times the market P&L volatility, or approximately 10 bps/week. While the DTS and RPV hedges come close to this target, the beta-hedged version of the trade significantly exceeds it.

We can conduct a simple performance attribution to separate between idiosyncratic volatility, which represents the opportunity to capitalize on one's views, and market volatility, which we are trying to avoid. Using data from the entire sample period, we calculate the empirical hedge ratio by regressing each security's return against the return of its industry. This ex post beta can be used to divide the weekly P&L of each security into a systematic part, defined simply as beta times the market return, and a non-systematic part, the time series of weekly residuals from the regression. This allows us to track how much of the weekly trade P&L is due to issuer-specific return, and how much is actually the result of systematic return from a poorly formed hedge. We can then measure the percentage of our trade P&L variance that results from systematic risk, which would ideally be as close to zero as possible. By this measure, we see that the beta-hedged strategy does not actually eliminate systematic risk as well as it seemed. Its 18.9% of variance from systematic risk is far greater than the 12.6% observed for the DTS hedge.

An additional red flag in the beta-hedged results was the instability of the hedge ratios. For each traded pair, we measured the standard deviation of the hedge ratio between the two legs of the trade. The average of this quantity is shown in Table 8.1. It is zero for the RPV strategy, for which the hedge ratio is constant at one, 0.3 for the DTS strategy, and a much larger 1.3 for the beta-weighted strategy.

What is happening here? A closer look at the time series data for the various traded pairs indicates that the beta-hedged strategy was indeed unstable, experiencing wild swings in its hedge ratio. The problem was most acute when the estimates of market beta of the hedge security over the trailing 24-week window fell to near-zero levels. This could happen either to an issuer whose spread remains very stable while the market exhibits considerable variation, or to one that experiences a lot of issuer-specific changes. In either case, it results in a very large position in the hedged security. If the low estimated beta turns out to be inaccurate, then we find ourselves seriously over-hedged. Rather than merely hedging out the market risk of the long position, we would actually have taken a leveraged short position in the market! If the low-beta estimate was obtained for the long position, then the opposite would be true, and we would be significantly under-hedged.

If the hedge produced by our trailing 24-week empirical betas was so poor, why did it produce such a pleasing result of low correlation with the market? The answer is simple: The estimation of empirical betas did not break down in a systematic way that would introduce a specific directional bias. While there were occasional large market exposures, these happened at random times and in random directions (long or short) for any given pair. For an exaggerated illustration, imagine a simple strategy that randomly goes long or short one unit of the market each week at the flip of a coin. This strategy takes nothing but market risk; yet the correlation of its return with the market return over the long term will be zero.

One can take various steps to make the estimation of empirical betas more robust. The most obvious one is to use more data points to form the estimates. To explore this possibility, we repeat our hedging analysis using a 52-week trailing window to calculate betas. The results are shown in Table 8.2.[3]

The evidence in Table 8.2 indicates that increasing the trailing window used to estimate beta has improved the stability of the beta-hedged strategy. The average P&L volatility has decreased from 18.0 bps/week to 15.2 bps/week, and its dispersion across pairs has decreased from 6.9 bps/week to 6.2 bps/week. Similarly, the percentage of variance from systematic risk has decreased from 18.9% to 13.9%, and the time variation of the hedge ratio has come down from 1.3 to 0.7. Nevertheless, by all of these measures, the DTS hedge retains its advantage over the empirical beta approach. Interestingly, the one apparent advantage that was enjoyed by the beta-based strategy, the low correlation between the net trade P&L and the market P&L, has now been mostly eliminated. Table 8.2 indicates that the correlations of the beta-hedged strategy are similar in magnitude to those of the DTS strategy. This confirms that the low correlations observed previously were spurious values due solely to the instability of the market exposure remaining in the hedged position.

## The Minimum Variance Hedge

In our discussion of the DTS hedge, we questioned whether the fact that this hedge achieves the lowest P&L volatility of the three schemes should be considered an advantage. According to a simple model of spread movement based on our DTS research, the hedge presented above can be shown to be the one that maximizes the information ratio, as well as generating a zero correlation with the market. It does not, however, result in the smallest

**TABLE 8.2** Performance Statistics by Hedging Mechanism for Intra-Industry Pairwise CDS Trades Based on a 52-Week Period

|  | RPV | DTS | Empirical Beta | DTS/2 | (1 + Beta)/2 |
|---|---|---|---|---|---|
| Average P&L volatility (bps/week) | 12.2 | 10.4 | 15.2 | 9.0 | 11.2 |
| Std. deviation of P&L volatility (over pairs) | 5.4 | 2.5 | 6.2 | 2.1 | 3.4 |
| Average absolute market correlation | 0.36 | 0.20 | 0.20 | 0.42 | 0.27 |
| Mean market correlation | −0.01 | 0.02 | −0.02 | 0.41 | −0.01 |
| Standard deviation of market correlation | 0.42 | 0.25 | 0.25 | 0.21 | 0.33 |
| Mean hedge ratio | 1.0 | 1.2 | 1.7 | 0.8 | 1.1 |
| Standard deviation of hedge ratio | 0.0 | 0.3 | 0.7 | 7.6 | 0.2 |
| Systematic percentage of variance | 17.5% | 8.9% | 13.9% | 24.1% | 12.9% |
| Market beta of trade P&L | −0.04 | 0.03 | −0.07 | 0.50 | −0.04 |

*Note:* Based on weekly data between April 2004 and December 2006. Empirical betas are computed using a trailing time window of 52 weeks. The column labeled "DTS/2" is discussed in the section titled "The Minimum Variance Hedge." The column labeled "(1 + Beta)/2" corresponds to an adjusted beta discussed in the section titled "A Closer Look at Forecasting Beta."
*Sources:* Barclays Capital and Markit.

possible trade volatility. This distinction goes to a different trade, in which we go long $h_L^{DTS}$ of issuer $L$, but short only $\frac{1}{2} \times h_S^{DTS}$ of issuer $S$.[4] The rationale can be explained as follows (a formal detailed proof is presented in the appendix): If we start with a naked long position in issuer $L$, we have exposures to both systematic and issuer-specific risk. As we start to go short issuer $S$ by incremental amounts, two things happen simultaneously to our position: While we slowly decrease the systematic exposure, we also add additional issuer-specific risk. At a certain point, the incremental reduction in systematic risk obtained by further growing the hedge is more than offset by the increase in non-systematic risk. However, given that our stated goal is to express a relative view on the two issuers without taking a view on the market, we continue to increase the size of the hedging leg of the trade until the market exposure is eliminated (so that the risk exposures are entirely focused on issuers' views), even if that results in a greater overall P&L volatility of the trade.

To illustrate the minimum variance hedge, we include a fourth column in Tables 8.1 and 8.2, in which we used only half the original size of the short position. As expected, this hedge achieves a lower P&L volatility than any of the other strategies explored. However, its performance has a much higher correlation with that of the market. In particular, the average beta of the trade P&L with respect to the market is about 0.5, as only half of the market exposure of the long position has been hedged away.

## A Closer Look at Forecasting Beta

Essentially, success or failure at our goal of constructing a trade that will isolate issuer-specific risk lies in our ability to forecast the market beta of each security over the return horizon. Suppose we are constructing a trade as of December 31, and plan to hold it for three months. The ideal betas for this hedge are the as-yet-unknown ones that we would calculate ex post using realized returns from January through March. What is the best forecast possible given the data at our disposal?

Let us compare two different methods for forecasting the market betas of individual CDS: (1) using the current ratio of an individual credit default swap's DTS to that of the market and (2) using the empirical beta of the individual CDS to the market from the prior period.[5] We divide the data set, containing roughly three years of weekly data, into non-overlapping periods of equal length, either 26 weeks or 52 weeks each. At the beginning of each period (except the first), we forecast the beta of each security using both methods. We then regress the actual beta that was observed during the period against each of these two candidate predictors. As we have 84 issuers in each period, our regressions have $5 \times 84$ observations when using the 26-week estimation window and $2 \times 84$ observations when using the 52-week estimation window. The results of these regressions are shown in Table 8.3.

Several things are apparent from Table 8.3. First, we see that the DTS ratio generates a better prediction of next-period beta, with $R$-squared values approximately twice as high as those using the prior-period empirical betas. Second, the regression results tell a very different story for the two models. When using the DTS ratio, the intercept is not statistically significant, and the coefficient is very close to one; that is, the DTS ratio as of the start of the period is an unbiased estimate of market beta in the coming period. For the empirical betas, this is not the case. The intercept plays nearly an equal role to the prior period beta, both in terms of the coefficients and the $t$-statistics. This means that if we want to forecast the next-period beta based on the

**TABLE 8.3** A Comparison of DTS Ratios and Past Empirical Betas as Predictors of Realized Market Betas

| Explanatory Variable for Predicting Beta | Time Period for Beta Estimation | $R^2$ | Regression Results | | |
|---|---|---|---|---|---|
| | | | Variable | Coefficients | t-stat. |
| Prior-period empirical beta | 26 weeks | 0.19 | Intercept | 0.56 | 9.83 |
| | | | Prior-period beta | 0.44 | 9.85 |
| Prior-period empirical beta | 52 weeks | 0.23 | Intercept | 0.49 | 5.63 |
| | | | Prior-period beta | 0.51 | 6.97 |
| DTS ratio | 26 weeks | 0.36 | Intercept | −0.09 | −1.10 |
| | | | DTS ratio | 1.09 | 15.31 |
| DTS ratio | 52 weeks | 0.50 | Intercept | −0.04 | −0.50 |
| | | | DTS ratio | 1.05 | 12.86 |

*Source:* Barclays Capital.

empirical beta observed in the prior period, the best forecast would be to assume that the beta will be halfway between the prior observation and 1. That is, betas are mean-reverting. This observation dovetails nicely with the established literature on empirical betas in equity markets:

> *A stock with a high historical beta in one period will most likely have a lower (but still higher than 1.0) beta in the subsequent period. Similarly, a stock with a low beta in one period will most likely have a higher (but less than 1.0) beta in the following period. In addition, forecasts of betas based on the fundamental attributes of the company, rather than its returns over the past, say, 60 months, turn out to be much better forecasts of future betas.* (Grinold and Kahn, 2000)

Just as Grinold and Kahn (2000) show that the predictive power of fundamentally based betas is superior to history-based betas for equities, the DTS-based hedge ratios are superior to empirical betas for bonds. This reflects the fact that spreads fully capture the most current information on the company fundamentals on average, unlike empirical betas which rely on historical data.

Rosenberg (1985) provides empirical evidence supporting this statement and shows how the predicted betas from Barra's E1 risk model do a much better job of forecasting next-period betas than just using historical betas. Rosenberg (1985) finds that a simple regression of the beta in one period on the historical beta from the prior period gives a coefficient of 0.58. Weinraub and Kuhlman (1994) note as well that "low beta stocks have greater beta variability.... This explains results of previous research that betas less than 1.0 are poor predictors of future returns."

The convincing results of these regressions, together with the corroboration from the published literature on equity market betas, suggests that when constructing trades using empirical betas, one should first adjust the betas toward one in this manner. Therefore, we repeat the historical back-testing using adjusted betas, defined as the average of 1.0 and the prior-period empirical beta. The results are reported in the last column of Table 8.2, under the heading "(1 + Beta)/2." The adjusted empirical beta exhibits improved performance according to some, but not all, of our metrics. In particular, the stability of the betas is far improved; the average standard deviation of the hedge ratio is reduced from 0.7 to 0.2, even lower than the 0.3 reported for the DTS hedge. The P&L volatility is reduced as well, coming quite close to that reported using DTS. However, there is a slight increase in both the correlation of the trade P&L with that of the market and the percentage of variance due to systematic risk.

## CONCLUSION

By the time we have finished adjusting our beta-hedge, we achieve performance that is not too different from that achieved by the DTS hedge, but still not quite as good. Along the way, we have run into a few of the complications that must be faced by anyone whose investment approach employs empirical betas. How much history should be used to estimate betas? How should extremely low or extremely high betas be treated? Should historical betas be used directly to form hedges, or adjusted toward 1?

Granted, if one has high-quality daily data to work with, one might be able to produce better estimates of beta than those we obtained. However, evidence from the equity market indicates that the difficulties in forecasting beta do not stem simply from a lack of daily data, but are rather fundamental in nature.

The DTS approach to forming hedges has several clear advantages. First, the calculation of the hedge ratio is simple and unambiguous. Second, the DTS ratio has shown itself to be both a good predictor of market beta at the individual issuer level and a reliable mechanism for neutralizing the market exposure of long–short trades. Finally, when dealing with long–short trades in swaps of matched maturities, the DTS-neutral trade will be carry-neutral as well, neatly avoiding the possibility of constructing a port-folio with negative carry.

It should be noted that the use of DTS ratios does not cover all pos-sible applications of empirical betas. The DTS ratio of two securities is highly indicative of the relative magnitudes of their future volatilities, but says nothing about their correlation. For the same-industry paired trades considered here, we assume that the systematic component of the issuers' spread changes are perfectly correlated; the calculation of the empirical betas of each security merely measure their sensitivities to industry-wide spread changes. For cross-sector trades, empirical betas would play the additional role of estimating the correlations between industries. However, cross-sector trades should be related to industry views, and are not pure expressions of issuer views.

While we have restricted our investigation to paired long–short trades in CDS, the results are applicable to a much broader portfolio context. Even portfolio managers who are able to take long–short positions in CDS do not necessarily hedge each trade on its own. Rather, long and short positions are established according to the manager's views, and the aggregate exposures of the portfolio are hedged to achieve the desired systematic exposures, either to be passive to the index or to actively reflect the manager's macro views. We believe that the right way to manage spread risk, consistent with the hedging mechanism illustrated in this chapter, is to measure industry exposures in terms of net DTS contributions. To maintain a neutral exposure, one would attempt to zero out the exposures in each industry. If a portfolio incorporates active industry exposures, the calculation of the overall risk should include correlations of relative spread movements across sectors.

## APPENDIX: HEDGING PAIR-WISE TRADES WITH SKILL

Throughout the chapter, we focus on hedging the systematic risk component of a long–short trade involving two individual securities. While setting the ratio of the two securities as the inverse of the ratio of their sensitivities to the market $h^*$ (irrespective of how the sensitivity measure is defined, such as empirical betas, DTS, or otherwise) should eliminate the exposure to systematic market moves, is this hedging approach optimal in terms of the expected profitability of the trade?

This approach may lead to large losses if the two securities move in the opposite directions than those predicted at the initiation of the trade. Clearly, one should take into account not just the systematic risk but also the idiosyncratic risk which results. Stated differently, the probability and magnitude of losses that may arise if the two securities diverge rather than converge should affect the construction of the trade. The probability of making the wrong directional call on the trade is inversely related to the investor's skill whereas the magnitude of loss in such a case is affected by the volatilities of the two securities.

In this appendix, we provide a more formal treatment of the problem facing a skilled investor who sets a pair-wise trade in two individual securities. (The framework can be easily extended to multiple securities.) We explicitly solve for the hedge ratios that minimize the total P&L volatility of the trade and alternatively maximize its information ratio.

Denote by $l, s$ the two securities that constitute the two legs of the trade and by $H$ the number of units we hold in security $s$ for each unit of security $l$ (i.e., the "hedge ratio"). The P&L of the trade for each period (month, day, etc.) is then

$$\Pi = \tilde{R}_l - H\tilde{R}_s \tag{8.5}$$

The return earned by the securities can be expressed as a combination of the market return and an idiosyncratic component:

$$R_i = \beta_i \tilde{R}_m + \tilde{\varepsilon}_i \quad i \in l, s \tag{8.6}$$

where $\tilde{\varepsilon}_l, \tilde{\varepsilon}_s$ are uncorrelated and have volatilities of $\sigma_l, \sigma_s$ respectively. The investor forms views on the idiosyncratic component of the securities' returns based on a set of signals. As in Grinold and Kahn (2000), we define skill as the correlation between the investor's predictions $\tilde{\varepsilon}_i^P$ and the actual realizations $\tilde{\varepsilon}_i$.[6] The actual idiosyncratic return realization can be written as a function of manager forecasts:

$$\tilde{\varepsilon}_i = \gamma_i \tilde{\varepsilon}_i^P + \upsilon_i$$

where

$$\upsilon_i \sim N\left(0, \sigma_{\upsilon_i}^2\right) \tag{8.7}$$

Based on our definition of skill, for a manager with skill level $\rho$, we have $\gamma_i = \sqrt{\rho^2 \sigma_{\upsilon_i}^2 / (1 - \rho^2) \sigma_{\varepsilon_i^P}^2}$. Also note that since $\text{Var}(\tilde{\varepsilon}_i | \tilde{\varepsilon}_i^P) = \sigma_{\upsilon_i}^2$ we get that $\sigma_{\upsilon_i}^2 = (1 - \rho^2)\sigma_i^2$. Therefore, the idiosyncratic return volatility conditional on the investor forecast ranges from zero (for a perfectly skilled investor) to the total (or unconditional) volatility of idiosyncratic return for an investor with no skill.[7]

## Minimum Volatility Hedge

The volatility of the trade conditional on the investor predictions is

$$\text{Var}\left(\Pi|\tilde{\varepsilon}_l^P, \tilde{\varepsilon}_s^P\right) = \text{Var}(\tilde{R}_l) - H^2\text{Var}(\tilde{R}_s) - 2\text{Cov}(\tilde{R}_l, H\tilde{R}_s)$$

$$= \sigma_m^2(\beta_l - H\beta_s)^2 + \text{Var}\left(\tilde{\varepsilon}_l|\tilde{\varepsilon}_l^P\right) + H^2\text{Var}\left(\tilde{\varepsilon}_s|\tilde{\varepsilon}_s^P\right)$$

Differentiating this expression with respect to $H$ and setting to zero yields:

$$H_{\text{min variance}} = \left(\frac{\beta_l}{\beta_s}\right)\left[\frac{1}{1 + (1 - \rho^2)(\sigma_s^2/\beta_s^2\sigma_m^2)}\right] \tag{8.8}$$

Looking at equation (8.8), we see that in addition to the ratio of market betas, the hedge ratio is influenced by two terms: the manager skill and the ratio of security's idiosyncratic and systematic volatilities. The first represents the likelihood that the manager made a wrong call in forming the trade since the lower the skill the more likely is this to happen. This is why except for the case of perfect skill ($\rho = 1$), the hedge ratio is always smaller than $b^* = \beta_l/\beta_s$, which means the trade is not fully immune against market movements. The second term represents the relative magnitude of losses from systematic risk versus idiosyncratic risk. Essentially, by departing from $b^*$ we are willing to accept some exposure to systematic risk in order to offset the loss that is realized should the securities' prices diverge.

When the idiosyncratic and systematic volatilities are roughly equal, the minimum variance hedge would converge to one half of $b^*$ (i.e., $H_{\text{min variance}} \to \frac{1}{2}(\frac{\beta_l}{\beta_s})$ as $\rho \to 0$).

## Maximum Information Ratio Hedge

If the investor goal were instead to maximize the information ratio of the trade, potentially taking more risk in exchange for higher expected return, we have

$$\frac{\partial\left(E(\Pi|\tilde{\varepsilon}_l^P, \tilde{\varepsilon}_s^P)/\text{Var}(\Pi|\tilde{\varepsilon}_l^P, \tilde{\varepsilon}_s^P)\right)}{\partial H} = 0 \tag{8.9}$$

From equation (8.7), we get that $E(\tilde{\varepsilon}_i|\tilde{\varepsilon}_i^P) = \gamma_i\tilde{\varepsilon}_i^p$ and, therefore, $E(\Pi|\tilde{\varepsilon}_l^P, \tilde{\varepsilon}_s^P) = \gamma_l\tilde{\varepsilon}_l^p - H\gamma_s\tilde{\varepsilon}_s^p$.[8] After differentiating and some tedious algebra we get the following quadratic equation for $H_{\max IR}$

$$H^2 \gamma_s \varepsilon_s^p \left(\frac{1}{b^*}\right) - 2H\gamma_l \varepsilon_l^p \left(\frac{1}{b^*}\right) + \left(\frac{1}{1+\phi_s}\right) \left[2\gamma_l \varepsilon_l^p - \gamma_s \varepsilon_s^p b^*(1+\phi_l)\right] = 0$$

(8.10)

where $\phi_i = \frac{(1-\rho^2)\sigma_s^2}{\sigma_m^2 \beta_s^2}$ is the ratio of (conditional) idiosyncratic volatility to systematic volatility.

Again relying on our previous findings that idiosyncratic volatility is roughly equal to systematic volatility, we get that at the limit $H_{\max IR} \rightarrow \left(\frac{\beta_l}{\beta_s}\right)$ as $\rho \rightarrow 0$.[9]

## NOTES

1. The results were qualitatively similar when trades were hedged relative to a broad market index instead.
2. The appendix presents an analytical framework for deriving a closed-form solution for the hedge ratio that would maximize the trade information ratio.
3. Note that when comparing Table 8.2 to Table 8.1, only results for the beta-hedged strategy change materially; the differences in the performance of the other hedging strategies is due solely to the change in the reporting period that was necessary for the formation of the first beta estimate.
4. The key assumption that leads to this result is that the magnitude of relative spread volatility is the same for systematic and idiosyncratic risk, as discussed above. If this is not the case, the formula for the minimum variance hedge will depend on the ratio of these volatility levels.
5. In this part of the analysis, we do not use separate industry-specific indexes for each issuer. Rather, we investigate the betas of each issuer to a broad market index formed as an equal-weighted average of all 84 issuers in our data set. This helps us avoid statistical problems for issuers from poorly represented industries.
6. In the case of a zero skill investor the correlation would be zero whereas for a 100% skilled investor the correlation would be 1. We assume that the investor is equally skillful across all securities.
7. This can be shown by taking the unconditional volatilities of the terms in equation (8.7) and substituting the expression for $\gamma_i$.
8. Recall that the investor has no skill in predicting systematic market changes and in addition we assume that the unconditional expected market return over the period is zero.
9. Equation 8.10 can now be written as $H(\frac{1}{b^*} - 1)[(H(\frac{1}{b^*}) + 1)\gamma_s \varepsilon_s^p - 2\gamma_l \varepsilon_l^p] = 0$ with $H = b^*$ being one solution.

### CHAPTER 9

# Positioning along the Credit Curve

## Risk and Reward in Credit Slope Trades

**D**oes the risk-reward profile of corporate bonds vary with maturity? A common theme among credit portfolio managers is that short-dated corporate bonds outperform long-dated corporates. To capitalize on this idea, many managers implement duration-neutral *credit steepener trades* (which combine a long position in short-dated corporates and a corresponding short position in long-dated corporates), with the goal of earning consistent spread carry as well as potentially benefiting from a steepening of the credit curve. Naik, Devarajan, and Wong (2007), for example, examine the performance of such trades over the economic cycle, and find that duration-neutral credit steepeners generate positive alpha over the long run, with high performance in bullish credit markets and lower performance in bearish markets.

This chapter analyzes the merits of a "credit steepener" as a carry trade across sectors and time-periods. We do not express active views on changes in the slope of the credit curve, but attempt to earn spread carry while remaining hedged against changes in spread levels. Consistent with the DTS approach espoused throughout this book, we use DTS rather than spread duration as the basis for sizing the hedges. Such trades, when constructed mechanically based on index partitions, can be exposed to substantial idiosyncratic risk. We therefore investigate a strategy that matches long and short bond positions on an issuer by issuer basis.

Consistent with Naik et al. (2007), we find that a credit steepener strategy earns significant positive returns over the long run. The use of DTS to scale the long and short positions results in lower return volatility as compared with a duration-neutral credit steepener. In addition, employing the same set of issuers in the construction of the long and short positions substantially reduces idiosyncratic risk and, consequently, drawdowns that could otherwise result from downgrades or defaults. Incorporating DTS and issuer-matching into the construction of the credit steepener strategy, and exploiting the fairly low correlations of the trade across sectors, generate high information ratios in historical back-testing. This strategy is potentially an attractive source of alpha for credit managers.

## DATA AND METHODOLOGY

A credit steepener entails long positions in short-dated bonds and offsetting (short) positions in long-dated bonds that are combined to neutralize the overall exposure to secular spread changes. Traditionally, this neutrality has been implemented by hedging spread duration. The return of the duration-hedged steepener strategy can be written as

$$R = ER_S - \left(D_S/D_L\right) ER_L \tag{9.1}$$

where $D_S$ and $D_L$ are the spread durations of the short- and long-dated corporate bonds, respectively. $ER_S$ and $ER_L$ are excess returns over duration-matched treasuries for the short- and long-dated corporates, respectively. These can be expressed in terms of spread carry and spread change returns (ignoring second order effects), as follows:

$$ER_S \approx S_S \Delta t - D_S \Delta S_S \tag{9.2}$$
$$ER_L \approx S_L \Delta t - D_L \Delta S_L$$

where $S_S$ and $S_L$ denote spread levels. Hence, (9.1) can be rewritten as

$$R \approx \underbrace{D_S \left( \frac{S_S}{D_S} - \frac{S_L}{D_L} \right) \Delta t}_{\text{CarryReturn}} + \underbrace{D_S \left( \Delta S_L - \Delta S_S \right)}_{\text{CurveReturn}} \tag{9.3}$$

By construction, the strategy is unaffected by parallel shifts in spreads, and benefits when the credit curve steepens (i.e., $\Delta S_L > \Delta S_S$). In addition, the strategy can deliver gains even in periods of mild flattening due to the positive spread carry it earns. To understand why this typically has been the case, we examine historical spread data from the U.S. Corporate Index between February 1993 and November 2007. Each month, we partition the

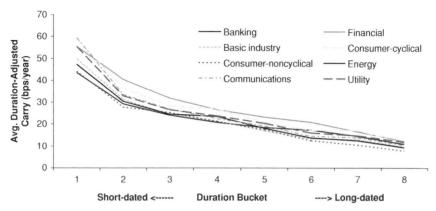

**FIGURE 9.1** Duration-Adjusted Carry by Sector and Duration Bucket
*Note:* Bonds in each sector are partitioned into eight equally populated buckets based on spread duration. Average spread over duration for a bucket is computed as the market-weighted average of the ratio of spread to spread duration of each bond in the bucket.
*Source:* Barclays Capital.

bonds in each index sector into eight equally populated duration buckets.[1] The partition is designed to strike a balance between having an adequate number of bonds in each bucket and achieving a wide range of maturities.

Figure 9.1 shows the average *duration-adjusted carry* over the sample period for the eight duration buckets, separately by sector. Duration-adjusted carry is computed as the (market-weighted) average of the ratio of spread to spread duration. While Table 9.1 suggests that the spread curve is generally upward sloping, the duration-adjusted carry curve is inverted, with shorter-maturity bonds offering higher spread per unit of duration. As a result, a duration-hedged credit steepener would earn a positive carry return (see equation 9.3) on average. In addition, the steepener strategy benefits from the roll-down effect. Since the short-to-intermediate part of the credit curve is typically steeper than the intermediate-to-long part, the long position in the short-dated bonds gains more (as it rolls down the curve) than the losses incurred on the short position, provided the spread curve is unchanged.

If changes in the slope of the spread curve are indeed proportional, then based on the results in Chapter 8, a credit steepener strategy which is DTS-neutral should exhibit a better risk-return profile compared to an otherwise similar duration-neutral steepener.[2]

**TABLE 9.1**  Summary Statistics for Corporate Bonds by Duration Buckets

| Bucket | Average Duration (years) | Average Maturity (years) | Average Spread (bps) |
|--------|--------------------------|--------------------------|----------------------|
| 1 | 1.6 | 1.8 | 77 |
| 2 | 2.7 | 3.1 | 87 |
| 3 | 3.7 | 4.3 | 97 |
| 4 | 4.7 | 5.7 | 105 |
| 5 | 5.8 | 7.5 | 119 |
| 6 | 6.8 | 9.2 | 109 |
| 7 | 9.0 | 16.2 | 125 |
| 8 | 11.9 | 30.1 | 124 |

*Note:* Based on corporate bonds comprising the U.S. Corporate Index between February 1993 and November 2007. Bonds in each sector are first assigned monthly into one of eight equally populated buckets based on spread duration. The bond population in each duration bucket (with a similar ranking) is then combined across sectors.
*Source:* Barclays Capital.

Using the previous notation, the return to a "DTS-neutral steepener" can be written as:[3]

$$R = ER_S - \left(DTS_S / DTS_L\right) ER_L \qquad (9.4)$$

$$\approx \underbrace{S_S \left(1 - D_S / D_L\right) \Delta t}_{\text{CarryReturn}} + \underbrace{D_S S_S \left(\frac{\Delta S_L}{S_L} - \frac{\Delta S_S}{S_S}\right)}_{\text{CurveReturn}}$$

We have seen that the duration-neutral steepener usually earns a positive spread carry; equation (9.4) makes it clear that for the DTS-neutral steepener this is always the case. The source of this positive carry is that the dollar amount in the (short-dated) long position is much larger than the dollar amount in the short position of this trade. However, because the strategy is net long (in dollar terms), it is exposed to loss given default.

Figure 9.2 plots average excess returns by sector and duration bucket, after scaling each bucket return by the ratio of its DTS to that of bucket 1. The resulting curve is downward sloping, implying that for the same DTS level, short-dated corporates provide higher excess returns on average than long-dated corporates. Therefore, the credit steepener strategy is primarily a carry trade, while the exposure to changes in spread curve slope drive the

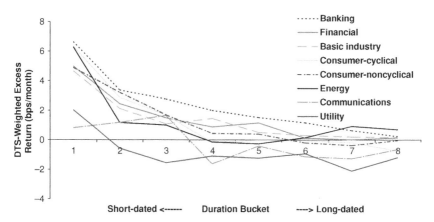

**FIGURE 9.2** Average DTS-Weighted Excess Returns by Sector and Duration Bucket

*Note:* Bonds are assigned monthly (February 1993–November 2007) to one of eight equally populated buckets based on their spread duration. Excess returns (over treasuries) of each bucket are scaled by the ratio of its DTS to that of the shortest maturity bucket (bucket 1) within each respective sector.

*Source:* Barclays Capital.

volatility in returns. In general, the DTS steepener boasts higher carry than the duration-hedged steepener. Since the spread curve is typically upward sloping, the DTS steepener has a smaller dollar position in the long-dated bucket for a given dollar position in the short-dated bucket.[4]

Figure 9.2 also reveals some differences across sectors. From February 1993 to November 2007, the banking sector provided one of the highest performance differentials across duration buckets, while utility and communications provided the lowest. This is in contrast to Figure 9.1, in which all sectors exhibit similar duration-adjusted carry curves. The smaller performance differential between short-dated and long-dated buckets for utility and communications can therefore be attributed to the spread curve rather than the carry component of returns. We examine this issue in more detail later.

## EMPIRICAL ANALYSIS

In the following sections, we examine the performance of credit steepeners constructed using DTS-based weightings. In order to magnify the spread-carry component of the strategy, we obtain long exposure to bonds in the shortest duration bucket (bucket 1) and short exposure to bonds in the longest duration bucket (bucket 8).

With performance measured in terms of excess returns over duration-matched treasuries, the strategy is basically a box trade: It buys bonds in bucket 1, going short treasuries with the same market value and duration, and sells bonds in bucket 8, going long treasuries with the same market value and duration. In a cash-only portfolio, position sizes are therefore limited by the amount of capital that results from selling the short end of the treasury component of the portfolio.

Table 9.2 displays several performance statistics for the strategy. The median strategy returns are in the range of 5 to 6 bps/month, and are quite similar to the average spread carry. This shows that in a typical month, the strategy accomplishes its goal of earning the carry. However, the average return varies significantly across sectors, from a low of 1.4 bps/month (communications) to a high of 6.4 bps/month (banking).

The difference between the mean and median return reflects the risks inherent in the strategy. Its performance can exhibit large negative tails as a result of issuer downgrades and defaults that occur in some months. For example, in April 2002, the strategy would have realized a loss of 5.04% in the Communications sector due to the downgrades surrounding WorldCom. The strategy in that month included long positions in short-dated WorldCom debt, while the offsetting short position in the longest-duration communications bucket did not happen to contain any exposure to WorldCom.

### Idiosyncratic Risk Reduction with Issuer Matching

The results in Table 9.2 highlight the large issuer-specific risk that could be involved in a credit-steepener. We therefore refine the strategy such that the long and short DTS exposures are matched not just at the sector level, but at the level of individual issuers. To accomplish this, we first identify the subset of issuers that have outstanding bonds in both the short- and long-duration buckets (i.e., buckets 1 and 8). We then weight the trade such that the overall exposures to each issuer are matched to have the same DTS contribution on the long and short side of the trade.

Formally, the return of the strategy $R$ is the (weighted) sum of returns $R_i$ of the DTS-neutral positions in each issuer $i$,

$$R = \sum_{\text{issuer } i} w_i R_i \qquad (9.5)$$

**TABLE 9.2** Performance of DTS-Neutral Steepener (bps/month)

| | Banking | Financial | Basic Industry | Consumer Cyclical | Consumer Non-cyclical | Energy | Communications | Utility |
|---|---|---|---|---|---|---|---|---|
| Average spread carry | 4.3 | 5.4 | 5.8 | 6.6 | 5.1 | 5.8 | 6.9 | 6.4 |
| **Performance Statistics** | | | | | | | | |
| Median | 5.9 | 5.4 | 5.6 | 6.2 | 5.5 | 4.7 | 4.9 | 6 |
| Average | 6.4 | 4.8 | 4.5 | 7.1 | 4.9 | 5.6 | 1.4 | 3.2 |
| Volatility | 11.9 | 20.5 | 18.8 | 21.7 | 15.5 | 17.7 | 62.1 | 41.6 |
| IR (annualized) | 1.9 | 0.8 | 0.8 | 1.1 | 1.1 | 1.1 | 0.1 | 0.3 |
| Maximum loss | −40 | −116 | −148 | −99 | −81 | −115 | −504 | −3.58 |
| Maximum gain | 64 | 82 | 51 | 91 | 71 | 61 | 377 | 141 |
| 95% VaR | −10 | −21 | −22 | −35 | −17 | −16 | −45 | −16 |

*Note:* Bonds are partitioned into eight equally populated buckets based on spread duration, monthly during February 1993–November 2007. The strategy is long one unit of the shortest duration bucket versus a DTS-weighted short position in the longest duration bucket.

*Source:* Barclays Capital.

where $w_i$ represents the relative weight of an issuer in the short-duration bucket (bucket 1), and $R_i$ is the return on a single-issuer DTS steepener trade:

$$w_i = MV_{i,S}/MV_S \qquad (9.6)$$

$$R_i = ER_{i,S} - (DTS_{i,S}/DTS_{i,L})ER_{i,L}$$

$MV_{i,S}$ is the total market value of long positions in issuer $i$ bonds (bucket 1), while $MV_S$ is the total market value of included bonds in that bucket. $ER_{i,S}$ (excess return) and $DTS_{i,S}$ are calculated as the market value-weighted averages of excess return and DTS across all issuer $i$ bonds in the short-duration bucket, and similarly for the long-duration bucket. Since the long and short positions of each issuer have the same DTS, the aggregate portfolio is DTS-neutral by construction.

How well does the issuer-matched steepener protect against spread widening in specific issuers? Comparing the revised strategy's performance (Table 9.3) with that of the basic (unmatched) steepener (Table 9.2) reveals that issuer matching leads to a significant reduction in various measures of risk (volatility, VaR, maximum loss). Information ratios are typically higher, ranging from 0.2 (utility) to 1.8 (banking).

While using the same set of issuers on the long and short sides of the steepeners reduces idiosyncratic risk, the strategy is not totally immune to extreme events. When an issuer is near default, its bonds tend to trade on price rather than spread. To protect against default, any long-short positions should be matched on a market-value basis rather than DTS-hedged. Since steepener strategies (irrespective of the hedging approach) are net long market value, they are exposed to loss given default.

Figure 9.3 plots the historical performance of the issuer-matched DTS steepener in the Utility sector. The strategy experienced a large loss of 4.73% in July 2002 as a result of defaults and extreme spread widening in several issuers (e.g., El Paso Energy Corp, PSEG Energy Holdings, and Williams Holdings of Delaware).[5] Excluding the July 2002 performance figure increases the information ratio of the strategy from 0.2 to 0.8. This highlights the potential for incurring a large loss even after positions are issuer-matched and DTS-hedged, as well as the impact a single event can have on the performance statistics of an entire strategy.

### Combining Issuer-Matched DTS Steepeners across Sectors

As a credit steepener consists of offsetting long and short positions within a sector, its performance should be independent of sector-specific factors. In practice, when we back-tested the performance of the strategy in each

**TABLE 9.3** Performance of DTS-Neutral Steepener with Issuer Matching (bps/month)

| | Banking | Financial | Basic Industry | Consumer Cyclical | Consumer Non-cyclical | Energy | Communications | Utility |
|---|---|---|---|---|---|---|---|---|
| Average spread carry | 4.0 | 4.5 | 4.9 | 5.2 | 3.9 | 4.7 | 5.0 | 5.9 |
| Performance Statistics | | | | | | | | |
| Median | 4.7 | 5.4 | 5.1 | 5.4 | 3.8 | 4.7 | 4.6 | 5.9 |
| Average | 5.9 | 5.5 | 4.9 | 6.7 | 4.2 | 5.5 | 4.8 | 3.1 |
| Volatility | 11.6 | 14.6 | 13.3 | 15.1 | 9.1 | 12.7 | 19.9 | 44.2 |
| IR (annualized) | 1.8 | 1.3 | 1.3 | 1.5 | 1.6 | 1.5 | 0.8 | 0.2 |
| Maximum loss | −38 | −80 | −66 | −80 | −30 | −57 | −121 | −473 |
| Maximum gain | 61 | 51 | 52 | 54 | 40 | 50 | 73 | 146 |
| 95% VaR | −10 | −11 | −13 | −13 | −10 | −14 | −19 | −25 |

*Note:* Bonds are partitioned into eight equally populated buckets based on spread duration, monthly during February 1993–November 2007. Issuers that do not have outstanding bonds in both the short- and long-duration buckets are excluded. Bonds (aggregated by issuers) are matched to have the same DTS contribution on the long and short side of the trade. The strategy is long one unit of the shortest duration bucket versus a DTS-weighted short position in the longest duration bucket.
*Source:* Barclays Capital.

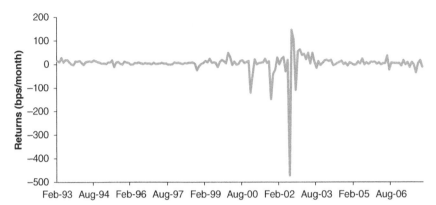

**FIGURE 9.3**   Performance of Issuer-Matched Utilities Steepener
*Note:* Utility bonds are partitioned monthly into eight equally populated buckets
based on spread duration during February 1993–November 2007. Issuers that do
not have outstanding bonds in both the short- and long-duration buckets are
excluded. Bond positions are scaled such that the aggregate DTS contributions to
each issuer are matched on the long and short sides of the trade. The strategy is
long one unit of the shortest duration bucket versus a DTS-weighted short
position in the longest duration bucket.
*Source:* Barclays Capital.

sector separately, we found that the pairwise correlations of strategy returns
in different sectors ranged from 0.3 to 0.6. While these figures suggest the
existence of at least one systematic (common) slope factor that drives performance, the fairly low correlations also indicate that implementing the
strategy simultaneously across multiple sectors can further diversify risk.

Table 9.4 reports performance statistics for the U.S. Credit Index and
for several variants of the credit steepener strategy when implemented
simultaneously across all sectors. The total size of the positions in each
sector is based on its market value relative to the aggregate value of the U.S.
Credit Index.[6]

Several important conclusions can be drawn from Table 9.4. First,
the aggregate issuer-matched DTS steepener has lower volatility and a
more symmetric distribution when compared to the sector-level results in
Table 9.3. Second, replacing spread duration with DTS and the introduction
of issuer-matching does not affect performance but reduces risk considerably. Volatility declines from 17.5 bps/month to 11.4 bps/month, and tail
risk, as measured by the 95% Value at Risk (VaR), is cut in half, from
−27 bps/month to −13 bps/month. Consequently, the annualized information ratio increases from 1.0 to 1.6.

Third, as a passive carry trade, the issuer-matched DTS steepener compares favorably to simply holding the U.S. Credit Index over the same time

**TABLE 9.4** Performance of Aggregate Credit Steepener vs. U.S. Credit Index

| Statistics (bps/mo) | Duration Steepener | Issuer-Matched Duration Steepener | Issuer-Matched DTS Steepener | U.S. Credit Index Excess Returns |
|---|---|---|---|---|
| Median | 6 | 5.3 | 5.5 | 11.7 |
| Average | 5.1 | 5.4 | 5.1 | 1.2 |
| Volatility | 17.5 | 13.3 | 11.4 | 61 |
| IR (annualized) | 1 | 1.4 | 1.6 | 0.1 |
| 95% VaR | −27 | −13.3 | −13 | −89 |
| Maximum loss | −73 | −52 | −49 | −270 |
| Maximum gain | 63 | 52 | 43 | 242 |

*Note:* The aggregate credit steepener is based on combining the sector-level strategy positions across all eight sectors weighted by their market values in the U.S. Credit Index. Excess returns are computed relative to a duration-matched portfolio of treasuries.
*Source:* Barclays Capital.

period. While the index performed well in many months, with a median return of 11.7 bps/month, it experienced high volatility (61 bps/month) and large drawdowns. Because of these drawdowns, the U.S. Credit Index had low average excess returns of 1.2 bps/month, with an information ratio of just 0.1. In contrast, the aggregate issuer-matched DTS steepener earned an average return of 5.1 bps/month and boasted an information ratio of 1.6.

How did the aggregate issuer-matched DTS strategy fare in different market periods? Figure 9.4 shows the histogram of strategy returns for months in which the U.S. Credit Index realized negative excess returns. The strategy had positive performance in 73% of these months, with an average return of 3.5 bps/month, compared with 6 bps/month when credit excess returns were positive. Hence, while the strategy performs better when credit as an asset class outperforms treasuries, it performed well even in most months when credit underperformed. It is not surprising, therefore, that the correlation between the strategy and the U.S. Credit Index was only 0.24.

Table 9.5 demonstrates that the annual performance of the strategy was positive in all years except 2007. The performance in 2007 illustrates that while the strategy performs well over the long term, it is susceptible to losses during market selloffs. The drawdowns stem from the fact that spread carry is not enough to cushion losses from a flattening of the credit curve due to a sharp rise in short-term default expectations. Moreover, the strategy is negatively convex, which can hurt performance during periods of high volatility.

The strategy's risk-return profile is akin to a passive strategy of writing out-of-the-money puts on the market. Writing out-of-the-money puts is

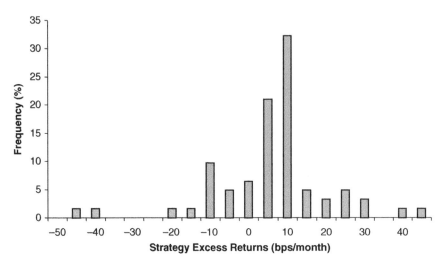

**FIGURE 9.4** Aggregate Issuer-Matched DTS Steepener Performance by Market State Source (strategy performance in months of negative excess returns for the U.S. Credit Index)
*Note:* The aggregate Issuer-matched DTS steepener is based on combining the sector-level strategy positions across all eight sectors weighted by their market values in the U.S. Credit Index. Excess returns are computed relative to a duration-matched portfolio of treasuries.
*Source:* Barclays Capital.

profitable in the long run, earning a consistent premium while being protected from small decreases in the price of the underlying asset. It is only during sharp selloffs that the strategy suffers large drawdowns.

Table 9.6 further illustrates the nature of the strategy in several historical episodes of a sharp increase in market risk aversion (characterized by large negative excess returns for the U.S. Credit Index and spikes in the VIX index). While the long-term performance of the issuer-matched DTS steepener is not highly correlated across sectors, the correlation rises in periods of widespread market turmoil, with returns being mostly negative.

## Implementing Credit Steepeners with Credit Default Swaps

Can the credit steepener strategy as a carry trade be implemented using CDS? The CDS market offers at least two attractive features: higher liquidity and larger scale. The positions that can be established in cash-only

**TABLE 9.5** Aggregate Issuer-Matched DTS Steepener Yearly Performance

| Year | Issuer-Matched DTS Steepener (bps) | U.S. Credit Index Excess Returns (bps) | Relative Performance (bps) |
|------|------|------|------|
| 1993 | 11.6 | 7.7 | 3.9 |
| 1994 | 4.7 | 4.7 | 0 |
| 1995 | 6.1 | 9.4 | −3.3 |
| 1996 | 3.8 | 10.2 | −6.4 |
| 1997 | 2.1 | −2.3 | 4.4 |
| 1998 | 0.9 | −18.3 | 19.2 |
| 1999 | 6.9 | 14.5 | −7.6 |
| 2000 | 10.2 | −34.7 | 44.9 |
| 2001 | 0.4 | 21.1 | −20.7 |
| 2002 | 8.1 | −14.5 | 22.6 |
| 2003 | 12.3 | 42.1 | −29.8 |
| 2004 | 6.0 | 13.5 | −7.5 |
| 2005 | 3.1 | −7.0 | 10.1 |
| 2006 | 4.1 | 9.6 | −5.5 |
| 2007 | −2.9 | −40.7 | 37.8 |

*Source:* Barclays Capital.

portfolios are limited by the total size of the short end of the treasury portion of the portfolio, which is sold to finance the long position in short-dated corporates. Implementing the strategy with CDS provides flexibility in sizing the trade.

We examine the performance of the DTS-neutral steepener using investment grade CDS from February 2004 through November 2007. Monthly CDS returns are calculated (from the perspective of the protection seller) as follows:

$$R_{CDS} = \left( \underbrace{s_0 \Delta t}_{\text{CarryReturn}} + \underbrace{RPV01_t \, (s_0 - s_t)}_{\text{SpreadChangeReturn}} \right) \Big/ \text{Notional} \qquad (9.7)$$

where $s_0$ and $s_t$ are the swap spread at the beginning and end of the period, respectively. $RPV01_t$ is the risky PV01 at the end of the calculation period.[7]

The strategy involves selling 5-year protection and buying 10-year protection, in the ratio of their $RPV01$ times spread (Ranguelova [2004] provides a discussion of duration-neutral CDS steepeners). Returns for this

**TABLE 9.6** Performance of Issuer-Matched DTS Steepener during Historical Risk Flares (bps/month)

| Month | U.S. Credit Index Excess Returns | Percent Change VIX | Banking | Finance | Basic Industry | Consumer Cyclical | Consumer Non-cyclical | Energy | Communications | Utility |
|---|---|---|---|---|---|---|---|---|---|---|
| Nov-07 | -270 | 23% | 3 | -33 | -31 | -6 | -29 | -22 | -31 | -13 |
| Aug-98 | -266 | 79% | -15 | -2 | -32 | -1 | -30 | -16 | -17 | 8 |
| Sep-01 | -204 | 28% | -15 | 15 | -3 | -18 | 1 | -21 | -11 | 13 |
| Jul-07 | -159 | 45% | 10 | -5 | 9 | -2 | 1 | 0 | -6 | -2 |

*Note:* Returns are in bps/month. VIX, an index of implied volatilities of S&P 500 options, is a widely used barometer of market volatility and investor sentiment.
*Source:* Barclays Capital.

strategy can therefore be written as

$$R = R_5 - \left( \frac{RPV01_5s_5}{RPV01_{10}s_{10}} \right) R_{10} \tag{9.8}$$

where $R_5$ and $R_{10}$ are monthly returns on the 5-year and 10-year CDS, respectively, calculated using equation (9.7). *RPV01* and spread $s$ in the hedge ratio are as of the beginning of the month.

Over the sample period (February 2004–November 2007), an equal-weighted portfolio of all 373 issuers earned an average of 1.6 bps/month, with an annualized information ratio of 0.6. For comparison, the strategy performance was 2.3 bps/month (with an annualized information ratio of 0.84) when implemented over the same period in the cash market.

However, the strategy returns using CDS and bonds are not directly comparable. First, bond excess returns are computed over treasuries, whereas CDS returns are relative to swaps. Second, the cash strategy is implemented on the extreme ends of the credit curve in order to maximize spread carry, while the synthetic strategy is implemented with 5- and 10-year contracts, which are the most liquid. Third, the issuer compositions of the two strategies are drastically different. The cash strategy selects issuers that have outstanding debt in the two selected maturity buckets, and weights them by market-value; the CDS strategy selects issuers for which CDS data are available for 5-year and 10-year contracts, and weights all issuers equally.

The performance of the strategy using CDS can possibly be improved by selling protection in shorter maturities, rather than at the five-year tenor. Nevertheless, because of the relatively short history available for CDS data, it is not yet possible to draw conclusions about the long-term performance of the strategy. Also, while the DTS steepener using CDS may be valuable for investors looking to express active views on specific issuers, it may not be appropriate as a passive strategy.

## CONCLUSION

A popular theme among credit portfolio managers in the U.S. investment-grade market is that short-dated credit offers a more attractive risk-return profile than longer-dated credit. Naik et al. (2007) show that duration-neutral credit steepeners generate positive alpha in the long run, but their performance decreases during bearish market conditions.

This chapter reexamines the properties of credit steepeners while making several improvements to the strategy. First, systematic spread exposure is neutralized using DTS rather than spread duration, leveraging the results from Chapter 1 showing that spread changes are proportional to spread levels. Second, we use the extreme ends of the credit curve in order to maximize spread carry. Third, to reduce idiosyncratic risk, the same set of issuers is used for both the long and short positions. Finally, positions are established separately in each sector and then combined based on relative market weights to take advantage of the fairly low correlations across sectors.

We find that these modifications to the basic duration-neutral steepener strategy result in consistent and significant positive performance over a period of 15 years, achieving an information ratio of 1.6. The strategy earns positive returns, on average, even in months when the U.S. Credit Index has negative excess returns. However, we also show that the strategy is susceptible to large draw-downs during market selloffs.

Overall, as a passive strategy, the issuer-matched DTS steepener performs well over the long run, with a low correlation to credit excess returns (0.24). Credit portfolio managers can, therefore, use this trade to generate alpha in their portfolios. Additionally, managers can then use their views on the slope of the credit curve, carry strength, and risk aversion in the markets to make judgment calls on top of this passive strategy.

## NOTES

1. Bonds are classified into one of the following sectors: banking and brokerage, finance, basic industry and capital goods, consumer cyclical, consumer non-cyclical, energy, communications, technology, and utility.
2. The DTS-neutral steepener may experience a negative return even if the curve steepens. For example, this could occur if the long end of the curve widens by more than the short end, but less than predicted by DTS.
3. Equation (9.4) approximates the DTS of a portfolio as the product of spread duration and spread of the portfolio. This is not exact since the DTS of a portfolio is the weighted sum of DTS for all bonds, and the average of the product of duration and spread is not equal to the product of the average duration and average spread.
4. The DTS-hedge ratio $DTS_S/DTS_L$ is smaller than the duration hedge ratio $D_S/D_L$ whenever the curve is upward sloping ($S_S < S_L$).
5. The entire utility sector had a $-7.77\%$ excess return in July 2002 because of the extreme spread widening of these issuers.
6. There are various alternative-weighting schemes, for example, based on historical volatilities and correlations of the sectors. We use market weights since they are objective and transparent.
7. Risky PV01 is defined as the expected present value of 1 bps paid on the premium leg until default or maturity, whichever is sooner.

### CHAPTER 10

# The 2007–2009 Credit Crisis

## Benefits of DTS in Risk Management

T he first part of this book introduced the notion of DTS as a better measure for managing the spread risk of credit portfolios. Although the evidence supporting this concept relies on a long historical perspective spanning multiple markets, the 2007–2009 credit crisis exhibited unprecedented spread behavior and, thus, provides a remarkable testing ground for the DTS concept. Did the behavior of spread volatility change during the crisis, or did the linear relation between spread volatility and spread level still hold true? Did DTS-based risk estimates adjust in a timely manner given the unprecedented speed and magnitude of corporate spread widening? Was DTS still superior to other risk sensitivity measures, such as spread duration and empirical betas?

In this chapter, we re-examine the relationship between the level and volatility of spreads over the 2007–2009 period and how it compares with historical results. We also evaluate the efficacy of DTS during this three-year period, from a portfolio manager's point of view, in the context of volatility forecasting, index replication, and the hedging of CDS trades. Finally, we offer a brief overview of the advantages offered by DTS in constructing models of portfolio risk.

## SPREAD BEHAVIOR DURING THE CREDIT CRISIS

The financial crisis of 2007–2009 produced unprecedented spread behavior. Spreads of U.S. investment-grade bonds widened to an all-time high of more than 6%, from lows of around 1% in the benign 2003–2006 period. Similarly, spreads of high-yield bonds rose to more than 18%, and CDX spreads increased by a factor of five. Figure 10.1 plots the time series of monthly spread levels for the U.S. Investment-Grade Corporate and High

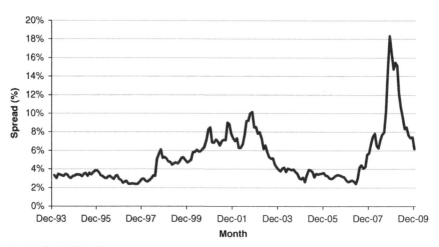

**A. High Yield Index**

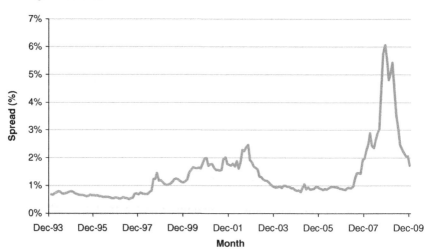

**B. Corporate Index**

**FIGURE 10.1** Spreads of U.S. Investment Grade, High Yield, and CDS Indexes
*Sources:* Barclays Capital and Markit.

Yield indexes, as well as for the on-the-run five-year CDX.NA.IG contract. As the charts for the three indexes demonstrate, credit portfolio managers and risk officers were challenged not only by unprecedented spread levels, but also by the extraordinary speed at which spreads widened. This episode serves as a remarkable out-of-sample test to the validity of the DTS concept,

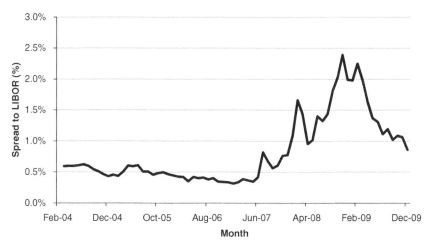

C. Investment Grade CDX (Markit CDX.IG.NA)

**FIGURE 10.1** (*Continued*)

which had been introduced in 2005, prior to the onset of the crisis. Indeed, the behavior of spreads during the crisis was very different than that reflected in the historical data between 1989 and 2006 used in Chapters 1 and 2.

To examine whether the fundamental relationship between systematic spread volatility and spread level was affected by the extreme market conditions, we repeat the analysis we presented in Chapter 1, using monthly data on all constituents of the Corporate and High Yield indexes (bonds rated B or better) between January 2007 and December 2009. Figure 10.2 displays the relation between the time series volatility of systematic spread changes and the average beginning-of-month spread. Each observation represents one of the 48 cells in the spread partition.[1]

The scatter plot illustrates that the relation between spread volatility and spread level remained fairly linear even in the turbulent 2007–2009 period, extending through spreads of 800 bps. A linear regression model yields a slope estimate of 14.1% (with an insignificant intercept), compared with a long-term slope estimate of 9.4% based on the 1989–2005 period. Hence, the realized spread volatility for corporates trading at a spread of 100 bps was about 14 bps/month, an increase from the roughly 9.5 bps/month implied by our previously reported long-term slope estimate.

The dispersion for observations around the regression line increased, relative to the original analysis, with the explanatory power ($R^2$) declining from 92% to 85%. The divergence from the straight line is mostly due to the spread dislocation during September and October 2008, and the fact that

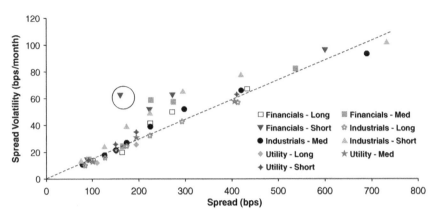

**FIGURE 10.2**  Volatility of Systematic Spread Changes versus Spread Level
*Note:* Based on monthly data for all constituents of the U.S. Corporate and High
Yield indexes (rated B or higher) between January 2007 and December 2009.
*Source:* Barclays Capital.

financials generally experienced higher spread volatility relative to industrial
and utility bonds. For example, the 125 to 200 bps spread cell populated by
short duration financial bonds (circled) widened by an average of 227 bps
in September 2008, a very large change relative to the beginning-of-month
average spread of 184 bps.[2]

In spite of the slight deterioration in explanatory power, the results
suggest that the linear relation between the level of spread and subsequent
spread volatility persisted during the crisis, albeit with a 50% increase in the
proportionality factor. Figure 10.3 illustrates the increase in the volatility
of relative spreads further by comparing the volatility during the pre-crisis
period 1999–2006 (x-axis) with that in 2007–2009 (y-axis). Volatilities are
calculated based on absolute and relative spread changes during the periods
(relative spread changes are the monthly changes in spread divided by the
beginning-of-month spreads). Each point on the graph represents one of the
8 × 3 industry-quality cells that form a partition of the investment-grade
universe.[3]

Two main patterns are evident in Figure 10.3. First, while relative
spread volatility was not constant, absolute spread volatility increased by
a factor of 2 to 3 depending on the sector, as reflected by the location far
above the diagonal line. Second, relative spread volatilities of various sectors
are quite tightly clustered, ranging from 9.1% to 15.7%, whereas the
range of absolute volatilities is much wider, from 14 bps/month to 35 bps/
month. The results indicate that relative spreads remained more stable than

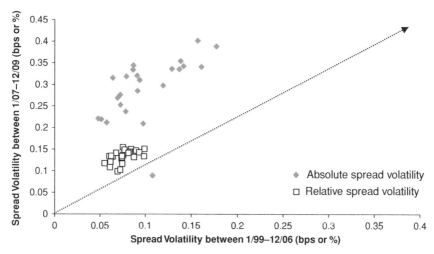

**FIGURE 10.3** Relative and Absolute Spread Volatility: Pre-Crisis versus Crisis
*Note:* Based on eight sectors × three credit ratings partition of the U.S. Corporate Index (January 2007–December 2009). To enable both absolute and relative spread volatility to be shown on same set of axes, both measures are expressed in units with similar magnitudes. An absolute spread change of 0.1 represents a 10 bps parallel shift across a sector, while a relative spread change of 0.1 implies that all spreads in the sector move by 10% of their current values.
*Source:* Barclays Capital.

absolute spreads and generated a more accurate forward-looking estimate of spread volatility.

How do we interpret the large increase observed in relative spread volatility relative to the pre-crisis value? If we look back at the theoretical derivation of DTS in Chapter 4, we find that the Merton model predicts a direct proportional relationship between the volatility of a firm's asset value and its relative spread volatility. If we take equity market volatility as a proxy for the harder-to-observe asset value volatility, this would predict that when equity volatility increases, relative spread volatilities should increase as well. A simple empirical test of this relation is shown in Figure 10.4. We take long-term time series of relative OAS changes of the U.S. Corporate Index and total returns of the S&P 500 index, and separate them into non-overlapping windows of 24 months. We plot the relative spread volatility in each of these windows against the contemporaneous equity return volatility and find that the two, indeed, exhibit a striking linear relationship. The data point at the right upper corner of the figure corresponds to the period from June 2007 through May 2009, during which the equity return volatility was

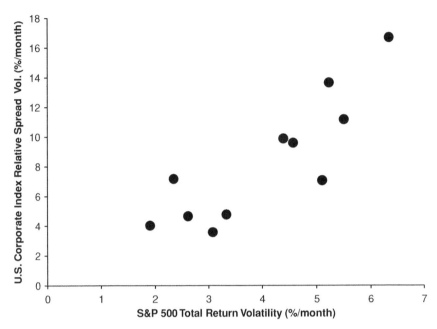

**FIGURE 10.4**   Relative Spread Volatility of the U.S. Corporate Index versus Total Return Volatility of S&P 500 Index
*Note:* Using non-overlapping 24-month periods from June 1989 through May 2011.
*Source:* Barclays Capital.

6.3%/month (or 21.9% annualized) and the relative spread volatility of the Corporate Index was 16.7%/month. Both of these figures are well above the values observed over the long term, but their ratio is certainly consistent with the historical relationship between the two.

## APPLICATIONS OF DTS

The results in the previous section establish that the fundamental relationship between spread level and subsequent changes in spread was maintained through the crisis. Credit portfolio managers may be more interested, however, in seeing whether using DTS during the crisis would have helped generate better performance. We therefore compare DTS with other spread risk measures in three key applications: risk projection, index replication, and hedging.

## Risk Projection: Predicting Spread Volatility

The ability to measure risk accurately is perhaps the most important requirement for managing a credit portfolio. A key benefit of DTS in the context of generating volatility forecasts is its use of current spread levels to quickly adapt to changing market conditions. In contrast, estimates based on past realized spread volatility can take longer to adapt, depending on the time window used for calibration. The selected historical time period is inherently subjective, and may not perfectly reflect the current state of the market.

The 2007–2009 credit crisis caught many investors off guard, with risk estimates calibrated to the sustained "volatility drought" of the previous few years severely underestimating the spread risk of corporate portfolios. It therefore provides an opportunity to compare forecasts based on DTS with those using realized spread volatilities over a trailing window.

Figure 10.5 shows the monthly spread changes of the U.S. Corporate Index normalized by several projections of spread volatility from January 2006, well before the first signs of the crisis were observed, through December 2009, when markets were already in recovery mode. The first forecast of volatility, based on DTS, is the product of the spread level at the beginning of the month and the (approximate) relative spread volatility of 10%/month from Chapter 1, that would have been available to investors at the beginning of the period. The plot also includes two estimates based on realized historical volatility, one over a trailing 36-month window and the other using the entire history (since September 1989) available at the start of each month.

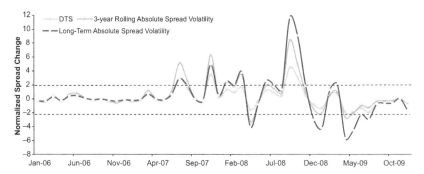

**FIGURE 10.5** Comparison of Volatility Forecasts Based on DTS and Historical Absolute Spread Changes

*Note:* Normalized spread changes are monthly changes in spreads divided by the forecast volatility based on DTS with a 10% slope, absolute spread volatility computed over the trailing 36 months, or the entire available history since September 1989. The results are reported monthly between January 2006 and December 2009.

*Source:* Barclays Capital.

The chart illustrates that the forecast based on the trailing 36 months would have fit the low volatility level during the pre-crisis period quite well, but was susceptible to large sudden shocks such as in July 2007 and November 2007, which resulted in 5.1 and 6.3 standard deviation realizations respectively. Although this spread volatility estimator gradually adjusted to the changing market conditions, it continued to understate the level of risk more than a year after the crisis began, with the spread widening of September 2008 being equivalent to an 8.4 standard deviation event.

In contrast, the "long-term" forecast was better prepared at the beginning of the crisis since it incorporated information from previous extreme market events such as the 1998 and 2002 crises. While its forecast of volatility for July 2007, for example, was higher than that of the "short-term" estimator, it generated grossly underestimated risk projections toward the end of 2008. Because the long-term volatility forecast adjusts to changing market conditions very gradually, the realized spread change in September 2008 would have corresponded to an 11.6 standard deviation event! Similarly, it underestimated the magnitude of the spread tightening beginning in early 2009 as market conditions started to improve.

Over the period, the DTS volatility estimator was consistently superior to both forecasts based on historical volatilities. The DTS-based forecasts quickly (albeit not perfectly) reflected both the increased level of risk once the crisis erupted and the reversal in market conditions in 2009, with most spread change realizations corresponding to less than two standard deviations. A notable exception was September 2008. Despite the already heightened level of spreads, the combined effect of the Lehman Brothers and Washington Mutual defaults and the bailout of AIG resulted in a 4.5 standard deviation event. However, as discussed previously, the forecasts using realized absolute spread volatility underestimated the risk by two to three times more than the DTS-based forecast.

Figure 10.5 provides an illustration of the advantage of the DTS approach compared with risk estimation based on absolute spread changes. In addition to the fact that it does not require a subjective selection of an historical calibration period, the rapid incorporation of market conditions, as reflected in the level of spreads, proved especially valuable during the crisis and the abrupt deterioration in credit markets. Furthermore, the DTS-based risk forecasts could have been improved further by using higher frequency spread information (for example, from the credit default swap market) to update the DTS intra-month, rather than just the beginning-of-month spread.

## Replication: Creating Index Tracking Portfolios

Portfolio managers often need to build portfolios that closely track the returns of a selected benchmark. Constructing a portfolio of cash instruments to replicate a target index can be accomplished using various methods, but a commonly used approach is stratified sampling. It relies on partitioning the index into "cells," which represent the manager's view of common risk factors affecting a given market (e.g., for credit these might be sector and rating). Bonds are then selected from each cell based on certain criteria and weighted such that they match various characteristics of the cell, such as the contribution to spread duration. The advantage of this approach is its simplicity and flexibility; its disadvantage is that it ignores the correlations among cells.[4] We compare the results of replicating the U.S. Corporate Index using stratified sampling and matching only a single characteristic at a time: DTS or spread duration. Our intention is not to design the "optimal" replicating portfolio, but rather to focus on the relative efficacy of one characteristic relative to the other.

To construct the two replicating portfolios, we employ the index partition used in Figure 10.3, with a total of 24 cells. Bonds in each cell are assigned monthly to one of four quadrants. The quadrants are defined using a $2 \times 2$ grid based on the cell market-weighted spread duration and DTS as illustrated in Figure 10.6. Bonds with spread duration and DTS above the respective weighted means are allocated to the upper-right quadrant, denoted HH. Similarly, bonds with spread duration above the mean but DTS below the mean are allocated to the upper-left quadrant (HL) and so on.

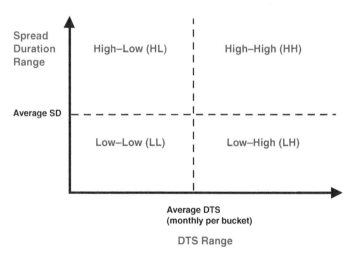

**FIGURE 10.6** Illustration of Cell Partition by DTS and Spread Duration in Replication Algorithm
*Source:* Barclays Capital.

Five bonds are then selected from the high-spread duration-low DTS quadrant (HL), and from the low-spread duration-high DTS quadrant (LH).[5] This set of 10 bonds is used in both variants of the replicating portfolio, to reduce noise from issuer selection and focus attention on the differences in systematic risk exposures.[6] Within a quadrant, each bond is allocated a weight based on its relative market value. The weight of the two quadrants is determined such that the overall DTS (or spread duration) of the 10 bonds matches that of the cell.

The key difference is in how we weight the bonds within each cell: in the DTS-based portfolio, we match the DTS exposure of the index in each cell, while in the spread duration–based portfolio we match the index spread duration exposure. For example, Table 10.1 displays a market structure report of the U.S. Corporate Index along the sector/quality partition used in our replication exercise, at the beginning of the sample on December 29, 2006. For each cell of the partition, the report characterizes the exposure of the index to that market segment in three different ways: market weight, contribution to *option-adjusted spread duration* (OASD), and contribution to DTS. The spread duration–based replicating portfolio is constructed such that it matches the contributions to OASD in each of the index sectors (the second column from the right), whereas the DTS-based replication matches the DTS contributions in the rightmost column.

The last stage in our replication exercise is selecting the bonds that form the replicating portfolio. In a real-life portfolio management, security selection plays an important role in determining performance and several different criteria can be employed in the security selection process, depending on the portfolio setting. If minimizing tracking error is the primary goal, then the security weights within each cell should focus on the primary issuer exposures of the benchmark. Alternatively, managers may aim to maximize liquidity or add value by choosing securities that they believe will outperform. Ideally, however, as long as the portfolio has matched the benchmark allocations on the macro level, it should track well in the event of any major industry rally or decline. The key is to match the right set of macro exposures.

Our interest is not in the issuer selection mechanism, but in evaluating which set of macro exposures is most important to match. So, we test our replication methods using several different issuer selection mechanisms, to ensure that differences between the two replicating portfolios (DTS matched and spread duration matched) are independent of the specific bonds that were selected. One approach is simulation, where bonds in each cell are randomly selected, the replication results recorded and the analysis repeated multiple times. Another approach, which we use, is to specify explicit selection criteria based on bond characteristics. While this approach leads to a

**TABLE 10.1**  Sector Quality Profile of U.S. Corporate Bond Index (as of 12/29/2006)

| | Market Value (%) | OASD | OAS | DTS | OASD Contribution | DTS Contribution |
|---|---|---|---|---|---|---|
| *Total* | *100.00* | *6.21* | *87.7* | *3.81* | *6.21* | *3.81* |
| Aaa–Aa | 24.09 | 5.03 | 57.2 | 1.29 | 1.21 | 0.31 |
| A | 40.85 | 6.40 | 80.1 | 3.31 | 2.62 | 1.35 |
| Baa | 35.06 | 6.80 | 117.5 | 6.13 | 2.38 | 2.15 |
| *Banking* | *26.09* | *5.19* | *65.5* | *1.91* | *1.35* | *0.50* |
| Aaa–Aa | 14.07 | 4.88 | 58.2 | 1.33 | 0.69 | 0.19 |
| A | 11.20 | 5.59 | 72.2 | 2.51 | 0.63 | 0.28 |
| Baa | 0.82 | 5.07 | 99.5 | 3.74 | 0.04 | 0.03 |
| *Finance* | *17.20* | *5.47* | *74.8* | *2.43* | *0.94* | *0.42* |
| Aaa–Aa | 5.94 | 4.65 | 53.1 | 0.95 | 0.28 | 0.06 |
| A | 7.28 | 5.93 | 75.9 | 2.65 | 0.43 | 0.19 |
| Baa | 3.98 | 5.84 | 105.0 | 4.23 | 0.23 | 0.17 |
| *Basic industry* | *9.09* | *6.62* | *93.7* | *4.42* | *0.60* | *0.40* |
| Aaa–Aa | 0.42 | 5.88 | 55.1 | 0.92 | 0.02 | 0.00 |
| A | 3.88 | 5.82 | 67.2 | 2.05 | 0.23 | 0.08 |
| Baa | 4.80 | 7.33 | 118.5 | 6.63 | 0.35 | 0.32 |
| *Consumer cyclical* | *7.53* | *6.40* | *108.2* | *5.41* | *0.48* | *0.41* |
| Aaa–Aa | 1.19 | 5.21 | 55.6 | 1.54 | 0.06 | 0.02 |
| A | 1.87 | 7.28 | 86.9 | 4.02 | 0.14 | 0.08 |
| Baa | 4.47 | 6.35 | 131.1 | 7.02 | 0.28 | 0.31 |
| *Consumer noncyclical* | *8.41* | *6.77* | *86.5* | *3.65* | *0.57* | *0.31* |
| Aaa–Aa | 1.67 | 6.90 | 61.5 | 1.78 | 0.12 | 0.03 |
| A | 3.94 | 7.32 | 81.9 | 3.62 | 0.29 | 0.14 |
| Baa | 2.80 | 5.92 | 107.8 | 4.82 | 0.17 | 0.13 |
| *Communications* | *15.70* | *6.74* | *112.3* | *6.08* | *1.06* | *0.95* |
| Aaa–Aa | 0.06 | 1.19 | 48.5 | 0.15 | 0.00 | 0.00 |
| A | 8.12 | 6.80 | 97.0 | 5.02 | 0.55 | 0.41 |
| Baa | 7.53 | 6.72 | 129.4 | 7.27 | 0.51 | 0.55 |
| *Energy* | *6.31* | *7.84* | *100.6* | *5.50* | *0.50* | *0.35* |
| Aaa–Aa | 0.58 | 4.64 | 59.7 | 1.55 | 0.03 | 0.01 |
| A | 1.73 | 8.15 | 83.7 | 4.05 | 0.14 | 0.07 |
| Baa | 4.00 | 8.17 | 113.8 | 6.69 | 0.33 | 0.27 |
| *Utility* | *9.66* | *7.33* | *101.6* | *4.97* | *0.71* | *0.48* |
| Aaa–Aa | 0.16 | 11.81 | 87.8 | 4.76 | 0.02 | 0.01 |
| A | 2.84 | 7.58 | 82.6 | 3.64 | 0.21 | 0.10 |
| Baa | 6.66 | 7.12 | 110.0 | 5.54 | 0.47 | 0.37 |

*Source:* Barclays Capital.

single replicating portfolio (per criterion), it more closely mimics a realistic process of constructing replicating portfolios for index tracking purposes.

We examine five potential bond selection criteria. The first criterion, based on market value, selects the largest ten bonds in each market cell (five from each quadrant). Hence, it results in the most investible and liquid portfolios (as larger size is generally associated with increased liquidity—see Chapter 5). The remaining four criteria are designed primarily to maximize our ability to distinguish between the two replication strategies. The second and third criteria rely on spread and select bonds with the highest (lowest) level of spread. This represents a replication strategy that tries to maximize carry (minimize risk).

The last two criteria are designed to maximize the dispersion of spread duration or DTS between the replicating portfolios. One selects bonds with the largest and lowest spread duration from the HL and LH quadrants respectively, while the other selects bonds with the lowest and highest DTS from the same two quadrants. Selecting bonds with the maximum potential dispersion in the characteristics that are also used to match the index helps to magnify the weight differential between the DTS and spread duration matched portfolios. This in turn would facilitate the comparison between the replication results of the two sensitivity measures.

Table 10.2 compares the *tracking error volatilities* (TEV) of the various replicating portfolios during the 24-month period beginning in January 2007. Irrespective of the selection criteria, matching each cell's DTS achieves lower-tracking error volatility than matching its spread duration, although the TEV improvement varies widely, from 1.2 bps/month to almost 15 bps/month. Looking at the difference in weight given to each bond under the two matching schemes (reported in the third column) suggests that the reduction in TEV is generally more meaningful as the weight differential increases (i.e., as the replicating portfolios are less similar to each other).

For example, if the selection criterion is market value the average (absolute) difference in the weight of each selected bond under the two replication schemes (in proportion to the total index market value) is 0.46%, and the TEV declines from 22.9 bps/month for matching spread duration exposures to 21.4 bps/month when matching DTS exposures. If the maximum spread criterion is used instead, the weight differential rises to 0.72%, and the decline in TEV when matching DTS, rather than spread duration exposures, is 14.7 bps/month.

It is important to mention that the superior tracking achieved by matching the index DTS does not come at the expense of performance. The last two columns in Table 10.2 display the average tracking errors of the replicating portfolios. The results indicate that while our simple replication exercise tends to underperform the index for any bond selection criterion, the

**TABLE 10.2** Index Replication Using Stratified Sampling

| Selection Criteria | Tracking Error Volatility (bps/month) | | Weight Differential per Bond (% of total Index market volume) | Average Tracking Error (bps/month) | |
|---|---|---|---|---|---|
| | SD Match | DTS Match | | SD Match | DTS Match |
| Market value (largest) | 22.9 | 21.4 | 0.46% | −11.5 | −8.0 |
| Spread (lowest) | 20.7 | 15.6 | 0.89% | −10.6 | −14.0 |
| Spread (highest) | 33.0 | 18.3 | 0.72% | −11.7 | −4.4 |
| Spread duration dispersion | 17.0 | 15.8 | 0.47% | 1.9 | 5.8 |
| DTS dispersion | 28.2 | 24.7 | 0.59% | −6.1 | −1.5 |

*Note:* Replication of the U.S. Corporate Index is performed through matching the spread or DTS characteristic of each of the 24 cells in the partition (8 sectors × 3 credit ratings). Based on monthly observations (January 2007–December 2008). The weight differential per bond is computed as the average of the absolute value of the weight difference assigned to a bond under the DTS and spread duration matched portfolios (as a proportion of the index aggregate market value).
*Source:* Barclays Capital.

DTS-based approach gives better average tracking errors (with one exception) than the spread duration–based one.

The use of DTS exposures to replicate an index by stratified sampling is far from a theoretical exercise. This approach has been used to form a highly liquid portfolio of bonds to track the U.S. Corporate and Credit indexes. A purely rules-driven sampling methodology ensures transparency. The replication methodology uses a partition of five sectors by five duration categories, with each cell represented by two bonds. The bonds are selected based on the Liquidity Cost Scores (LCS) introduced in Chapter 5, and are weighted such that the index DTS exposure in each cell is matched. Historical back-testing of this strategy indicates that it tracks the index much more closely than an alternative strategy based on liquid derivatives including Treasury futures, swaps, and CDX. Chapter 14 describes the methodology and performance of this strategy in more detail.

## Hedging

Another natural application of DTS is hedging. In Chapter 8, we analyzed the efficacy of various measures (including DTS) in hedging out the market exposure of pair-wise long-short trades using single-name credit default swaps. We repeat the analysis with weekly CDS data from 2007–2008 using the original set of 63 issuers. All issuers were part of the CDX.NA.IG at the beginning of 2007 and belong to one of the following five industries: consumer cyclical, consumer staples, industrials, financials, and utilities.[7] Trades are formed by constructing all available same-industry pairs with a randomly assigned directional view. The long–short positions in each trade are implemented based on one of three hedging approaches. The DTS approach is compared to one that matches Risky Present Value (RPV, the equivalent of spread duration for CDS) and one based on empirical betas estimated over a trailing window. (For a detailed description, see Chapter 8.)

Table 10.3 presents various statistics on the trades, including the overall P&L volatility, the correlation of trade performance with the market return for the industry, and the beta of the trade performance with that of the market for all hedging approaches. The statistics are computed separately for each pair and then averaged across all 392 pairs. Empirical betas are estimated based on a trailing window of 26 weeks in order to allow the betas to adapt faster to the market conditions in 2007–2008.

How should we determine which hedge is the most successful? Ideally, one would like to maximize the information ratio: the return per unit of risk. However, because of the lack of ability to measure alpha in this framework, this is not feasible. A possible approach might be to minimize the total risk of the hedged position. Table 10.3(A) shows that the beta-hedged strategy has a larger P&L volatility (137.3 bps/week compared with 117.5/week for DTS), and the dispersion of volatility across pairs (138.7 bps/week) is also larger, indicating that many pairs produced a trade volatility of 275 bps/week or more (i.e., more than one standard deviation away from the mean).

However, while overall volatility may be easy to quantify, it does not necessarily align with the goals of investors. After all, our goal is not to minimize all risks; we are trying to get exposure to both of these securities in order to translate our issuer-specific views into alpha. This point is made clear in Table 10.3(B), which reports the same statistics when issuers from the financial sector are excluded (a total of 272 pairs). The exclusion of financials leads to a dramatic decline in the trades' volatility level and dispersion by factors of more than two and four, respectively (regardless of the hedging mechanism). This reflects the extreme fluctuations in credit default spreads of financials issuers (mostly in September and October 2008). While the ranking of the hedges in Table 10.3(B) is similar to that in Table 10.3(A) (with the DTS hedge generating the lowest volatility), it highlights the inadequacy of overall P&L volatility as a measure of the hedging success.

An alternative could be to seek a trade whose returns have the lowest possible correlation with the market. This metric, presumably, should tend

**TABLE 10.3** Performance of Same-Industry CDS Pairs by Hedging Mechanism

| A. Entire Issuer Set, January 2007–December 2008 | Hedging Method | | |
| --- | --- | --- | --- |
| | RPV | DTS | Empirical Beta |
| Average P&L volatility (bps/week) | 159.1 | 117.5 | 137.3 |
| Standard deviation of P&L volatility (over pairs) | 221.1 | 105.4 | 138.7 |
| Average absolute market correlation | 0.40 | 0.25 | 0.17 |
| Mean market correlation | 0.00 | 0.00 | −0.01 |
| Standard deviation of market correlation | 0.47 | 0.31 | 0.22 |
| Mean hedge ratio | 1.0 | 1.5 | 1.9 |
| Standard deviation hedge ratio | 0.1 | 0.6 | 1.5 |
| Systematic percentage of variance | 21.6% | 25.6% | 41.1% |

| B. Excluding Financials, January 2007–December 2008 | Hedging Method | | |
| --- | --- | --- | --- |
| | RPV | DTS | Empirical Beta |
| Average P&L volatility (bps/week) | 73.0 | 57.7 | 66.0 |
| Standard deviation of P&L volatility (over pairs) | 50.8 | 23.2 | 26.9 |
| Average absolute market correlation | 0.30 | 0.18 | 0.12 |
| Mean market correlation | 0.04 | −0.01 | −0.01 |
| Standard deviation of market correlation | 0.48 | 0.31 | 0.22 |
| Mean hedge ratio | 1.0 | 1.5 | 1.8 |
| Standard deviation hedge ratio | 0.0 | 0.6 | 1.4 |
| Systematic percentage of variance | 23.3% | 19.2% | 28.6% |

| C. Entire Issuer Set, November 2004–December 2006 | Hedging Method | | |
| --- | --- | --- | --- |
| | RPV | DTS | Empirical Beta |
| Average P&L volatility (bps/week) | 13.3 | 11.2 | 18.0 |
| Standard deviation of P&L volatility (over pairs) | 5.6 | 2.7 | 6.9 |
| Average absolute market correlation | 0.37 | 0.23 | 0.11 |
| Mean market correlation | 0.01 | 0.04 | 0.01 |
| Standard deviation of market correlation | 0.43 | 0.28 | 0.14 |
| Mean hedge ratio | 1.0 | 1.2 | 1.9 |
| Standard deviation hedge ratio | 0.0 | 0.3 | 1.3 |
| Systematic percentage of variance | 18.6% | 12.6% | 18.9% |

*Note:* Statistics are first computed for each pair and then averaged across pairs. Empirical betas are estimated using a trailing 24-week window. For detailed definitions of the statistics calculated in the table, see Chapter 8.
*Source:* Barclays Capital and Markit.

to select hedging strategies that take more issuer risk and less market risk. The empirical beta-based hedge looks better by this measure, whether we measure correlation by the average of the absolute value of the correlation or by the cross-sectional standard deviation of these correlations across all pairs. So is the empirical beta-based hedge better?

In Chapter 8, we documented a similar result and show that it reflects the instability of hedge ratios based on empirical betas. We argued that the estimation of beta did not break down in a systematic way that would introduce a bias in one direction or another. Occasionally, the beta-hedged strategy takes a big market exposure, either long or short, and because of the random timing of this systematic exposure, the overall market correlation over the entire time period is low. To demonstrate this, we also report the mean and standard deviation of the hedge ratio between the two legs of the trade, for each pair. While the average hedge ratios implied by the DTS and empirical beta approaches are not very different (in Table 10.3(B), for example, 1.5 and 1.8, respectively), the average standard deviation of the beta-based hedge ratios (1.4) is more than double that of the DTS-based hedge ratios (0.6).

Another possibility would be to attribute the risk of the hedged position to systematic and issuer-specific components and then seek the hedge that derives the lowest percentage of its variance from systematic risk.[8] Based on this metric, DTS is again more effective, with only 19.2% of overall variance stemming from systematic risk, versus 28.6% and 23.3% for the empirical beta and RPV hedges, respectively.

Comparing the results in Table 10.3(A) and (B) with those in Table 10.3(C), suggests that all hedging methods were less effective during 2007–2008 than in the pre-crisis period. However, we find that the DTS hedge is still far superior to the simple duration (RPV) hedge, according to any of our performance metrics. The case is a little less clear with empirical betas: The DTS hedge produces lower-risk trades, but the empirical-beta hedge produces returns that are less correlated with the market. Upon closer examination, however, it appears that the low correlations are a result of unstable hedge ratios; the percentage of systematic risk is lowest for the DTS-hedged trades.

## ADVANTAGES OF DTS IN RISK MODEL CONSTRUCTION

Many portfolio managers rely on multi-factor risk models to help them measure and control portfolio risk, either in absolute terms or relative to a benchmark. The DTS approach is ideally suited to estimate spread risk in such models. For example, a risk model might contain modules for measuring exposures to three different types of adverse credit events: systematic changes in spreads, either market-wide or across a particular sector; issuer-specific spread changes; and defaults. The use of DTS can improve the modeling of the first two of these three types of credit risk.

Exposures to systematic changes in credit spreads in a particular market segment can be measured as the sum of the DTS contributions of all portfolio investments within that segment. The risk factor, which relates to these exposures, is a relative shift in spreads across the sector—for example, that all financial spreads increase by 10% of their current levels. The alternative to this, in a model not based on DTS, would be to assume that the risk factor is a parallel shift in spreads across a sector (e.g., all financials widen by 10 bps)—and that the exposures are therefore contributions to spread duration. Thus, in the DTS-based model, the key risk factor volatility for a particular sector would be its estimated volatility of relative spread changes, while the alternative model would estimate the volatility of absolute spread changes.

The DTS-based approach offers three distinct advantages. First, it offers a better assessment of the relative risks of different portfolios. If two portfolios have the same market weight and average spread duration in a given sector, but portfolio A implements this allocation with higher-spread assets than portfolio B, only the DTS-based model will correctly show that portfolio A has a greater exposure to a widening across this sector than does portfolio B. Second, the DTS-based approach improves the accuracy of the risk projection by reducing the uncertainty in the estimation of risk factor volatilities. As we have seen, relative spread volatilities are much more stable than absolute spread volatilities. Therefore, even if we do continually update our estimates of relative spread volatilities within each sector, we find that they change much more slowly than the corresponding estimates of absolute spread volatility and that they are less sensitive to the choice of the time window used in this estimation process.[9]

The third advantage offered by DTS is perhaps more subtle, but opens the door to the most profound change in the structure of the model. Up to this point, we have discussed the exposure to "a given segment of the market" in the abstract, without specifying exactly how the market is to be partitioned. However, choosing the partition along which to measure systematic exposures is one of the most critical elements of risk model design, involving careful trade-offs among various goals. It is desirable to limit the model to a small number of intuitive factors, both to maximize the clarity and practical applicability of the risk reports produced, and to ensure that a sufficient number of bonds are available to accurately calibrate each risk factor. Conversely, it is important to include enough factors to achieve sufficient explanatory power. For example, a single risk factor that measures portfolio exposure to U.S. corporates would measure the effect on the portfolio of a potential rally or decline across the corporate bond universe, but not the effect of a relative widening of financials versus industrials. We would like to partition the universe finely enough to capture all major sector rotation effects.

Prior to the introduction of the DTS framework, when constructing a model of systematic spread risk for U.S. corporates, we used to partition this universe into a sector/quality grid. The partitioning by quality was made absolutely necessary by the assumption that the systematic spread movement in a given market cell tends to take the form of a parallel shift in spreads. When we calibrated such a model to market data, we found that the volatility of absolute spread changes for Baa financials was much greater than that of Aa financials. Although the risk factors representing these two cells might be highly correlated, the substantial difference in volatilities precluded us from combining these cells.

If we instead assume that the spread change across an industry is a relative shift, we no longer need to segregate our model by credit quality. The fact that Baa financials tend to have greater risk than Aa financials is reflected in the higher spreads. This higher volatility of Baa bonds will now show up as a larger exposure to the same (relative) spread volatility risk factor rather than as an exposure to a different risk factor with greater (absolute) spread volatility. This puts the risk model designer at a great advantage with regard to the tradeoff between compactness and explanatory power. The model can be designed with roughly the same explanatory power as before using a much smaller number of risk factors; alternatively, finer industry breakdown can be employed to create a model with a similar number of factors but greater explanatory power.

## CONCLUSION

Despite the unprecedented nature of the 2007–2009 credit crisis, we find that using DTS would have improved the ability of portfolio managers to forecast risk, hedge, and track their benchmarks. The fundamental linear relation between the level of spread and spread volatility underlying DTS persisted during the period across all sectors and credit ratings, although the proportionality factors increased from 10% to about 15% as equity volatility rose. While this implies that the long-term calibrated DTS model would not have fully captured spread risk during the crisis months, it was far more effective than any other spread duration–based risk measure.

The speed at which market conditions deteriorated highlights the need for risk measures that are able to adjust quickly without relying on historical data which may not properly reflect current market conditions. The explicit use of spread as a barometer of risk in the context of DTS proved to be of paramount importance and should continue to benefit market practitioners in the future.

## NOTES

1. The spread partition used to generate Figure 10.2 is different than that used in Figure 1.8. Duration buckets for financials, industrials, and utilities are divided into five, seven, and four cells, respectively, with breakpoints ranging from 100 bps to 500 bps. Because of the large spread widening during the sample period, some low-spread cells are not populated in the latter half of 2008 and some high-spread cells are not populated in the first half of 2007.
2. Of the 41 bonds in that cell, 16 were issued by GE Capital, whose spreads widened by about 300 bps during that month.
3. The industry groups are banking, finance, basic industry, consumer cyclical, consumer non-cyclical, communications, energy, and utilities.
4. A stratified sampling approach is "blind" to the relationships among cells. This can be remedied by complementing a stratified sampling approach with the use of an optimizer that accounts for the correlations among cells.
5. This approach guarantees exact replication with positive weights for all bonds since five of the bonds have a higher DTS (or spread duration) than the average, whereas the other set of selected bonds has a lower DTS (or spread duration) than the average. If the HL or LH quadrants do not have at least five bonds, bonds are selected from the low-spread duration-low DTS (LL) and the high-spread duration-high DTS quadrants (HH).
6. Selecting 10 bonds from each cell strikes a good balance between having a realistic size for the replicating portfolio (240 bonds) and reducing idiosyncratic risk. If fewer bonds are used to represent each cell, the variation in tracking errors may reflect not only the difference between the two systematic risk measures (DTS and spread duration), but also the idiosyncratic performance of the set of bonds selected.
7. None of the other industry groups had sufficient issuer population to participate in the study. Only issuers for which spread data for the entire 2007–2008 period were available were selected.
8. This is done by regressing weekly trade P&L against the contemporaneous market return. The systematic percentage of variance is the product of the estimated market coefficient with the volatility of the market return, divided by the overall trade volatility.
9. Earlier in this chapter, we have seen clear evidence that relative spread volatility does change over time. Nevertheless, we have also seen that even if we worked through this period with an estimate of relative spread volatility frozen at the pre-crisis average level of 10%, the performance through the crisis was superior to using absolute spread volatilities.

# CHAPTER 11

# A Framework for Diversification of Issuer Risk

In sizing credit exposures, investors must strike the right balance between two opposing needs. To control risk, it is important not to take a concentrated position in a single issuer. However, to generate alpha, the recommended names must have sufficient weight in the portfolio to affect outperformance. An overemphasis on diversification dilutes the value of issuer selection skills. As a result, investors often seek guidance on the "correct" level of diversification for a given portfolio.

We approach this dilemma from two different angles. One approach addresses this question head-on, relying on a model of portfolio downgrade risk and an empirical study of the performance cost of downgrades. As we will show, the historically observed performance cost of a downgrade is typically much greater for Baa securities than for those rated A or above, and the level of downgrade risk depends strongly on credit rating. Therefore, while precise issuer limits depend on each investor's appetite for risk, they should differ by quality, according to the ratios of downgrade risk between the different quality groups.

The second approach relies on the use of DTS (see Chapter 1). While portfolio diversification was not the driver of DTS-related research, nevertheless, its findings apply to portfolio diversification as well. The portfolio's contribution-to-DTS exposure to a particular issuer is proportional to the excess return volatility produced by that exposure. Furthermore, the spread-based approach to estimating risk often provides a much more timely response to credit events than does a ratings-based approach. Therefore, the DTS framework suggests a different approach to controlling portfolio concentrations: Rather than imposing a limit on the portfolio market weight in a given issuer (possibly making that limit dependent on the issuer's rating), set a limit on the DTS contribution of any issuer, regardless of credit quality. While this idea is attractive in principle, its implementation creates several practical problems.

We conducted our first study of sufficient diversification as early as 2002.[1] Our motivation for revisiting this topic is twofold. First of all, most pre-2008 credit studies now would be considered unreliable, or at least incomplete, unless they are extended to include the 2007–2009 credit crisis. Second, we asked ourselves what our research on DTS might add to the downgrade-centric analysis of issuer diversification. How do these two approaches relate to each other? What are the strengths and weaknesses of each? Can they be integrated into a single consistent scheme?

## DOWNGRADE RISK BEFORE AND AFTER THE CREDIT CRISIS

The first approach to optimal diversification places the emphasis on downgrade risk. There is a strong motivation for it. We want to prevent a single issuer-specific event from causing a large loss in the portfolio. So, we model both the frequency and intensity of such events. Ultimately, the primary issuer-specific risk in credit portfolios is default and, theoretically, one could approach diversification using models of default risk. In practice, however, this is not the most effective route for investment grade portfolios, for several reasons. First, most distressed issuers do not go directly to default from an investment-grade rating; it is much more typical for an issuer to be downgraded below investment grade, after which it may eventually default, or recover. Immediate defaults are rare events whose probability is very hard to estimate. Downgrades are a more likely cause of significant losses in such portfolios—and are more easily modeled.

We therefore use ratings downgrades as proxies for issuer events in the corporate market. This does not imply that rating agency actions themselves are the primary source of risk; rather, we expect a significant change in an issuer's creditworthiness eventually to be reflected in its rating. In many cases, the market reacts to this change before the rating shift is announced. We study that by looking at the performance of downgraded bonds and measuring both the magnitude and the time course of their underperformance relative to their peer groups. These empirical results, combined with rating agency data on the historical frequency of ratings transitions, allow us to model the risk of portfolio losses from downgrades.

Not surprisingly, the results change significantly with the inclusion of the credit crisis of 2007–2009. To demonstrate this, we first truncate the data sample shortly before the onset of the crisis, and then compare the results to those obtained using all available data through the end of 2010.

**TABLE 11.1** Average Underperformance due to Downgrades (August 1988–December 2007)

| Months Prior to Downgrade | Initial Quality | Observations | Monthly Underperformance (%/month) | | Quarterly or Annual Underperformance (%/quarter or %/year) | | |
|---|---|---|---|---|---|---|---|
| | | | Mean | Std. Dev. | Mean | Std. Dev. | t-stat |
| 0–2 | Aaa–Aa | 791 | −0.06 | 1.37 | −0.18 | 2.29 | −2.2 |
| | A | 1,328 | −0.80 | 3.76 | −2.39 | 6.83 | −12.7 |
| | Baa | 1,058 | −3.12 | 10.41 | −9.35 | 20.90 | −14.6 |
| 3–5 | Aaa–Aa | 791 | −0.04 | 1.13 | −0.13 | 1.47 | −2.5 |
| | A | 1,328 | −0.27 | 1.71 | −0.81 | 2.67 | −11.1 |
| | Baa | 1,058 | −1.00 | 5.20 | −2.99 | 7.50 | −13.0 |
| 6–8 | Aaa–Aa | 791 | −0.06 | 0.91 | −0.18 | 1.50 | −3.4 |
| | A | 1,328 | −0.10 | 1.35 | −0.29 | 2.21 | −4.7 |
| | Baa | 1,058 | −0.56 | 2.80 | −1.69 | 5.04 | −10.9 |
| 9–11 | Aaa–Aa | 791 | 0.00 | 0.87 | 0.01 | 1.28 | 0.1 |
| | A | 1,328 | 0.03 | 1.20 | 0.09 | 1.93 | 1.8 |
| | Baa | 1,058 | −0.08 | 1.94 | −0.25 | 3.52 | −2.3 |
| Full year | Aaa–Aa | 791 | | | −0.49 | 2.79 | −4.9 |
| | A | 1,328 | | | −3.39 | 7.81 | −15.8 |
| | Baa | 1,058 | | | −14.28 | 22.29 | −20.8 |

*Note:* The last three columns show the quarterly statistics for each three-month period in the body of the table and the annual statistics for the full year preceding a downgrade in the bottom section.
*Source:* Barclays Capital.

Table 11.1 shows the performance of downgraded bonds relative to their peer groups from August 1988 through December 2007. We find that the majority of the price impact from a downgrade occurs in the final few months before the event, with the largest underperformance in the month of the downgrade and the two months preceding it. As we look further back, we find a noticeable underperformance three to five months before a downgrade. The effect can be felt as far back as eight months before a downgrade. Nine or more months before a downgrade, bonds do not significantly underperform their peer groups.

For example, securities downgraded from Baa experienced an average peer group underperformance of −14.28% during the year leading up to the downgrade. This amount accumulates unevenly through the year. The average quarterly underperformance was −9.35% in the quarter immediately preceding a downgrade, but only −2.99% and −1.69%, respectively, in the previous two quarters. The *t*-statistic shows all of these numbers to be highly significant. In contrast, the much smaller average underperformance of −0.25% in the fourth quarter preceding the downgrade is barely significant.

Severe return consequences are usually limited to downgrades from lower-rated credits. The most drastic underperformance is found when bonds are downgraded from Baa to below investment grade. The crossing of the investment grade boundary can create major price dislocations because many portfolios (forced, for example, by the investment policy) must sell into a falling market.[2] For bonds downgraded from single-A, the resulting underperformance in the two to three quarters preceding the event is roughly one fourth of the losses realized in downgrades from Baa. The time distribution of these losses roughly mirrors the Baa pattern. For securities rated Aaa and Aa, we did not detect any statistically significant underperformance due to downgrades.

In all cases, the standard deviation of underperformance is much larger than the average underperformance. This means that a downgraded bond may do much worse than the average. In fact, several bonds downgraded from Baa lost more than half of their value during the year preceding the downgrade.

The historical losses realized by downgraded bonds can be combined with the probabilities of downgrades to build a simple model of downgrade risk for a single bond or a portfolio. The results, based on the full-year data from the bottom section of Table 11.1, are summarized in Table 11.2. These numbers can be interpreted as follows. For any bond rated Baa, the expected

**TABLE 11.2** Downgrade-Based Model for Diversification (August 1988–December 2007)

| Initial Rating | Downgrade Probability (%/year) | Statistics of Losses for Downgraded Bonds (%/year) | | Resulting Statistics for Expected Loss on a Single Bond (%/year) | | Ratio of Position Sizes Relative to Baa (inverse volatility) |
|---|---|---|---|---|---|---|
| | | Mean | Std. Dev. | Mean | Std. Dev. | |
| Aaa–Aa | 6.35 | −0.49 | 2.79 | −0.03 | 0.71 | 8.9 |
| A | 5.79 | −3.39 | 7.81 | −0.20 | 2.05 | 3.1 |
| Baa | 5.78 | −14.28 | 22.29 | −0.82 | 6.36 | 1.0 |

*Source:* Moody's and Barclays Capital.

loss due to downgrades over a one-year horizon is 82 bps, but with a very large standard deviation of 636 bps. This measure of downgrade-related risk combines the probability of a downgrade with the uncertainty about the losses that could be realized should one occur. This risk is much smaller for bonds rated A and nearly non-existent for debt rated Aa.

We use this model to define an optimal portfolio structuring problem in which we seek to track the U.S. Corporate Index using a given number of bonds, such that the portfolio loss volatility due to downgrades is minimized. The portfolio is assumed to match the index exposures to all systematic risk factors, including yield curve, sector, and quality. We further assume that the portfolio matches the market weights of the benchmark in each quality group, and that both the portfolio and the benchmark allocate equal weight to each bond within a given credit quality. The goal of the optimization is to determine how many bonds (out of the given total) the portfolio should have in each credit quality to minimize the risk from downgrades. We show that the optimal solution requires greater diversification in the higher-risk quality groups; in particular, the optimal position sizes in different quality groups should be inversely proportional to the dispersion of the downgrade loss. Thus, because the standard deviation of downgrade loss for a single Baa bond is 8.9 times that of an Aaa–Aa bond, the portfolio position limits for Aaa–Aa bonds should be 8.9 times as large as those for Baa bonds.

In Table 11.3, we extend the analysis shown in Table 11.1 through the end of December 2010. Our conclusions regarding the time course of downgrade losses do not change. The majority of losses is incurred in the quarter preceding the downgrade; significant additional losses are observed two quarters preceding the downgrade, and for Baa issuers, up to nine months ahead. However, when we examine the magnitudes of losses shown for different qualities, we find some striking differences between Table 11.1 and Table 11.3. The mean and standard deviation of downgrade loss for Baa-rated issuers do not change much with the addition of the data from the 2007–2009 credit crisis; however, those for the two higher-rated categories show substantial increases in both columns. The average annual under-performance of issuers downgraded from single-A increase from 3.39% to 5.55%; for Aaa–Aa issuers, the increase is from 0.49% to 2.10%.

Table 11.4 shows the implications of the increase in realized downgrade losses for portfolio structuring. The ratio of downgrade loss volatilities be-tween issuers with different ratings has become markedly smaller; so has the recommended ratio of position sizes. The crisis of 2007–2009 strongly affected higher-rated issuers. As a result, the optimal position size ratios have become much less skewed.

It is not particularly surprising that an empirical study of the credit markets of 2008 assigns greater risk to securities rated A. After all, the

**TABLE 11.3** Average Underperformance due to Downgrades (August 1988–December 2010)

| Months Prior to Downgrade | Initial Quality | Observations | Monthly Underperformance (%/month) | | Quarterly or Annual Underperformance (%/quarter or %/year) | | |
|---|---|---|---|---|---|---|---|
| | | | Mean | Std. Dev. | Mean | Std. Dev. | t-stat |
| 0–2 | Aaa–Aa | 1,036 | −0.37 | 3.40 | −1.12 | 6.36 | −5.7 |
| | A | 1,635 | −1.30 | 7.86 | −3.89 | 13.46 | −11.7 |
| | Baa | 1,217 | −2.82 | 10.66 | −8.46 | 20.95 | −14.1 |
| 3–5 | Aaa–Aa | 1,036 | −0.19 | 1.80 | −0.57 | 2.76 | −6.6 |
| | A | 1,635 | −0.48 | 3.30 | −1.44 | 5.77 | −10.1 |
| | Baa | 1,217 | −1.07 | 5.58 | −3.20 | 8.36 | −13.4 |
| 6–8 | Aaa–Aa | 1,036 | −0.08 | 1.08 | −0.24 | 1.79 | −4.3 |
| | A | 1,635 | 0.01 | 2.72 | 0.02 | 4.58 | 0.2 |
| | Baa | 1,217 | −0.59 | 3.42 | −1.76 | 5.56 | −11.1 |
| 9–11 | Aaa–Aa | 1,036 | −0.06 | 0.97 | −0.17 | 1.55 | −3.6 |
| | A | 1,635 | −0.08 | 2.25 | −0.24 | 3.56 | −2.7 |
| | Baa | 1,217 | −0.13 | 2.60 | −0.40 | 4.66 | −3.0 |
| Full year | Aaa–Aa | 1,036 | | | −2.10 | 7.83 | −8.6 |
| | A | 1,635 | | | −5.55 | 15.01 | −14.9 |
| | Baa | 1,217 | | | −13.83 | 21.79 | −22.1 |

*Note:* The last three columns show the quarterly statistics for each three-month period in the body of the table, and the annual statistics for the full year preceding a downgrade in the bottom section.
*Source:* Barclays Capital.

**TABLE 11.4** Downgrade-Based Model for Diversification (August 1988–December 2010)

| Initial Rating | Downgrade Probability (%/year) | Statistics of Losses for Downgraded Bonds (%/year) | | Resulting Statistics for Expected Loss on a Single Bond (%/year) | | Ratio of Position Sizes Relative to Baa (inverse volatility) |
|---|---|---|---|---|---|---|
| | | Mean | Std. Dev. | Mean | Std. Dev. | |
| Aaa–Aa | 8.24 | −2.10 | 7.83 | −0.17 | 2.33 | 2.6 |
| A | 6.12 | −5.55 | 15.01 | −0.34 | 3.96 | 1.6 |
| Baa | 5.66 | −13.83 | 21.79 | −0.78 | 6.14 | 1 |

*Source:* Moody's and Barclays Capital.

headline event of this crisis was the default of Lehman Brothers, which carried an A credit rating when it filed for bankruptcy. Could this single event be sufficient to explain the differences between the results in Tables 11.2 and 11.4? While there is a noticeable change in the results for debt rated A when Lehman Brothers is excluded from the sample, the overall conclusion remains essentially unchanged; the position size ratio changes from 2.6 : 1.6 : 1 to 2.9 : 1.9 : 1. Even after excluding the performance effect of the Lehman Brothers default, the optimal ratings remain far less skewed than indicated by the data through the end of 2007.

Performance of downgraded issuers varies over time, reflecting different credit market environments. In the yearly numbers from 1989 through 2010, shown in Table 11.5, one can recognize the major disturbances and crises of

**TABLE 11.5** Average Underperformance Due to Downgrades: Yearly Results, 1989–2010

|      | Observations | | | Mean (%/month) | | | Standard Deviation (%/month) | | |
|------|--------|-----|-----|--------|-------|-------|--------|------|-------|
|      | Aaa–Aa | A   | Baa | Aaa–Aa | A     | Baa   | Aaa–Aa | A    | Baa   |
| 1989 | 15     | 30  | 18  | −0.34  | −0.20 | −0.35 | 1.42   | 1.22 | 1.97  |
| 1990 | 100    | 85  | 24  | 0.02   | −0.26 | −1.62 | 0.69   | 1.56 | 6.52  |
| 1991 | 134    | 86  | 52  | −0.05  | −0.09 | −0.85 | 0.70   | 1.38 | 3.74  |
| 1992 | 85     | 129 | 29  | 0.02   | −0.09 | −0.30 | 1.13   | 1.08 | 2.35  |
| 1993 | 33     | 14  | 35  | 0.06   | 0.02  | −0.28 | 1.00   | 0.72 | 1.57  |
| 1994 | 8      | 38  | 15  | −0.08  | −0.08 | −0.37 | 0.41   | 0.96 | 1.84  |
| 1995 | 51     | 59  | 25  | 0.05   | −0.08 | −0.45 | 0.67   | 1.23 | 2.52  |
| 1996 | 32     | 56  | 35  | 0.01   | −0.05 | −0.50 | 0.51   | 0.76 | 4.01  |
| 1997 | 5      | 77  | 9   | −0.05  | −0.16 | −0.12 | 0.43   | 0.64 | 0.76  |
| 1998 | 44     | 59  | 46  | −0.10  | −0.27 | −0.53 | 0.86   | 1.19 | 2.83  |
| 1999 | 37     | 58  | 45  | 0.00   | −0.12 | −0.96 | 1.00   | 1.23 | 3.40  |
| 2000 | 46     | 89  | 49  | −0.05  | −0.46 | −3.13 | 0.56   | 1.80 | 8.70  |
| 2001 | 30     | 135 | 111 | −0.26  | −0.44 | −1.92 | 1.98   | 2.78 | 10.20 |
| 2002 | 68     | 178 | 222 | −0.14  | −0.63 | −2.08 | 2.04   | 4.50 | 8.74  |
| 2003 | 59     | 78  | 72  | −0.03  | −0.40 | −0.80 | 1.42   | 3.03 | 5.07  |
| 2004 | 8      | 39  | 59  | 0.07   | −0.08 | −0.13 | 0.71   | 1.19 | 2.28  |
| 2005 | 8      | 31  | 99  | −0.03  | −0.21 | −0.95 | 0.30   | 1.08 | 2.86  |
| 2006 | 4      | 18  | 45  | −0.01  | −0.09 | −0.37 | 0.21   | 0.72 | 2.65  |
| 2007 | 24     | 69  | 68  | −0.11  | −0.40 | −0.66 | 0.51   | 1.46 | 2.48  |
| 2008 | 192    | 158 | 61  | −0.66  | −1.95 | −1.47 | 3.81   | 9.93 | 5.10  |
| 2009 | 46     | 134 | 71  | −0.32  | −0.66 | −0.79 | 3.34   | 9.53 | 10.57 |
| 2010 | 7      | 15  | 27  | −1.21  | 1.11  | 0.13  | 3.81   | 3.61 | 6.12  |

*Source:* Barclays Capital.

these two decades. For example, the leading role played by bonds rated Aa and A (mostly financials) in the credit crisis of 2007–2009 is clearly apparent. The magnitude of the underperformance in these qualities is unprecedented both in absolute terms and relative to Baa.

Of course, the possibility of downgrades is not the only source of nonsystematic risk. Even securities that do not experience rating changes exhibit "natural" spread volatility. This source of return variance may also motivate portfolio diversification. To estimate the magnitude of this type of idiosyncratic volatility, not related to either secular changes in sector spreads or downgrade events, we proceed as follows. From the same data set used to quantify downgrade risk, we isolate a set of bonds whose ratings remained unchanged for at least the next six months. Every month, we measure the cross-sectional standard deviation of spread changes across all the bonds within each peer group and average this quantity over time. The resulting spread volatilities are higher for lower-rated credits, as was the case for downgrade risk, but in a much less drastic manner. After adjusting these spread volatilities to the same units as downgrade risk (excess return, in percent per year), we combine the two sources of risk by adding the variances.

Table 11.6 shows the results of this analysis, for the period up to December 2007 and including all data through December 2010.[3] For the data not including the 2007–2009 crisis, the overall nonsystematic risk volatilities, including both downgrades and natural spread volatility, are much less differentiated by quality than those from downgrade risk alone.

**TABLE 11.6**  Sources of Return Volatility (%/year) by Credit Rating

|  | Due to Downgrade | Other Nonsystematic | Total Nonsystematic Volatility |
|---|---|---|---|
| **April 1990–December 2007** | | | |
| Aaa–Aa | 0.70 | 1.60 | 1.75 |
| A | 2.08 | 1.90 | 2.81 |
| Baa | 6.42 | 2.94 | 7.06 |
| Position-size ratio | 9.2 : 3.1 : 1.0 | 1.8 : 1.5 : 1.0 | 4.0 : 2.5 : 1.0 |
| **April 1990–December 2010** | | | |
| Aaa–Aa | 2.37 | 1.76 | 2.95 |
| A | 4.02 | 2.42 | 4.69 |
| Baa | 6.19 | 3.63 | 7.17 |
| Position-size ratio | 2.6 : 1.5 : 1.0 | 2.1 : 1.5 : 1.0 | 2.4 : 1.5 : 1.0 |

*Source:* Barclays Capital.

A comparison shows that while downgrade risk dominates in Baa, natural spread volatility may dominate in the higher qualities. When based on these pre-crisis data, the recommended position size ratios are $9.2:3.1:1$ if we base them on downgrade risk alone. However, if we include all the sources of non-systematic risk, we obtain optimal position size ratios of $4.0:2.5:1$.

In contrast to the pre-crisis period, accounting for additional sources of non-systematic risk makes less of a difference to the optimal position size ratios when looking at the entire sample. Considering just the higher estimated downgrade risk for Aaa-Aa and A-rated issuers, we find a large reduction in the optimal ratios. Incorporating natural spread volatility now makes only a very minor difference, bringing the ratios from $2:6:1.5:1.0$ to $2.4:1.5:1.0$.

The changes in the output of our model in the aftermath of the credit crisis reflect tensions that have been widely discussed in the industry. The reliability of credit ratings has been called into question as investors in highly rated instruments suffered large losses, particularly in structured products. However, finding a suitable alternative is difficult. Investment mandates need concise, transparent and reasonably stable mechanisms for specifying what instruments may be included in a portfolio; credit ratings were developed to meet this need and, despite their shortcomings, remain the primary reference for investment policy.

One alternative that we investigate in the next section is based on the DTS model, which relies on spread as the key indicator of risk in credit markets. The model can be applied to the task of setting issuer limits in a framework that may or may not consider credit ratings.

## USING DTS TO SET POSITION-SIZE RATIOS

As discussed in Chapter 1, spread volatility depends on spread level in a near-linear fashion and, therefore, excess return volatility has a similar dependence on DTS. This holds true for systematic risk exposures to industry groups and for non-systematic exposures to individual issuers. Therefore, a prudent way to limit the risk exposure to issuers could be to impose a cap on the total DTS contribution of an issuer (duration times spread times market weight), rather than a cap on its market weight. This would allow a portfolio to have large concentrations in low-spread issuers while enforcing stricter constraints on high-spread issuers.

This DTS-based approach is in some ways similar to the downgrade-based one that defines issuer caps in terms of market weight limits that depend on credit quality; yet there are some crucial differences. In both schemes, the basic principle is to allow greater concentrations to issuers perceived to be less risky and require more diversification where risk is greater. The fundamental difference between the two methods is the choice of the risk indicator: the quality assigned by the rating agencies or the spread determined by the market. Each has its own merits; ratings are more stable and transparent but spreads react to market events much more quickly. As the credit quality of a particular issuer deteriorates, a spread-based indicator will register the increase in risk much faster than a ratings-based indicator. Nevertheless, while this may give a clear advantage when measuring risk, the cost of a policy forcing managers to transact on spread gyrations could be prohibitive. A rigid cap on DTS exposure would make the limits dependent on spreads and could lead to inefficient forced selling.

How can we incorporate the DTS measure into a practical approach to setting issuer limits? One modest step in this direction would be to maintain the structure of the original scheme, but use DTS periodically to recalibrate the limits in response to market conditions. That is, issuer caps can be specified as limits on market weight that can differ by quality—but the ratios of position limits for different ratings groups can be periodically updated to market conditions rather than relying on a long-term historical study of the performance effect of downgrades.

The key conclusion of the downgrade-based study is that the optimal ratio of portfolio position sizes in two qualities is given by the inverse of the ratio of their volatilities, defined as the projected volatility of a bond's monthly return relative to its peers. In the previous section, we calculated this ratio based on our empirical model of downgrade risk; however, the relationship could be based on other estimates of risk as well.

We can therefore maintain the grouping by credit quality and use a simple DTS-based approach to measure the relative risks in different credit ratings. The ratio of the projected non-systematic volatilities of two asset classes can be approximated by the ratio of their DTS. Figure 11.1 shows the average DTS levels of different quality subsets of the U.S. Corporate Index and how they have evolved. The figure shows how spreads widened in 2000–2002, tightened steadily over the next several years, and then exploded in 2008.

We use the data shown in Figure 11.1 to calculate the optimal position size ratios by inverting the ratio of DTS levels. Figure 11.2 shows the resulting position limits for bonds rated Aaa–Aa and A, respectively, in relation to the Baa position limit. For example, as of December 2001, the ratio of the largest allowed positions in the three quality groups was 4.3 : 1.7 : 1.0. (That is, a position in a bond rated Aa that is 4.3 times as large as one in a bond rated Baa will carry the same amount of non-systematic risk.) These numbers are in line with the downgrade-based results that we published around that time. As market volatility (and spreads) ground lower in the following years, these ratios increased, peaking in March 2005 at 6.6 : 3.0 : 1. However, when spreads skyrocketed in 2008, the ratio was not preserved,

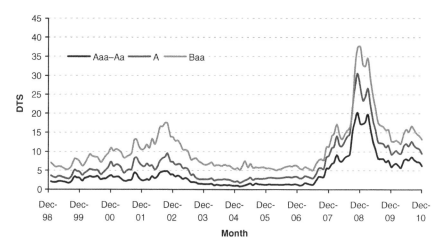

**FIGURE 11.1** Average DTS of Corporate Index by Quality (January 1999–December 2010)
*Source:* Barclays Capital.

and no credit quality was deemed free of risk. As all spreads widened, the ratio of position sizes declined to 1.4 : 1.0 : 1.0 as of September 2008. The last data point in the sample, as of December 2010, indicates a ratio of 2.1 : 1.4 : 1.

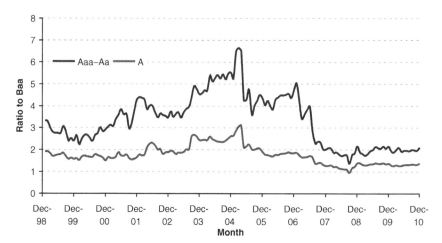

**FIGURE 11.2** Ratios of Position Limits Based on the DTS Model
*Note:* Positions of Aaa–Aa and A-rated issuers relative to the limits for Baa-rated issuers, January 1999–December 2010.
*Source:* Barclays Capital.

A comparison of these results to those in Table 11.6 suggests a close agreement between the two models. Given that DTS is a predictor of overall excess return volatility, not just downgrade risk, we focus on the total non-systematic return volatility from the rightmost column of Table 11.6. Figure 11.2 shows that the DTS approach would have justified position size ratios of about $4:2:1$ from 2005 through early 2007, based on the tight spreads prevalent at the time. This is in line with the 1990–2007 results shown in the top half of Table 11.6. However, by the end of 2007, the DTS model would have already signaled a shift to a less skewed ratio closer to $2:1.5:1$, which agrees fairly well with the downgrade-based results through the end of 2010. This very clearly highlights the difference between the two approaches. As is typical for analyses based on long-term historical averages, downgrade-based assumptions necessarily lag market events. A portfolio manager who, in summer 2007, was deciding on allocation limits across qualities would have been better served by relying on DTS-implied ratios.

Lastly, one needs to be careful not to misinterpret the position-size ratios discussed here. The lack of change in the size of the Baa position limit does not imply that it remained constant throughout this period in market-weight terms. It is meant to highlight our focus on the *ratio* of the limits in different quality groups, rather than absolute constraints. A ratio of 4:2:1, for example, means only one thing: If the manager decides to limit the allocation to a single Baa issuer to 0.5% of the portfolio, the maximum allocations to single-A and Aaa–Aa issuers should be 1% and 2%, respectively. The precise sizing of these limits needs to reflect the plan sponsor's risk appetite and may be adjusted from time to time to reflect the market environment.

## COMPARING AND COMBINING THE TWO APPROACHES TO ISSUER LIMITS

We have presented two different approaches to setting issuer limits. In the first, issuer limits are expressed in terms of market weights and vary by credit quality. This corresponds to the way many plan sponsors specify investment policy constraints to their portfolio managers. The second approach is based on the assumption that to maintain a desired limit on the risk exposure to any given issuer, one should ensure that all issuer DTS contributions remain below some threshold. However, as discussed, this approach leads to practical difficulties in implementation. A realistic compromise could be to use DTS on a periodic basis to recalibrate the issuer limits in the market-weight scheme. This section discusses these issues in more detail.

The sufficient diversification approach to setting limits on issuer market weights has some clear advantages that make it very well suited for specifying an investment policy. A permitted position is easy to identify and is not subject to debate. Furthermore, because ratings evolve rather slowly, the guidelines are stable and do not force a manager to churn the portfolio as markets move.

This is not true for a strict implementation of a policy that limits DTS contributions. Suppose the maximum allowed DTS contribution from any issuer is 3.0 and the manager establishes a 0.5% position in issuer XYZ with a spread of 100 bps and a duration of 5 years, for a DTS contribution of $100 \times 5 \times 0.5\% = 2.5$. If the spread widens to above 120 bps, the manager would be required to sell off some of the position to stay within the limits. This example highlights some difficulties with this arrangement. First, pricing uncertainty can make it unclear whether a given position is within the guidelines. Second, the need to adjust positions as spreads change imposes a hardship on managers and increases transaction costs for investors.

Another difficulty with a policy based exclusively on DTS contributions is that it can potentially allow very large exposures to short-maturity bonds. While the risk of such a position may not be large in terms of spread volatility or excess return volatility, it is clearly undesirable from a tail risk point of view. A prudent approach to tail risk is to limit the overall portfolio exposure to any single name.

Nevertheless, it is hard to ignore the evidence that credit ratings do not always present the full, or even true, picture. The broad-brush treatment that allows the same position size for all A-rated issuers, even with large differences in spreads across this peer group, clearly leaves room for improvement. There is no question that incorporating information on issuer DTS contributions improves our ability to estimate issuer risk; the difficulty is how to set up rules or guidelines that incorporate this information without causing unreasonably high turnover. With some ingenuity, it might be possible to reap the benefits of DTS-based risk controls without imposing too much of an operational burden. For example, one could establish a two-tiered constraint with different thresholds for new and existing positions. For instance, in the above example, if the DTS contribution limit were 3.0 for new purchases and 4.0 for existing positions, the XYZ position would remain within the guidelines unless the spread widened from 100 to beyond 160. Presumably, the requirement to reevaluate the exposure to an issuer after a spread move of this magnitude would not be perceived as overly intrusive.

A more difficult challenge for a system of limits on issuer DTS contributions would be a general rise in corporate spreads, as in 2008. In a crisis environment, virtually every issuer in the credit portfolio might exceed the previously established caps on issuer exposures. Should managers be forced to rebalance their portfolios massively into a market with no liquidity?

Forced selling is never a good thing. Indeed, Chapters 12 and 13 demonstrate how the performance of corporate bond indexes is affected by the forced selling of bonds downgraded to below investment grade. We conclude that investors would be better served by holding onto fallen angels well beyond the downgrade month, because on average they tend eventually to recoup the unjustifiably large losses they sustain when managers of investment-grade portfolios are forced to sell them at once. How might these results apply to a policy of selling upon a spread widening, even without any change in ratings? This is not at all clear. One might argue that this could help encourage the sale of weakening credits before a downgrade strikes, thus reducing losses in the long run. Conversely, this could just serve to lock in losses in many bonds that will recover and never suffer a downgrade. Generally, a momentum strategy like this one does well in trending markets and poorly in choppy markets. If enough market participants adopt this approach, it could lead to destabilizing behavior in which spread widening and asset sales reinforce each other in a vicious cycle.[4]

Even when DTS limits are in place, one would probably want to include a hard limit on market value weights, to prevent extremely large concentrations in short-maturity or low-spread securities.

In short, when specifying hard limits on issuer exposures in a portfolio, plan sponsors should retain the time-honored tradition of market-weight limits. An update of our original study to include the effects of the credit crisis suggests that the differentials between the concentrations for different ratings brackets should be less skewed than in our earlier findings. However, we also believe that managers should track and control the DTS exposures to issuers and ensure that no single exposure grows too large. Rather than implementing this rule via a hard cutoff, managers should have a roughly defined upper limit for issuer DTS exposures and use their judgment in managing these exposures according to market conditions.

## CONCLUSION

The credit crisis of 2007–2009 reminded us yet again to be wary of issuer concentrations. Plan sponsors may no longer wish to allow positions in higher-rated credits to be much greater than those in lower-rated credits.

Keeping track of the DTS exposures to individual issuers within a portfolio is a good way to monitor issuer risk and can often highlight problem issuers before they are subject to rating agency actions. While there are some practical issues with explicitly setting limits on DTS exposures in an investment policy, we recommend that both managers and sponsors employ this valuable tool as part of their efforts to control issuer risk.

# NOTES

1. See Chapter 14 in Dynkin, Gould, Hyman, Konstantinovsky, and Phelps (2007).
2. A detailed treatment of this issue can be found in Chapters 12 and 13. In the former, we investigate how the credit index excess returns are affected by rules that require selling bonds immediately after downgrades to high yield. The latter focuses on the price dynamics of these "fallen angels."
3. Historical spread data were available only from April 1990. This explains the different starting point and the small differences in the downgrade risk between this table and Tables 11.2 and 11.4.
4. This danger that de-risking trades in cash markets could create a destabilizing force is probably very small compared with the corresponding danger from speculative activity in the CDS market. Furthermore, if portfolio managers respond to a general widening of spreads by attempting to diversify, no net selling pressure will develop. Imagine two similar portfolios, one with a position in issuer XYZ and another with a position in ABC; while the first manager sells half his XYZ to buy ABC, the other might be happy to take the other side of the trade.

### CHAPTER 12

# How Best to Capture the Spread Premium of Corporate Bonds?

Periods of poor credit bond returns often cause investors to reassess whether credit should be a permanent part of their fixed income allocation. In fact, from 1990 through 2009, the average annual excess return (over duration-matched Treasuries) of the U.S. Corporate Index was only 27 bps with a standard deviation of 741 bps, despite a strong credit market rally in 2009.[1] For investors looking to credit bonds as a way to clip higher returns with modest additional risk relative to treasuries, such performance is not particularly attractive. In response, investors began to wonder if they should abandon a persistent allocation to credit altogether, relying on the asset class solely as a market-timing tool.

Despite the historical record, we suspect that many investors maintain a persistent allocation to credit because they believe that if they can endure transitory spread volatility, credit bonds will, in time, earn an excess return net of default losses—a credit spread premium—over comparable duration Treasury bonds. To avoid confusion, we use the term *reported index excess return* to refer to excess returns that include the impact of spread changes, in addition to default losses. We use the term *spread premium* to refer to excess returns net of realized default losses but not including the impact of credit spread changes. A buy-and-hold credit investor will earn the spread premium at maturity (or default.) Before maturity, the investor's mark-to-market will reflect the reported index excess return.

We first explore the magnitude of the credit spread premium. We show that credit has produced a surprisingly large credit spread premium—so large that some refer to it as a *credit spread puzzle*.

But, are investors able to capture this credit spread premium? This may seem an odd question. If an investor has a persistent allocation to credit, then should not the credit spread premium just flow through? Not necessarily. Most investors use the IG Corporate Index to represent their corporate portfolio allocation. However, the IG Corporate Index is not a static set of bonds. Indeed, the index follows a set of pre-defined rules that sometimes force selling certain bonds. If these bonds are sold at a time when their spreads are particularly wide, for reasons not necessarily related to expected default losses, then index rules may be constraining investors' ability to capture the credit spread premium. We measure the impact of these constraints and show that an alternative corporate index might enable investors to capture almost 80% more spread premium.

The results also suggest a stable, low-volatility, long-term outperformance strategy for investment managers who use the standard Corporate Index as their performance benchmark. Managers should be able to harvest the additional credit spread premium and outperform the benchmark if they can, at least for a while, retain bonds that the Corporate Index discards.

## THE CREDIT SPREAD PREMIUM

At issuance, a credit bond offers a positive yield spread over a comparable maturity Treasury bond. Investors demand additional yield as compensation for the possibility that the credit bond, unlike the Treasury bond, may default before maturity with a recovery value less than 100% of par. In addition, it is more expensive to execute a roundtrip trade in a credit bond than it is for a Treasury bond. An investor who anticipates selling the bond at some point would like to be compensated for this expected liquidity cost by requiring a wider spread at the time of purchase. Another factor affecting credit spread is the uncertainty regarding future default losses and liquidity costs. In particular, both tend to increase during tough macroeconomic times when investors need their credit assets to perform well. In such a world, risk-averse investors demand additional spread, a risk premium, beyond the expected default and liquidity costs, to compensate them for the possibility that the credit bond may have to be sold exactly during economic times when both default and liquidity costs are high. (See Chapters 5 and 6.)

There are investors who can ride out difficult times with little need to liquidate portfolio holdings. These investors have an opportunity to recoup a credit bond's spread, net of realized default losses. Indexes should also earn, over time, this credit spread premium.

## MEASURING THE CREDIT SPREAD PREMIUM FOR THE IG CORPORATE INDEX

What has been the magnitude of the credit spread premium, that is, excess returns over Treasuries net of losses from defaults? We use two approaches to measure the spread premium. The traditional approach is to take the beginning of period spread (to Treasuries) for a credit bond or index, and then subtract off the realized default loss experience of the bonds. We use Moody's historical default and recovery data along with the historical spread and composition data for the Corporate Index as our representation of the corporate market. A second approach is to take the Corporate Index reported excess returns (versus treasuries), reflecting the mark-to-market performance of the bonds (including default), and add back the component of the reported index excess return attributable to market spread changes. While both methods should reach the same broad conclusion over long periods, there may be differences over shorter periods. Fortunately, we have historical data extending back to 1990 that allow us to use both methods to measure the credit spread premium over long horizons.

## Measuring the Spread Premium Using Historical Default and Recovery Data

We first measure the spread premium using the default and loss-given-default record as reported by Moody's. Using the average ratings distribution and OAS of the Corporate Index since 1990, and Moody's cumulative default and average recovery rates,[2] we estimate the realized corporate spread premium with a simple calculation shown in Table 12.1. For example, over the period 1990–2009, Baa bonds had an average share of 33% of the index with an average OAS of 174 bps. During this period, their average annual default rate was 0.41% and their average recovery rate was 44.6% (meaning that the average loss given default was 55.4%). Multiplying the annual

**TABLE 12.1** Estimated Average Annual Credit Spread Premium Using Historical Default Data, IG Corporate Index (1990–2009)

| Rating | Average Weight in IG Corporate Index | Average OAS (bps) | Annual Default Rate[a] | Average Loss Given Default (1 – Recovery rate) | Annual Loss Due to Defaults (bps) | Annual Excess Return (bps) |
|---|---|---|---|---|---|---|
| Aaa | 4.50% | 79 | 0.02% | 55.40% | 1 | 78 |
| Aa | 16.50% | 86 | 0.05% | 55.40% | 3 | 83 |
| A | 46.00% | 118 | 0.16% | 55.40% | 9 | 109 |
| Baa | 33.00% | 174 | 0.41% | 55.40% | 22 | 152 |
| | | **130** | | | | **118** |

[a]From Moody's Corporate Default and Recovery Rates, 1920–2009, February 2010.
*Source:* Moody's and Barclays Capital.

default rate by the average loss given default, we obtain realized average annual default losses of 22 bps/year for the Baa cohort. Given an average OAS of 174 bps/year, the realized spread premium for Baa corporate bonds should average 152 bps/year over the 20-year period. After conducting the same computation for the other three investment-grade rating categories, we sum the market value–weighted results and find that investment-grade corporate bonds have earned an average annual spread premium of 118 bps/year. Although the figure is produced using a simple calculation, similar results have been found by Elton, Gruber, Agrawal, and Mann (2001) and others.

To get a sense of the volatility of the credit spread premium, we repeat the estimation exercise and examine overlapping five-year periods starting in 1990. We choose five-year periods because this interval lines up with the average duration of the index and it approximates the length of an economic cycle. The results in Table 12.2 suggest that the credit spread premium is consistently positive and consequential. In other words, corporate spreads are considerably and persistently larger than realized losses from default. (This finding is the "credit spread puzzle" mentioned previously.)[3] Considering that the average corporate bond spread during this period was 130 bps, spread premium accounted for over 91% of corporate spread levels.

Figure 12.1 shows that the credit spread premium is highly correlated with the market spread level at the beginning of the period. This is not too surprising. We show in Chapter 6 that, in addition to expected default cost, spread levels are driven by market risk premium and liquidity cost. Assuming these are largely mean-reverting over a five-year period, the realized spread premium would be highly correlated with the market spread level at the beginning of the period.

### Measuring the Spread Premium Using Index Excess Returns

The historical default experience indicates that corporates have earned a significant spread premium over the past 20 years. This supports the case for investors to have a persistent allocation to IG credit as part of their fixed income benchmark. We now proceed to measure the credit spread premium for the IG Corporate Index using index reported excess returns.

Barclays Capital reports excess returns that equal the difference in total return between a bond and a portfolio of hypothetical par Treasury bonds matching the bond's key rate duration exposures.[4] Unlike the credit spread premium calculated using Moody's realized default loss data, the reported index excess returns include a market spread change component. Table 12.3

**TABLE 12.2** Estimated Average Annual Credit Spread Premium Using Historical Default Data, IG Corporate Index, Five-Year Periods (1990–2005)

| | Beginning Year (bps) | | | | | | | | | | | | | | | |
|---|---|---|---|---|---|---|---|---|---|---|---|---|---|---|---|---|
| | 1990 | 1991 | 1992 | 1993 | 1994 | 1995 | 1996 | 1997 | 1998 | 1999 | 2000 | 2001 | 2002 | 2003 | 2004 | 2005 |
| Annual excess return over five-year period | 100 | 157 | 111 | 88 | 72 | 74 | 60 | 46 | 49 | 99 | 97 | 186 | 166 | 183 | 87 | 65 |
| Corporate index OAS at beginning of five-year period | 102 | 158 | 109 | 89 | 73 | 79 | 65 | 57 | 67 | 117 | 113 | 204 | 178 | 187 | 95 | 81 |
| Excess return as percent of OAS | 98% | 99% | 102% | 98% | 98% | 93% | 92% | 81% | 73% | 85% | 86% | 91% | 93% | 98% | 92% | 80% |

*Source:* Moody's and Barclays Capital.

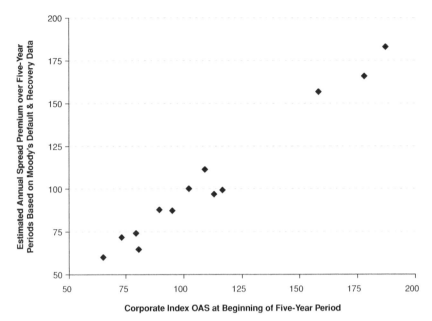

**FIGURE 12.1** Relationship between OAS and Annual Credit Spread Premium Using Historical Default Data, Five-Year Periods (1990–2005)
*Source:* Moody's and Barclays Capital.

shows the one-year reported index excess returns over the sample period for the IG Corporate, High Yield, and the Fixed-Rate MBS indexes.

Over the past 20 years, the IG Corporate Index has averaged 27 bps/year of annual reported index excess returns, compared to 305 bps/year for the High Yield Index and 25 bps/year for the MBS Index. Given the volatility of reported index excess returns, the annual information ratios for the IG Corporate (0.04), High Yield (0.15), and MBS (0.15) indexes are low.

Figure 12.2 shows the cumulative reported index excess returns for the IG Corporate Index over five-year periods. We measure the cumulative five-year index excess returns by first calculating the annual compounded excess return over each of the next five years and then summing these annual returns. Over five-year periods, index excess returns are still volatile and can be significantly negative (five of the 15 overlapping five-year periods).

Reported index excess returns exhibit more volatility than the spread premium estimated using historical defaults as reported in Table 12.2. The reason for this is that index excess returns also include a spread-widening/tightening component missing from the spread premium calculated using default losses alone. Investors with a persistent allocation to

**TABLE 12.3** Annual Reported Index Excess Returns for the IG Corporate, High Yield, and Fixed-Rate MBS Indexes (1990–2009)

| Year | IG Corporate Index (%) | High Yield Index (%) | MBS Index (%) |
|---|---|---|---|
| 1990 | −1.93 | −5.94 | 1.25 |
| 1991 | 2.72 | 20.08 | 0.13 |
| 1992 | 1.17 | 5.91 | −1.11 |
| 1993 | 0.86 | 7.55 | −1.04 |
| 1994 | 0.53 | 2.49 | 0.93 |
| 1995 | 1.36 | 0.66 | −0.49 |
| 1996 | 1.14 | 8.26 | 0.83 |
| 1997 | 0.18 | 3.81 | 1.30 |
| 1998 | −2.25 | −8.43 | −0.90 |
| 1999 | 1.47 | 4.82 | 1.13 |
| 2000 | −5.27 | −18.87 | −0.77 |
| 2001 | 2.72 | −2.85 | −0.75 |
| 2002 | −2.45 | −13.29 | 1.73 |
| 2003 | 5.80 | 26.42 | 0.11 |
| 2004 | 1.63 | 8.00 | 1.42 |
| 2005 | −1.15 | 0.47 | −0.37 |
| 2006 | 1.26 | 8.42 | 1.22 |
| 2007 | −5.22 | −7.73 | −1.85 |
| 2008 | −19.88 | −38.32 | −2.55 |
| 2009 | 22.76 | 59.55 | 4.82 |
| Average (bps/year) | 27 | 305 | 25 |
| Annual standard deviation (bps) | 741 | 1,916 | 161 |

*Source:* Barclays Capital.

credit and the ability to hold bonds through economic cycles try to ride out any transient spread widening/tightening and hold bonds to maturity. Consequently, using index data to estimate the spread premium requires neutralizing the spread component of reported index excess returns. To do so, we add back to the reported index excess return the annual change in index OAS multiplied by the average OASD for the year. For example, in 1995, the OAS of the index tightened by 14.5 bps. With an average OASD over the year of 5.53, we estimate that 80 bps of excess return stemmed from spread tightening. We subtract this from the reported index excess return of 136 bps to compute an estimated realized credit spread premium of 56 bps. We report the estimated annual spread premium calculated using index data in Table 12.4.

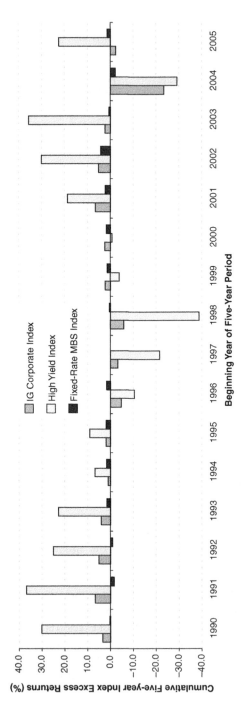

**FIGURE 12.2** Five-Year Cumulative Excess Returns for IG Corporate, High Yield, and Fixed-Rate MBS Indexes (1990–2005)
*Source:* Barclays Capital.

**TABLE 12.4** Estimated Average Annual Spread Premium Using Index Data, for IG Corporate, High Yield, and Fixed-Rate MBS Indexes (1990–2009)

| Year | IG Corporate Index (%) | High Yield Index (%) | MBS Index (%) |
|---|---|---|---|
| 1990 | 0.74 | 7.84 | 2.69 |
| 1991 | 0.43 | 7.59 | −0.51 |
| 1992 | 0.22 | 1.08 | −0.84 |
| 1993 | 0.01 | 4.28 | −0.54 |
| 1994 | 0.88 | 3.04 | −0.89 |
| 1995 | 0.56 | 3.54 | −0.79 |
| 1996 | 0.70 | 3.18 | 0.85 |
| 1997 | 0.74 | 3.86 | 0.71 |
| 1998 | 0.70 | 2.97 | 0.12 |
| 1999 | 1.25 | 1.04 | 0.26 |
| 2000 | −0.22 | −2.46 | 0.68 |
| 2001 | 1.27 | −7.00 | −1.49 |
| 2002 | −1.93 | −7.63 | 0.98 |
| 2003 | 0.40 | 4.48 | −0.01 |
| 2004 | 0.79 | 3.16 | 1.23 |
| 2005 | −0.08 | 2.86 | 0.54 |
| 2006 | 0.57 | 5.38 | 0.56 |
| 2007 | 1.49 | 5.22 | −0.10 |
| 2008 | 2.16 | 9.76 | −0.72 |
| 2009 | −1.05 | 16.09 | 1.58 |
| Average (bps/year) | 48 | 341 | 22 |
| Annual standard deviation (bps) | 88 | 525 | 100 |

*Source:* Barclays Capital.

The average annual credit spread premium in Table 12.4 is somewhat comparable (48 bps/year versus 27 bps/year) to the average annual reported index excess return over the past 20 years. This is not too surprising as spreads have exhibited mean-reverting behavior over time. Notice that the annual realized spread premium can be negative for any of the three asset classes. For example, the IG Corporate Index had four years in which the credit spread premium was negative—2000, 2002, 2005, and 2009—reflecting periods of credit-quality stress and a large number of downgraded and defaulted bonds.

As expected, after removing the spread change component, the annual volatility of the realized spread premium is much lower (80% lower) than that of the reported index excess returns. The large drop in excess return volatility produces much higher annual information ratios for the IG Corporate (0.54) and High Yield (0.65), but only slightly higher for MBS (0.22).

Figure 12.3 shows the cumulative spread premium for the IG Corporate Index over five-year overlapping periods. For IG and MBS, there are no five-year periods with negative cumulative spread premium. In contrast, High Yield suffered through five consecutive years where the cumulative spread premium was negative over a five-year interval (1997–2001). This period must have been very discouraging for long-horizon high-yield investors who were trying to ride out the spread volatility.

Table 12.5 compares the two methods of estimating spread premium. As shown, spread premium calculated using adjusted index excess returns for the IG Corporate Index is substantially lower than that estimated using historical default loss data. For the 16 five-year (overlapping) periods since 1990, the IG Corporate Index data imply a credit spread premium averaging 52 bps/year less than the spread premium estimated with Moody's historical data.

## The Spread Premium Shortfall of the Corporate Index

Why are the two spread premium estimates so far apart? To be sure, the calculation methods are very different and, so, the two estimates should not be expected to agree over short periods. In addition, the credit spread premium based on Moody's data is only a rough estimate and should not be seen as an obtainable target. However, the persistently large relative shortfall of the spread premium measured using reported index excess returns needs to be explained.

Estimating spread premium using historical default data implicitly assumes the investor has a buy-and-hold approach and the set of bonds held in his portfolio does not change except for defaults. In contrast, the IG Corporate Index is not a static buy-and-hold set of bonds. Table 12.6 provides a snapshot of the Corporate Index as of two separate dates (December 31, 1989, and February 28, 2010). The index's composition is constantly changing, not only as a result of newly issued and maturing bonds, but also due to index inclusion rules. Any impact of the index's rules will be reflected in the reported index excess returns. Is it possible that structural features of the index might be constricting its realized spread premium?

In addition to new issuance and redemptions, three particular index rules have a significant impact on the index's composition over time. First, any issue that is downgraded below investment grade is removed at the end of the month (at the bid-side price); second, issues are excluded if their

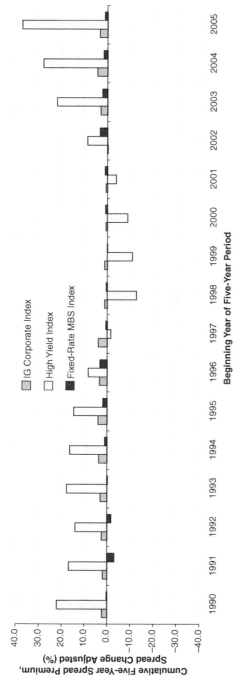

**FIGURE 12.3** Cumulative Five-Year Spread Premium Using Index Data for the IG Corporate, High Yield, and Fixed-Rate MBS Indexes (1990–2005)

*Source:* Barclays Capital.

**TABLE 12.5** Comparison of Annual Credit Spread Premium Estimates for IG Corporate Index, Five-Year Periods (1990–2005)

| | | | | | | | | | (bps) | | | | | | | |
|---|---|---|---|---|---|---|---|---|---|---|---|---|---|---|---|---|
| | 1990 | 1991 | 1992 | 1993 | 1994 | 1995 | 1996 | 1997 | 1998 | 1999 | 2000 | 2001 | 2002 | 2003 | 2004 | 2005 |
| Credit spread premium based on historical default loss experience | 100 | 157 | 111 | 88 | 72 | 74 | 60 | 46 | 49 | 99 | 97 | 186 | 166 | 183 | 87 | 65 |
| Credit spread premium based on spread adjusted index excess returns | 46 | 42 | 47 | 58 | 72 | 79 | 63 | 75 | 21 | 15 | 6 | 9 | −5 | 64 | 99 | 62 |
| Difference | 55 | 115 | 64 | 30 | 0 | −5 | −3 | −29 | 27 | 84 | 91 | 177 | 171 | 119 | −11 | 3 |

*Source:* Moody's and Barclays Capital.

**TABLE 12.6** Attributes of the IG Corporate Index

| | Average OAD | Average OAS | No. of Issues | No. of Tickers | Index Liquidity Constraint (millions) | Average Issue Size (millions) | Average Maturity (years) | Market Value (%) | | | |
|---|---|---|---|---|---|---|---|---|---|---|---|
| | | | | | | | | Aaa | Aa | A | Baa |
| 12/31/1989 | 4.76 | 100 | 3,826 | ~750 | 25 | 119 | 12.9 | 10% | 26% | 39% | 25% |
| 2/28/2010 | 6.35 | 172 | 3,376 | 561 | 250 | 707 | 10.2 | 1% | 16% | 45% | 38% |
| Average over period | 5.62 | 131 | | | | 364 | 11.4 | 4% | 17% | 46% | 33% |

*Source:* Barclays Capital.

remaining maturity is less than one year; and third, issues are removed if their amount outstanding falls below the index's liquidity requirement, which is periodically revised upward ($250 million as of May 2011).

There are some a priori reasons why these index rules may be constricting the realized spread premium. In general, as portfolio constraints are loosened or removed, performance is likely to improve. The same applies to indexes. Consider the index's downgrade rule: bonds downgraded below investment grade are removed from the index at the end of the downgrade month. It is very likely that when a downgraded bond is excluded, its spread is wider than when it was added to the index. In addition, the bond may be trading at a wider spread than is justified by the bond's new rating because of increased credit uncertainty about the bond arising from its rating transition. Furthermore, as discussed in detail in Chapter 13, the group of institutional investors forced to sell the bond must sufficiently entice the relatively small group of high-yield investors to add the new name to their portfolios. This has two implications for the index's spread premium. First, since the bond is no longer part of the index, the bond does not participate in the spread adjustment when calculating the Corporate Index's spread premium as the bond's spread widening is not added back. Second, most downgraded bonds end up maturing as scheduled. Consequently, the spread premium realized by these bonds up until their maturity is not captured by the IG Corporate Index.

Removing bonds with less than one year to maturity may also reduce the index's credit spread premium. Bonds with less than a year to maturity are seasoned bonds that may trade at wider spread levels to compensate investors for their lower liquidity.[5] When these bonds are sold out of the index, they leave at wider bid-ask spreads, and likely at a lower bid price, suggesting that there is a lot of credit spread premium still in them. Investors have less incentive to hold onto these bonds because they are not part of the index and because they offer low nominal spreads relative to longer-duration bonds of the same issuer. Although such short-duration bonds may be of interest to some investors such as managers of money market funds, the lack of attention from institutional IG investors may cause these bonds to leave the index at particularly wide spreads.

Finally, the index revises the minimum amount outstanding constraint (also called the "liquidity constraint") from time to time. For example, in early 1990, the liquidity constraint for the IG Corporate Index was $25 million, but as of May 2011 the constraint was $250 million. When the constraint is increased, all bonds in the index that are below the constraint threshold are sold out en masse from the index. Contrary to when the bonds were first included in the index, these relatively small bonds would trade at a spread concession to larger bonds included in the index due to their relative illiquidity.[6] This cheapening and forced sale may result in a drag on the index's realized spread premium.

## ALTERNATIVE CORPORATE INDEXES

To assess the impact of index rules on the magnitude of the credit spread premium, we construct several alternative corporate indexes using the same machinery and pricing as the IG Corporate Index, but relax one or more of the index rules. Specifically, we consider five alternative corporate indexes, all incepted on December 31, 1989, as follows:

1. *Downgrade Tolerant.* Bonds in the IG Corporate Index downgraded below investment grade are allowed to remain in the index until they default; bonds still need to satisfy the liquidity and minimum maturity constraints.
2. *Remaining Maturity Tolerant.* Bonds in the IG Index are not removed if their remaining maturity reaches less than one year; bonds are still excluded upon being downgraded below investment grade or violating the liquidity constraint.
3. *Liquidity Constraint Tolerant.* Once eligible for the IG Index, bonds are not required to satisfy the liquidity constraint going forward; bonds are still excluded upon being downgraded below investment grade or having a remaining maturity of less than one year.
4. *Fully tolerant.* The downgrade, liquidity, and remaining maturity rules are all relaxed.
5. *IG-Only Fully Tolerant.* This alternative version incorporates both numbers 2 and 3 above. Bonds that violate the index's maturity or liquidity rules are not excluded, but this index holds only investment-grade bonds, so upon a downgrade to high yield, bonds are sold out of the index.

Table 12.7 presents summary statistics for each of the five alternative corporate indexes, as well as the standard IG Corporate and High Yield indexes, as of February 28, 2010. (The table also includes data for two composite indexes that are discussed later.) Of course, the alternative indexes have more issues and issuers (i.e., tickers), than the IG Corporate Index. Both the Downgrade Tolerant and Fully Tolerant indexes have a 6% exposure to the high-yield sector. This high-yield exposure is more heavily skewed to issues rated Ba compared to the High Yield Index. It is important to note that the characteristics reported in the table for these alternative corporate

**TABLE 12.7** Alternative Corporate Indexes (as of February 28, 2010)

|  | | Alternative Corporate Indexes | | | | | | Composite Indexes | |
|---|---|---|---|---|---|---|---|---|---|
|  | IG Corporate Index | Downgrade Tolerant Corporate Index | Remaining Maturity Tolerant Corporate Index | Liquidity Constraint Tolerant Corporate Index | IG-Only Fully Tolerant Corporate Index | Fully Tolerant Corporate Index | High Yield Index | IG-HY Composite Index | IG-Ba Composite Index |
| OAD | 6.35 | 6.28 | 6.04 | 6.38 | 6.06 | 5.99 | 4.28 | 6.24 | 6.3 |
| OAS | 1.73 | 1.96 | 1.72 | 1.73 | 1.72 | 1.95 | 6.51 | 1.99 | 1.85 |
| No. of issues | 3,376 | 3,662 | 3,562 | 4,385 | 4,660 | 5,056 | 1,674 | 5,050 | 4,003 |
| No. of tickers | 561 | 654 | 571 | 623 | 630 | 747 | 772 | 1299 | 770 |
| Aaa (%) | 1 | 1 | 1 | 1 | 1 | 1 | 0 | 1 | 1 |
| Aa (%) | 16 | 15 | 16 | 16 | 16 | 15 | 0 | 15 | 16 |
| A (%) | 46 | 43 | 46 | 45 | 46 | 43 | 0 | 43 | 44 |
| Baa (%) | 37 | 35 | 37 | 38 | 38 | 36 | 0 | 35 | 36 |
| Ba (%) | 0 | 4 | 0 | 0 | 0 | 4 | 37 | 2 | 4 |
| B (%) | 0 | 1 | 0 | 0 | 0 | 1 | 37 | 2 | 0 |
| ≤ Caa (%) | 0 | 1 | 0 | 0 | 0 | 1 | 25 | 1 | 0 |

*Source:* Barclays Capital.

indexes are a function of their inception date. For example, the composition of high-yield bonds in the Downgrade Tolerant Index depends on when the index started accepting downgraded investment-grade bonds.

Our goal is to measure the realized credit spread premium for the alternative indexes and compare them to the IG Corporate Index. We follow the same procedure as before and estimate the spread premium using reported index excess returns adjusted for spread changes. For each index, we take the annual reported index excess returns and add back the impact of spread changes. Table 12.8 shows the results.

The alternative corporate indexes have higher annual average spread premium than the IG Corporate Index. For example, the Liquidity Constraint Tolerant Index has an annual realized spread premium of 54 bps/year compared to the 48 bps/year for the IG Corporate Index, with similar volatility. The Remaining Maturity Tolerant and the IG-Only Fully Tolerant indexes both have modest improvements in their realized spread premium compared to the IG Corporate Index (3 bps/year and 8 bps/year, respectively). Although these alternative indexes slightly underperform the IG Corporate Index in some years, they generally outperform.[7]

The Downgrade Tolerant and Fully Tolerant indexes consistently outperform the IG Corporate Index, with the exception of 1993 when both alternative indexes underperform the IG Corporate Index by 5 bps. The average annual credit spread premia for the Downgrade Tolerant and Fully Tolerant alternatives were 80 bps/year and 86 bps/year, respectively (32 bps/year and 38 bps/year more than the IG Corporate Index). From 1990 to 2010, the Fully Tolerant Corporate Index captured 79% more credit spread premium than the IG Corporate Index. In addition, the volatility for both alternatives was lower than the IG Corporate Index. As a result, the annual information ratio improves from 0.54 for the IG Corporate Index to 1.00 and 1.11, respectively, for the Downgrade Tolerant and Fully Tolerant alternatives.

Considering that the U.S. Aggregate Index has had an 18% average allocation to the Corporate Index, replacing the IG Corporate Index with one of these alternative corporate indexes would have improved the Aggregate's performance by approximately 6 to 7 bps/year. Given that the average alpha (before fees) from fixed income active management is approximately 44 bps/year (see Desclée and Phelps [2010]), the magnitude of the performance boost from the alternative corporate indexes is not negligible.

Table 12.9 shows the annual credit spread premium for the various corporate indexes for five-year holding periods. The Fully Tolerant Index (bottom row) consistently outperformed the IG Corporate Index. The additional annual credit spread premium earned by the Fully Tolerant Index ranges from 8 bps/year to 63 bps/year for a given five-year period.

**TABLE 12.8** Estimated Annual Credit Spread Premium Using Index Data, Alternative and Traditional Corporate Indexes (1990–2009)

| Year | IG Corporate Index | Downgrade Tolerant Corporate Index | Remaining Maturity Tolerant Corporate Index | Liquidity Constraint Tolerant Corporate Index | IG-Only Fully Tolerant Corporate Index | Fully Tolerant Corporate Index |
|---|---|---|---|---|---|---|
| | | | Alternative Corporate Indexes (percent per year) | | | |
| 1990 | 0.74 | 1.11 | 0.83 | 0.86 | 0.83 | 1.06 |
| 1991 | 0.43 | 1.06 | 0.44 | 0.43 | 0.44 | 1.03 |
| 1992 | 0.22 | 0.34 | 0.22 | 0.14 | 0.14 | 0.24 |
| 1993 | 0.01 | -0.04 | -0.07 | 0.07 | 0.00 | -0.04 |
| 1994 | 0.88 | 1.06 | 0.92 | 0.89 | 0.93 | 1.07 |
| 1995 | 0.56 | 0.76 | 0.53 | 0.55 | 0.53 | 0.70 |
| 1996 | 0.70 | 0.78 | 0.69 | 0.73 | 0.72 | 0.80 |
| 1997 | 0.74 | 0.83 | 0.72 | 0.74 | 0.72 | 0.80 |
| 1998 | 0.70 | 0.79 | 0.66 | 0.70 | 0.67 | 0.75 |
| 1999 | 1.25 | 1.33 | 1.14 | 1.34 | 1.21 | 1.30 |
| 2000 | -0.22 | 0.26 | -0.16 | -0.10 | -0.04 | 0.30 |
| 2001 | 1.27 | 1.73 | 1.27 | 1.29 | 1.30 | 1.73 |
| 2002 | -1.93 | -1.02 | -1.69 | -1.72 | -1.49 | -0.71 |
| 2003 | 0.40 | 0.83 | 0.53 | 0.50 | 0.63 | 1.11 |
| 2004 | 0.79 | 0.98 | 0.70 | 0.89 | 0.80 | 1.02 |
| 2005 | -0.08 | 0.44 | -0.22 | 0.05 | -0.08 | 0.31 |
| 2006 | 0.57 | 1.08 | 0.64 | 0.56 | 0.58 | 1.07 |
| 2007 | 1.49 | 2.01 | 1.15 | 1.48 | 1.18 | 1.69 |
| 2008 | 2.16 | 2.37 | 2.77 | 2.24 | 2.83 | 2.94 |
| 2009 | -1.05 | -0.65 | -0.86 | -0.86 | -0.65 | -0.05 |
| Average (bps/year) | 48 | 80 | 51 | 54 | 56 | 86 |
| Annual standard deviation (bps) | 88 | 80 | 89 | 84 | 85 | 77 |

*Source:* Barclays Capital.

**TABLE 12.9** Estimated Annual Credit Spread Premium Using Index Data, Alternative and IG Corporate Indexes, Five-Year Periods (1990–2005)

| | | | | | | | | (bps/year) | | | | | | | | |
|---|---|---|---|---|---|---|---|---|---|---|---|---|---|---|---|---|
| | 1990 | 1991 | 1992 | 1993 | 1994 | 1995 | 1996 | 1997 | 1998 | 1999 | 2000 | 2001 | 2002 | 2003 | 2004 | 2005 |
| IG Corporate Index | 46 | 42 | 47 | 58 | 72 | 79 | 63 | 75 | 21 | 15 | 6 | 9 | −5 | 64 | 99 | 62 |
| Downgrade Tolerant Corporate Index | 71 | 64 | 58 | 68 | 84 | 89 | 80 | 99 | 62 | 63 | 56 | 59 | 46 | 107 | 138 | 105 |
| Remaining Maturity Tolerant Corporate Index | 47 | 41 | 46 | 56 | 71 | 75 | 61 | 73 | 24 | 22 | 13 | 12 | −1 | 56 | 101 | 70 |
| Liquidity Constraint Tolerant Corporate Index | 48 | 42 | 48 | 60 | 72 | 81 | 68 | 79 | 30 | 26 | 17 | 20 | 6 | 69 | 104 | 69 |
| IG-Only Fully Tolerant Corporate Index | 47 | 41 | 46 | 58 | 71 | 77 | 66 | 77 | 33 | 32 | 24 | 23 | 9 | 62 | 106 | 77 |
| Fully Tolerant Corporate Index | 67 | 60 | 56 | 67 | 83 | 87 | 79 | 98 | 67 | 75 | 69 | 69 | 56 | 104 | 141 | 119 |
| Credit Spread Premium Pickup by Fully Tolerant Corporate Index | **22** | **18** | **8** | **9** | **11** | **8** | **16** | **23** | **46** | **59** | **63** | **60** | **61** | **40** | **42** | **57** |

*Source:* Barclays Capital.

The IG-Only Fully Tolerant Index underperforms in a few periods, but never by more than 2 bps/year.

We saw in Table 12.4 that the High Yield Index also had greater spread premium than the IG Corporate Index. However, the annual volatility of the High Yield spread premium (525 bps) was six times as large as that of the IG Corporate Index (88 bps). What is impressive about the results for the alternative indexes is that they are able to generate additional spread premium with no additional volatility.

Nevertheless, it is prudent to ask if the improvement for the alternative indexes stems from increased risk. A skeptic may argue that the Fully Tolerant Index earns a higher spread premium because an investor in that index takes on more risk compared to the IG Corporate Index. To examine this issue, Table 12.10 shows various risk attributes of reported index excess returns, for the traditional and alternative indexes between 1990 and 2010. All five alternative corporate indexes had similar or even better risk profiles than the IG Corporate Index. For example, the standard deviation of monthly excess returns for the Fully Tolerant Index is 118 bps/month, equal to that of the IG Corporate Index. In terms of tail risk (e.g., worst cumulative reported index excess returns over a period, worst 5% of months, and worst month), the Fully Tolerant compares very favorably. The same holds for the other alternative indexes.

Figure 12.4 plots the reported monthly index excess returns for the IG Corporate Index against those for the Fully Tolerant Index. As the figure shows, the reported index excess returns for the two indexes were highly correlated (correlation coefficient = 0.996).[8] Note that although the two sets of returns fall smartly along a line, the monthly reported index excess returns for the Fully Tolerant Corporate Index generally fall along a line with an angle slightly less than 45 degrees relative to those for the IG Corporate Index, again highlighting the better performance of the Fully Tolerant Corporate Index.[9]

Perhaps the higher realized spread premium for the Downgrade Tolerant and Fully Tolerant indexes is the result, in large part, of the presence of high-yield bonds in those indexes? If so, then why not just add high yield directly to the IG Corporate Index? Table 12.10 shows that the risk properties (standard deviation and tail risk measures) of the High Yield Index are more than double those of the IG Corporate Index. Since the alternative indexes have only a small allocation to high yield, we construct two composite indexes: The IG Corporate-High Yield Index Composite and the IG Corporate-High Yield Ba-Only Composite. Each composite is constructed to mimic dynamically the allocation to high yield found in the Downgrade Tolerant Index. For example, in a month when the Downgrade Tolerant Index had an $x$% weight to high-yield bonds, the IG-HY Composite would

TABLE 12.10 Risk Properties, Alternative Corporate Indexes (January 1990–February 2010)

| | | Alternative Corporate Indexes | | | | | | | |
| | IG Corporate Index | Downgrade Tolerant Corporate Index | Remaining Maturity Tolerant Corporate Index | Liquidity Constraint Tolerant Corporate Index | IG-Only Fully Tolerant Corporate Index | Fully Tolerant Corporate Index | High Yield Index | IG-HY Composite Index | IG-Ba Composite Index | MBS Index |
|---|---|---|---|---|---|---|---|---|---|---|
| Average monthly reported index excess returns (bps) | 2.2 | 4.1 | 2.5 | 2.6 | 2.9 | 4.7 | 18 | 3.1 | 2.7 | 2.2 |
| Standard deviation of monthly reported index excess returns (bps) | 118 | 126 | 112 | 117 | 111 | 118 | 297 | 125 | 120 | 38 |
| Information ratio (annual) | 0.06 | 0.11 | 0.08 | 0.08 | 0.09 | 0.14 | 0.21 | 0.09 | 0.08 | 0.2 |
| Kurtosis | 17.4 | 15.6 | 17.9 | 17.3 | 17.6 | 15.9 | 7.7 | 15.9 | 16.5 | 2.3 |
| Worst cumulative reported index excess returns over | | | | | | | | | | |
| 12-months (bps) | −2,249 | −2,335 | −2,136 | −2,246 | −2,120 | −2,206 | −4,138 | −2,328 | −2,268 | −386 |
| 24-months (bps) | −2,695 | −2,855 | −2,541 | −2,710 | −2,539 | −2,691 | −4,736 | −2,817 | −2,732 | −469 |
| 36-months (bps) | −2,600 | −2,674 | −2,450 | −2,627 | −2,458 | −2,535 | −4,083 | −2,671 | −2,614 | −373 |
| Reported index excess returns in worst 5% of months | | | | | | | | | | |
| Average | −308 | −331 | −290 | −307 | −288 | −309 | −816 | −330 | −317 | −97 |
| Worst month's reported index excess returns (bps) | −838 | −858 | −806 | −812 | −776 | −795 | −1,650 | −840 | −832 | −163 |
| Month | Sep-08 | Sep-08 | Sep-08 | Sep-08 | Sep-08 | Sep-08 | Oct-08 | Sep-08 | Sep-08 | Oct-08 |

Source: Barclays Capital.

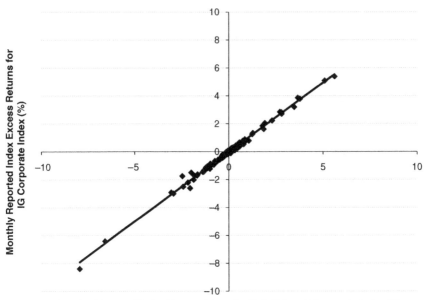

Monthly Reported Index Excess Return for Fully Tolerant Corporate Index (%)

**FIGURE 12.4** Reported Monthly Index Excess Returns, Fully Tolerant and IG Corporate Indexes (January 1990–February 2010)
*Source:* Barclays Capital.

have a weight of $(1 - x\%)$ to the IG Corporate Index and $x\%$ to the High Yield Index. The IG-Ba Composite is constructed slightly differently as we take the weight of the Downgrade Tolerant in Ba-bonds only and ignore the rest (assuming an investor would not hold sub-Ba bonds). We then form the composite by taking the proportional shares of IG and Ba in the Downgrade Tolerant Index and then resize those share weights as the weights for the IG-Ba Composite Index.

Summary statistics for these two composite indexes as of February 28, 2010, are included in Table 12.7; reported index excess returns and risk properties from January 1990 through February 2010 are in Table 12.10. Table 12.10 shows that the two IG-HY composites exhibit risk behavior similar to that of the Downgrade Tolerant Index. However, the relative reported index excess return advantage of the Downgrade Tolerant Index persists. For example, the IG-HY Composite has an average monthly reported index excess return of 3.1 bps/month compared to 4.1 bps/month for the Downgrade Tolerant Index.

The data on realized spread premium confirm that the advantage of the Downgrade Tolerant Index cannot be attributed solely to the increased allocation to High Yield. Table 12.11 indeed shows that both the

**TABLE 12.11** Estimated Annual Credit Spread Premium for Traditional, Alternative, and Composite Corporate Indexes (1990–2009)

| Year | IG Corporate Index (%) | Alternative Corporate Indexes | | Composite Indexes | |
|------|------|------|------|------|------|
| | | Downgrade Tolerant Corporate Index (%) | Fully Tolerant Corporate Index (%) | Composite IG Corporate + HY Indexes (%) | Composite IG Corporate + HY Ba-Only Indexes (%) |
| 1990 | 0.74 | 1.11 | 1.06 | 0.95 | 0.82 |
| 1991 | 0.43 | 1.06 | 1.03 | 0.96 | 0.80 |
| 1992 | 0.22 | 0.34 | 0.24 | 0.29 | 0.05 |
| 1993 | 0.01 | −0.04 | −0.04 | −0.03 | 0.11 |
| 1994 | 0.88 | 1.06 | 1.07 | 1.12 | 0.99 |
| 1995 | 0.56 | 0.76 | 0.70 | 0.65 | 0.63 |
| 1996 | 0.70 | 0.78 | 0.80 | 0.85 | 0.82 |
| 1997 | 0.74 | 0.83 | 0.80 | 0.81 | 0.77 |
| 1998 | 0.70 | 0.79 | 0.75 | 0.76 | 0.71 |
| 1999 | 1.25 | 1.33 | 1.30 | 1.16 | 1.26 |
| 2000 | −0.22 | 0.26 | 0.30 | −0.30 | −0.30 |
| 2001 | 1.27 | 1.73 | 1.73 | 1.35 | 1.43 |
| 2002 | −1.93 | −1.02 | −0.71 | −1.22 | −1.81 |
| 2003 | 0.40 | 0.83 | 1.11 | 0.62 | 0.22 |
| 2004 | 0.79 | 0.98 | 1.02 | 0.81 | 0.90 |
| 2005 | −0.08 | 0.44 | 0.31 | 0.31 | 0.37 |
| 2006 | 0.57 | 1.08 | 1.07 | 1.05 | 0.53 |
| 2007 | 1.49 | 2.01 | 1.69 | 1.87 | 1.73 |
| 2008 | 2.16 | 2.37 | 2.94 | 2.42 | 2.14 |
| 2009 | −1.05 | −0.65 | −0.05 | −0.87 | −0.63 |
| Average (bps/year) | 48 | 80 | 86 | 68 | 58 |
| Annual standard deviation (bps) | 88 | 80 | 77 | 84 | 86 |

*Source:* Barclays Capital.

IG-HY and IG-Ba composite indexes produce a higher annual spread premium (68 bps/year and 58 bps/year, respectively) than the IG Corporate Index (48 bps/year) with a lower annual volatility (84 bps and 86 bps versus 88 bps). However, the two composite indexes clearly underperformed the Downgrade Tolerant Index, both in terms of annual spread premium

(80 bps/year) and volatility (80 bps). The intuition is that the IG Corporate Index suffers from the automatic selling of downgraded bonds at the end of their downgrade month. The risk premium and liquidity cost of these bonds spike in their downgrade month, causing the IG Corporate Index to discard considerable spread premium. On a relative basis, the Downgrade Tolerant Index captures more of this discarded spread premium than do the composites that hold predominantly high-yield bonds that never carried an investment-grade rating.

## CAPTURING SPREAD PREMIUM: ADOPTING AN ALTERNATIVE CORPORATE BENCHMARK

We now examine more closely the Fully Tolerant and IG-Only Fully Tolerant indexes. Although the Fully Tolerant Index is the least constrained, and has the highest realized credit spread premium, it may be unacceptable to investors with hard requirements to avoid high-yield bonds. The IG-Only Fully Tolerant Index tries to be as unconstrained as possible without ever holding a high-yield bond at the beginning of a month.

Figures 12.5 and 12.6, respectively, show the market value percentage breakdown of bond types excluded from the IG Corporate Index but remaining in the Fully Tolerant and IG-Only Fully Tolerant indexes. As of February 28, 2010, the Fully Tolerant Corporate Index contains approximately 15% of its market value in bonds that are excluded from the IG Corporate Index. This 15% is roughly evenly distributed across downgraded (now high yield) bonds, small-issue-size bonds and bonds with remaining maturity of less than one year.

For the Fully Tolerant Index, the percentage of market value in high yield has been increasing over time, although it does wax and wane along with macroeconomic trends. The percentage in bonds with a remaining maturity of one year or less is quite stable, at approximately 5%. The percentage of small-sized bonds is generally decreasing over time except when the Corporate Index liquidity constraint changes and there is a large spike in the market value weight of these bonds. For example, in July 1999, when the liquidity constraint increased from $100 million to $150 million, the percentage market value weight of small-sized bonds increased from about 3% to 16%. These spikes in market value arising from changes in the liquidity constraint cause the overall weight of "excluded" bonds to sometimes exceed 20%, at times approaching 30%, of the Fully Tolerant Index.

How would an investor go about adopting either the Fully Tolerant or IG-Only Fully Tolerant Index as their credit benchmark? Unlike other Barclays Capital indexes, there is an element of time-dependence for these

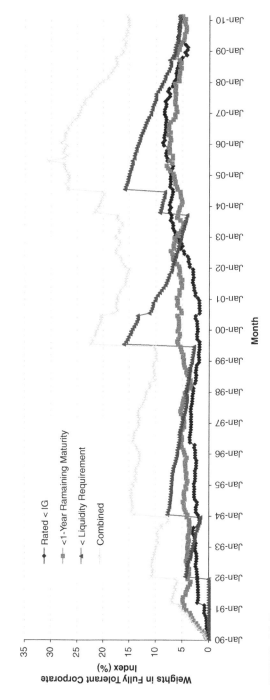

**FIGURE 12.5** Composition of Fully Tolerant Corporate Index (January 1990–February 2010)
*Source:* Barclays Capital.

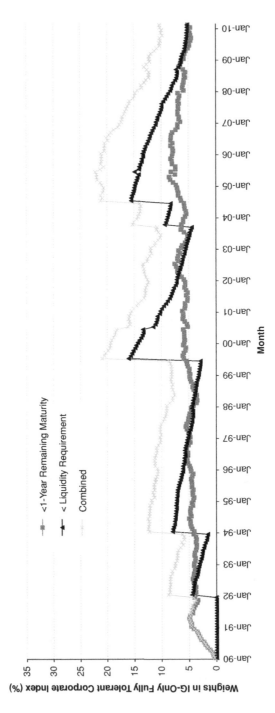

**FIGURE 12.6** Composition of IG-Only Fully Tolerant Corporate Index (January 1990–February 2010)
*Source:* Barclays Capital.

indexes as their current composition depends on when the index rules were relaxed. For example, we commenced construction of the Fully Tolerant Index on December 31, 1989. From that date onward, any bond in the IG Corporate Index downgraded to high yield was eligible for the Fully Tolerant Index. However, bonds that already carried a high-yield rating at inception were not included.

The investor has some choices. He or she could select the Fully Tolerant Index that began on December 31, 1989. However, this would require the portfolio manager to find that 15% market value of the index that he or she does not currently hold. This may be difficult. Alternatively, the investor could adopt the Fully Tolerant Index prospectively. In other words, as of Date MM/DD/YYYY, the investor will relax the rules for the IG Corporate Index. When an investment-grade bond is downgraded, the bond will not leave the index. There is no reason to believe that the portfolio manager is suddenly unable to evaluate the credit. In fact, this is a strong argument for adopting the Fully Tolerant Index: The portfolio manager, who analyzed the bond when it was an investment-grade credit, is probably still able to continue evaluating it. Why throw away this expertise (not to mention selling the bond when it is plump with unrealized spread premium) just because the bond was downgraded? The manager is still at liberty to underweight the bond based on his or her view.

## CONCLUSION

Despite the high level of spread volatility, credit bonds have generated a substantial spread premium. On average, more than 90% of a bond's spread has been in excess of that needed to cover default losses. Investors willing to tolerate the spread volatility can potentially harvest this credit spread premium.

However, to capture as much of this spread premium as possible, investors adhering to index rules need to ensure that their credit benchmark does not have rules that may inadvertently discard some of this spread premium. We show that the index inclusion rules for the IG Corporate Index have constrained the ability of investors to capture a larger credit spread premium.

We propose some alternative credit benchmarks that would have allowed investors with a persistent credit allocation to capture a spread premium (86 bps/year) almost 80% larger than that offered by the IG Corporate Index (48 bps/year) without taking additional risk.

For portfolio managers benchmarked against the IG Corporate Index, these results suggest a long-term strategy for benchmark outperformance. If managers have permission to hold bonds that the Corporate Index discards, managers should be able to harvest the additional spread premium and outperform the benchmark.

## NOTES

1. This chapter follows closely Ng and Phelps (2011). Excluding the volatile 2007–2009 period does not significantly improve the information ratio for the asset class. Between 1990 and 2007, the average annual reported index excess return was 14 bps/year, with an annual standard deviation of 278 bps.
2. Moody's Corporate Default and Recovery Rates, 1920–2009, Moody's Investors Service, February 2010.
3. As with the equity risk premium puzzle, there have been many suggested explanations for the "credit spread puzzle." For example, realized defaults have been better than expected so far. However, the worse is still yet to come. (Yikes!) Another explanation is that corporate coupon income is taxable at the state level whereas Treasury coupon income is not. A third explanation is that Treasury yields are artificially low due to a liquidity premium, an effect that would exaggerate the credit spread puzzle. However, other studies have measured the credit spread premium using swap rates as the pricing benchmark and still find a substantial credit spread premium. Also, the credit spread premium may be compensation for the fact that credit returns are asymmetrical, negatively skewed with substantial kurtosis, which are undesirable for investors. Chapter 6 analyzes three likely sources of the credit spread premium: expected liquidity cost; expected default cost; and a risk premium accounting for the likelihood that these costs are likely to be high when the financial markets are performing poorly.
4. In January 2001, Barclays Capital changed its index excess return method from a "duration bucketing" approach to the current "key-rate duration" approach. Although there are important differences between these methods, the results are not sensitive to the particular method used.
5. Our Liquidity Cost Score (LCS)™ analysis shows that a bond's bid-ask spread widens as the bond ages. See Chapter 5.
6. We currently estimate that a bond's spread is expected to widen 0.43 bps per $100 million reduction in its amount outstanding. See Chapter 5.
7. The Liquidity Constraint Tolerant Index and, to a lesser extent, the IG-Only Fully Tolerant Index have spikes of outperformance versus the Corporate Index. This is because the liquidity constraint changes episodically: 1992, 1994, 1999, 2003, and 2004. In a year where the liquidity constraint is unchanged, the spread premium performance of the Liquidity Constraint Tolerant and IG Corporate Index tends to be similar.
8. In addition, the correlations of reported monthly index excess returns for the Fully Tolerant Corporate Index with the MBS Index and the S&P 500 (total returns) are virtually the same as for the IG Corporate Index. This is so for the

entire 20-year period and also for the worst 5% of months for the IG Corporate Index.

9. Using OLS regression, the slope of the regression line is 0.99 with an intercept of –0.025, indicating the better performance of the Fully Tolerant Corporate Index relative to the IG Corporate Index.

### CHAPTER 13

# Risk and Performance of Fallen Angels

The U.S. Corporate Index is widely used by investors as the benchmark against which they manage their U.S. investment-grade corporate allocation. Because of the index dominance, changes in its constituents have the potential to affect not only the composition of investors' portfolios, but also the pricing of its underlying securities.

One of the key reasons the index population varies over time is due to changes in credit ratings. In particular, corporate bonds that are part of the index and are downgraded below investment-grade status (commonly termed *fallen angels*) are excluded from the index at its next monthly rebalancing. Investors who are benchmarked to the index and own fallen angels have a strong incentive to sell them at the time of downgrade, for two main reasons. First, many investors have explicit constraints on their ability to hold non-investment-grade bonds. As a result, pension funds' mandates, for example, typically require selling fallen angels within a predefined period following the downgrade. Similarly, insurance companies are subject to regulation that imposes large capital charges on speculative-grade bonds. Second, holding out-of-benchmark securities, particularly those that are likely to be more volatile than the average high-grade bond, can lead to an increase in the tracking errors of investors' portfolios.

Fallen angels as a group represent a significant proportion of the overall supply of high-yield securities, as much as 15% to 25% in some years. As a result, when a large number of investors are forced to sell their holdings in these bonds within a short period around the downgrade date, it can depress prices beyond any negative effects from the information contained in the rating change announcement. In such scenarios, the prices of fallen angels may temporarily drop below their fundamental values, but would return to equilibrium levels over time as the selling imbalance abates. The limited demand from prospective buyers is another factor that can facilitate a temporary price distortion. Investors in high-yield bonds are usually active only in this market, which has different characteristics than the high-grade market. Consequently, the two markets are highly segmented, as discussed in Chapter 7.

Determining whether fallen angels are subject to price pressures induced by forced selling has important implications for investors. Is there an optimal time for credit investors benchmarked against the U.S. Corporate Index to sell their holdings of fallen angels after a downgrade? Should these investors adopt more flexible investment mandates that do not necessitate the disposal of fallen angels? Can the price dynamics of fallen angels offer attractive profit opportunities for absolute return investors such as hedge funds?

The evidence on the price behavior of fallen angels around their downgrades is mixed. Ellul, Jotikasthira, and Lundblad (2010) examined this issue using transaction data from insurance companies, which hold more than one-third of all outstanding investment-grade corporate bonds. They found that companies that were more constrained by regulation were, on average, more likely to sell downgraded bonds. In addition, downgraded bonds that were widely held by constrained insurance companies experienced significantly elevated selling pressures and larger price reversals. However, Ambrose, Cai, and Helwege (2009) reached the opposite conclusion and documented negligible, if not nonexistent, price pressure effects using the same database.[1] As we showed in Chapter 12, not removing fallen angels from the U.S. Corporate Index after their downgrade would lead to a significant performance pickup without a corresponding increase in risk. Furthermore, combining the index instead with the same proportion of bonds from the U.S. High Yield Index did not generate nearly as much improvement, consistent with the existence of price pressures.

Our first goal is therefore to provide a conclusive answer to the question of whether fallen angels are subject to price pressures due to forced selling. Using a large sample of more than 1,400 bonds that migrated from investment-grade to high-yield status since 1990, we analyze the characteristics and price dynamics of fallen angels during the three-year period around their downgrade date. Consistent with the implications of price pressures, we find that after their downgrade, fallen angels initially underperform high-yield bonds with similar characteristics, with a subsequent reversal lasting up to two years after the rating change. Moreover, the magnitude of price recovery by individual issuers tends to increase with the size of their initial underperformance. In contrast, price reversal is not evident for bonds that were upgraded from high-yield to high-grade status and were not subject to selling (or buying) induced by investment constraints.

An alternative explanation for these patterns is based on investor overreaction. Under this scenario, selling is voluntary and motivated by behavioral biases rather than investment constraints. Investors *overreact* to the negative informational content of the downgrade event, which depresses bonds' prices below their fundamental value. Over time, these misevaluations are gradually corrected and fallen angels outperform high-yield bonds as their prices mean revert. We examine this claim but find no evidence supporting it.

To establish an explicit link between the magnitude of forced selling and the performance of fallen angels, we analyze two possible measures of price pressures. First, we examine the interplay between trading volumes and the liquidity of fallen angels. Under typical market conditions, an increase in trading volumes is associated with a decrease in trading costs and improved liquidity. However, if higher volumes are a result of forced selling, liquidity should decline rather than rise. Such a scenario reflects the execution immediacy demanded by investors and the fact that trading activity mostly represents down-volume. Indeed, we find that trading volumes in the six-month window centered on the downgrade event increase by a factor of four, but the bid-ask spreads for fallen angels increase simultaneously, well beyond those for high-yield peers.

Second, we look at the behavior of the cash-CDS spread basis. Credit default swaps are not subject to the same investment constraints that motivate the selling of fallen angels' bonds. As a result, the spread basis between the bonds and credit default swaps of fallen angels should also exhibit mean reversion, widening initially and then gradually converging to their long-term equilibrium levels. We indeed find that while swap spreads widen as expected, they do so to a lesser degree than the spreads of cash bonds. Consequently, the cash-CDS basis widens, on average, to about 225 bps in the first three months after the downgrade and then declines steadily to the long-term mean of about 40 bps.

Our results suggest that fallen angels that experience a deterioration in liquidity despite higher turnover and a widening of their cash-CDS basis between the downgrade month and the end of the following quarter perform worse than other downgraded bonds, but exhibit greater outperformance in the subsequent 12 months. Overall, the two measures are able to explain about 30% of the cross-sectional variation in the performance of fallen angels.

Can investors exploit the price pressures following the downgrade of fallen angels? We analyze the performance of a dynamic strategy that is dedicated to these bonds. The risk-return profile of such a strategy reflects not only the typical price behavior of fallen angels after their downgrade but also their supply dynamics. Therefore, while the findings based on the event-study approach used in the first part of the chapter are indicative, one needs to examine the results from a portfolio perspective.

We analyze the characteristics and performance of several rules-based portfolios with different investment guidelines over time. We find that portfolios of fallen angels consistently outperform high-yield peers by about 8.5% per year on average, with information ratios in excess of one, using a relatively simple set of rules based on time relative to the downgrade event and a rich or cheap indicator. While the magnitude of the outperformance is not constant, primarily because of the variation in the supply of fallen angels, it is not confined to a specific period and is evident throughout the sample. Even incorporating the higher costs of trading fallen angels compared with other high-yield bonds does not significantly diminish their attractiveness. The chapter concludes with a short discussion of the implications of these findings for investors.

## DATA AND METHODOLOGY

### Sample Construction

The sample used in our analysis consists of all bonds that were part of the U.S. Corporate Index and experienced a "rating event" between January 1990 and December 2009. A rating event is defined as a removal from the index due to a downgrade from any investment-grade rating to high-yield status or, conversely, an inclusion in the index following an upgrade to investment-grade status from any high-yield rating.[2] The credit ratings used throughout the analysis reflect the rating method used by the index at each date.[3] The final sample contains a total of 2,251 bonds (representing 761 unique issuers) of which 1,485 were downgraded and 766 were upgraded. The difference between the number of unique issuers and the number of individual bonds reflects the fact that some issuers experienced several rating events or had multiple bonds outstanding at the time of the rating event.

The period in which prices may be affected by investors selling their holdings in fallen angels is likely to be short-lived and concentrated around the month during which the rating event took place. It is not clear, however, how fast the ensuing price recovery process may be, and we therefore employ a relatively long analysis window during which we track all bonds in the sample. The analysis window starts a year before the rating event month and ends 24 months after it, with the exception of defaulted bonds.[4] Since investing in defaulted bonds requires specialized knowledge, we postulate that once a bond defaults, most investors do not continue to hold it. Therefore, bonds that default exit the sample at the month-end following the default month, and their prices at that time constitute their final value.[5]

Each of the statistics that we analyze for fallen angels (such as performance) is adjusted by the contemporaneous value of a peer group with similar characteristics. Peer groups are defined based on industry (financials, industrials, and utilities) and credit quality (A and higher, Baa, Ba, B, and Caa and lower). In addition, with the exception of the lowest credit-quality category, separate buckets are constructed for bonds with remaining maturity of below or above 10 years, resulting in a total of 27 peer groups. Our goal in defining such partitions is to capture the primary risk factors of corporate bonds while keeping the peer groups sufficiently populated to minimize idiosyncratic effects.

Peer groups are populated monthly using the universe of bonds that compose the U.S. Corporate or High Yield indexes and had not experienced a rating event in the previous 24 months to prevent possible contamination due to overlap. To compute flow statistics such as relative returns and turnover, bonds are matched to their appropriate peer group at the beginning of each month (based on industry, credit quality, and remaining maturity at that time). In contrast, for point-in-time measures such as spreads and trading costs, a bond's peer group is determined once, based on its characteristics immediately following the rating event, and held constant throughout the analysis window. A static peer group (as opposed to matching every month) is used to avoid the discontinuity in the rating event month resulting from the change in credit quality.[6]

Monthly relative statistics for each bond are computed whenever the peer group is populated by at least 20 bonds. Otherwise, they are recorded as missing. Relative statistics are then aggregated by issuer using the market values of the underlying bonds throughout the first part of the study. The second part employs individual bonds to examine the performance of a strategy of investing in fallen angels.

We examine the joint behavior of trading volumes and the liquidity of fallen angels using monthly data since January 2007 from two separate sources.[7] Transactions data are retrieved from TRACE (Trade Reporting and Compliance Engine) files, which contain individual trades at the CUSIP level.[8] To analyze liquidity, we employ LCS, our measure of bond liquidity discussed in Chapter 5. We also use data from Markit to compare the behavior of fallen angels' bonds with credit default swaps on the same underlying entity. The cash-CDS basis is constructed as the difference between each issuer's LIBOR-OAS and a weighted combination of 5-year and 10-year swaps with the same risky PV01 as the issuer's spread duration. CDS returns are computed in a similar fashion.

## Descriptive Statistics

Table 13.1 reports the number of issuers and the market value of their outstanding bonds (as of the beginning of the rating event month) in dollar

**TABLE 13.1** Issuer Population and Market Value by Year and Rating Event Type

| | Downgrades | | | | Upgrades | | |
|---|---|---|---|---|---|---|---|
| Year | Number of Issuers | Market Value ($millions) | Market Value as Percent of HY Index | Corporate Index Average OAS (bps) | Number of Issuers | Market Value ($millions) | Market Value as Percent of Corporate Index |
| 1990 | 15 | 4,095 | 7.8% | 106 | 5 | 2,463 | 0.5% |
| 1991 | 15 | 8,459 | 14.2% | 107 | 14 | 8,888 | 1.5% |
| 1992 | 9 | 4,913 | 6.9% | 92 | 9 | 2,519 | 0.4% |
| 1993 | 15 | 7,676 | 5.9% | 78 | 21 | 7,651 | 1.1% |
| 1994 | 9 | 6,725 | 4.8% | 73 | 10 | 2,877 | 0.4% |
| 1995 | 7 | 4,840 | 3.2% | 66 | 16 | 10,459 | 1.4% |
| 1996 | 12 | 10,194 | 5.4% | 59 | 19 | 6,774 | 0.9% |
| 1997 | 8 | 2,148 | 0.9% | 58 | 34 | 9,452 | 1.0% |
| 1998 | 27 | 18,823 | 5.8% | 95 | 39 | 31,933 | 3.0% |
| 1999 | 20 | 12,937 | 3.7% | 113 | 27 | 16,230 | 1.4% |
| 2000 | 16 | 14,345 | 4.7% | 161 | 22 | 13,092 | 1.1% |
| 2001 | 37 | 41,771 | 13.7% | 172 | 21 | 21,632 | 1.5% |
| 2002 | 64 | 100,611 | 28.8% | 197 | 9 | 5,428 | 0.3% |
| 2003 | 51 | 37,733 | 7.9% | 127 | 9 | 12,327 | 0.7% |
| 2004 | 20 | 33,207 | 5.8% | 92 | 15 | 12,184 | 0.7% |
| 2005 | 17 | 93,211 | 15.4% | 90 | 22 | 18,133 | 1.1% |
| 2006 | 16 | 18,329 | 3.0% | 90 | 16 | 22,387 | 1.4% |
| 2007 | 20 | 30,767 | 4.7% | 124 | 22 | 34,253 | 1.9% |
| 2008 | 25 | 36,257 | 6.6% | 356 | 15 | 19,343 | 1.0% |
| 2009 | 39 | 46,797 | 8.1% | 326 | 9 | 7,718 | 0.3% |

*Note:* Market value of downgraded and upgraded bonds is measured as of the beginning of the rating event month. The market value and OAS of the indexes are based on averaging monthly values in each year.
*Source:* Barclays Capital.

terms and as a proportion of the index to which they migrated, as well as the average OAS of the Corporate Index by year.

Two key observations emerge from the table. First, the number of downgrades generally varied with the business cycle (proxied by the average OAS of the Corporate Index), while the number of upgrades was distributed more uniformly over time. The largest spikes in downgrades in terms both of absolute number and total market value occurred during the 2001–2002 recession and the 2007–2009 financial crisis. The year 2005 was an

**TABLE 13.2** Distribution of Beginning and Ending Credit Qualities in Rating Event Month

A. Rating Transitions for Downgraded Bonds

| Rating at Start of Event Month | Rating at End of Event Month | | | | | | Percent of Total |
|---|---|---|---|---|---|---|---|
| | Ba1 | Ba2 | Ba3 | B | Caa–C | Total | |
| Aaa–Aa | 0 | 0 | 0 | 1 | 0 | 1 | 0.1% |
| A | 7 | 19 | 1 | 14 | 4 | 45 | 3.0% |
| Baa1 | 38 | 18 | 7 | 2 | 4 | 69 | 4.6% |
| Baa2 | 209 | 66 | 10 | 27 | 3 | 315 | 21.2% |
| Baa3 | 626 | 268 | 110 | 46 | 5 | 1,055 | 71.0% |
| Total | 880 | 371 | 128 | 90 | 16 | 1,485 | |
| Percent of total | 59.3% | 25.0% | 8.6% | 6.1% | 1.1% | | |

B. Rating Transitions for Upgraded Bonds

| Rating at Start of Event Month | Rating at End of Event Month | | | | | | Percent of Total |
|---|---|---|---|---|---|---|---|
| | Aaa–Aa | A | Baa1 | Baa2 | Baa3 | Total | |
| Ba1 | 2 | 14 | 27 | 54 | 441 | 538 | 71.3% |
| Ba2 | 1 | 1 | 5 | 4 | 53 | 64 | 8.5% |
| Ba3 | 5 | 4 | 4 | 9 | 28 | 50 | 6.6% |
| B | 4 | 9 | 18 | 19 | 48 | 98 | 13.0% |
| Caa–C | 0 | 3 | 2 | 0 | 0 | 5 | 0.7% |
| Total | 12 | 31 | 56 | 86 | 570 | 755 | |
| Percent of total | 1.6% | 4.1% | 7.4% | 11.4% | 75.5% | | |

*Note:* The results are based on all bonds in the sample except for 11 bonds that were upgraded to investment-grade status and were not rated before the rating event.
*Source:* Barclays Capital.

exception because of the downgrade of Ford and GM. Second, the market value of downgraded bonds as a percentage of the High Yield Index was much larger than the share of upgraded bonds in the Corporate Index. Downgrades made up more than a quarter of the High Yield Index in some years, while upgrades represented at most 3% of the Corporate Index. The significant proportion of fallen angels in the high-yield universe explains why they may be susceptible to price pressures after their downgrades.

Table 13.2 displays the distribution of beginning and ending credit qualities in the rating event month separately for upgraded and downgraded bonds. Table 13.2(A) shows that of the 1,485 fallen angels, 1,055 (71%) were rated Baa3 just before the rating event, and 626 of those were

**TABLE 13.3** Status of Bonds 24 Months after the Rating Event

| Rating Event Year | Total Number of Bonds | Active | | Inactive | | |
|---|---|---|---|---|---|---|
| | | High Yield | Investment Grade | Matured | Defaulted | Called |
| Downgraded Bonds | | | | | | |
| 1990–1994 | 173 | 69.9% | 9.8% | 7.5% | 2.9% | 9.8% |
| 1995–1999 | 211 | 71.6% | 15.2% | 8.5% | 0.5% | 2.8% |
| 2000–2004 | 678 | 66.2% | 9.3% | 5.9% | 15.5% | 2.1% |
| 2005–2009 | 404 | 80.4% | 5.0% | 6.7% | 6.4% | 1.5% |
| Upgraded Bonds | | | | | | |
| 1990–1994 | 112 | 2.7% | 64.3% | 7.1% | 0.0% | 23.2% |
| 1995–1999 | 273 | 4.8% | 72.2% | 6.2% | 0.0% | 12.5% |
| 2000–2004 | 168 | 15.5% | 54.8% | 6.0% | 6.0% | 17.9% |
| 2005–2009 | 202 | 4.5% | 73.3% | 3.0% | 1.5% | 15.3% |

*Note:* The table reports the status of bonds in the sample at the end of the analysis window, 24 months after the rating event month. A bond that was still trading at that time was defined as "active," and its credit rating (investment grade or high yield) was recorded. Inactive bonds were classified as matured, defaulted, or called. The exact classification for 30 inactive bonds could not be determined.
*Source:* Barclays Capital.

downgraded only one notch, to the highest non-investment-grade credit quality (Ba1). Almost the same proportion of upgraded bonds migrated from a Ba1 rating (71.3%), of which 441 switched to the lowest investment-grade quality rating (Baa3). Given that public information on bond issuers is updated regularly, these statistics suggest that both downgrades and upgrades should not have come as a surprise to the market. The rating events would have been anticipated by many investors; thus, their informational content would have been limited on average.

Before analyzing performance, we examine how the population of bonds in the sample evolved between the rating event month and the end of the analysis window. In particular, did fallen angels maintain their high-yield rating or were they likely to return to investment-grade status? What proportion of fallen angels ended up in default?

Table 13.3 summarizes the status of bonds at the end of the 24-month period following the rating event month.[9] If a bond was still trading at the end of the analysis window, it was defined as "active" and its status was recorded as either investment grade or high yield. Inactive bonds were assigned to one of three categories: matured, defaulted, or called. The table reports the total number of bonds and the proportion each classification represented in the overall population of rating events in each year.

The results indicate that the vast majority of fallen angels were still trading two years after their downgrade. Most (70%–80%) maintained their high-yield status, although a non-negligible percentage regained investment-grade ratings. In fact, the actual percentage of fallen angels that returned to investment-grade status was higher, because most bonds that were ultimately called were first upgraded to investment-grade rating. Upgraded bonds exhibited a similar pattern and generally preserved their new credit status with the exception of 2001, when almost a third of the upgraded bonds eventually returned to a high-yield rating.[10]

The relative number of bonds that matured was fairly stable, reflecting the minimum of one year remaining to maturity required of all bonds in the U.S. Corporate Index. In contrast, the short-term default rate among fallen angels exhibited considerable variation. Default rates surged in 2000–2004 (mostly because of 2001, which had a 25% default rate—20% in terms of market value), but were generally much lower, reaching a nadir of 0.5% in 1995–1999. Altman (2004) found similar results and reported that the annual default rate among bonds rated below investment-grade at issuance was almost uniformly higher between 1985 and 2004. Interestingly, the number of defaults did not surge during the recent financial crisis.[11]

## PERFORMANCE DYNAMICS AROUND RATING EVENTS

Table 13.4 reports the performance of downgraded and upgraded issuers during the analysis window by quarter relative to the event month.[12] For each quarter, the table displays the number of observations, average monthly relative returns, and associated $t$-statistics, as well as the cumulative relative returns as of the end of the quarter.[13] For downgraded issuers, these statistics are calculated using both equal and value weighting (based on the total market value of bonds outstanding for each issuer).

The value-weighted monthly relative returns earned by downgraded issuers were negative and highly significant during the three quarters prior to the rating event month and in the downgrade month itself, resulting in a cumulative underperformance of 15.09%. The fact that performance turned negative well before the actual downgrade is not surprising. Hite and Warga (1997); Steiner and Heinke (2001); Hull, Predescu, and White (2004); and Norden and Weber (2004), among others, found evidence suggesting that downgrades are anticipated well in advance based on changes in bond prices and credit default swaps spreads. In addition, many of the issuers in the

**TABLE 13.4** Quarterly Average and Cumulative Relative Returns around Rating Events

| | Downgraded Issuers | | | | | | | Upgraded Issuers | | | |
| | Market Value Weighted | | | | Equal Weighted | | | Market Value Weighted | | | |
| Quarter Relative to Rating Event Month | Number of Observations | Average Relative Monthly Returns (bps) | t-statistic | Relative Cumulative Returns | Average Relative Monthly Returns (bps) | t-statistic | Relative Cumulative Returns | Number of Observations | Average Relative Monthly Returns (bps) | t-statistic | Relative Cumulative Returns |
|---|---|---|---|---|---|---|---|---|---|---|---|
| −4 | 1,114 | −23.6 | −1.82 | −0.69% | −4.1 | −0.22 | −0.12% | 842 | 35.4 | 2.46[a] | 1.05% |
| −3 | 1,150 | −71.3 | −4.10[b] | −2.79% | −32.6 | −1.79 | −1.09% | 887 | 26.8 | 1.61 | 1.89% |
| −2 | 1,194 | −103.6 | −4.31[b] | −5.78% | −112.7 | −3.72[b] | −4.40% | 944 | 44.3 | 2.48[a] | 3.25% |
| −1 | 1,231 | −247.6 | −6.91[b] | −12.66% | −145.6 | −3.69[b] | −8.51% | 965 | 47.3 | 4.18[b] | 4.72% |
| 0 | 415 | −277.6 | −5.86[b] | −15.09% | −345.7 | −5.71[b] | −11.67% | 319 | 89.3 | 8.68[b] | 5.66% |
| 1 | 1,201 | −8.8 | −0.18 | −15.29% | 71.2 | 1.48 | −9.76% | 1,090 | −16.7 | −1.81 | 5.10% |
| 2 | 1,143 | 12.1 | 0.46 | −15.01% | 64.9 | 1.87 | −7.99% | 1,017 | −3.1 | −0.20 | 5.01% |
| 3 | 1,141 | 15.7 | 0.70 | −14.61% | 38.2 | 1.17 | −6.94% | 966 | −13.9 | −0.98 | 4.57% |
| 4 | 1,149 | 69.0 | 3.26[b] | −12.82% | 27.8 | 0.97 | −6.15% | 937 | −16.5 | −0.88 | 4.05% |
| 5 | 1,134 | 65.5 | 3.53[b] | −11.12% | 53.6 | 2.20[a] | −4.65% | 903 | −0.8 | −0.04 | 4.03% |
| 6 | 1,056 | 35.2 | 1.81 | −10.18% | 13.5 | 0.48 | −4.26% | 873 | 11.3 | 0.76 | 4.39% |
| 7 | 1,013 | 11.5 | 0.63 | −9.87% | 48.8 | 1.30 | −2.86% | 846 | 6.4 | 0.36 | 4.58% |
| 8 | 980 | 7.5 | 0.50 | −9.67% | 1.5 | 0.05 | −2.82% | 808 | −10.2 | −0.65 | 4.26% |

[a]Denotes significance at the 5% level.
[b]Denotes significance at the 1% level.

*Note:* This table reports the performance of issuers during the analysis window by quarter relative to the rating event month (defined as quarter zero). Average monthly relative returns are computed by pooling relative returns across all issuers and months in each quarter using either value or equal weighting. t-statistics are adjusted for serial and cross sectional correlation. Cumulative relative returns are calculated by first averaging issuers' relative returns by month and then cumulating them since the beginning of the analysis window. Cumulative relative returns are reported as of the end of each quarter.
*Source:* Barclays Capital.

sample had already been downgraded within investment-grade in the year before the eventual downgrade to high-yield status.

The underperformance of downgraded issuers persisted in the first three months after the downgrade but weakened substantially (with monthly relative returns being marginally negative and no longer significant). Price dynamics then reversed course, and downgraded issuers consistently outperformed their peers until the end of the analysis window by a total of 6.63%. Interestingly, about two-thirds of the overall outperformance was concentrated in just six months (quarters 4 and 5). These results are very similar in spirit to the findings by Hradsky and Long (1989), who analyzed the performance of defaulted bonds from 1977 through 1988. In their study, cumulative excess returns over the four-year period centered on the default date, also declined sharply as investors uncovered the signs of financial distress long before the default announcement, followed by a strong price reversal. Furthermore, Hradsky et al. (1989) reported that a large part of the price correction of bankrupt securities occurred between the fifth and tenth months after the default.

While the evidence of a price reversal is consistent with the existence of forced selling, it does not rule out an alternative explanation based on investor overreaction. Under this scenario, investors process the negative information that served as the basis for the rating event, but overreact to it. As a result, bond prices decline below their fundamental value even before the actual change in credit rating. Following the rating event, the misevaluations are gradually corrected, and fallen angels outperform high-yield bonds as their prices mean revert. Therefore, the overreaction theory implies that the performance patterns reflect investors' behavioral biases, leading to *voluntary* selling, while we posit that selling is *involuntary* and driven by regulatory and investment constraints.

To disentangle the theories, we first contrast the value-weighted and equal-weighted returns of downgraded issuers. If the strong price reversal after downgrade were a correction to investors' earlier overreaction, we would expect the effect to be more pronounced for smaller issuers. Generally, larger issuers are followed more closely by market participants since they typically play a bigger role in investors' portfolios. As a result, their prices, on average, are more likely to reflect their "true" intrinsic values than are those of smaller issuers. In contrast, if selling activity is mostly involuntary, the magnitude of initial underperformance and subsequent recovery should increase with issuers' size. This is exactly what we observe in practice. The effect of a downgrade on larger issuers is much more severe; using value weighting leads to a cumulative underperformance (relative to peers) of 9.67% over the entire period, while equally weighting all issuers results in a total underperformance of only 2.82%. Furthermore, the strong performance reversal in quarters 4 and 5 is not evident when returns are equally weighted.

Another way to distinguish between the two explanations is to compare the performance of upgraded and downgraded issuers. In the case of forced selling, upgraded issuers should not exhibit a reversal since they are not subject to induced buying (or selling) by investors. The overreaction theory, on the other hand, implies that the performance of upgraded issuers is likely to be the reverse image of what we observe for downgraded issuers. This is based on the notion that if investors have a tendency to overreact, it is reasonable to expect that they would do so for both negative and positive information. In fact, Easterwood and Nutt (1999) even found that equity analysts underreact to negative information but overreact to positive information.

The results in Table 13.4 suggest that upgraded issuers outperform their peers in the rating event month and throughout the prior year, but the magnitude (in absolute terms) is only about a third of the underperformance observed for downgraded issuers (5.66% versus –15.09%). In addition, despite the evidence in Table 13.2 that the distribution of rating transitions for downgraded and upgraded issuers is fairly symmetric, fallen angels underperform their peers by 277 bps in the rating event month, whereas upgraded bonds outperform only modestly (89 bps), consistent with the effects of forced selling. Most important, while the prices of fallen angels following the rating event exhibit a clear reversal, such a pattern is not evident for upgraded issuers, and their performance is in line with that of their peers.

In another attempt to corroborate our findings and distinguish between the two competing explanations, we identify a subset of downgraded issuers for which the information component contained in the rating event was likely to be limited. Specifically, we focus on issuers that were rated Baa3 throughout the year before the rating event and were then downgraded only one notch, to Ba1. These issuers then maintained their new ratings until the end of the analysis window. While it is certainly possible that the downgrade did come as a surprise in some cases, it is likely that the magnitude of new information contained in the downgrade event was more limited for such issuers relative to other issuers in the sample. If overreaction was an important driver of the reversal pattern, we would expect its effect to be smaller for this subset of issuers.

Figure 13.1 plots the median beginning-of-month relative spreads for the entire group of downgraded issuers, upgraded issuers, and the subset of issuers that experienced a rating change from Baa3 to Ba1 during the analysis window.[14] Not surprisingly, spreads of upgraded issuers were initially much wider than their (future) investment-grade peers, but the gap declined consistently from 78 bps at the start of the analysis window to 13 bps at

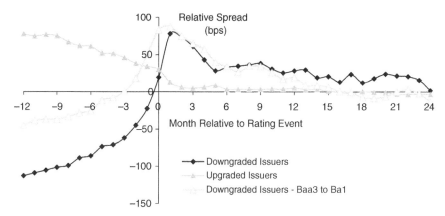

**FIGURE 13.1** Relative Spreads of Upgraded and Downgraded Issuers
*Note:* The graph plots the median beginning-of-month relative spread for issuers
included in the three groups during the analysis window.
*Source:* Barclays Capital.

the end of the rating event month (which corresponds to month 1 in the
plot). Following the upgrade, relative spreads continued to compress until
they became essentially zero or even slightly negative in the second year.

In contrast, the spreads of all downgraded issuers, as well as the subset
that migrated only from Baa3 to Ba1, exhibited very different behavior.
Their spreads widened rapidly by about 130 bps from at the beginning of
the analysis window until just before the rating event (−112 bps to 19.5
bps and −45 bps to 83 bps for all issuers and the subset, respectively), as
the market apparently anticipated (on average) the eventual downgrade.
The rating change brought further widening, as relative spreads increased
to 78 bps (for the full set of downgraded issuers) immediately following
the downgrade month. Spreads then reversed course and declined fairly
consistently until they reached parity with spreads of other high-yield bonds.
Hence, there does not seem to be any meaningful difference in the spread
dynamics between the subset of issuers downgraded from Baa3 to Ba1 and
the overall sample, suggesting that it is unlikely that the price (and spread)
reversal reflected investor overreaction.

## Cross-Sectional Variation in the Performance of Fallen Angels

The performance results in Table 13.4 point to a strong recovery, on average,
of fallen angels in the two years following the rating event, but do not capture

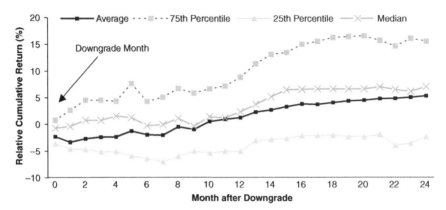

**FIGURE 13.2** Distribution of Relative Cumulative Performance since the Downgrade

*Note:* The distribution of relative cumulative returns was generated by first compounding the total returns of each issuer starting at the rating event month and then subtracting the contemporaneous cumulative return of its peer group. If an issuer left the sample before the end of the analysis window, because all its outstanding bonds matured, were called, or defaulted, we assumed that it continued to earn the same return as its peer group for all remaining months.

*Source:* Barclays Capital.

the degree of variability among issuers. While many of the downgraded issuers outperformed their peers and even regained investment-grade status, others were downgraded further, and some ended in default, as shown in Table 13.3. To better understand the cross-sectional differences among downgraded issuers, Figure 13.2 displays the mean cumulative returns of downgraded issuers over peers since the beginning of the rating event month alongside the 25th, 50th, and 75th percentiles of the distribution.

The distribution of relative cumulative returns was generated by first compounding the total returns of each issuer over different horizons starting at the rating event month and then subtracting the contemporaneous cumulative return of its peer group.[15] If an issuer left the sample before the end of the analysis window because all of its outstanding bonds matured, were called, or defaulted, we assumed that it continued to earn the same return as its peer group for all remaining months in order to prevent any survivorship bias that would alter the shape of the distribution.

The chart clearly illustrates that fallen angels were not all created alike. The top quartile of issuers outperformed their peers throughout the entire period, including the downgrade month, by a total of 15.5%. This suggests that some issuers may not have been subject to forced selling in large scale or that most of the selling activity took place before the rating event. In contrast, the performance of the bottom quartile of issuers deteriorated over time, reaching a minimum seven months after the downgrade (−7.1%). Even the worst-performing issuers exhibited a modest reversal, however, as the 25th percentile of the return distribution at the end of the analysis window was –2.3%, higher than the corresponding –3.7% figure in the rating event month. Similar to Ellul et al. (2010), Figure 13.2 also suggests that the minimum (average) return was reached only one month following the downgrade, at which point the price reversal process began.

Another important cross-sectional dynamic that was not addressed in Table 13.4 is the relation between the magnitude of initial underperformance and the subsequent price reversal. Did issuers that experienced worse performance (relative to their peers) shortly after their downgrades also exhibit a larger bounce-back afterward? To answer this question, we first need to determine over what periods the initial underperformance and ensuing reversal should be measured.

Figure 13.3 presents the distribution of the time (by quarter) in which the minimum relative cumulative return (measured since the beginning of the rating event month) for each downgraded issuer occurred. The histogram

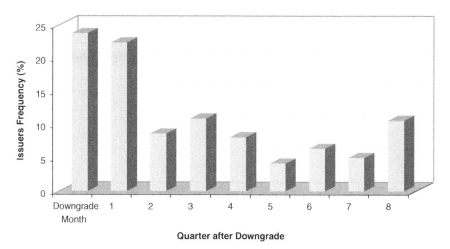

**FIGURE 13.3** Time of Minimum Relative Cumulative Return Since Downgrade by Quarter
*Note:* The histogram displays the proportion of fallen angels (out of the total number of downgraded issuers in the sample) that realized their minimum relative cumulative return (measured since the beginning of the rating event month) in each quarter. Relative cumulative returns are calculated as in Figure 13.2.
*Source:* Barclays Capital.

indicates that for almost half of the issuers (46.1%), the minimum relative (cumulative) performance was realized in the downgrade month or during the three months immediately following it. In contrast, the relative performance of only 10.6% of the issuers continued to deteriorate up to eight quarters after the rating event.

The highly skewed distribution in Figure 13.3 has two implications. First, for those considering an investment in fallen angels, it indicates a potential optimal buying time (on average) of about three months after the downgrade. We explore this issue further in the second part of the chapter. Second, it suggests that the period of initial underperformance can be represented by the time between the downgrade month and the end of the quarter following it.

To study the relation between the magnitude of initial underperformance and the subsequent price reversal, issuers were first sorted based on their average relative returns during a "formation period" of four months, starting at the rating event month. They were then assigned to one of 20 performance buckets, with the worst-performing 5% of all issuers populating the first bucket, and so on. Figure 13.4 displays median average relative returns of issuers in each of the buckets during the formation period and three subsequent separate six-month periods.

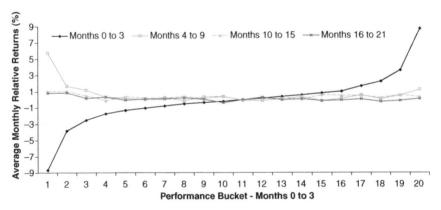

**FIGURE 13.4**   Median of Issuers' Average Monthly Returns Conditional on Formation Period Performance
*Note*: Downgraded issuers were first sorted based on their average relative returns during a "formation period" of four months starting at the rating event month. They were then assigned to one of twenty performance buckets, with the first bucket containing the worst performing 5% of all issuers, and so on. Each observation represents the median average relative returns of issuers in each of the buckets during the formation period or three separate six-month periods following it.
*Source*: Barclays Capital.

The chart suggests an asymmetric relation between the performance during the formation period and subsequent periods. Issuers that were assigned to one of the bottom four buckets experienced a strong rebound in relative performance, whereas high performing issuers during the formation period earned substantially lower returns but still managed to outperform their peers slightly.[16] Furthermore, the reversal pattern in the six months immediately after the formation period was much stronger than in the other two periods. For example, the worst performing issuers outperformed peers by 5.75%, 1.04%, and 0.86% in the first, second, and third six-month periods, respectively, compared with an average monthly relative return of −8.66% in the formation period.

Both results are consistent with the implications of price pressures. Ellul et al. (2010) found that issuers that were more widely held by constrained insurance companies experienced significantly elevated selling pressure and larger price reversals. Hence, forced selling may not uniformly affect all issuers. Poor performers during the formation period are more likely to have been subject to forced selling and, therefore, to experience a subsequent reversal, unlike top performers. Similarly, the magnitude of the reversal should be larger soon after the selling pressures abate, as shown in Figure 13.4.

## The Relation between Forced Selling and Performance

While the results in the previous sections are fully consistent with the implications of forced selling, the evidence is indirect. To establish an explicit link between the magnitude of forced selling and the performance of fallen angels, we investigate two possible measures of price pressure: The interplay between trading volumes and liquidity and the dynamics of the cash-CDS basis. We first establish the relation at the aggregate level and then employ a set of regressions to show that it also holds for the cross-section of issuers.

### Volume, Liquidity, and Cash-Derivative Basis as Proxies for Price Pressure

Under typical market conditions, increased trading volumes are associated with lower trading costs and improved liquidity. However, if higher volumes are a result of forced selling, liquidity should decline rather than rise. This reflects the execution immediacy demanded by investors and the fact that trading activity mostly represents down-volume.

Figure 13.5 plots the median relative LCS alongside the median absolute and relative turnover around the rating event month for a group of 84 issuers that were downgraded between January 2007 and December 2009.[17]

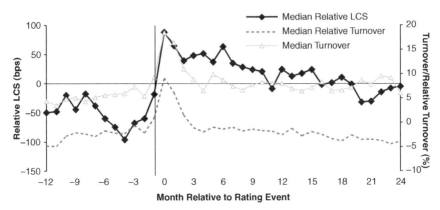

**FIGURE 13.5**   Relative Turnover and Liquidity of Downgraded Issuers
*Note*: Turnover is the ratio of monthly aggregate volume to the amount outstanding of all bonds by the same issuer. Relative turnover is the difference in turnovers between an issuer and its peer group. LCS represents the cost of an institutional-size roundtrip transaction in a bond as a percentage of its market price based on traders' quotes. All values represent median values based on 84 issuers that were downgraded between January 2007 and December 2009.
*Sources*: Barclays Capital and TRACE.

The patterns that emerge from the graph are striking. Absolute turnover increased by factor of almost four, from 5.1% to just over 18%, in the rating event month, but then declined rapidly within four months, to almost the same level as in the beginning of the analysis window. This pattern is similar to what was reported by Ellul et al. (2010), who found that the net dollar volume of fallen angels turned negative from about 20 weeks before the downgrade and then spiked up in the event week. Starting the week following the downgrade, the selling pressure dropped sharply, by 60% in just five weeks.[18] Furthermore, Ellul et al. (2010) reported that the net selling volume of fallen angels in the event week was almost three times larger than that of the control group, composed of investment-grade bonds that were downgraded to just a notch above high-yield status (Baa3). The dynamics of the relative turnover in Figure 13.5 indicate a similar behavior.

The timeline of the selling imbalance in Ellul et al. (2010) also ties in well with the changes in relative LCS. At the beginning of the sample window, the trading costs of downgraded issuers were 50 bps lower than their soon-to-be high-yield peers and declined even further on a relative basis, to 96 bps, only four months before the rating event. The relative LCS then shot up by almost 200 bps, rising to 88 bps in the downgrade month, and started to decline consistently until it converged to about the same level as other high-yield bonds two years after the rating event.

A second measure we use to proxy for the magnitude of price pressures while controlling for the possible effect of information contained in the rating event is the basis between the spread of cash securities and CDS. Credit default swap contracts should not be subject to the same level of fire sales as bonds (if any). This reflects the fact that investors who are subject to the investment constraints that motivate the sale of fallen angels do not generally obtain credit exposure through the use of credit default swaps. Consequently, while default swap spreads are expected to rise around the rating event, they should do so to a lesser extent than the spreads of bonds from the same issuers, causing the basis to widen initially and then slowly converge to its long-term equilibrium level.[19]

Figure 13.6 illustrates the changes in the spread basis during the analysis window using the median value across the 65 downgraded issuers for which data is available since January 2004.[20] The results point to the same dynamics as in Figure 13.1. The basis widened consistently from about 40 bps to more than 100 bps in the rating event month and rose even further, to almost 225 bps, three months after the downgrade. The additional widening of the cash-CDS basis is consistent with the significant selling activity of fallen angels shortly after the rating event, which exacerbated any existing price declines due to negative information. As before, once the selling pressures

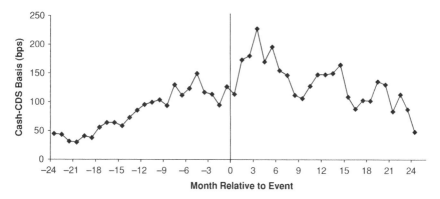

**FIGURE 13.6** Median Cash-CDS Basis Relative to Rating Event Month
*Note:* The cash-CDS basis was constructed as the difference between each issuer's Libor-OAS and a weighted combination of 5-year and 10-year swaps on the same underlying entity with RPV01 equal to the issuer's spread duration. Median value is based on a sample of 65 issuers that we were able to match since January 2004.
*Sources:* Barclays Capital and Markit.

abated, we observe a strong reversal pattern, and the basis declined again to roughly the same level as 18 to 24 months before the downgrade. Notice also that these results are again inconsistent with the overreaction theory. If our findings were driven by investors' overreaction to negative information, then the cash-CDS basis should have remained fairly stable around the rating event, as both spreads would have moved in tandem.

**Predictability in the Cross-Section of Fallen Angels' Returns**    If the performance of fallen angels is affected by forced selling, then any measure that is correlated with the magnitude of price pressures should explain the cross-sectional variation in their performance. Based on the evidence in Figure 13.5, issuers that experienced a larger widening of their cash-CDS basis relative to other downgraded issuers would be expected to perform worse initially but earn higher returns subsequently. The same pattern should hold for issuers that saw a higher increase in turnover accompanied by a simultaneous rise in their trading costs.

To test these predictions, we use two separate regression models. The first investigates the relation between the performance of downgraded issuers during the "underperformance period" in which they are subject to selling pressures and their *contemporaneous* liquidity, turnover, and cash-CDS basis. We define the "underperformance period" to be the same as the "formation period" in Figure 13.4—the four months between the start of the rating event month and the end of the next quarter. In contrast, the second regression is predictive in nature. It examines whether the realizations of these variables in the "underperformance period" can explain the future returns of downgraded issuers during the 12-month "reversal period" immediately following.

Table 13.5(A) presents the estimation results for the first regression model, in which the dependent variable is the relative return (of an issuer) in any of the four months of the underperformance period. The first specification examines whether the performance of downgraded issuers relative to peers can be explained by information contained in the rating event.[21] The performance during the rating event month and shortly after, however, should be affected only by new information that the market did not anticipate previously. Therefore, we include three proxies for the magnitude of possible "surprise" embedded in the rating event.

The first variable, "HY at Downgrade" is a dummy variable that equals one if an issuer carried an investment-grade rating from all three major rating agencies (Moody's, Standard & Poor's, and Fitch) at the time of the "rating event" and zero otherwise. We find this to be the case for only 74% of issuers. A second dummy variable, "Rating Change Size," controls for the magnitude of the rating revision. As shown in Table 13.2(A), about 76%

**TABLE 13.5** Cross-Sectional Regressions of Fallen Angels Performance

A. Contemporaneous Regressions

| | Model I | | | Model II | | | Model III | | |
|---|---|---|---|---|---|---|---|---|---|
| | Coef. | t-stat. | p-value | Coef. | t-stat. | p-value | Coef. | t-stat. | p-value |
| Intercept | −1.23 | −1.32 | 0.19 | −1.52 | −1.30 | 0.19 | 2.95 | 0.57 | 0.57 |
| *Measures of New Information* | | | | | | | | | |
| HY at downgrade | −0.39 | −0.43 | 0.67 | 0.43 | 0.41 | 0.68 | | | |
| Rating change size | −1.00 | −0.82 | 0.41 | −0.99 | −0.55 | 0.58 | | | |
| Lagged 1-month relative return | 0.07 | 1.31 | 0.19 | 0.06 | 0.93 | 0.35 | | | |
| *Measures of Price Pressure* | | | | | | | | | |
| Change in cash-CDS basis | | | | −1.63 | −5.80 | <.0001 | −1.68 | −6.33 | <.0001 |
| Lag change in cash-CDS basis | | | | −0.31 | −1.29 | 0.20 | | | |
| Change in relative LCS times relative turnover | | | | | | | −0.13 | −6.08 | <.0001 |
| Size | | | | | | | −0.38 | −0.52 | 0.61 |
| Number of observations | 411 | | | 246 | | | 173 | | |
| Adjusted $R^2$ | 0.013 | | | 0.144 | | | 0.298 | | |

(Continued)

**TABLE 13.5** (Continued)

**B. Predictive Regressions**

| | Model I | | | Model II | | | Model III | | |
|---|---|---|---|---|---|---|---|---|---|
| | Coef. | t-stat. | p-value | Coef. | t-stat. | p-value | Coef. | t-stat. | p-value |
| Intercept | 0.74 | 3.96 | <.0001 | 0.21 | 1.66 | 0.10 | 0.18 | 0.11 | 0.91 |
| Average relative return month 0–3 | −0.09 | −2.61 | 0.01 | −0.01 | −0.56 | 0.58 | −0.10 | −2.76 | 0.01 |
| *Measures of Price Pressure* | | | | | | | | | |
| End of month 3 cash-CDS basis | | | | 0.15 | 2.69 | 0.01 | | | |
| $\sum$ change in relative LCS × turnover | | | | | | | 0.004 | 2.05 | 0.05 |
| Size | | | | | | | 0.11 | 0.47 | 0.64 |
| Number of observations | 64 | | | 58 | | | 55 | | |
| Adjusted $R^2$ | 0.085 | | | 0.089 | | | 0.152 | | |

*Note:* The dependent variable in panel A is the relative return for each issuer in the rating event month or in one of the following three months (underperformance period). The dependent variable in panel B is the average relative return of each issuer over the 12-month period following the underperformance period. HY at downgrade is a dummy variable that equals one if an issuer carried an investment-grade rating from all three major rating agencies (Moody's, S&P, and Fitch) at the time of the rating event and zero otherwise. Rating change size is a dummy variable that equals one for issuers that were downgraded by more than two notches during the month of downgrade and zero otherwise. The change in the cash-CDS basis and relative LCS are the differences between the cash-CDS basis and relative LCS at the end of the current and previous months. Relative turnover is the ratio of the monthly aggregate volume to the amount outstanding for each issuer in excess of the peer group. Size is the natural logarithm of each issuer's market value as of the end of its downgrade month. $\sum$Relative LCS × Turnover is the sum of the product of relative LCS and turnover between the downgrade month and the end of the following quarter.
*Source:* Barclays Capital.

of fallen angels were downgraded by only one or two notches. Therefore, a rating change of more than two notches, on average, may not be expected by the market. The "Rating Change Size" is set to one if the downgrade was more than two notches and zero otherwise. The lagged one-month relative return of each issuer is also included to control for the possibility that informational effects may be incorporated over several months. The estimation results, however, indicate that none of the variables have any significant explanatory power, and the adjusted $R^2$ is only 0.013.

The second specification includes the first measure of price pressure, the change in the cash-CDS basis, in addition to the proxies for information. The lagged change in the cash-CDS basis is included as well to control for the possibility that the CDS market will react before the cash market does. We find that the coefficient of the change in the cash-CDS basis is highly significant (*t*-statistic of –5.80) and implies that a 1% widening of the basis leads to an additional underperformance of 1.63% per month in the cash market relative to peers during the "underperformance period." In contrast, the coefficients of the lagged change in cash-CDS basis, as well as the variables controlling for information, are all insignificant.

The findings in Figure 13.5 suggest that increased trading volume coupled with a simultaneous rise in illiquidity (as measured by a widening of bid-ask spreads) may signal the existence of price pressures. To capture the joint dynamic of volume and liquidity, the third specification includes the product of the change in relative LCS and relative turnover. The product term reflects the notion that if a larger trading volume for an issuer (relative to peers) is due to forced selling, its LCS should rise as well, reflecting the one-sided nature of the market and the increased risk premium demanded by dealers for holding the security in their inventory. The value of the product term in this case would be positive, and a negative coefficient would be consistent with the effect of price pressure. Notice that for the more common cases in which LCS rises because of lack of sufficient trading volume (i.e., negative relative turnover) or declines as a result of abnormally high trading activity, the product term would be negative.

The results of the third specification support the view that the combination of high volume and bid-ask spreads is a likely sign of price pressure.[22] The coefficient of the product term is negative, as expected, and significant at the 1% level (*t*-statistic of –6.08). Moreover, the coefficient of the change in the cash-CDS basis remained highly significant and essentially unchanged (–1.68 instead of –1.63). This implies that the two measures capture different aspects of price pressure and combined are able to explain 30% of the cross-sectional variation in the performance of fallen angels.

Two additional results are worth mentioning. First, although the coefficient of size is negative (consistent with the evidence in Table 13.4, which suggests a size effect), larger issuers did not earn significantly lower returns, This is likely due to the difference in sample composition and the small subset used in the estimation, which reduces the power of the regression considerably.[23] Second, the intercept changed sign, from negative in the first specification to positive (albeit insignificant in both). This implies that the relative return of downgraded issuers during the underperformance period is no longer negative, on average, once the effects of price pressure on performance are removed.

To test the second prediction, Table 13.5(B) examines the relation between our two proxies for price pressure and future returns. In particular, in the second regression, issuers' average relative returns during the 12-month "reversal period" (the dependent variable) are regressed against the cash-CDS spread basis and a combination of volume and the bid-ask spread level at the end of the "underperformance period" (i.e., the end of month 3 after the downgrade). Issuers that experience a greater degree of price pressure during the "underperformance period" based on these measures are expected to exhibit a larger performance reversal.

To set the stage, the first specification includes only each issuer's average relative return in the "underperformance period" as an explanatory variable. Therefore, it almost exactly corresponds to the analysis in Figure 13.4, which showed the relation between performance in the "formation period" and returns in three subsequent six-month periods. Indeed, the performance reversal observed in Figure 13.4 is now manifested by the negative and significant coefficient (at the 1% confidence level) of the "Average Relative Return Month 0–3." This implies that issuers with worse initial underperformance experienced a stronger rebound.

However, once the proxies for price pressure are added to the regression model, the coefficient of past performance is no longer significant. In the second specification, the coefficient of the level of the cash-CDS basis is positive and significant, suggesting that a 1% widening of the basis during the "underperformance period" leads to an average of 15 bps per month in the next 12 months. In the third specification, the cash-CDS basis is replaced by $\sum$Change in relative LCS × turnover, which is the sum of the monthly product of relative LCS changes and turnover during the "underperformance period" and the issuer's size. As in the second specification, past performance has no explanatory power, whereas issuers that experienced higher volume coupled with a decrease in liquidity relative to other issuers enjoyed greater outperformance than their peers.[24] Overall, the results in Table 13.5(B) confirm that the observed relation between the degree of initial underperformance and subsequent outperformance is a reflection of the magnitude of price pressure.

## FALLEN ANGELS AS AN ASSET CLASS

The evidence so far suggests that fallen angels as a group exhibit a strong reversal pattern starting shortly after their downgrade. The primary driver of this phenomenon does not seem to be overreaction to information, but rather the structural inefficiency stemming from the segmentation between the investment and non-investment-grade markets. The collective need by many investors to divest former investment-grade issues in a short period of time temporarily brings the price of fallen angels below their equilibrium level.

What would be the performance of a strategy that seeks to exploit this structural inefficiency? The second part of the chapter investigates the properties and performance of a dynamic, rules-based strategy that invested in fallen angels over the sample period. While results in the previous sections are indicative, they reflect an event study approach in which all events (downgrades) were time-aggregated. However, as Table 13.1 demonstrates, the supply of fallen angels varies considerably over time, which can greatly affect the risk-return profile of such a strategy. Its performance would reflect not only the typical price behavior of fallen angels after they are downgraded but also their frequency over time.

A strategy that focuses solely on fallen angels can be viewed as an addition to an existing portfolio of high-yield bonds or as a separate strategy for absolute return investors who find its risk-return profile appealing. Our goal in constructing this strategy is to emulate the experience of a portfolio manager who consistently buys fallen angels. While the strategy does not engage in individual name selection as an actual portfolio manager would, we incorporate several features into the construction process to reflect the findings above and the way that bond portfolios are managed in practice as well as accounting for trading costs. We, therefore, believe the results provide a good illustration of the potential benefits and risks of investing in fallen angels relative to other high-yield bonds.

### Construction Method

We construct three dynamic portfolios of fallen angels that differed in their bond inclusion and exclusion criteria (Table 13.6 provides a summary of the criteria). The portfolios are fully seeded with cash at inception (January 1991), with no leverage allowed. All portfolios are rebalanced thereafter at the end of each month employing the same approach for sizing the positions of individual bonds.

**TABLE 13.6** Bond Inclusion/Exclusion Criteria by Portfolio

| Portfolio | | Buy All | Three-Month Reversal | Flexible Reversal |
|---|---|---|---|---|
| Buy conditions (if all are satisfied) | Timing | Downgrade month | Month 3 | Month 1–6 |
| | Minimum relative spread | N/A | ≥ 40 bps | ≥ 40 bps |
| | Minimum price | N/A | N/A | ≥ $40 |
| | Change in relative spread | N/A | N/A | Tighten |
| Sell triggers (if any one is satisfied) | Technical | Yes | Yes | Yes |
| | Timing | Month 24 | Month 24 | Month 24 |
| | Relative spread | N/A | Negative | Negative |

*Note:* The technical trigger for selling a bond refers to bonds that matured, defaulted, or were called. The relative spread change condition requires a bond relative spread to tighten compared with the previous month.
*Source:* Barclays Capital.

The first portfolio, "Buy All," is meant to represent the performance of the overall universe of fallen angels after downgrade. Hence, every fallen angel bond is acquired at the end of its rating event month. For issuers with multiple bonds, only the bond with the highest market value is purchased to limit issuer concentration.[25] In addition, a position size limit is imposed to reduce the exposure to any single issuer. In general, the tighter the cap, the more it reduces the effect of a default or sharp price decline, but in periods in which the population of fallen angels is limited, it likely results in the portfolio's not being fully invested. We therefore set the maximum position size at 10% and assume that any uninvested cash portion earns a return equivalent to the one-month LIBOR rate.

At each rebalancing date, bonds that satisfied either of the following two conditions were removed:

1. The bond has defaulted, been called, or matured during the month.
2. Two years have passed since the rating event month.

The first trigger can be seen as technical in nature, since the bonds had stopped trading. Otherwise, bonds were sold at the end of the analysis window (24 months after the downgrade). In both cases, the end-of-month sale price represents the bond's final value for performance calculation purposes.

Once the list of bonds to be added and removed was finalized, the new set of bonds that constituted the portfolio for the following month is equally weighted. For example, suppose that after the portfolio is rebalanced at the end of June 2009, it includes eight bonds with a 10% weight each and a 20% allocation to cash. Assume further that at the end of the next month, two of the bonds are sold and five new bonds are added. The total number of bonds in the portfolio increases to eleven, with each having an equal weight of 9.09% of the total portfolio value.

While this weighting scheme is not likely to be used in practice, it is better suited for our purpose, which is to capture the performance of fallen angels as a group, for two reasons. First, using differential weights would make the strategy more sensitive to the performance of certain issuers. Second, our approach guarantees that all fallen angels that satisfy the inclusion criteria are represented in the portfolio even if it is already fully invested. Under alternative weighting schemes, some fallen angels may not be purchased simply because they are downgraded in a period in which the portfolio is fully invested. This, in turn, introduces a subjective component to the analysis. The clear disadvantage of using equal weighting in practice, on the other hand, is the relatively high turnover it introduces.

In the second portfolio, termed "Three-Month Reversal," fallen angels are purchased at the end of the third month following their downgrade. This is motivated by the evidence in Figure 13.3, which indicates that for more than 45% of fallen angels, the price reversal process starts in the first three months after the downgrade. Another aspect in which this portfolio differed from the "Buy All" portfolio is the incorporation of pricing data. Only bonds trading at relative spreads of at least 40 bps are eligible for purchase, in order to screen out bonds that are not "cheap" on a relative basis and are, therefore, less likely to outperform their peers. When the relative spreads of bonds already in the portfolio become negative, they are sold, as their potential upside is limited.

The last portfolio, "Flexible Reversal," aims to not only exploit the general pattern of price reversion, but also to acknowledge that not all fallen angels exhibit the same behavior. Some fallen angels never experience any reversion and continue straight to default. In addition, even when fallen angels do experience a price reversal, the timing may vary.

A bond qualified for purchase by the "Flexible Reversal" portfolio if it satisfies *all* the following:

1. Its relative spread is higher than 40 bps but also has tightened compared with the previous month.
2. No more than six months have passed since the downgrade month (e.g., months one through six after the rating event).

3. The end-of-month bond price is over \$40 (per \$100 par amount).
4. It was not previously part of the portfolio.[26]

The first condition can be seen as an indicator for the timing of a possible reversal. A tightening of relative spreads may suggest that the selling imbalance caused by the downgrade has mostly diminished. The second requirement is motivated by the notion that since price pressures due to "fire sales" are temporary, price reversals should occur within a fairly short period of time following the downgrade. The selection of a six-month window is driven by the evidence in Figure 13.5, which suggests that selling activity declines sharply after that time frame, as well as those in Figure 13.3.

The condition for a minimum purchase price is imposed to avoid buying bonds for which the price decline may have been driven primarily by (negative) information rather than price pressures. Including such bonds would likely result in higher portfolio volatility and reduce our ability to properly measure the benefit related to exploiting reversals resulting from price pressures.[27] Existing bonds, however (i.e., after they are initially purchased), are not subject to this requirement, and their prices could drop below the \$40 threshold. The exclusion criteria for the "Flexible Reversal" portfolio are similar to those of the "Three-Month Reversal" portfolio.

## Portfolio Characteristics

Before evaluating performance, we examine various properties of the three portfolios reported in Table 13.7. Not surprisingly, the "Buy All" portfolio had the largest number of bonds per month on average, 47.1, compared with 11.7 and 13.4 for the "Three-Month Reversal" and "Flexible Reversal" portfolios, respectively. The larger population of the "Buy All" portfolio reflects, in part, its formulation, as all fallen angels are purchased unconditionally. The primary reason, however, is the difference in selling triggers. In the "Buy All" portfolio, bonds are held for the duration of the two-year period after the downgrade, unless they become inactive, whereas in the two other portfolios, they could be sold earlier if their spreads relative to peers are sufficiently tight.

The effect of the additional sale trigger is illustrated in Table 13.8, which reports the percentage of bonds in every portfolio that are sold in order to satisfy each exclusion criterion. Whereas the passage of the two-year period represented 81% of the sales in the "Buy All" portfolio, consistent with the evidence in Table 13.3, it constitutes less than 18% in the "Three-Month Reversal" and "Flexible Reversal" portfolios. Instead, the main reason in these portfolios is the relative spread trigger, which is responsible for about 75% of the bonds that are sold. As a result, the average holding period for

**TABLE 13.7** Portfolio Composition Summary Statistics

| | Mean | Median | Minimum | Maximum |
|---|---|---|---|---|
| **Buy All** | | | | |
| Number of bonds | 47.1 | 36.0 | 0.0 | 148.0 |
| Holding period (months) | 21.7 | 24.0 | 1.0 | 24.0 |
| Turnover | 15.2% | 12.6% | 0.0% | 51.0% |
| Percent of Financials relative to HY Index | 13.0% | 8.9% | −8.3% | 48.2% |
| Percent of Industrials relative to HY Index | −22.8% | −25.0% | −81.4% | 18.0% |
| Percent of Utilities relative to HY Index | 9.9% | 8.8% | −11.8% | 35.7% |
| Percentage of cash in portfolio | 1.6% | 0.0% | 0.0% | 100.0% |
| **Three-Month Reversal** | | | | |
| Number of bonds | 11.7 | 9.0 | 0.0 | 52.0 |
| Holding period (months) | 9.7 | 8.0 | 1.0 | 21.0 |
| Turnover | 19.0% | 16.6% | 0.0% | 84.2% |
| Percent in Financials relative to HY Index | 17.5% | 7.8% | −9.6% | 96.5% |
| Percent in Industrials relative to HY Index | −15.7% | −10.0% | −91.7% | 18.5% |
| Percent in Utilities relative to HY Index | −1.8% | −5.9% | −12.5% | 41.7% |
| Percentage of cash in portfolio | 30.8% | 10.0% | 0.0% | 100.0% |
| **Flexible Reversal** | | | | |
| Number of bonds | 13.4 | 11.0 | 1.0 | 60.0 |
| Holding period (months) | 9.8 | 7.5 | 1.0 | 23.0 |
| Turnover | 19.4% | 15.8% | 0.1% | 80.0% |
| Percent in Financials relative to HY Index | 12.4% | 5.8% | −9.6% | 96.5% |
| Percent in Industrials relative to HY Index | −12.8% | −7.7% | −89.6% | 18.6% |
| Percent in Utilities relative to HY Index | 0.8% | −4.9% | −12.5% | 53.7% |
| Percentage of cash in portfolio | 26.0% | 0.0% | 0.0% | 90.0% |

*Note:* Turnover is calculated as the sum of the absolute changes in weights of all bonds based on the portfolio composition before and after the monthly rebalancing.
*Source:* Barclays Capital.

**TABLE 13.8** Distribution of Bonds Sales by Exclusion Triggers

| | Buy All | | Three-Month Reversal | | Flexible Reversal | |
|---|---|---|---|---|---|---|
| Passage of 24 months since downgrade | 369 | 81.1% | 47 | 17.6% | 53 | 17.4% |
| Relative spread is negative | 0 | 0.0% | 199 | 74.5% | 230 | 75.7% |
| Matured | 34 | 7.5% | 7 | 2.6% | 8 | 2.6% |
| Called | 18 | 4.0% | 1 | 0.4% | 0 | 0.0% |
| Defaulted | 34 | 7.5% | 13 | 4.9% | 13 | 4.3% |
| Total Sells | 455 | | 267 | | 304 | |

*Source:* Barclays Capital.

the "Buy All" portfolio is 21.7 months, whereas the average holding periods for the "Three-Month Reversal" and "Flexible Reversal" portfolios are only 9.7 and 9.8 months, respectively (Table 13.7). Note also that although the default rate in the "Buy All" portfolio (7.5%) is almost double that of the two other portfolios, its net effect on performance cannot be easily determined, since the larger population of the "Buy All" portfolio results in a much smaller weight allocated to each bond. Another implication of the additional sale trigger is more frequent trading. The "Three-Month Reversal" and "Flexible Reversal" portfolios have higher turnover rates (19.0% and 19.4% per month, respectively) than the "Buy All" portfolio (15.2%). The unusually high turnover rates reflect the unrealistic equal-weighted scheme that we adopt, and we examine their effect on performance in the next section.

Two additional portfolio characteristics of interest are presented in Table 13.7. First, relative to the High Yield Index, all three portfolios over-weight the financial sector and underweight the industrial sector, but with considerable variation over time. During the recent crisis, for example, all three portfolios have an overweight to financials of about 40%. Second, the 10% position limit causes the "Three-Month Reversal" and "Flexible Reversal" portfolios to have a 25% to 30% allocation to cash on average. These averages, however, mask the large change in the number of bonds between the first and second halves of the sample. Figure 13.7 displays the number of bonds in the portfolio over the sample period for each of the three portfolios. Irrespective of the portfolio, the population exhibits large variations over time, consistent with the evidence in Table 13.1, peaking in 2001–2003 period and during the 2007–2009 financial crisis as the deterioration in market conditions increased the supply of fallen angels. As a result, the average cash holdings in the second half of the sample for the

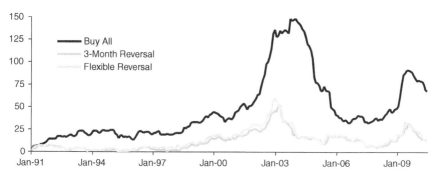

**FIGURE 13.7** Monthly Portfolio Bond Population
*Source:* Barclays Capital.

"Three-Month Reversal" and "Flexible Reversal" portfolios are only 3.1% and 1.6%, respectively.

## Performance and Analysis

Table 13.9(A) reports various statistics for the three portfolios regarding their absolute and relative returns between January 1991 and June 2010.[28] Several key results are evident from the table.

Despite the simple construction rules underlying the "Buy All" portfolio, it outperforms its peers by about 3.6% a year on average during the analysis period, leading to an information ratio of 0.64. The higher volatility of the portfolio compared with the peer group (2.77% versus 2.14%) is at least partly a reflection of the larger number of bonds in the peer group. To have a more proper comparison, the column titled "Modified Peer Group" presents the performance of an alternative peer benchmark with the same number of bonds as the portfolio.[29] The volatility of the Modified Peer Group is indeed somewhat higher than that of the broad peer group we use, but so is its performance (0.80% versus 0.73%), and this pattern holds irrespective of the portfolio and time period. As a result, information ratios are lower when the Modified Peer Group serves as the benchmark, but fallen angels still handsomely outperform these high-yield bonds. The tail statistics of the "Buy All" portfolio are similar to those of the peer group and better than the Modified Peer Group. The worst one-month and three-month returns are −12.36% and −24.89%, respectively, compared with −13.53% and −26.49% for the modified peer group; similarly, the fifth percentile of the portfolio monthly return distribution is −2.33%, compared with −3.12% for the modified peer group.

**TABLE 13.9** Performance of Fallen Angels Portfolios

**A. Full Sample**

| | Portfolio | Peer Group | Return over Peer Group | Modified Peer Group | Return over Modified Peer Group |
|---|---|---|---|---|---|
| **Buy All** | | | | | |
| Average (monthly) | 1.04% | 0.73% | 0.31% | 0.80% | 0.24% |
| Volatility (monthly) | 2.77% | 2.14% | 1.68% | 2.50% | 1.77% |
| SR/IR (annualized) | 0.87 | 0.64 | 0.64 | 0.64 | 0.48 |
| Worst month | −12.36% | −14.24% | −5.81% | −13.53% | −5.37% |
| Worst three-month | −24.89% | −23.51% | −5.19% | −26.49% | −7.56% |
| 5th percentile of return distribution | −2.33% | −2.57% | −1.90% | −3.12% | −2.52% |
| **Three-Month Reversal** | | | | | |
| Average (monthly) | 1.46% | 0.67% | 0.78% | 0.74% | 0.72% |
| Volatility (monthly) | 3.83% | 2.11% | 2.62% | 2.63% | 2.69% |
| SR/IR (annualized) | 1.01 | 0.56 | 1.03 | 0.53 | 0.93 |
| Worst month | −10.76% | −14.46% | −8.45% | −12.72% | −10.94% |
| Worst three-month | −26.01% | −22.74% | −9.29% | −27.48% | −8.90% |
| 5th percentile of return distribution | −3.81% | −1.93% | −2.64% | −2.00% | −2.90% |
| **Flexible Reversal** | | | | | |
| Average (monthly) | 1.21% | 0.68% | 0.53% | 0.76% | 0.45% |
| Volatility (monthly) | 3.54% | 2.09% | 2.27% | 2.68% | 2.37% |
| SR/IR (annualized) | 0.85 | 0.57 | 0.81 | 0.54 | 0.66 |
| Worst month | −13.34% | −13.75% | −7.01% | −12.08% | −6.78% |
| Worst three-month | −29.66% | −22.92% | −14.60% | −27.68% | −11.05% |
| 5th percentile of return distribution | −3.95% | −2.14% | −2.59% | −2.75% | −2.88% |

**B. Three-Month Reversal Portfolio by Period**

| | Portfolio | Peer Group | Return over Peer Group | Modified Peer Group | Return over Modified Peer Group |
|---|---|---|---|---|---|
| **January 1991–December 2000** | | | | | |
| Average (monthly) | 0.92% | 0.52% | 0.40% | 0.54% | 0.38% |
| Volatility (monthly) | 1.90% | 0.81% | 1.71% | 0.92% | 1.86% |
| SR/IR (annualized) | 0.89 | 0.40 | 0.80 | 0.42 | 0.71 |
| Worst month | −5.70% | −3.05% | −6.25% | −2.15% | −6.11% |
| Worst three-month | −5.76% | −6.24% | −8.98% | −3.62% | −8.90% |
| 5th percentile of return Distribution | −1.03% | −0.78% | −1.83% | −1.25% | −2.30% |

**TABLE 13.9** (*Continued*)

B. Three-Month Reversal Portfolio by Period (continued)

|  | Portfolio | Peer Group | Return over Peer Group | Modified Peer Group | Return over Modified Peer Group |
|---|---|---|---|---|---|
| **January 2001–June 2010** |  |  |  |  |  |
| Average (monthly) | 2.02% | 0.83% | 1.19% | 0.94% | 1.08% |
| Volatility (monthly) | 5.09% | 2.90% | 3.28% | 3.64% | 3.32% |
| SR/IR (annualized) | 1.21 | 0.72 | 1.25 | 0.68 | 1.13 |
| Worst month | −10.76% | −14.46% | −8.45% | −12.72% | −10.94% |
| Worst three-month | −26.01% | −22.74% | −9.29% | −27.48% | −8.38% |
| 5th percentile of return distribution | −5.51% | −2.91% | −2.97% | −4.31% | −3.69% |

*Note:* The returns for the portfolios' peer and modified peer groups are computed as the equal-weighted performances of the individual bonds' peer groups (as explained in the "Data and Methodology" section) and single matched peer bonds. The Sharpe ratio (SR) is calculated using the one-month LIBOR rate and applied to absolute returns of the portfolio or peer group. The information ratio (IR) is the ratio of average and standard deviation of relative returns of the portfolio over its peer group.
*Source:* Barclays Capital.

Comparing the results across portfolios suggests that the "Three-Month Reversal" and "Flexible Reversal" portfolios have substantially higher performance than the "Buy All" portfolio, with information ratios for the "Three-Month Reversal" portfolio (based on both peer benchmarks) almost doubling, from 0.64 and 0.48 to 1.03 and 0.93. Despite the attempt to improve performance by using a bond-specific signal for the beginning of the reversal process, the "Flexible Reversal" portfolio actually generates lower returns than the "Three-Month Reversal" portfolio. An important reason for this is that by trying to identify the inflection point for each issuer, the portfolio gives up, by construction, some spread tightening. Hence, timing an investment in individual fallen angels (as opposed to using a uniform rule) may be difficult to achieve.

The two portfolios experience higher volatility and slightly worse tail properties than the "Buy All" portfolio. For example, the fifth percentile of the distribution of *relative* returns and the worst three-month period declines from –2.52% and –7.56% respectively, using the Modified Peer Group benchmark for the "Buy All" portfolio, to –2.90% and –8.90% for the "Three-Month Reversal." This increased risk is mostly related to the

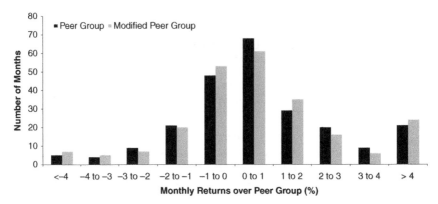

**FIGURE 13.8** Distribution of Monthly Relative Returns for the "Three-Month Reversal" Portfolio
*Source:* Barclays Capital.

difference in the number of bonds between the two portfolios and the "Buy All" portfolio.

Figure 13.8 presents the distribution of relative returns for the "Three-Month Reversal" portfolio. It indicates that the distribution is symmetric and exhibits "fat tails" (skewness and kurtosis are 0.72 and 4.38 respectively, using the Modified Peer Group benchmark), with positive relative performance in 63% of months.

**Robustness Tests**   Is there a relation between the performance of fallen angels and their supply dynamics? As Figure 13.7 illustrates, the population of bonds in the portfolios is characterized by two distinct states that correspond quite closely to the first and second halves of the sample period. The number of bonds is fairly stable until 1999, but rose sharply thereafter following the two credit episodes of 2001–2002 and 2008–2009.

To address this question, Table 13.9(B) displays the same statistics for the "Three-Month Reversal" portfolio as in Table 13.9(A), separately for the first and second halves of the sample. The results show a clear difference in portfolio risk and performance between the two periods. Volatility almost doubles despite the larger portfolio population, but the monthly average relative return is higher by a factor of three (1.19% versus 0.40%). Consequently, the information ratio increases from 0.8 in the first half to 1.25 in the second half. These changes in performance are driven in part by the difference in cash holdings between the two periods. During most of

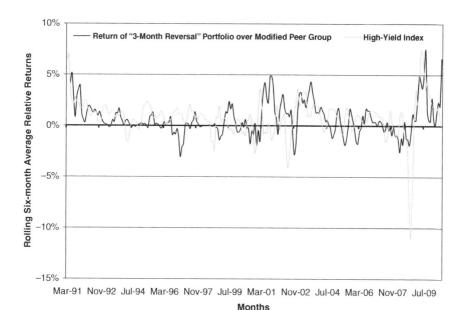

**FIGURE 13.9** Rolling Six-month Average Relative Returns of the Three-Month Reversal Portfolio and U.S. High Yield Index
*Source:* Barclays Capital.

the first decade, the portfolio is not fully invested and has an average cash position of 54%, contributing to the lower returns and volatility.[30]

The portfolio's relative performance is also sensitive to the macroeconomic environment and overall conditions in the high-yield market. This is illustrated in Figure 13.9, which displays the rolling six-month average relative returns of the "Three-Month Reversal" portfolio against the average absolute returns of the High Yield Index over the same time frame. The chart shows that the portfolio relative returns tend to co-vary with the absolute performance of the high-yield market, with a monthly correlation of 0.22.

One possibility for this phenomenon is that the peer group (and modified peer group) formulation that we use do not properly capture all relevant risk factors. As a result, the relative returns of the "Three-Month Reversal" portfolio still reflect exposures to systematic risks that are also present in the broader market. We tested several alternative peer group specifications, but all produced similar results.

Another explanation, which is also supported by evidence in Ellul et al. (2010), is that the performance of the High Yield Index serves as a proxy for the level of demand for high-yield securities. Past research has shown that investors' inflows tend to follow strong positive performance and vice versa. This is especially the case for individual investors, who constitute a large part of the high-yield investor base through mutual funds holdings. Ellul et al. (2010) found that the degree of initial price declines and subsequent reversals was related to the potential demand for fallen angels, which they measured using the assets under management of high-yield mutual funds and distressed focused hedge funds. Their results indicate that the initial drop in price and subsequent reversal are indeed larger when the capital of potential buyers is relatively scarce.[31]

Another important question is the degree to which our results are sensitive to the parameter values. Table 13.10 reports the relative performance statistics over the entire period for the "Three-Month Reversal" portfolio using various alternative parameter specifications. Comparing the importance of the timing confirms again that the optimal buying time of fallen angels is three months after their downgrade (represented by the original portfolio formulation). The table also suggests that the properties of the "Three-Month Reversal" portfolio are fairly robust to changes in other key parameters. In fact, using a 5% position limit would generate lower risk and a higher information ratio compared with the original results based on a 10% position limit.

**Performance Net of Transactions Costs**    Overall, the findings in this section suggest that inefficiency in the pricing of fallen angels can be exploited using a simple set of rules based on time since the downgrade event and pricing relative to peers. While the benefit from the mispricing of fallen angels certainly varies over time as a function of supply dynamics and market conditions, outperformance is not confined to a single episode, but is evident throughout the sample. However, given the high turnover associated with the "Three-Month Reversal" Portfolio, would the strategy still be attractive to investors after trading costs are explicitly factored in?

While it is not feasible to provide an exact answer, an estimate of net performance can be computed as follows (all values are based on averages):

$$\text{Net performance} = \text{Portfolio monthly return} - \frac{1}{2} \times \text{LCS} \times \text{Turnover}$$

Notice that, since LCS represents the roundtrip trading cost of a bond and our turnover calculation combines "buys" and "sells," the product of the two should be divided by two to get a correct estimate of the portfolio rebalancing costs.

Figure 13.5 indicates that the average round-trip trading cost for a fallen angel shortly after downgrade is about 50 to 60 bps higher than a similar

**TABLE 13.10** Performance of "Three-Month Reversal" Portfolio over Peer Group with Alternative Specifications

| | Original Formulation | Buy Bonds Instead in | | | | Position Limit | Minimum Relative Spread | Minimum Absolute Price |
| --- | --- | --- | --- | --- | --- | --- | --- | --- |
| | | Month 1 | Month 2 | Month 4 | Month 5 | 5% | 20 bps | $40 |
| Average (monthly) | 0.78% | 0.64% | 0.67% | 0.75% | 0.66% | 0.64% | 0.70% | 0.61% |
| Volatility (monthly) | 2.62% | 2.52% | 2.72% | 3.02% | 3.11% | 2.10% | 2.59% | 2.05% |
| Information ratio (annualized) | 1.03 | 0.87 | 0.85 | 0.86 | 0.73 | 1.07 | 0.93 | 1.03 |
| Worst month | −8.45% | −7.41% | −9.13% | −8.52% | −9.97% | −8.45% | −7.77% | −6.25% |
| Worst three-month | −9.29% | −14.00% | −11.12% | −11.67% | −11.53% | −7.67% | −10.55% | −9.29% |
| 5th percentile of return Distribution | −2.64% | −2.51% | −2.54% | −3.08% | −3.47% | −1.65% | −2.75% | −2.33% |

*Source:* Barclays Capital.

high-yield bond, or about 4% to 5% in absolute terms. Combining the LCS data with the average "Three-Month Reversal" portfolio turnover (19%) and relative performance translates into a net average monthly relative performance of 72.7 bps. The average monthly total return, which is of greater interest to absolute return investors, can be computed similarly and is equal to 103.25 bps per month (146 bps – 0.5 × 450 bps × 19%), or about 12.39% a year since 1991. This translates into an annualized information ratio of 0.94 and a Sharpe ratio of 0.63 after trading costs.[32]

Two additional observations are worth mentioning. First, the LCS data underlying Figure 13.5 coincides with a severe liquidity crisis. Hence, the trading costs of fallen angels over the long-term should be lower. Second, since the LCS data reflects bid-ask spreads quoted by a single dealer (Barclays Capital), the "effective" spreads for investors are likely to be tighter.

## CONCLUSION

Typical mandates for investment-grade corporate bond portfolios and the current regulatory environment either explicitly or implicitly require portfolio managers to sell bonds that are downgraded to non-investment-grade status. The collective need to divest downgraded bonds in a short period of time can create pressures that temporarily bring fallen angel prices below equilibrium.

The findings in this chapter support the existence of such price pressures. We document strong price reversal patterns at both the aggregate and cross-sectional levels. Our results suggest that investors begin to sell their soon-to-become fallen angels before the rating change event in anticipation of the downgrade and continue to sell for up to about three months afterwards. As the selling intensity dissipates, price declines reverse, and fallen angels outperform high-yield peers by a total of 6.63% in the two-year period after the downgrade. In addition, the price recovery of individual issuers is negatively correlated with the magnitude of their initial underperformance. Furthermore, we find no support for an alternative behavioral explanation to these results based on investors' overreaction to the negative information of the downgrade event.

We also provide direct evidence linking price pressures to the performance of fallen angels in the two-year period after their downgrade. Cross-sectional regressions indicate that the extent of initial underperformance in the three months following the downgrade (as well as the downgrade month) relates to the magnitude of the contemporaneous cash-CDS spread basis widening, as well as to changes in relative liquidity and turnover. These factors are also shown to have predictive power for issuers' relative performance in the subsequent twelve months. In particular, a wider cash-CDS basis and higher liquidity costs at the end of the first quarter after the downgrade are positively and significantly related to future relative performance across issuers.

In the second part of the chapter, we analyze the characteristics and performance of several dynamic portfolios with different guidelines for investing in fallen angels over time. We show that these portfolios consistently outperform high-yield peers by about 8.5% per year on average, with information ratios in excess of one, using a relatively simple set of rules based on time relative to the downgrade event and a "rich/cheap" indicator. While the magnitude of the outperformance is not constant, it is not confined to a specific period and is evident throughout the sample. Even incorporating the higher costs of trading fallen angels compared with other high-yield bonds does not significantly diminish their attractiveness.

These findings have several important implications for investors. First, traditional credit investors who use the U.S. Corporate Index as their benchmark and own fallen angels at the time of their downgrade may be better off not liquidating their holdings at once, but unwinding them gradually instead, starting about three months after the rating change. Second, investors such as plan sponsors should consider the merits of adopting more flexible investment mandates that do not necessitate the disposal of fallen angels. In Chapter 12, we demonstrate that an alternative index that is similar to the Corporate Index but does not exclude fallen angels offers a significant performance improvement without a commensurate increase in risk. Even investors who are not willing to implement such dramatic changes should, at a minimum, allow for a longer period of time (perhaps two years) during which fallen angels can be sold. Our findings suggest that the vast majority of fallen angels do not default during that time frame and that their spreads decline consistently relative to those of their high-yield peers, reaching parity only at the end of that period. Third, for absolute return investors such as hedge funds, the pricing inefficiency and return predictability of fallen angels can provide attractive profit opportunities. This may be especially the case if we enhance the simple portfolio construction rules we tested and use an overlay of credit default swaps to eliminate default risk.

# NOTES

1. Ambrose et al. (2009) restrict their sample to include only bonds for which the issuers' stock had no significant reaction to the rating change to control for any new information revealed in the downgrade event. They argue that the trading

activity by insurance companies in their data set is therefore more likely to be driven by regulatory pressure than information-motivated trading.

2. Bonds that qualified under the second category serve as a control group. Since these bonds were not subject to selling (or buying) induced by investment constraints or regulation, their performances were unlikely to be affected by price pressures.

3. The index method for determining a bond's credit rating has changed several times during the sample period. Prior to October 2003, it was based on Moody's or S&P if Moody's was unavailable. From October 2003 to July 2005, it was the lower of Moody's and S&P. Since July 2005, it has been the middle rating of Moody's, S&P, and Fitch.

4. Rating events that occurred less than 36 months after an earlier rating event were excluded to avoid spillover effects. For example, fallen angels that were upgraded to investment-grade status less than three years before the later downgrade may have been subject to less selling pressure if they were being held by different clientele than fallen angels that had originally been issued as high-grade bonds.

5. Another reason for excluding bonds from the sample shortly after they default is that the quality of pricing data tends to deteriorate as time passes after the default date.

6. To illustrate this point, consider a case in which we examine the relative spreads of fallen angels when peer groups are determined monthly. The relative spreads would likely be positive for some time before the rating event (i.e., wider than their peers) as investors anticipate the pending downgrade, but may become negative immediately after the downgrade, as the spreads of the new peer groups containing high-yield bonds are much higher.

7. LCS estimates are available monthly for all bonds in the U.S. Corporate and High Yield Indices only since January 2007. TRACE market coverage before that date is also incomplete.

8. TRACE truncates the sizes of large transactions at $1 million and $5 million for high-yield and investment-grade bonds, respectively, which may cause our estimates of turnover to be downward biased. Alternative transaction caps can be imputed based on equating the sum of individual trades with the aggregate volume figures reported by TRACE. This procedure yields higher transaction limits of $4 million and $12.5 million for high-yield and investment-grade bonds, respectively. In addition, in order to focus on trading activity by institutions, transactions of less than $100,000 were excluded.

9. If the rating event occurred less than 24 months before the last sample month (June 2010), we record the bond status as of the last available date.

10. The large proportion of upgraded bonds that were called reflects the prevalence of the call feature among bonds that were rated high-yield at issuance. As the financial health of their issuers improved, they were called and replaced by other funding alternatives at a lower cost.

11. This is consistent with the evidence from decomposing credit spreads in Chapter 6, which suggests that most of the widening in credit spreads during the

2007–2009 financial crisis reflected an increase in illiquidity rather than expectations of future defaults.

12. The rating event month was defined as quarter zero. The three months following it correspond to quarter one, and so on.

13. Formally, the relative cumulative return of downgraded ($D$) or upgraded ($U$) issuers from the start of the analysis window until month $T$ is given by

$$R_j^T = \prod_{t=-12}^{T} \left( 1 + \sum_i w_{i,t}(R_{i,t} - R_{i,t}^p) \right) - 1 \quad j \in D, U$$

where $w_{i,t}$, $R_{i,t}$ are the relative weight and total return of issuer $i$ in month $t$, respectively, and $R_{i,t}^p$ is the contemporaneous weighted return of all the peer groups corresponding to issuer $i$'s outstanding bonds.

14. Recall that the peer group was determined once, based on each bond's characteristics at the rating event month. Issuers that were downgraded or upgraded again following the rating event month may have traded at very large positive or negative spreads relative to their peers. The use of the median rather than the average spread was meant to neutralize such effects.

15. Formally, the cumulative return of issuer $i$ relative to its peers over $t$ months since the rating event month is given by

$$R_j^T = \prod_{0 \le t \le T} (1 + R_{i,t}) - \prod_{0 \le t \le T} \left(1 + R_{i,t}^p\right)$$

where, as in note 13, $R_{i,t}$ is the total return of issuer $i$ in month $t$ and $R_{i,t}^p$ is the contemporaneous (weighted) return of all the peer groups corresponding to issuer's i outstanding bonds.

16. Of the 17 issuers in the best performing bucket (20), 11 were downgraded in 2009 and 8 belonged to the financial sector. For example, Lincoln National Corp. and Hartford Financial had monthly average relative returns of 39% and 24%, respectively, during months 0 to 3.

17. As before, issuer-level LCS and turnover were calculated by weighting the LCS of outstanding bonds by their respective market values and aggregating all trading volume and amount outstanding linked to the underlying CUSIPs, respectively.

18. Ellul et al. (2010) report that the average total volume per bond for this sample is almost $2.5 million in the event week, declining to less than $1 million just five weeks later.

19. Hence, this argument is unrelated to the long-term level of the cash-CDS basis, which is beyond the scope of this chapter.

20. To reduce the likelihood of stale quotes, months with 10 or more daily consecutive unchanged observations were excluded.

21. Because of the limited amount of data available for LCS, turnover, and CDS, the number of issuers used in each specification varies and is only a subset of the overall sample.

22. Given the limited number of observations in the third specification, the variables that were found to be insignificant before were excluded in order to maximize statistical power.

23. In other words, the small number of observations increases the likelihood that the estimated size coefficient is insignificant even if there is a relation between issuer performance and size.

24. The third specification does not include the cash-CDS basis because it would have decreased the sample size even further.

25. Specifically, the largest bond in the bucket with bonds having remaining maturity of 10 years or less. If none of the qualifying bonds were in this bucket, then the largest bond in the longer maturity bucket (10 years or more) was selected. The reason for this procedure was to reduce the frequency of missing peer group returns, as the population of the long-maturity bucket was typically smaller.

26. This was meant to prevent a situation in which, for example, a bond that was purchased a month after the downgrade and sold two months later, when its relative spread became negative, would have returned to the portfolio because it widened again to 45 bps within three months.

27. Portfolio volatility is likely to rise since, over time, these bonds would proceed to default or recover, resulting in large positive returns.

28. Peer groups returns were calculated by equal weighting the performance of the peer groups matched to every fallen angel in the portfolio, as explained in the Data and Methodology section. When a fallen angel's peer group was populated by fewer than 20 bonds, the High Yield Index return was used instead. The relative return of any unused cash allocation was set to zero.

29. The Modified Peer Group was constructed by matching each fallen angel with the largest bond (in terms of market value) that had the same quality, industry, and maturity characteristics and had not yet been matched to another fallen angel in the portfolio. The Modified Peer Group returns were computed as the equal-weighted returns of all bonds that were matched to fallen angels.

30. Similar patterns were also observed for the "Buy All" and "Flexible Reversal" portfolios but were not reported for the sake of brevity.

31. Ellul et al. (2010) found that the median cumulative abnormal return in the downgrade week during periods of low demand was –17.3%, compared with –3.4% for high demand periods.

32. The results were unchanged when we repeated the calculation of the net performance and volatility using the individual monthly turnover.

### CHAPTER 14

# Obtaining Credit Exposure Using Cash and Synthetic Replication

Investors often seek exposure to easily tradable credit market beta (long or short). They have several choices that differ in their liquidity, cost, and replication accuracy. In this chapter we analyze the liquidity, cost, and replication performance of these choices.

One possibility is a *total return swap* (TRS) that guarantees to pay an investor the total return on the underlying credit index in return for a periodic floating rate plus a spread. However, credit total return swaps are not always available because they may trade only on a "matched-book" basis. Broker-dealers must bear the risk of tracking error between the index return and their hedges, so they tend to charge more for swaps executed on an unmatched basis.

Alternatively, an investor can replicate a credit index with a small proxy portfolio of cash bonds. However, cash replication is difficult. The investor must be able to identify which bonds are liquid (i.e., obtainable at a reasonable cost) and, once identified, know how to combine them into a portfolio that would track the index. An additional complication of unfunded cash replication is the necessity to finance positions in the repo market.

In this chapter, we introduce a cash replication method that uses a small proxy portfolio of liquid bonds and, typically, provides very good tracking. Because the underlying index is also, in essence, a cash bond portfolio, cash replication does not generate tracking errors owing to basis risk (discussed below) between the cash and derivative markets. However, it does involve significant idiosyncratic risk because the proxy portfolio, by necessity, has higher issuer concentration than the underlying index.

The final alternative is a "synthetic" replication with a combination of derivatives, such as interest rate and CDX swaps. In this chapter, we will assume that the replication is executed via a credit *Replicating Bond Index* (RBI) basket swap. A Credit RBI basket consists of interest rate and

CDX swap indexes, weighted to match the exposures of the underlying credit index, and rebalanced monthly. An investor gets synthetic credit exposure by receiving the total return on the RBI swap and paying a floating LIBOR rate plus a spread. Consequently, the investor bears the tracking error between the RBI and the underlying index.

Synthetic credit replication is generally inexpensive and very liquid because the underlying components of a Credit RBI basket are among the most actively traded financial instruments. However, we demonstrate that, over short time periods, Credit RBI tracking errors may be very high owing to the substantial volatility of the CDS-cash basis. Investors who look for credit beta to capitalize on expected short-term spread movements may be disappointed with the performance of synthetic replication. Nevertheless, because the CDS-cash basis tends to mean revert, the Credit RBI's tracking improves considerably over longer horizons. Given its liquidity and low cost, investors who seek long-term credit beta exposure and can tolerate short-term tracking errors, may find a Credit RBI to be an effective replication solution.

## CASH CREDIT REPLICATION (TCX)

We present a methodology for constructing a small basket ("TCX") of liquid cash bonds to track the monthly excess returns of an underlying credit index. To identify liquid bonds, we rely on Liquidity Cost Scores (LCS)™ introduced in Chapter 5. For the purposes of this chapter, our goal is to track the U.S. Credit Index. It is important to note that the TCX methodology can be used to replicate virtually any credit benchmark (Pan-Euro Credit, HY Credit, Sterling Credit, etc.). The TCX methodology is fully transparent and replicable, using stratified sampling rather than optimization.[1]

### Construction Rules for a TCX Portfolio

To create the TCX portfolio, we divide the U.S. Credit Index into five sectors (basic industrial, consumer, financial, technology, and other) and five duration categories (0–3, 3–5, 5–7, 7–10, and 10+). For each of the resulting 25 buckets, we identify the top 20% most liquid ("top LCS quintile") index bonds according to their LCS rank. Then, for each of the 25 sector-duration buckets, we use stratified sampling to select bonds from the eligible universe to match the contribution to DTS (duration times spread, introduced in Chapter 1) and the market value weight in the Credit Index.

Matching contribution to DTS does not ensure that the TCX matches the OAD or key rate duration (KRD) profile of the Credit Index. Consequently, there may be a mismatch (usually minor) in OAD between the TCX and

Credit Index. Investors looking to match duration as well may need to make a duration adjustment elsewhere in their portfolio or use a Treasury futures overlay.

The TCX construction methodology follows a set of rules:

- TCX contains 50 bonds (two bonds from each of the 25 sector-duration buckets).
- Each bond must be part of the TCX eligible universe (i.e., a member of IG Credit Index and in the top LCS quintile in its sector-duration bucket) at the beginning of the month.
- For each sector duration bucket, we calculate a market value-weighted mean DTS ($DTS_{avg}$). We then calculate a mean DTS for all bonds in the index within the same bucket but with a DTS larger than $DTS_{avg}$, and for all bonds with a DTS smaller than $DTS_{avg}$. We label these "higher" and "lower" means, $DTS_{hi}$ and $DTS_{lo}$, respectively. We then select two eligible bonds, one closest to $DTS_{hi}$ and the other closest to $DTS_{lo}$, and weight them to match $DTS_{avg}$ and the bucket's market value percentage.
- To ensure issuer diversification, TCX imposes a maximum issuer market value constraint of 5%. There is also a minimum market value per bond of 0.5%.
- TCX composition is held fixed for a month, and then rebalanced. To minimize turnover, if a bond in the current TCX remains in the eligible universe, the bond will remain in the new month's TCX (provided the other TCX construction constraints are satisfied), although its market value weight may change. Any bond downgraded below investment-grade remains in the TCX until the following month.

Table 14.1 presents the composition of the TCX as of March 31, 2010. Based on its LCS, the TCX overall liquidity score is almost twice as good (i.e., lower) as that of the index (0.43 versus 0.84). The superior liquidity of the TCX also appears in other dimensions: The average daily volume (from TRACE) of the securities in TCX was approximately 80% higher than that of the bonds in the index ($298 million versus $163 million), as of the same date.

Note that we select bonds for the TCX based entirely on their risk and liquidity characteristics, without any consideration of their relative value. Nevertheless, investors using the TCX have latitude to make substitutions reflecting their views.

## Properties of the TCX Portfolio

We now discuss some properties of the TCX portfolio.

**TABLE 14.1** TCX Portfolio Composition (as of March 31, 2010)

| Identifier | Ticker | Description | Coupon | Maturity Date | Market Value (%) | LCS |
|---|---|---|---|---|---|---|
| 002819AB | ABT | ABBOTT LABORATORIES-GLOBAL | 5.60 | 11/30/2017 | 0.89 | 0.35 |
| 002824AU | ABT | ABBOTT LABORATORIES | 5.13 | 4/1/2019 | 0.61 | 0.36 |
| 037411AV | APA | APACHE CORP | 6.90 | 9/15/2018 | 2.28 | 0.66 |
| 032510AC | APC | ANADARKO PETROLEUM | 6.20 | 3/15/2040 | 1.83 | 0.61 |
| 025816BB | AXP | AMERICAN EXPRESS CO | 8.13 | 5/20/2019 | 1.27 | 0.66 |
| 59018YN5 | BAC | MERRILL LYNCH & CO.-GLOBAL | 6.15 | 4/25/2013 | 4.51 | 0.16 |
| 055451AG | BHP | BHP BILLITON FINANCE | 5.50 | 4/1/2014 | 1.57 | 0.18 |
| 055451AH | BHP | BHP BILLITON FINANCE | 6.50 | 4/1/2019 | 1.38 | 0.34 |
| 105756AE | BRAZIL | BRAZIL (FED REP OF)-GLOBAL | 10.13 | 5/15/2027 | 1.27 | 0.24 |
| 12189TAT | BRK | BURLINGTON NORTH SANTA FE | 6.75 | 7/15/2011 | 1.70 | 0.19 |
| 172967CQ | C | CITIGROUP INC-GLOBAL | 5.00 | 9/15/2014 | 1.90 | 0.40 |
| 172967DR | C | CITIGROUP INC-GLOBAL | 6.13 | 8/25/2036 | 1.61 | 1.08 |
| 18683KAA | CLF | CLIFFS NATURAL RESOURCES IN | 5.90 | 3/15/2020 | 0.74 | 0.38 |
| 14040HAQ | COF | CAPITAL ONE FINANCIAL | 5.70 | 9/15/2011 | 3.33 | 0.22 |
| 17275RAF | CSCO | CISCO SYSTEMS INC | 5.50 | 1/15/2040 | 2.31 | 0.76 |
| 126650BN | CVS | CVS CORP | 6.60 | 3/15/2019 | 1.05 | 0.43 |
| 24702RAG | DELL | DELL INC | 5.63 | 4/15/2014 | 0.97 | 0.36 |
| 260543BW | DOW | DOW CHEMICAL | 7.60 | 5/15/2014 | 1.60 | 0.36 |
| 25459HAR | DTV | DIRECTV HOLDINGS LLC | 5.20 | 3/15/2020 | 0.50 | 0.56 |
| 29273RAJ | ETP | ENERGY TRANSFER PARTNERS LP | 7.50 | 7/1/2038 | 3.54 | 1.19 |
| 349631AQ | FO | FORTUNE BRANDS INC | 3.00 | 6/1/2012 | 0.50 | 0.28 |
| 36962GXZ | GE | GENERAL ELECTRIC CAPITAL-GLOBA | 6.75 | 3/15/2032 | 2.40 | 0.57 |
| 38141EA2 | GS | GOLDMAN SACHS GROUP-GLOBAL | 7.50 | 2/15/2019 | 5.00 | 0.54 |
| 437076AS | HD | HOME DEPOT INC-GLOBAL | 5.88 | 12/16/2036 | 1.63 | 0.63 |
| 459056JS | IBRD | INTERNATL BANK RECON DEV | 8.25 | 9/1/2016 | 2.81 | 0.53 |

| | | | | | | |
|---|---|---|---|---|---|---|
| 46625HBV | JPM | JP MORGAN CHASE & CO-GLOBAL | 5.13 | 9/15/2014 | 5.00 | 0.22 |
| 500630BG | KDB | KOREA DEVELOPMENT BANK-GLOBAL | 5.75 | 9/10/2013 | 3.87 | 0.25 |
| 50075NAU | KFT | KRAFT FOODS INC-GLOBAL | 6.13 | 2/1/2018 | 2.42 | 0.55 |
| 02209SAC | MO | ALTRIA GROUP INC | 8.50 | 11/10/2013 | 1.29 | 0.31 |
| 637432LR | NRUC | NATIONAL RURAL UTILS CFC-GLOBA | 10.38 | 11/1/2018 | 2.34 | 0.60 |
| 68389XAC | ORCL | ORACLE CORP | 5.75 | 4/15/2018 | 1.39 | 0.64 |
| 72650RAV | PAA | PLAINS ALL AMER PIPELINE | 4.25 | 9/1/2012 | 2.52 | 0.23 |
| 10138MAH | PEP | BOTTLING GROUP LLC | 6.95 | 3/15/2014 | 1.61 | 0.27 |
| 743410AW | PLD | PROLOGIS | 6.88 | 3/15/2020 | 0.69 | 0.35 |
| 743410AX | PLD | PROLOGIS | 6.25 | 3/15/2017 | 3.32 | 0.28 |
| 748148RM | Q | QUEBEC PROV CANADA-GLOBAL | 4.88 | 5/5/2014 | 2.28 | 0.43 |
| 448814DC | QHEL | HYDRO-QUEBEC | 8.50 | 12/1/2029 | 2.45 | 0.17 |
| 822582AD | RDSALN | SHELL INTERNATIONAL FINANCE | 6.38 | 12/15/2038 | 2.03 | 0.66 |
| 515110BA | RENTEN | LANDWIRTSCHAFT RENTENBK-GLOBAL | 1.88 | 9/24/2018 | 5.00 | 0.18 |
| 87938WAA | TELEFO | TELEFONICA EMISONES SAU-GLOBAL | 5.98 | 6/20/2011 | 1.30 | 0.12 |
| 40049JAX | TELVIS | GRUPO TELEVISA S.A. DE CV | 6.00 | 5/15/2018 | 1.27 | 0.64 |
| 87927VAV | TITIM | TELECOM ITALIA CAPITAL-GLOBAL | 7.72 | 6/4/2038 | 1.23 | 1.01 |
| 8935268Y | TRP | TRANSCANADA PIPELINES | 7.13 | 1/15/2019 | 2.18 | 0.34 |
| 88732JAW | TWC | TIME WARNER CABLE INC | 5.00 | 2/1/2020 | 0.90 | 0.38 |
| 00184AAF | TWX | AOL TIME WARNER-GLOBAL | 6.88 | 5/1/2012 | 2.55 | 0.19 |
| 91913YAD | VLO | VALERO ENERGY | 6.88 | 4/15/2012 | 1.09 | 0.19 |
| 947075AF | WFT | WEATHERFORD INTL LTD | 9.63 | 3/1/2019 | 1.42 | 0.58 |
| 931142CK | WMT | WAL-MART STORES-GLOBAL | 6.50 | 8/15/2037 | 2.16 | 0.65 |
| 984121BS | XRX | XEROX CORP | 5.50 | 5/15/2012 | 1.10 | 0.20 |
| 984121BZ | XRX | XEROX CORP | 4.25 | 2/15/2015 | 1.39 | 0.24 |
| | | TCX | | | | **0.43** |
| | | U.S. Credit Index | | | | **0.84** |

*Source:* Barclays Capital.

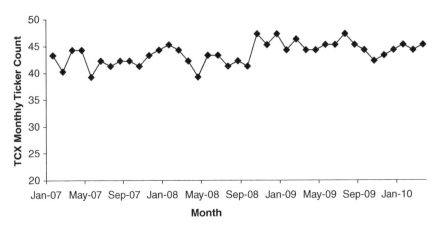

**FIGURE 14.1** Number of Issuers in TCX (February 2007–April 2010)
*Source:* Barclays Capital.

**Number of Issuers**    Since February 2007 (the inception of LCS), the number of issuers in the TCX portfolio has ranged from 39 to 47, with an average of 43 (Figure 14.1), compared with approximately 650 issuers in the Credit Index.

**Liquidity**    Figure 14.2 demonstrates the TCX liquidity advantage: Its average LCS has been approximately 48% lower than that of the index, with the absolute difference varying with the aggregate LCS of the market. Furthermore, not only does the TCX have a better average LCS, but also the

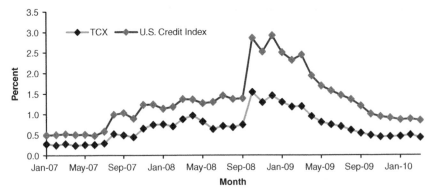

**FIGURE 14.2** Average LCS of the TCX and Credit Index (January 2007–March 2010)
*Source:* Barclays Capital.

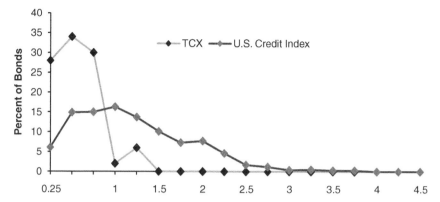

**FIGURE 14.3** Cross-Sectional Distribution of LCS for the TCX and Credit Index (March 2010)
*Source:* Barclays Capital.

cross-sectional distribution of its LCS scores is much tighter than that of the index (Figure 14.3).

**OAD** Because the TCX does not explicitly match the OAD of the index, there may, at times, be a mismatch between the two. The TCX tends to have a slightly higher OAD than the index, owing to the positive relationship between LCS and OAS (see Chapter 5). Liquid bonds eligible for TCX are likely to have relatively tighter spreads than their bucket peers in the index. All else constant, to match DTS, the TCX has to select longer-duration bonds. Figure 14.4 shows the TCX and index OADs. The largest absolute OAD

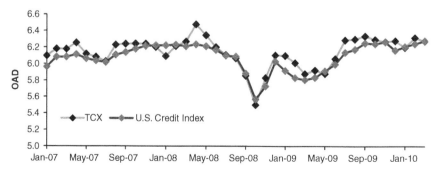

**FIGURE 14.4** Monthly OAD of TCX and Credit Index (January 2007–March 2010)
*Source:* Barclays Capital.

**TABLE 14.2** Monthly Excess Returns of the TCX and Credit Index (February 2007–March 2010)

|  | TCX ExRet | Credit Index ExRet | TCX–Credit Index |
|---|---|---|---|
| **Entire Period (bps)** | | | |
| Mean | −4.7 [0.6] | −0.5 | −4.2 [1.1] |
| Standard Deviation | 284.3 [263.5] | 238.5 | 89.9 [66.7] |
| Maximum | 567.2 [567.2] | 482.9 | 215.2 [215.2] |
| Minimum | −1,154.8 [−954.8] | −716.9 | −438.0 [−238.0] |
| **2/07–7/08** | | | |
| Mean | −50.8 | −43.5 | −7.2 |
| Standard Deviation | 129.6 | 115.7 | 27.9 |
| Maximum | 285.0 | 253.7 | 31.4 |
| Minimum | −260.5 | −262.5 | −67.1 |
| **8/08–3/10** | | | |
| Mean | 36.8 [46.8] | 38.3 | −1.5 [8.5] |
| Standard Deviation | 372.2 [339.8] | 309.0 | 122.6 [88.6] |
| Maximum | 567.2 [567.2] | 482.9 | 215.2 [215.2] |
| Minimum | −1,154.8 [−954.8] | −716.9 | −438.0 [−238.0] |

*Note:* The results shown in brackets exclude the overweight to Lehman Brothers.
*Source:* Barclays Capital.

gap (0.24) occurred in May 2008. The average OAD gap since February 2007 was 0.06.

## TCX Performance vs. U.S. Credit Index

The objective of TCX is to match the monthly excess returns of the Credit Index. Table 14.2 compares the TCX and Index excess returns between February 2007 and March 2010. For the 38-month period, the average monthly excess return for the TCX was –4.7 bps, compared with –0.5 bps for the Credit Index, a difference of –4.2 bps per month. Figure 14.5 shows that in terms of monthly excess returns, the TCX and Index closely followed each other during the sample period.

Most of the average monthly excess return difference between the TCX and Index occurred in September 2008, when the TCX held a 3.5% position in Lehman Brothers, much higher than the Credit Index's 1.2% weight. Had the TCX held the same weight of Lehman as the index during that month,

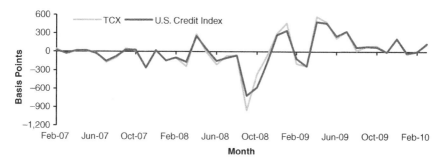

**FIGURE 14.5** Excess Returns of the TCX and Credit Index (February 2007–March 2010)
*Source:* Barclays Capital.

the average monthly excess return difference between the TCX and Index would have been 1.1 bps. For reference, Table 14.2 shows, in brackets, the excess return statistics assuming the TCX did not have the 2.3% overweight to Lehman in September 2008.

Over the 38-month period, the standard deviations of excess returns were 284 bps and 239 bps for the TCX and the Credit Index, respectively, and the correlation of their monthly excess returns was 0.96. Excluding the overweight to Lehman Brothers, the TCX excess returns would have had a lower standard deviation of 264 bps, and a higher correlation with the index of 0.97.

Table 14.2 also reports the tracking effectiveness of TCX separately before and after the onset of the credit crisis. Before the crisis, the TCX tracked the Credit Index with relatively low volatility (27.9 bps/month), as expected. However, some months with large return differences, resulting in an average tracking error of –7.2 bps/month. These outlier months were the result of some poor-performing financial bonds held by the TCX, particularly from March 2008 onward.

As mentioned, the TCX's overexposure to Lehman produced a large tracking error in September 2008 (–438 bps) that caused the TEV of the TCX with respect to the Credit Index to increase to 122.6 bps for the second period. Overall, the TCX tracked the Credit Index excess returns reasonably well despite a particularly volatile three-year period. Figure 14.6 shows the time series of the monthly difference in excess returns between the TCX and the Credit Index.

Finally, Figure 14.7 shows the cumulative excess return difference between the TCX and the Credit Index. Until the crisis, the TCX had a maximum cumulative underperformance of about 160 bps. However, by the

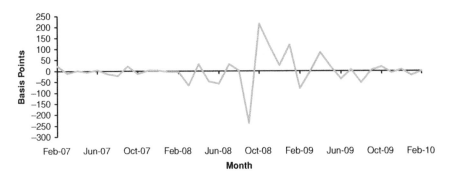

**FIGURE 14.6** Difference in Excess Returns of the Credit Index and TCX (February 2007–March 2010)
*Source:* Barclays Capital.

end of September 2008, the cumulative underperformance was 567 bps. This underperformance was relatively modest given that the Credit Index's cumulative excess return at that point was –2,500 bps (see Figure 14.13). As the crisis evolved and the TCX's highly liquid bonds performed better than the many illiquid bonds in the Index, the cumulative excess return underperformance quickly reversed. By March 2010, the net cumulative underperformance was 160 bps, reflecting mostly the permanent effect of the September 2008 Lehman bankruptcy. Without the overweight to Lehman, the cumulative excess return difference between the TCX and the Index would have been +40 bps.

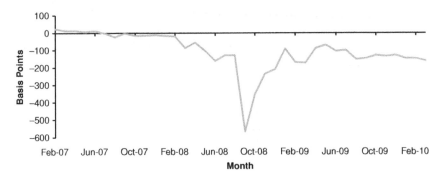

**FIGURE 14.7** Cumulative Excess Return Difference between TCX and Credit Index (February 2007–March 2010)
*Source:* Barclays Capital.

## TCX Turnover and Transactions Cost

As discussed in Chapter 5, a bond's liquidity (i.e., LCS) is persistent, but not constant. LCS fluctuates with changes in the bond's attributes (e.g., DTS and age) and with its level of trading volume and trader-quoted status. In addition, new bonds regularly enter the Credit Index. The attention bestowed on these new issues tends to make them relatively liquid. The fluctuating relative liquidity across bonds generates TCX monthly turnover as existing bonds lose eligibility and new, more liquid, bonds become eligible. Turnover also arises from the re-weighting of the bonds remaining in the TCX.

Figure 14.8 shows the monthly change in the market value percentages across all bonds entering, leaving, and remaining (after rebalancing) in the TCX. Over the entire three-year period, the TCX averaged monthly turnover of 35%. However, it varied throughout the period. For example, turnover was much higher in November 2008–December 2008 (average = 49%), when newly illiquid bonds needed to be replaced, and it fell below 30% in 2009 as credit markets stabilized.

While turnover is a good indicator of the cost of maintaining a TCX portfolio, we can use LCS to obtain a better estimate of transactions cost. Since the TCX uses the same bid-side pricing as the Credit Index, we can estimate its transactions cost by simply multiplying the bond's LCS by the transaction market value for all *buy* transactions (i.e., bonds entering the TCX or increasing their weight in it). For *sell* transactions, we assume that the bonds are sold at the index bid price with no additional cost. However, since bonds leaving the TCX are generally less liquid than they were when they entered it, we can estimate a more conservative (i.e., higher) value for

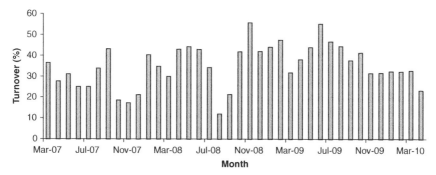

**FIGURE 14.8** Monthly TCX Turnover (March 2007–April 2010)
*Source:* Barclays Capital.

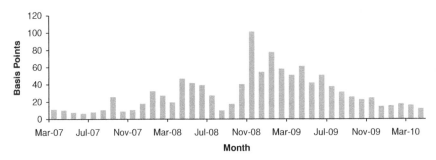

**FIGURE 14.9**   Monthly TCX Transactions Cost (March 2007–April 2010)
*Source:* Barclays Capital.

transactions cost by using 70% of a bond's LCS when the bond is purchased and 30% of its LCS when it is sold.[2]

The average monthly transactions cost over the 38-month period was 30 bps (Figure 14.9). Transactions cost was more volatile than turnover as it changed with the market aggregate LCS level. From March 2007 through July 2008, the average cost was 21 bps per month. Following the onset of the crisis, LCS scores increased significantly, resulting in an average monthly transactions cost of 38 bps, peaking at 102 bps in November 2008. This big increase in transactions cost is not surprising given the combination of high turnover and the elevated level of LCS. Monthly transactions cost for the TCX fell below 20 bps towards the end of 2009.

## Quarterly Rebalancing to Control TCX Transactions Cost

Given the TCX's high monthly turnover, investors seeking long-term credit exposure may wish to consider quarterly TCX rebalancing. While quarterly rebalancing may lead to increased TEV as the TCX and index drift apart, the increase might be tolerable because both turnover and transactions cost will be lower. We find that while the quarterly TCX does have significantly lower transactions cost, there is only a modest change in its TEV versus the Credit Index.

This strategy produces higher turnover at each quarterly rebalancing date, but the overall magnitude of rebalancing over the three-month period is lower. The main issue would then be the tracking error of the quarterly TCX.

**TABLE 14.3** Comparison of Performance Statistics for TCX and Three Quarterly TCX Portfolios (February 2007–March 2010)

| | TCX | V1 | V2 | V3 | Average Q | Credit Index |
|---|---|---|---|---|---|---|
| Mean return | −4.7 | −2.6 | −7.5 | 3.5 | −2.0 | −0.49 |
| Standard deviation of return | 284.3 | 264.5 | 287.4 | 257.8 | 273.1 | 238.5 |
| TEV (vs. Credit Index) | 89.9 | 75.1 | 88.4 | 60.5 | 73.1 | |
| Relative LCS (begin) | 53% | 54% | 52% | 52% | 52% | |
| Relative LCS (end) | 62% | 68% | 67% | 70% | 68% | |

*Note:* Relative LCS is the ratio of the TCX LCS to the Credit Index LCS.
*Source:* Barclays Capital.

We construct three versions (V1, V2, and V3) of a quarterly TCX portfolio, corresponding to different launch dates. V1 begins February 2007, V2 in March 2007, and V3 in April 2007. The portfolios are held unchanged for three months. Table 14.3 presents the monthly excess returns and tracking errors versus the Credit Index for the three quarterly TCX versions.

Over the 38-month sample period, the tracking performance of the three versions varied quite a bit, with an average TEV of 73.1 bps. This variability in tracking errors can be entirely attributed to September 2008 and name selection risk inherent in small proxy portfolios. As the quarterly versions of the TCX are rebalanced at different times, their compositions will vary and performances over identical time periods may differ. For example, V2 had a 2.3% overweight to Lehman and a 3.6% overweight to AIG during September 2008. In contrast, V1 had the same overweight to Lehman, but did not own AIG. V3 has the lowest tracking error of the quarterly versions as it did not own AIG *and* had less exposure to Lehman (0.8% overweight). As a result, V3 underperformed the index by −154.6 bps in September 2008, compared with underperformance of −320.7 bps and −438.7 bps for V1 and V2, respectively.

Table 14.3 also shows that the monthly TCX had higher TEV than any of the three quarterly TCX portfolios. This, too, can be largely explained by September 2008, when the holdings of the monthly TCX were the same as those of V2. With the overweight to Lehman and AIG, the monthly TCX underperformed V1 and V3 by 118.0 bps and 284.1 bps, respectively. This outlier month was enough to cause the TEV of the monthly TCX to be significantly higher than that of V1 and V3. To more clearly evaluate

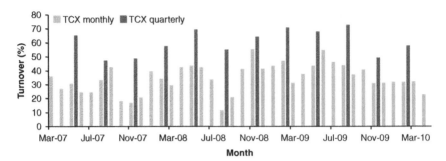

**FIGURE 14.10**   Turnover for Monthly and Quarterly TCX (March 2007–April 2010)
*Note:* Quarterly turnover should be divided by 3 to be comparable to monthly turnover.
*Source:* Barclays Capital.

the effect on TEV of holding a TCX constant for three months, we should compare the monthly TCX and V2, which had the same performance in September 2008. Their nearly identical TEVs mean that holding a TCX for three months produces comparable tracking error volatility to the monthly TCX. This result is not too surprising. Given that the composition of the Credit Index changes slowly over time, and the TCX contains highly liquid bonds that match the sector, duration, and DTS of the index, tracking should generally remain close over a three-month period.

Table 14.3 also shows the average relative LCS of the quarterly TCX (as a percentage of the Credit Index LCS at the beginning and end of its quarterly rebalancing periods) and compares it with the average relative LCS of the monthly TCX at the beginning and end of each month. As expected, the monthly and quarterly TCX show a drop-off in relative liquidity versus the Credit Index. However, the quarterly TCX has only a modest relative LCS deterioration, despite holding the portfolio constant for an additional two months. This result is not unexpected as a bond's liquidity is persistent over such a short period.

Figure 14.10 shows the turnover pattern for the monthly and quarterly TCX versions. The chart indicates that rebalancing the TCX quarterly does help reduce turnover. From February 2007 to February 2010, the average monthly turnover (i.e., quarterly turnover divided by 3) for the quarterly TCX was 20% for all three versions of the quarterly TCX, compared with 35% for the monthly TCX.

Rebalancing the TCX monthly generated 30 bps of transactions cost whereas rebalancing the TCX quarterly reduced the monthly cost to 17 bps (Table 14.4).[3]

**TABLE 14.4** Transactions Cost for TCX and Three Quarterly TCX Portfolios (March 2007–April 2010)

|  | TCX | V1 | V2 | V3 | Average Q |
|---|---|---|---|---|---|
| Monthly cost (bps) | 30.5 | 17.6 | 16.4 | 17.3 | 17.1 |
| Monthly turnover (%) | 35.1 | 20.3 | 20 | 20.1 | 20.1 |

*Source:* Barclays Capital.


## SYNTHETIC REPLICATION OF CASH INDEXES

For investors looking for credit beta over long periods, the high turnover of the TCX may be prohibitively costly. An alternative strategy is synthetic replication, which involves using baskets of liquid derivative instruments (e.g., interest rate and CDX/iTraxx swaps). The derivative instruments in the basket are weighted to match the risk exposures of the underlying cash index. As noted earlier, we label these replicating baskets of derivatives "RBIs." Before discussing credit index synthetic replication specifically, we take a brief detour to present a general overview of synthetic replication and some issues that pertain to its tracking performance.

The advantage of synthetic replication lies in its use of liquid derivative contracts. This means that RBI basket swaps are always available—for virtually any notional amount or term—since the broker/dealer can always hedge the position. This is in stark contrast to most total return swaps which, in volatile market environments, are either unavailable or trade only on a matched-book basis. In addition, RBI baskets have lower transactions cost than traditional cash bond replication. Finally, RBI basket swaps, unlike cash replication, allow investors to obtain beta exposure with little cash investment. Provided that the RBI basket has satisfactory tracking error properties, an RBI basket swap is an effective way for investors to synthetically manage fixed-income beta, including asset allocation, alpha-beta recombination, and passive replication strategies.

As we discuss next, the sources of tracking error from synthetic replication are closely related to the level of market liquidity. RBIs tend to outperform their underlying cash indexes when market liquidity worsens and underperform when it improves. These risks may be mitigated by including additional derivative instruments that may track fluctuations in market liquidity (e.g., short VIX futures and long the ED–FF futures spread, discussed next). We will examine if including such derivative instruments can help reduce tracking error volatility, especially during highly volatile markets.

## Drivers of Tracking Error in Synthetic Replication

There are some sources of tracking error in synthetic replication that are largely absent in cash replication. Whereas both use a small number of instruments to replicate a large index, replication generates more idiosyncratic risk as it often substantially overweights specific names. However, in RBI baskets this risk is lower because the liquid derivative instruments in the basket are generic and therefore have little idiosyncratic risk of their own.[4] This helps to improve synthetic replication performance relative to cash replication.

While the use of derivatives produces less idiosyncratic risk than cash replication, synthetic replication has a number of its own sources of tracking error. The primary ones are spread (or basis) risk, liquidity risk, arbitrage (or funding) risk, and rollover risk. As we discuss in the following sections, these drivers of tracking error are often interrelated.

## Spread and Liquidity Risk

For many segments of diversified bond indexes, synthetic replication uses a set of interest rate swaps to track the underlying subindex. However, since these asset classes often trade at a spread to the swap curve, fluctuations in their spread-to-swaps—that is, spread risk—are a source of tracking error. Most market participants perceive a cash credit bond as having more credit and liquidity risk than what is embedded in the LIBOR curve used to price an interest rate swap. As relative perceptions of credit and liquidity risk fluctuate, so will the cash-swap basis, and, hence, the performance of synthetic replication. Such fluctuations, however, would not affect cash replication as both the cash replication basket and index would move in tandem.

Spread risk can, at times, be substantial. For example, the monthly LIBOR-OAS volatilities of Aa-rated corporates, agency, ABS, and CMBS between January 2005 and September 2009 were 112 bps, 17 bps, 177 bps, and 319 bps, respectively (see Figure 14.11). Although spreads-to-swaps have a general tendency to mean-revert over time, this cash-swap basis risk may lead to monthly RBI tracking errors that can be very large and persist over long periods of time. Unfortunately, investors cannot always outlast a mean reversion process, so spread risk is an important factor in evaluating synthetic replication.

Another component of the spread risk between the cash market and derivatives arises from differences in liquidity. For example, compare the liquidity of a cash corporate bond with that of a par interest rate swap. The cost of executing a roundtrip transaction in U.S. investment-grade credit bonds in September 2009 was, on average, approximately 140 bps of the

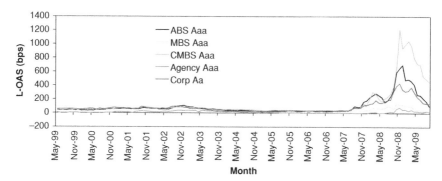

**FIGURE 14.11** Spread-to-Swap Levels for Various Sectors of the U.S. Aggregate Index (1999–2009)
*Source:* Barclays Capital.

bond's value (see Chapter 5). In February 2007, this execution cost was approximately 70 bps. For a comparable duration interest rate swap, the cost is, and has been, approximately 3 bps. If market impact costs were included, the liquidity difference would be even more pronounced.

As market liquidity worsens, the liquidity cost differential between less liquid and more liquid instruments widens. Assuming that spreads widen to reflect higher liquidity costs, we would expect cash bonds to underperform swaps and subsequently outperform when market liquidity improves. Consequently, fluctuations in market liquidity will lead to tracking errors in synthetic replication strategies.[5]

## Arbitrage Risk

Good performance of synthetic replication requires a close and stable link between the cash and derivatives markets. For example, successful replication of the Treasury Index using Treasury futures requires a stable cash-futures basis. Cash and derivatives typically have an arbitrage relationship. For example, the relationship between cash Treasuries and Treasury futures is governed by a *cost-of–carry model:* An investor can either hold a cash Treasury bond or obtain the same economic exposure by going long Treasury futures contracts (assuming the likely deliverable is the particular cash bond) and investing cash in a short-term deposit instrument. What holds this cash-futures relationship together is arbitrage activity. If the cash bond becomes relatively cheaper than futures, then arbitrageurs would buy the cash bond (financed via repo) and sell futures. If cash becomes relatively

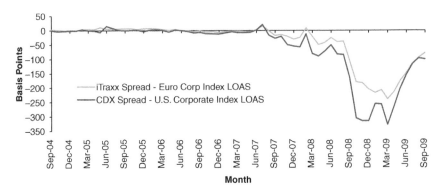

**FIGURE 14.12** CDX-Cash Basis and iTraxx-Cash Basis (April 2004–September 2009)
*Source:* Barclays Capital.

richer, then arbitrageurs would use reverse repo to obtain and sell the cash bond and buy futures.

Arbitrage activity requires reliable access to funding, at a known cost. However, during periods of market stress and volatility, funding becomes both expensive and uncertain; therefore, arbitrage activity can be significantly curtailed. Providers of arbitrage funding can grow impatient with arbitrage "convergence" trades, and during volatile markets quickly withdraw funding if convergence is too slow or perversely starts to move in reverse.

The lack of arbitrage activity wreaks havoc on synthetic replication strategies as it weakens the forces preventing the derivatives position from moving away from the underlying cash market. For example, as funding costs for investors increased during the credit crisis, carrying costs for cash credit bonds became high. Instead of holding cash bonds, investors chose to sell protection through CDS. This caused a widening of the CDS-cash basis, which became extremely negative. Both CDS and the CDX/iTraxx indexes (these indexes have their own arbitrage relationship with CDS) outperformed cash credit bonds for an extended period of time.

Typically, as the CDS-cash basis (or the CDX/iTraxx-cash basis) becomes very negative, investors use arbitrage funding to buy the relatively cheap cash bonds and buy protection through CDS. A cash bond-CDS portfolio is, to some extent, a hedged portfolio. Although convergence should produce arbitrage profits over time, the volatility of the basis in 2007–2008 made convergence seem more like a long-term theoretical prospect than a near-term certainty. As a result, funding for this arbitrage activity became very limited during this period. The lack of arbitrage capital, in turn, made it possible for the basis to become even more negative, producing losses for those who had earlier entered the arbitrage trade and further forestalling convergence.

As another example of how limits to arbitrage can drive synthetic replication tracking errors, consider the U.S. Treasury futures market in the last quarter of 2008. Repo rates were close to zero, which meant that those acquiring bonds through reverse repo suffered little penalty if they failed to return the bonds. Given the desire to hoard Treasury bonds during this period, many investors became reluctant to place their Treasuries out on repo. As a result, futures became cheap to cash bonds. Normally, in this situation, investors would buy futures and sell cash bonds (obtained *via* reverse repo). However, since cash bonds were difficult to obtain, there was limited arbitrage activity to bring cash and futures back in line.

Yet another example of arbitrage risk is the case of Agency MBS TBA contracts, which are essentially forward contracts on generic cash MBS pools. Many investors synthetically replicate long MBS beta through a strategy of rolling TBA contracts from month to month. The advantage of TBA contracts is that investors can delay settling the MBS purchase and invest cash elsewhere. In addition, since the MBS purchase has not settled, investors avoid having to deal with the monthly principal and prepayment cash flows. However, by rolling TBA positions, investors are effectively buying an MBS pool with financing from the broker-dealer. The financing cost is embedded in the roll drop level (i.e., the difference between the price of the near month TBA contract and that of the following month contract). The investor effectively pays this financing cost whenever he or she postpones the MBS cash purchase by rolling the TBA position for an additional month.[6]

During the height of the credit crisis, broker-dealers had difficulty obtaining financing themselves, much less extending it to the very large number of TBA investors who wished to roll. As a result, the roll drop reached a level that made rolling long TBA positions very uneconomic compared to holding cash MBS pools. In such a situation, long TBA investors have the option not to pay the implied expensive financing by simply taking delivery of pools on settlement date. However, this requires cash and many of these investors either had their cash invested in short-term securities that had suddenly become very illiquid and could not be sold, or they simply wanted to hoard cash. As a result, they chose to roll their TBA contracts despite the expense.

Other investors with available cash, seeing that forward TBA prices were higher than expected relative to cash prices, started to sell forward TBA contracts and buy MBS pools. In addition, the Federal Reserve announced its intervention in the MBS market, which included providing relatively cheap

**TABLE 14.5** Effect of Limits to Arbitrage on Synthetic Replication: U.S. Treasury and U.S. Fixed-Rate MBS

| Aggregate Index Sector | Replication Methodology | Average Monthly Replication Tracking Error | Replication TEV | Worst Monthly Tracking Error |
|---|---|---|---|---|
| | | 2005–2007 | | |
| Treasury (23.8%) | Treasury futures | −1.3 bps | 5.0 bps | 12.1 bps |
| Mortgages (35.8%) | TBAs | +1.0 bps | 4.7 bps | 9.5 bps |
| | | 2008 | | |
| Treasury (23.8%) | Treasury futures | +0.9 bps | 37.5 bps | 87.3 bps |
| Mortgages (35.8%) | TBAs | −6.9 bps | 18.5 bps | 54.3 bps |

Source: Barclays Capital

financing to the TBA roll market. As a result of these actions, financing rates in the TBA market returned to normal within a few months. During these months, however, a synthetic replication strategy of rolling long TBA contracts significantly underperformed simply holding cash MBS pools.

The breakdown of arbitrage activity in 2008 produced dramatic changes in the success of synthetic replication, which heretofore had impeccable tracking error performance. Table 14.5 shows the performance of replication strategies for the cash U.S. Treasury Index and Fixed-Rate MBS Index using Treasury futures and TBA contracts, respectively. For the three-year period up to 2008, both synthetic strategies produced excellent tracking performance. Synthetic replication using Treasury futures tracked the Treasury Index with an average monthly tracking error of −1.3 bps and a TEV of only 5.0 bps. The largest monthly tracking error was 12.1 bps. Similarly, for TBA replication of the MBS Index, the average monthly tracking error was 1.0 bp, with a TEV of only 4.7 bps. The largest monthly tracking error was 9.5 bps. However, the breakdown of arbitrage activity in 2008 led to a severe degradation in synthetic replication performance. TEVs for U.S. Treasury Index and MBS Index replication increased to 37.5 bps and 18.5 bps, respectively. The largest monthly tracking errors increased as well, more than fivefold, to 87.3 bps and 54.3 bps, respectively.

## Rollover Risk

These episodes highlight another risk in synthetic replication compared with cash bond replication. Suppose an investor decides to receive the return of a

RBI basket that includes, as one of the derivative instruments, a total return swap on the Treasury Index and/or the Fixed-Rate MBS Index. While the investor is guaranteed the total return on a cash index, the counterparty (i.e., the broker-dealer) is generally using a synthetic strategy (e.g., Treasury futures contracts or TBAs) to replicate that return. Since the broker-dealer is guaranteeing a cash market return within the RBI basket, the broker-dealer must adjust the pricing of the RBI basket swap for the risk that the synthetic replication strategy may not generate the exact cash market return. As a result, the cost of an RBI basket swap is variable and can increase in a market environment in which there are limits to arbitrage. Such an environment creates rollover risk for investors who need to renew or adjust the notional amount of an existing RBI basket swap.

Spread risk, liquidity risk, arbitrage risk, and rollover risk can be significant sources of tracking error for synthetic replication. As discussed previously, these risks are closely related to changes in market liquidity and financing availability. As liquidity becomes scarce, synthetic instruments (e.g., interest rate and CDX swaps) tend to outperform cash market instruments, and vice versa. Consequently, investors who use synthetic instruments to replicate a long cash market exposure benefit from illiquid environments. As discussed in Upbin et al. (2009), for alpha-beta recombination strategies, long synthetic replication exposure helps mitigate any illiquidity associated with a cash hedge fund investment. However, there are investors who use synthetic instruments to replicate short cash market exposure, and these investors will likely underperform during periods of market illiquidity. A good synthetic replication methodology needs to perform well across all market environments.

Perhaps we can improve the performance (i.e., minimize tracking errors) of synthetic replication by including positions in derivative instruments that track movements in market liquidity? If so, these instruments can be used to hedge fluctuations in liquidity risk. Two possibilities are futures on the CBOE Volatility Index (VIX) and a long-short spread combination of CME Eurodollar (ED) and CBOT Fed Funds (FF) futures contracts. The VIX measures the level of implied short-term equity market volatility, whereas ED futures track forward three-month LIBOR rates, and FF futures track the forward Fed funds overnight effective rate.

Increases in VIX are often associated with reduced liquidity in the fixed income markets. Increasing volatility raises the risk to market participants from holding positions, which, in turn, leads to wider bid-ask spreads and a greater preference for more liquid assets. In fact, as shown in Chapter 5, we observe a strong relationship between liquidity costs in the U.S. cash credit market and the level of the VIX (see Figure 5.6).

Another related measure of market liquidity is the spread between short-term Eurodollar deposit rates and overnight Fed funds. As market liquidity diminishes, there is usually increased concern about the creditworthiness of banks, which leads to a decline in the ED-FF futures spread.

Based on these relationships, we will investigate the addition of a short VIX futures position or a long ED-FF futures spread position to the RBI basket. If liquidity worsens, the short VIX and long ED-FF futures positions will likely have negative returns, offsetting the tendency of the RBI to out-perform in such environments. The reverse will occur as market liquidity improves. We first present the performance of the Credit RBI basket, and then examine the reduction in tracking error resulting from the use of these additional derivative positions to hedge movements in market liquidity.

## CREDIT RBIs

A Credit RBI basket designed to track the U.S. IG Credit Index, uses a combination of six par interest rate swaps to match the KRD profile of the index and a blend of 5-year and 10-year CDX swaps to match the Credit Index's LIBOR spread duration. An investor interested in obtaining long exposure to the index, can enter into a Credit RBI swap to receive the total return on the Credit RBI basket and pay LIBOR plus a spread.

Table 14.6 shows excess returns (to U.S. treasuries) for the Credit Index and Credit RBI. From February 2007 to March 2010 the mean excess return for the RBI was 4.1 bps, with a volatility of 140 bps, compared with –0.5 bps, and a volatility of 239 bps, for the Credit Index. Over the period, the monthly TEV between the Credit RBI and the underlying index was 188 bps, twice that of the TCX (see Table 14.2). Looking at the two subperiods, the Credit RBI performed much better than the index through July 2008 and performed worse since August 2008. The Credit RBI also had somewhat larger extreme returns than the index in the first subperiod, but much smaller extreme returns in the second. The TEV for the Credit RBI in the first subperiod was 140 bps (compared with the TCX's 28 bps; see Table 14.2), and in the second subperiod it was 226 bps (123 bps).

Figure 14.13 presents the cumulative excess returns over Treasuries for the TCX, Credit RBI, and Credit Index since February 2007. Unlike the TCX, the Credit RBI excess returns deviated from those of the Credit Index. The primary reason for this was the behavior of the cash-synthetic basis. The Credit RBI uses a blend of 5-year and 10-year CDX swaps to match index exposures to changes in credit spreads. However, during the crisis, spreads of cash bonds widened by much more than CDS due to liquidity effects. As a

**TABLE 14.6**   Monthly Excess Returns for the Credit Index and Credit RBI (February 2007–March 2010)

|  | Credit Index Excess Returns | Credit RBI Excess Returns | Credit RBI–Credit Index |
|---|---|---|---|
| **Entire Period (bps)** | | | |
| Mean | −0.5 | 4.1 | 4.6 |
| Standard deviation | 238.5 | 140.0 | 188.3 |
| Maximum | 482.9 | 305.7 | 511.5 |
| Minimum | −716.9 | −332.5 | −332.8 |
| **2/07–7/08** | | | |
| Mean | −43.5 | −22.1 | 21.4 |
| Standard deviation | 115.7 | 157.3 | 139.6 |
| Maximum | 253.7 | 305.7 | 347.8 |
| Minimum | −262.5 | −332.5 | −236.3 |
| **8/08–3/10** | | | |
| Mean | 38.3 | 27.7 | −10.6 |
| Standard deviation | 309.0 | 121.7 | 226.1 |
| Maximum | 482.9 | 266.7 | 511.5 |
| Minimum | −716.9 | −205.4 | −332.8 |

*Source:* Barclays Capital.

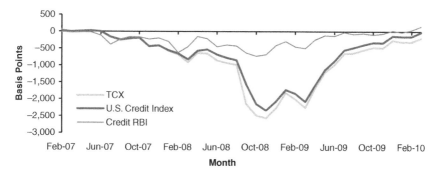

**FIGURE 14.13**   TCX, Credit Index, and Credit RBI Cumulative Excess Returns (February 2007–March 2010)
*Source:* Barclays Capital.

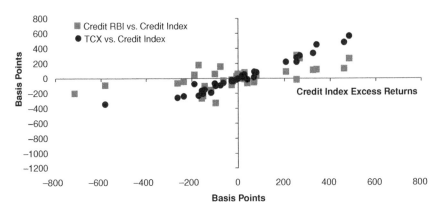

**FIGURE 14.14** TCX and Credit RBI Excess Returns versus the Credit Index
Excess Returns (February 2007–March 2010)
*Source:* Barclays Capital.

result, the CDX-cash basis became very negative as the credit crisis unfolded
but reverted back toward zero as the crisis abated. This caused the Credit
RBI to have positive tracking errors to the Credit Index during the crisis and
negative errors as the market recovered.

Whereas the correlation of monthly excess returns between the TCX and
Credit Index was 0.96 for the entire period, the correlation of the Credit RBI
and Credit Index excess returns was only 0.61. Another manifestation of the
difference in correlations can be seen by plotting the monthly excess returns
for the Credit RBI and TCX relative to those of the Credit Index. As shown
in Figure 14.14, the TCX versus Credit Index excess returns line up closely to
the 45 degree line, whereas those for Credit RBI versus Credit Index do not.

If investors are tolerant of monthly volatility, and if they have a view that
the movement in the CDX-cash basis will eventually reverse, they may find
the Credit RBI an efficient source of long-term credit beta (Figure 14.15). For
the Credit RBI, we have data covering a longer period (April 2004 to March
2010) than for TCX. For this period, the tracking error of excess returns
versus the Credit Index is lower (138 bps) than the recent three-year period
(188 bps). From April 2004 to January 2007, the excess return tracking error
volatility for the Credit RBI was only 22 bps. This suggests that for periods
with stable index excess returns, the Credit RBI does a good job tracking the
Credit Index. In this context, the advantage of the Credit RBI as a source of
long-term credit beta is its lower cost, compared with a TCX strategy.

How much does the performance of the Credit RBI improve if we include
additional derivative positions to hedge movements in market liquidity? We

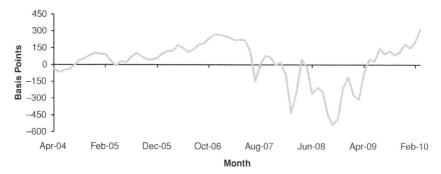

**FIGURE 14.15** Cumulative Excess Returns to Treasuries of the Credit RBI
(April 2004–March 2010)
*Source:* Barclays Capital.

calculate the VIX and ED-FF positions in the Credit RBI basket by examining
a sliding-window regression of their returns on tracking errors from synthetic
replication. Specifically, each month, we regress the past 12-month returns of
VIX futures against the respective tracking errors of a RBI basket versus the
Credit Index. We then use the estimated regression coefficient as the hedge
ratio for the following month. For example, if the hedge ratio is 7.42%,
we add a notional short position in the VIX futures equal to approximately
742 bps of the total market value.

Figure 14.16 shows that the addition of a short VIX futures position
generally had a noticeable effect on Credit RBI tracking errors, in particular
during the period of extreme market disruption in the fourth quarter of
2008 and the period of market recovery in 2009. The inclusion of VIX
significantly reduced RBI tracking errors in the former period. Similarly, in
the latter period, as market liquidity recovered in the first half of 2009, the
inclusion of VIX also reduced RBI tracking errors. During all other periods
the magnitude of the VIX position in the alternative RBI basket was small
and had only a negligible effect, as expected, on RBI tracking errors versus
the Credit Index.

Table 14.7 reports the performance of these two alternative RBI baskets
along with the standard RBI basket. The results suggest that the RBI with
short VIX to hedge changes in market wide liquidity conditions reduces the
average tracking error and also extreme tracking errors. The alternative RBI
with ED-FF has moderately higher TEV than the RBI without VIX. This lack
of improvement for the RBI with ED-FF is likely related to the problems of
LIBOR measurement during the credit crisis (discussed in Chapter 5). Figure 14.17 shows the cumulative performance of RBI and the two alternative

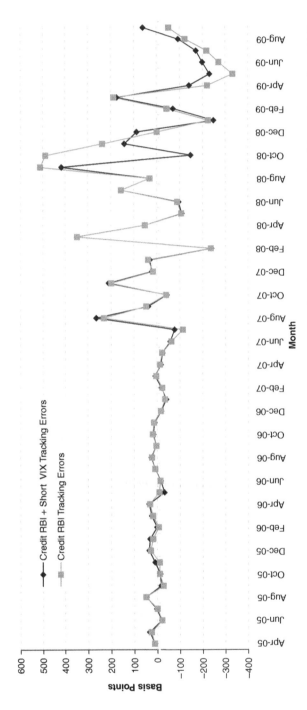

**FIGURE 14.16** Monthly Tracking Errors: Credit RBI and Credit RBI with a Short VIX Exposure (April 2005–September 2009)
*Source:* Barclays Capital.

**TABLE 14.7** Credit RBI and Alternative Credit RBIs, Tracking Errors (April 2005–September 2009)

| RBI Basket for U.S. IG Credit | Mean Monthly Outperformance | Realized Monthly Tracking Error Volatility | Worst Monthly Tracking Error |
|---|---|---|---|
| IR Swaps & CDX 5-yr + 10-yr | 6.2 bps | 141.3 bps | 511.5 bps |
| IR Swaps; CDX 5-yr + 10-yr; short VIX | 3.4 bps | 111.7 bps | 417.2 bps |
| IR Swaps; CDX 5-yr +10-yr; ED-FF futures | −3.7 bps | 155.6 bps | 582.6 bps |

*Source:* Barclays Capital.

RBIs. Both alternative RBIs have lower cumulative tracking errors versus the Credit Index making them appealing to investors seeking long-term credit beta exposure.

## CONCLUSION

TCX provides transparent tracking of the U.S. Credit Index with a small set of highly liquid cash bonds. Overall, it does it quite well, even in tumultuous periods. Between 2007 and 2010, the TCX proved to be a better tracking strategy than synthetic replication (Credit RBI), with a lower mean tracking error and significantly lower tracking error volatility. Nevertheless, cash replication involves relatively high transactions cost, which may make TCX most attractive for short-term tactical credit beta exposure.

For investors looking for credit beta exposure for longer than a month, a quarterly rebalanced TCX portfolio may be more appropriate. It has lower transactions cost, and comparable tracking ability. The properties of the quarterly TCX make it useful as the basis for a liquid credit index and total return swaps.

For investors interested in a long-term credit beta, synthetic replication with its lower transactions cost may be appealing. But it may not be a good strategy for investors who need short-term exposure. Such investors need to be keenly aware of the tracking error risks inherent in synthetic replication, especially during periods of changing market liquidity. During these market

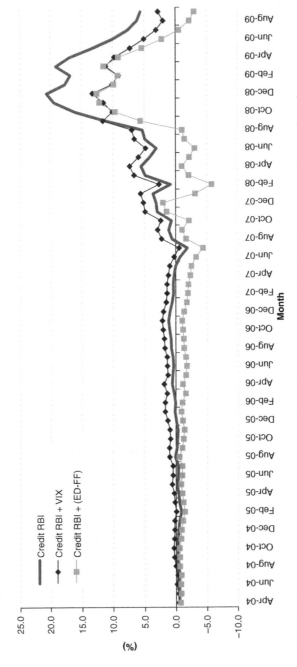

**FIGURE 14.17** Credit RBI and Alternative Credit RBIs, Cumulative Tracking Errors versus the Credit Index (April 2004–September 2009)
*Source:* Barclays Capital.

environments, short-term investors who must use synthetic replication may want a Credit RBI basket that includes a market liquidity hedge overlay.

## NOTES

1. We could have used a risk model and optimizer to construct TCX, but we prefer a stratified sampling approach that is broadly consistent with a risk model framework (i.e., sector/DTS). Stratified sampling offers two benefits. First, we can construct the TCX in a transparent manner, and second, it provides some robustness to the portfolio's construction by making it less susceptible to risk parameter estimation errors.
2. Liquidity Cost Scores (LCS)$^{TM}$ are based solely on the bid-ask spreads of Barclays Capital traders. The effective bid-ask spread faced by investors may be tighter as they have the benefit of approaching multiple broker-dealers. As such, the true cost of transacting on the TCX may be lower. The 70% to 30% split is arbitrary on our part as a way to be more conservative in estimating the TCX's transactions cost.
3. Allocating 100% of the transactions cost using the LCS at time of entering the TCX, we estimate the monthly transactions cost to be 15 bps.
4. However, the idiosyncratic risk is not zero. For example, the CDX index is a basket of 125 issuer names. While the CDX has more issuers than the TCX (50 names), it is still far less than the 600+ issuers in the U.S. Credit Index. In addition, the CDX issuer weighting scheme is very different than that of the Credit Index.
5. Hedge funds may use illiquid strategies to generate alpha. Since an RBI basket is essentially long liquidity, combining an RBI basket swap with cash investment in hedge funds provides a bit of a liquidity hedge. See Upbin, Konstantinovsky, and Phelps (2009).
6. For more information on the TBA roll market and MBS replication, see Chapter 6 in Dynkin, Gould, Hyman, Konstantinovsky, and Phelps (2007).

# References

Altman, E., and G. Bana. 2004. "Defaults and Returns on High-Yield Bonds." *Journal of Portfolio Management* 30(2): 58–73.

Ambastha, M., A. Ben Dor, L. Dynkin, J. Hyman, and V. Konstantinovsky. 2010. "Empirical Duration of Corporate Bonds and Credit Market Segmentation." *Journal of Fixed Income* 20(1): 5–27.

Ambrose, B., K. Cai, and J. Helwege. 2009. "Fallen Angels and Price Pressure." Working paper, Penn State University, December.

Arnott, R., J. Hsu, F. Lei, and S. Shepherd. 2010. "Valuation-Indifferent Weighting for Bonds." *Journal of Portfolio Management* 36(3): 117–130.

Asvanunt, A., and A. Staal. 2009a. "Corporate Default Probability model in the Barclays Capital POINT Platform." Barclays Capital, April.

Asvanunt, A., and A. Staal. 2009b. "The POINT Conditional Recovery Rate (CRR) Model." Barclays Capital, August.

Ben Dor, A., L. Dynkin, and J. Hyman. 2005a. "Empirical Duration of Credit Securities: Dependence on Spread." Lehman Brothers, *Global Relative Value*, March 14.

Ben Dor, A., L. Dynkin, and J. Hyman. 2005b. "DTS-Further Insights and Applicability." Lehman Brothers, August.

Ben Dor, A., L. Dynkin, and J. Hyman. 2005c. "DTS (Duration Times Spread)—Scope and Applicability. Empirical Duration and Debt Seniority." Lehman Brothers, *Global Relative Value*, November 7.

Ben Dor, A., L. Dynkin, P. Houweling, J. Hyman, E. Leeuwen, and O. Penninga. 2007. "DTS (Duration Times Spread): A New Measure of Spread Exposure in Credit Portfolios." *Journal of Portfolio Management* 33(2): 77–100.

Ben Dor, A., S. Polbennikov, and J. Rosten. 2007. "DTS (Duration Times Spread) for CDS: A New Measure of Spread Sensitivity." *Journal of Fixed Income* 16(4): 32–44.

Berd, A., R. Mashal, and P. Wang. 2004. "Consistent Risk Measures for Credit Bonds." Lehman Brothers, *Quantitative Credit Research Quarterly*, Q3/4.

Bhattacharya, B., and M. Trinh. 2006. "Anatomy of the Risk Premium in Credit Markets." Lehman Brothers.

Blanco, R., S. Brennan, and I. W. Marsh. 2005. "An Empirical Analysis of the Dynamic Relationship between Investment Grade Bonds and Credit Default Swaps." *Journal of Finance* 60(5): 2255–2281.

Collin-Dufresne, P., R. S. Goldstein, and J. S. Martin. 2001. "The Determinants of Credit Spread Changes." *Journal of Finance* 56(6): 2177–2207.

Dastidar, S., and B. Phelps. 2009. "Introducing LCS: Liquidity Cost Scores for US Credit Bonds," *Barclays Capital*, October 6.

Dastidar, S., and B. Phelps. 2011. "Credit Spread Decomposition: Decomposing Bond-Level Credit OAS into Default and Liquidity Components." *Journal of Portfolio Management* 37(3): 1–17.

Dastidar, S., A. Edelstein, and B. Phelps. 2010. "Liquidity Cost Scores (LCS) for Pan-European Credit Bonds." Barclays Capital, September 24.

Desclée, A., and B. Phelps. 2010. "Fixed Income Active Returns: Characteristics, Constraints and Competition." Barclays Capital, February 26.

Dhande S. S., and B. Phelps. 2007. "Tracking Error Performance of Synthetic Replicating Credit Portfolios: Attribution Methodology and Replication Refinements." Lehman Brothers, September 10.

Dynkin, L., A. Gould, J. Hyman, V. Konstantinovsky, and B. Phelps. 2007. *Quantitative Management of Bond Portfolios*. Princeton, NJ: Princeton University Press.

Easterwood, J. C., and S. Nutt. 1999. "Inefficiency in Analysts' Earnings Forecasts: Systematic Misreaction or Systematic Optimism?" *Journal of Finance* 54(5): 1777–1797.

Ellul, A., C. Jotikasthira, and C. Lundblad. 2010. "Regulatory Pressure and Fire Sales in the Corporate Bond Market." Working paper, University of North Carolina–Chapel Hill, March.

Elton, E., M. Gruber, D. Agrawal, and C. Mann. 2001. "Explaining the Rate Spread on Corporate Bonds." *Journal of Finance* 56(6): 2177–2207.

Grinold, R. C., and R. N. Kahn. 2000. *Active Portfolio Management*, 2nd ed. New York: McGraw-Hill.

Hite, G., and A. Warga, 1997. "The Effect of Bond-Rating Changes on Bond Price Performance." *Financial Analyst Journal* 53(3): 35–51.

Hotchkiss, E. S., and G. Jostova. 2007. "Determinants of Corporate Bond Trading: A Comprehensive Analysis." Working paper, Boston College.

Hradsky, G. T., and R. D. Long. 1989. "High-Yield Default Losses and the Return Performance of Bankrupt Debt." *Financial Analysts Journal* 45(4): 38–49.

Huber, P. J. 1967. "The Behaviour of Maximum Likelihood Estimates Under Nonstandard Conditions." In *Proceedings of the Fifth Berkeley Symposium in Mathematical Statistics 1*, edited by L. Lecam and J. Neyman, 221–233. Berkeley: University of California Press.

Hull, J., M. Predescu, and A. White. 2004. "The Relationship between Credit Default Swap Spreads, Bond Yields, and Credit Rating Announcements." *Journal of Banking and Finance* 28(11): 2789–2811.

Hyman, J. 2007. "Yield Curve Shift and Twist and Credit Spread Change: Re-Examining the Relationships." Lehman Brothers, *Global Relative Value*, October 15.

Lee, S. W., and B. E. Hansen. 1994. "Asymptotic Theory for the GARCH(1,1) Quasi-Maximum Likelihood Estimator." *Econometric Theory* 10(1): 29–52.

Merton, R. C. 1974. "On the Pricing of Corporate Debt: The Risk Structure of Interest Rates." *Journal of Finance* 29(2): 449–470.

Moody's Investors Service. 2010. "Corporate Default and Recovery Rates, 1920–2009," February.

Naik, V., M. Devarajan, and E. Wong. 2007. "The Anatomy of Credit Curve Trades over the Economic Cycle." Lehman Brothers Fixed Income Research, *Quantitative Credit Research Quarterly*, Q2.

Ng, K. Y., and B. Phelps. 2011. "Capturing Credit Spread Premium." *Financial Analysts Journal* 67(3): 63–75.

Norden, L., and M. Weber, 2004. "Informational Efficiency of Credit Default Swap and Stock Markets: The Impact of Credit Rating Announcements." *Journal of Banking and Finance* 28(11): 2813–2843.

Ranguelova, E. 2004. "CDS Steepeners." Lehman Brothers Fixed Income Research, *Structured Credit Research*, April.

Rosenberg, B. 1985. "Prediction of Common Stock Betas." *Journal of Portfolio Management* 12(2): 5–14.

Schönbucher, P. 1999. "A Libor Market Model with Default Risk." Working paper, University of Bonn.

Schuknecht, L., J. von Hagen, and G. Wolswijk. 2010. "Government Bond Risk Premiums in the EU Revisited: The Impact of the Financial Crisis." ECB Working Paper no. 1152, February.

Steiner, M., and V. G. Heinke. 2001. "Event Study Concerning International Bond Price Effects of Credit Rating Actions." *International Journal of Finance and Economics* 6(2): 139–157.

Upbin, B., V. Konstantinovsky, and B. Phelps. 2009. "Alpha-Beta Recombination: Can Synthetic Fixed Income Compete with Traditional Long-Only Managers." *Journal of Portfolio Management* 35(2): 80–101.

Weinraub, H. J., and B. R. Kuhlman. 1994. "The Effect of Common Stock Beta Variability on the Variability of the Portfolio Beta." *Journal of Financial and Strategic Decisions* 7(2): 79–84.

White, H. 1982. "Maximum Likelihood Estimation of Misspecified Models." *Econometrica* 50(1): 1–25.

# Index

**A**

Absolute spread change
  approach, 4
  risk projections, DTS approach, 66
  volatility, 7e
    comparison, 8f
Absolute spread volatility
  instability, 10
  relative spread volatility, contrast, 233f
Active credit exposure
  hedging, 187–189
  motivation, 189
Active portfolio managers, spread
    decomposition usage, 133–134
Adjustment factor (AdjF)
  liquidity dispersion, relationship, 93
  non-quoted adjustment factor, contrast,
    100
Aggregate credit steepener, U.S. Credit Index
    (performance contrast), 223t
Aggregate issuer-matched DTS steepener
  market state source, 224f
  volatility, reduction, 222
  yearly performance, 225t
Aggregate issuer-matched DTS strategy,
    performance, 223
Aggregate portfolio, DTS neutrality, 220
Aggregate $R^2$
  impact, 12
  report, 13
Alltel 30-year bond hedge ratio, variation,
    181f
Alpha, generation, 201
Alpha-beta recombination strategies, 357
Alternative corporate benchmark, adoption,
    288–291
Analytical duration
  empirical duration, relationship, 159–161
  hedging, 190

Analytical TEV, empirical TEV (contrast),
    188f
Annual credit spread premium, 281, 284
  estimates, comparison, 276t
  OAS relationship, historical default data
    (usage), 270f
Annual reported index excess returns, 271t
Arbitrage
  activity
    breakdown, 356
    requirements, 354
  relationship, 353
  risk, 353–356
Asset value volatility, observation, 233–234
Average annual credit spread premium
    (estimation), historical default data
    (usage), 267t
  IG Corporate Index, 269t
Average CDS spread, increase, 144
Average DTS-weighted excess returns,
    sector/duration bucket, 217f
Average excess returns, 216
Average hedge ratios, implication, 244
Average monthly returns, median, 310f
Average OAS, usage, 187

**B**

Barclays Capital
  Euro Treasury Index, spread volatility
    projections test, 65f
  excess returns, 268, 270
  Index Production Team, message
    collection/storage, 89
  traders, bid-ask data collection, 113, 115
  U.S. IG/HY Credit Indexes, Liquidity Cost
    Score, 83f
Barra's E1 risk model, betas (prediction),
    206–207
Bear Stearns, takeover, 137

Benchmark bond, defining, 91–92
Beta
  estimates, usage, 183
  estimation, 244
  history-based betas, 206
  prediction, 206–207
Beta-based hedge, 244
Beta-hedged strategy
  correlation, 203
  performance, 201
Beta-weighted hedge, 200–201
Bid-ask indications, 102t
  Bloomberg message screen, example, 89f
Bid-ask markets, estimation, 91
  LCS approach, 102t
Bid-ask quotes, absence, 109–110
Bid-ask spreads
  calculation, 88
  indicative only characteristic, 115
  liquidity measures, correlation, 81
  quotes, 89
Bid-ask trader indications, limitation, 90
Black-Scholes-Merton formulas, impact,
    75–76
Black-Scholes option pricing equation, usage,
    75
Bloomberg message screen, 89f
Bond-level expected default cost, variables
    (choice), 138
Bond-level indicatives, LCS (relationship),
    93, 96
Bond-level LCS, importance, 141
Bond-level risk premium variables, analysis,
    150
Bond-level spread decomposition,
    aggregation, 136–137
Bond-level trading volume data
  availability, 81
  measure, 117
Bonds
  age, 99
  amount outstanding, 99
  attributes, 98–102
    LCS regression, 99t, 118t
    regression, 119t
  average LCS, 107–108
  bid-ask spread indications, 90
  biweekly price returns, usage, 178–179
  bond-level persistence, 111–112
  characteristics, differences, 159

classification, 28
composition/volume, 175t
data set, 14
DTS/OAS, 99
eligible universe, TES filter restriction, 130
event study approach, 159
excess returns, 85–86
hedge ratios, 178f
idiosyncratic spread change, 17
interest rate sensitivity, decline, 159
issuance, investment-grade rating,
    180–181
LCS volatility, 150
liquidity
  costs, LCS measure, 129–130
  distribution, change, 83
Liquidity Cost Score (LCS)
  buckets, 110–111
  comparison, 106
  trading volume (relationship), 96
long-term statistical averages, 79
monthly relative statistics, 299
non-positive spreads, exclusion, 34
option-adjusted spread
  drivers, 139, 141
  modeling, 138
  stability/decline, 134–135
  variation, 134
option adjusted spread duration (OASD),
    82
peer group, risk characteristics, 10
population, variation, 185
pre-rating/post-rating event hedge ratios,
    184f
pre-rating/post-rating event regressions,
    182
price
  adjustment dynamic, cross-sectional
    variation, 174
  obtaining, 75
price-quoted bonds, 88
rating events
  experience, frequency, 180f
  summary statistics, 182t
relative trade efficiency, 130
removal, 278
return aggregation, frequency/period/level,
    161
sales (distribution), exclusion triggers
    (impact), 324t

selection, LCS (usage), 241
spread-quoted bonds, 88
trader ranks, 109
    bid-ask quotes, absence, 109–110
trading volume, 98–99
    control, 178
Bond-specific factors, impact, 143
Box trade, 218
Buy-and-hold credit investor, spread
    premium, 265

**C**

Callable bonds, exclusion, 34
Capital structure, 78
Cash basket proxies, creation, 129
Cash-CDS basis, 187
    change, 317
Cash-CDS spread basis, behavior, 297
Cash credit replication (TCX), 338–351
    arbitrage risk, 353–356
    average LCS, 342f
    average monthly excess return, difference,
        344–345
    cash indexes, synthetic replication,
        351–358
    CDX-Cash Basis/iTraxx-Cash Basis, 354f
    construction methodology, 339
    credit index, 344t, 345f, 359f
        cumulative excess return difference,
            346f
        excess returns, difference, 346f
    credit RBIs, 358–363
        cumulative excess returns, 359f
        excess returns, contrast, 360f
    cumulative excess returns, 361f
        difference, 346f
    ED-Ff futures spread, 351
    excess returns, 345f
    issuers, number, 342f
    LCS, cross-sectional distribution, 343f
    liquidity, 342–343
        risk, 352–353
    market value percentages, monthly
        change, 347
    monthly excess returns, 344t
    monthly OAD/TCX/Credit Index, 343f
    monthly/quarterly TCX, turnover, 350f
    monthly TCX transaction costs, 348f
    monthly TCX turnover, 347f
    monthly tracking errors, 362f

OAD, 343–344
overexposure, 345
performance, U.S. credit index (contrast),
    344–346
portfolio
    composition, 340t–341t
    construction rules, 338–339
    properties, 339–344
rollover risk, 356–358
spread, 352–353
spread-to-swap levels, 353f
synthetic replication, tracking error
    drivers, 351
transactions cost, 347–348, 351t
    control, quarterly rebalancing (usage),
        348–351
turnover
    cost, 347–348
    pattern, 350
Cash indexes, synthetic replication, 351–358
Cash-only portfolio, position sizes
    (limitation), 218
CDX-Cash basis, 354f
Chain rule, usage, 76
Committee on Uniform Security
    Identification Procedures (CUSIP), 89
Communications Sector, issuers (average
    spread/spread changes), 11f
Composite corporate indexes, estimated
    annual credit spread premium, 287t
Conditional default probability (CDP), 146
Conditional recovery rate (CRR), 138–139
    loss-given-default measure, 146
    model, results, 141
Consumer sectors
    default contribution, 137f
    liquidity contribution, 137f
Contemporaneous liquidity/turnover, 314
Contribution-to-DTS exposures, manager
    reliance, 33
Core-plus allocations, 157
Corporate benchmark, alternative
    (adoption), 288–291
Corporate bonds
    duration buckets, summary statistics, 216t
    estimation methodology, 161–163
    liquidity, quantification, 81
    market, illiquidity, 174
    monthly total spread volatility, range, 63
    risk-reward profile, variation, 213

Corporate bonds (*Continued*)
  spread premium, capture process, 265
  U.S. Treasury hedge ratios, 162t
Corporate bond spread
  behavior, analysis, 5–20
  risk-free rate, relationship, 75
  sensitivity (measurement), 3
  volatility, 48–50
Corporate default probability (CDP),
    138–139
  model, results, 141
Corporate Index
  average DTS, 259f
  credit rating categories, 161
  partition, 8–9, 14
Corporate index, spread premium shortfall,
    274–279
Corporate indexes
  alternatives, 279–288
    estimated annual credit spread
      premium, 287t
    list, 280t, 285t
    estimated annual credit spread premium,
      287t
Corporate issuers, spread (DTS-like
    behavior), 61
Cost-of-carry model, 353
Countries
  relative spread volatilities, 64
  spread dynamics, 64
Credit bond
  portfolio, hedging, 149–150
  roundtrip trade, execution, 266
Credit crisis (2007–2009), 229
  broker-dealer financing, difficulty, 355
  downgrade risk, 250–257
  DTS application, 234–244
  relative/absolute spread volatility, 233f
  risk model construction, DTS usage
    (advantages), 244–246
  spread behavior, 229–234
Credit curve
  data/methodology, 214–217
  empirical analysis, 217–227
  positioning, 213
Credit default swaps (CDSs), 39
  CDS-cash bonds basis, widening, 39
  changes, usage, 149
  coefficients, magnitude (change), 143
  communication sector, 46f

dataset, description, 42t
indexes, spreads, 230f
investment-grade bonds, 140t
investment-grade bonds-only regression,
    142t
Kraft, 134f
regression coefficients, 143
results, 5
sectors, estimates (comparison), 44
spread duration, 242
usage, 227
variables, 134
Credit default swaps (CDSs) spreads
  empirical analysis, 41–50
  increase, 144
  regression, 151t
    change, 151t
  systematic volatility, 42, 44
  volatility, analysis (QML procedure),
    48
  width, 137
Credit exposure (obtaining), cash/synthetic
    replication (usage), 337
Credit index
  excess returns, difference, 346f
  monthly excess returns, 359t
  RBI-2, empirical/analytical durations
    (basis), 188f
Credit markets
  change, 48
  extreme conditions, 158
  securities, risk (increase), 253, 255
  segmentation, 173
Credit ratings
  basis, 179–180
  hedge ratios, variation, 163–166
  spread, hedge ratios function, 164f
Credit RBIs, 358–373
  basket
    components, 337–338
    VIX/ED-FF positions, calculation,
      361
  monthly excess returns, 359t
  short VIX exposure, 362f
  tracking errors, 363t
Credit sector exposures, skewing, 124–125
Credit spreads
  decomposition, purposes, 133–134
  interest rates, negative correlation, 163
  liquidity cost, identification, 82

premium, 266
    market spread level, correlation, 268
    volatility, 268
    puzzle, 268
Credit steepeners
    implementation, CDSs (usage), 224–227
    trades, implementation, 213
Crossover names, spread change, 44
Cross-sectional high-yield OAS, explanation,
    147
Cumulative excess returns
    difference, portfolio contrast, 127f
    IG Corporate level, 272f
    performance, contrast, 127f
Cumulative relative returns, 304t

**D**

Daily corporate bond pricing data, 173
Daily spread change, absolute/relative
    volatility, 63f
Data description, 34–35
Default contribution, 137f
    market OAS, 144f
    sector-wise spread decomposition, 141f,
    146f
Defaulted bonds, investment, 298
Default losses, representation, 139
Default OAS components, 145f
Default risk
    accounting, 141
    joint dynamics, 133
Derivatives, usage, 352
Descriptive statistics, usage, 299–303
Developed markets sovereigns, DTS (usage),
    59–66
Diversification, downgrade-based model,
    252t, 254t
Downgraded bonds
    average spread level, 183
    hedge ratios, 183
    historical losses, 252–253
    pre-rating/post-rating event regressions,
    182
Downgraded issuers
    liquidity, 312f
    performance, 314
        variation, 255–256
    relative spreads, 307f
    relative turnover, 312f
    underperformance, 305

upgraded issuers, performance
    (comparison), 306
value-weighted returns, equal-weighted
    returns (contrast), 305–306
Downgrade event, 297
    negative informational content, investor
    overreaction, 297
Downgrade risk, 250–257
    estimation, 257
    quantification, 256
Downgrade rule, 278
Downgrades
    average underperformance, 251t, 254t
        yearly results, 255t
    loss, standard deviation, 253
    performance cost, 249
    performance effect, long-term historical
        study, 258
    possibility, 256
Downgrade tolerant corporate index, 279,
    281
Dummy variables, usage, 77
Duration-adjusted carry
    curves, 217
    sector/duration bucket categorization,
    215f
Duration-based bonds, 119–120
Duration buckets, summary statistics, 216t
Duration exposures, matching, 186
Duration-matched treasuries, excess returns,
    214
Duration-neutral credit steepener trades,
    implementation, 213
Duration-neutral steepener, positive spread
    carry, 216
Duration sample, 35f
Duration times spread (DTS), 3, 20–21
    advantages, 244–246
    applications, 234–244
    basis, 199–200
    contributions, 4
        limitations, 261
        matching, 338–339
    DTS-based approach, 245, 257–258
    DTS-based forecasts, 65
    DTS-based issuer caps, 32
    DTS-based models, implementation
        difficulty, 33
    DTS-based risk, 261
    DTS-hedged trades, systematic risk, 198

Duration times spread (DTS) (*Continued*)
  DTS-neutral positions, 218, 220
  DTS-neutral steepener, performance, 219t
    examination, investment grade CDS (usage), 225
    issuer matching, 221t
  DTS/OAS, 87
  DTS-weighted excess returns, sector/duration bucket, 217f
  DTS-weighted trade, volatility, 200
  excess return volatility
    contrast, 21f
    contrast, seniority classes, 30f
    relationship, 58
  exposure
    evolution, 69f
    matching, 198
    usage, 241
  hedge, generation, 242
  levels, ratio inversion, 258–259
  limits, placement, 262
  measure, incorporation, 258
  model, position limits (ratios), 259f
  paradigm, introduction, 33
  periodic usage, 260–261
  prediction, 20
  quintiles, 21
  ratio, 205
    comparison, 206t
    usage, 205–206
  seniority classes, 27–30
  summary statistics, 22t
  theoretical basis, 73
  theoretical derivation, 233
  usage, 190, 245
  usefulness, 73
  volatility estimator, quality, 236
Duration times spread (DTS) hedge
  advantage, 203
  observation, 202
  performance, 198

**E**
Emerging markets (EM)
  debt, spread dynamics, 55–59
  sovereign debt, DTS relation (evidence), 59f
Emerging Markets (EM) Dollar
    Denominated Index, 55–56

  countries spread level, 58f
  historical spread level, 56f
Empirical analysis, 161–163
Empirical beta-based hedge, 244
Empirical duration
  analytical duration, relationship, 159–161
  credit risk perception, impact, 164–165
  spread level, relationship, 171f
  theory/evidence, 159–172
  usage, 186–192
Empirical hedge ratios
  behavior instability, exhibition, 167
  credit rating/period, 169t
  projected hedge ratios, comparison, 167f
Empirical hedge ratios, projection, 166
Empirical RBI, level, 187
Empirical TEV, analytical TEV (contrast), 188f
Equity market betas, 207
Estimated annual credit spread premium, 287t
  index data, usage, 282t, 283t
Estimated average annual credit spread premium, historical default data (usage), 267t
Estimated average annual spread premium, index data (usage), 273t
Estimated return volatility, 67t
Estimation methodology, 40–41
Euro Aggregate Index
  DTS exposure, evolution/attribution, 69f
  estimated return volatility, 67t
  isolated return volatilities, 68f
  spread exposure, increase, 68, 70
Euro Corporate Indexes
  annualized excess return volatilities, 61f
  systematic spread volatility estimation, QML usage, 50t
Eurodollar (ED) futures contracts, 357
European credit markets, trading conventions, 113
European indexes, OAS (time series), 113
European sovereign crisis, 117–118
European Treasury Indexes, spreads, 60f
Euro sovereign crisis, 61–62
Euro Treasuries, DTS (usage), 59–66
Euro Treasury Index
  annualized excess return volatilities, 61f
  average spread, 59–60
  daily spread change, 64–66

DTS exposure, evolution/attribution, 69f, 70f
LIBOR spread, 60
progression, 68, 70
Eurozone economies, deficits/debt ratios, 55
Excess return, 20–21
standardized excess return, distribution, 24f
volatility
estimates, 24
forecasts, comparison, 22–25
Excess return volatility
DTS function, 59f
duration times spread, contrast, 21f, 27f
seniority classes, 30f
measure, 20–25
Execution strategies, 82
Expected default losses, alternative measure (usage), 145–147
Expected default probability measures, 146
Expected TEV, improvement, 123–124

**F**

Fallen angels, 81
analysis, 325–332
asset class, 319–332
construction method, 319–322
bonds sales (distribution), exclusion triggers (impact), 324t
Buy All portfolios, 322
construction, sample, 298–299
cumulative relative returns, 304t
data/methodology, 298–303
descriptive statistics, usage, 299–303
downgraded issuers, relative turnover/liquidity, 312f
dynamic portfolios, construction, 319–320
dynamic strategy, performance analysis, 297
flexible reversal portfolio, 321–322, 324–325, 327
high-yield securities proportion, 295–296
high-yield status, maintenance, 303
issuers
average monthly returns, median, 310f
population, 300t
market value, 300t
minimum relative cumulative return month, distribution, 309f
observations, 300–301
performance, 325–332
asymmetric relation, 311
cross-sectional regression, 315t–316t
cross-sectional variation, 307–311
forced selling, relationship, 297
portfolio
bond inclusion/exclusion criteria, 320t
characteristics, 322–325
composition summary statistics, 323t
performance, 326t–327t
price behavior, 296
price pressures, 296
volume/liquidity/cash-derivative, proxy basis, 311–314
price reversal, evidence, 305
quarterly average returns, 304t
rating event month, beginning/ending credit qualities (distribution), 301t
rating events
bonds, status, 302t
performance dynamics, 303–318
relative cumulative performance, distribution, 308f
returns, cross-section predictability, 314–318
reversal period, 318
risk/performance, 295
robustness tests, 328–330
rules-based portfolios, characteristics/ performance, 298
selling imbalance, 312–313
spreads, reversal, 307
strategy, 319
three-month reversal, 321, 325
three-month reversal portfolio
monthly relative returns, distribution, 328f
performance, 331t
properties, 330
rolling six-month average relative returns, 329f
transactions costs, performance net, 330–332
underperformance period, 318
value-weighted monthly relative returns, 303, 305
weighting scheme, 321
Fed Funds (FF) futures contracts, 357

Financial sectors
    default contribution, 137f
    liquidity contribution, 137f
Firm-specific fundamental information,
        usage, 138–139
Five-year spread premium, index data
        (usage), 275f
Fixed rate IG bonds, comparison, 121t–123t
Flexible Reversal portfolios, 321–324, 327
Flight-to-quality scenario, 73
Forced selling
    impact, 297
    performance, relationship, 297, 311–318
Forecasting data, examination, 205–207
Fully tolerant corporate index, 279, 281, 288
Fully Tolerant Corporate Index,
        composition, 289f
Future spread volatility, estimates, 64–65

**G**
Gamma, estimates (usage), 183
Gaussian conditional probability density
        function, usage, 53
Gauss-Wiener process, 74
German Treasury index, LIBOR spread, 60f
Greece, absolute spread volatility (increase),
        64

**H**
Hedged portfolios, excess returns, 149f
Hedge ratios
    aggregated data, usage (disadvantage), 179
    data/methodology, 179–181
    discontinuity, 165f, 185–186
    discontinuous behavior, 173
    empirical analysis, 181–183
    estimation, 185
    event study approach, 179–186
    exhibition, 165
    extrapolation, 166
    function, 177f
    implication, 244
    performance evaluation, relationship,
        183–186
    predictability, 166–172
    rating changes, 179–186
    reverse, 181
    spread level, relationship, 161, 163
    stability, 166–172
        pattern, 186

stale pricing, impact, 173–179
    variation, 163–166
        rating event categorization, 185f
Hedges (determination), metric (usage),
        198
Hedge security, market beta (estimates),
        202
Hedging, 241–244
    approaches, 199–200
        comparison, 197
    DTS application, 241–242
    mechanisms, 201t, 204t
    results, analysis, 200–207
    simulation methodology, 199–200
    strategies, 199
High beta, 3–4
High-profile bonds, two-way flow, 92
High-spread buckets, population, 57
High-Spread Euro Countries, spread
        volatility/level (contrast), 62f
High-volume bond, defining, 91–92
High-yield bonds
    analysis, 139
    boundary, 15
    callable issuance, 179
    core-plus investment, 189–192
    interest rate sensitivity, 189–190
        uncertainty, 157
    liquid subset, 177
    OAS regression, 154t
    performance, 325
    regressions, usage, 117
    research, 158
    variation, 18
High-yield data, usage, 16
High-yield debt
    effective duration, 158
    out-of-benchmark (core-plus) allocations,
        157
High Yield indexes, 229–230
High Yield Indexes, credit rating categories,
        161
High Yield indexes, spreads, 230
High-yield managers, total return/default
        risk perspective, 159
High-yield markets, investment-grade
        markets (hedge ratio discontinuity),
        165f
High-yield securities, 18–19
    fallen angel proportion, 295–296

High-yield spreads
 decomposition, 147
 impact, 147
Historical absolute spread changes, 235f
Historical back-testing, information ratio
  generation, 214
Historical default, usage, 267–268
Historical risk flares, performance, 226t
Historical time period, 235
History-based betas, comparison, 206
Hit ratio, elevation, 183
HY Index, 82

**I**

Idiosyncratic risk
 minimization, 123
 reduction, 352
  issuer matching, 218–220
Idiosyncratic spread
 level, volatility, 17f
 volatility, 16–18
  conditional relation, pooled estimation,
   47t
  measurement, collection, 17
Idiosyncratic spread change
 linear term coefficient, distributions, 46f
 volatility, 17f
Idiosyncratic volatility, 19–20, 44–48
IG bonds, index percentage, 120f
IG Corporate-High Yield BB-Only
  Composite, 284
IG Corporate Index
 annual average spread premium, 281
 annual reported index excess returns, 271t
 attributes, 277t
 average, 270
 credit spread premium
  measurement, 266–279
  negative level, 273
 data, implication, 274
 monthly index excess returns, 284
 risk, comparison, 284
 spread premium, index data (usage), 275f
 usage, 265–266
IG Credit Index, relationship, 87
IG-HY Composites, risk behavior, 286
IG Index, 82
 LCS relationship, 88f
 monthly estimated TEV, contrast,
  124f

IG-only fully tolerant corporate index, 279
 composition, 290f
IG-Only Fully Tolerant indexes, 288
IG Sector, out-of-sample test, 103f
Illiquid bonds, holding (mark-to-market
  impact), 86
Illiquidity, increase, 83
Indexes
 cumulative excess return performance,
  contrast, 127f
 downgrade rule, 278
 excess returns, 270–271
 replication
  derivatives, usage, 186–187
  stratified sampling, usage, 241t
Index-level LCS, 125f
Index tracking portfolios
 construction, 123
 creation, 236–241
Information ratio
 generation, 214
 maximization, 203–204, 242
In-sample monthly prediction error dataset,
  out-of-sample months (usage), 148
In-sample projection, 52
Interest rates, credit spreads (negative
  correlation), 163
Interest rate sensitivity
 difference, 177
 stale pricing, impact, 158–159
 uncertainty, 157
Intra-industry pairwise CDS trades,
  performance statistics (hedging
  mechanism), 201t, 204t
Investment-grade bonds
 analysis, 139
 boundary, 15
 daily quotes, changes (absence), 173
 LCS, regression, 140t
 liquidity cost cumulative distribution, 84f
 liquidity cost frequency distribution, 84f
 liquid subset, 177
 OAS/CDS spreads, regression, 140t
 OAS regression, 153t
 residual/confidence intervals, coefficient,
  148f
 spread decomposition methodology,
  136–137
Investment-grade bonds-only regression,
  142t

Investment Grade CDX, 231f
Investment-grade corporate universe, spread
    level partitioning, 6–7
Investment-grade data, usage, 16
Investment-grade markets, 319
    high-yield markets, hedge ratio
        discontinuity, 165f
Investment-grade rating categories,
    interest-rate sensitivities, 163–164
Investment managers, low-volatility
    long-term outperformance strategy,
    266
Involuntary selling, 305
Isolated return volatilities, 68
    Euro Aggregate Index, 68f
Issuer
    diversification, downgrade-centric
        analysis, 250
    DTS contributions, limitations,
        261–262
    limits, comparison/combination,
        260–262
    population, 300t
    risk, diversification framework, 249
Issuer-matched DTS steepener
    combination, 220–224
    historical performance, 220
    historical risk flares, performance, 226t
    passive carry trade, 222–223
Issuer-matched utilities steepener,
    performance, 222f
Issuers
    issuer-specific events, effect
        (minimization), 48
    one-year default probability, estimation,
        138
    recovery rate, estimation, 138
Issuer-specific risk, 204
iTraxx-Cash basis, 354f

**K**
Key rate durations (KRDs), 66–67
    profile, basis, 187
Kraft Foods (KFT)
    credit default swap (CDS), 134f
    duration-based group, 119
    LCS, 135f
    liquidity/default characteristics, 134–135
    option-adjusted spread (OAS), 134f
    spread decomposition, 136f

**L**
Lehman Brothers default
    impact, 236
    overweight, 345
    performance effect, exclusion, 255
Liquid basket, issuer representation, 109
Liquid cash basket proxies, creation, 129
Liquid credit benchmarks, 82
Liquidity
    abundance, 141, 143
    components, contributions, 144f
    conditions, worsening, 170
    constraint, 278–279
    contribution, 137f
        sector-wise spread decomposition, 141f,
        146f
    crisis, 128–129
    defining, 82
    differences, 137
    dispersion, adjustment factor
        (relationship), 93
    distribution, change, 83
    improvement, 123
    increase, 174
    OAS components, 145f
    penalty, 117–118
    proxy, 173–174
    risk, 352–353
        joint dynamics, 133
    subjective measures, LCS correspondence,
        108
Liquidity constraint tolerant corporate
    index, 279
Liquidity cost
    embedding, identification, 82
    LCS capture, 130
    market measure, 134
Liquidity Cost Score (LCS)
    bond-level indicatives, relationship, 93, 96
    Bucket, bonds (example), 112
    changes, usage, 149
    coefficients, magnitudes (change), 143
    comparison, out-of-sample test (usage),
        104t–105t
    computation, 81, 139
        bid-ask indications, usage, 93
    credit market segmentation, 91–92
    cross-sectional distribution, 343f
    cumulative excess return, difference,
        87f

distribution, 109f
  Pan-European/U.S. fixed rate IB bonds,
    120f
frequency distribution, 124
investment-grade bonds-only regression,
    142t
Kraft, 135f
LCS-sorted portfolios
  summary statistics, 111t
  transition matrices, 112t
liquidity, subjective measures
    (correspondence), 108
method, out-of-sample test (1-2-3
    rankings), 106–107
methodology, 88–92
  distinctions, 113
migration, potential, 111
1-2-3 rankings, 107
1-2-3 ranks, comparison, 108t
persistence, 110–112
  summary statistics, 111t
price percentage terms, measurement, 83
quintiles
  examination, 84–86
  excess return performance,
    examination, 86
regression, 99t
  coefficients, 143
  investment-grade bonds, 140t
relationship, 88f
sector analysis, 85f
segmentation, 92f
TRACE
  trading volume, relationship, 98f
  volume, relationship, 98f
usage, 82
variables, 134
volatility, 150
  regression, 151t
Liquidity Cost Score (LCS) model
specification, 98–102
support, out-of-sample test (usage), 110
test, 102–112
validation, LOW bond usage (example),
    103, 106
Liquidity Cost Score (LCS) value
consistency, 107
estimation, regression (usage), 117
generation, 96
persistence, 111

Liquidity quintiles
  bonds
    composition/volume, 175t
    hedge ratios, 178f
  examination, 174
  price return volatilities/correlations, 176t
  spread, hedge ratio function, 177f
Liquid tracking portfolios
  construction, 82
  maintenance, 128
Log-likelihood function, 51
  form, writing, 53
  logarithm, 52
London Interbank Offered Rate (LIBOR)
  spreads, 39
    duration, 358
  value calculation, problems, 87
Long-dated corporates
  duration-matched treasuries, excess
    returns, 214
Long-dated corporates, performance,
    213
Long DTS exposures, 218
Long-short trades, 197
Long-term credit beta, source, 360
Long-term statistical averages, impact, 79
Loss-given-default measures, 146
LOW bonds, 93
  LCS comparison, out-of-sample test
    (usage), 104t–105t
  non-quoted off-the-run issues, treatment,
    100, 102
  quotation, LCS results, 94t
  roundtrip execution cost, LCS
    representation, 107
Low-spread buckets, population, 57

**M**
Market beta
  estimates, 202
  forecasting methods, 205
Market exposures, 203
Market-level risk premium, representation,
    138
Market liquidity
  deterioration, 111
  increase, 125
Market OAS
  components, 145f
  contributions, 144f

Market risk
  aversion, increase, 224
  definition, determination, 198
  hedging, 197
  impact, 203
  premium
    contributions, 144
    importance, 143
Market's best bid-ask spread, 90
Market segmentation, 184
Market stress, 147
Market value, 300t
Market weights, usage, 187
Mark-to-market constraints, reduction, 136
Mark-to-market investors, short-term
    dislocations, 136
Maturity
  dependence, 78f
  slope dependence, 77–79
Maximum likelihood
  estimates, 41
  technique, 40
Maximum likelihood estimation (MLE)
    methodology, 40–41
Median cash-CDS basis, 313f
Median relative LCS, 311
Median spread levels, volatility (contrast),
    43f
Merton model, zero-coupon bond, 74–77
Minimum variance hedge, 203–205
Modified Peer Group, 325
Month-by-month regressions, estimation,
    146–147
Monthly estimated TEV, IG index (contrast),
    124f
Monthly excess returns, 359t
Monthly LIBOR-OAS volatilities, 352
Monthly portfolio performance, statistics,
    150t
Monthly TCX, turnover, 350f
Monthly tracking errors, 362f
Multicollinearity, concern, 139
Multi-factor risk models, 244–245

**N**
Natural spread volatility, 256
Net performance, equation, 330
Next-period beta, prediction, 205
Non-benchmark bond
  consideration, 117

off-the-run issue, 92
quote, 93
trading, 92–93
Non-benchmark quoted bonds, LCS
    computation (bid-ask indications), 93
Non-investment-grade bonds, allocation,
    189–190
Non-investment-grade markets, 319
Non-quoted adjustment factor (NQAdjF),
    usage, 100
Non-quoted bonds
  adjustment, 100
  identification, modeled LCS (usage), 103
Non-quoted bonds, LCS model
  specification, 98–102
  usage, 96–102
Non-quoted universes, comparison, 101t
Non-systematic risk, sources, 257
Normalized excess return realizations,
    mean/standard deviation, 23f
Normalized residuals, time series
    (mean/standard deviation), 23
Normalized spread changes, statistical
    properties (distribution), 66
Null hypothesis, $p$-values, 182

**O**
Off-the-run issue, 92
1-2-3 ranks, LCS (comparison), 108t
1-2-3 trader rankings, average LCS
    (correspondence), 108–109
One-month LIBOR rate, 320
One-month USD LIBOR rate, 190
On-the-run bond, 92f
  defining, 91–92
On-the-run CDX.NA.IG contract, 230
Option-adjusted duration (OAD) model, 179
Option adjusted spread (OAS)
  annual credit spread premium, historical
    default data (usage), 270f
  attribute levels, 147
  composition, change, 141–145
  drivers, 139, 141
  investment-grade bonds, 140t
  investment-grade bonds-only regression,
    142t
  Kraft, 134
  levels, comparison, 144–145
  percentage, market/default components,
    145f

regression, 151t
  residual, size, 148
  time series, 113, 115f
Option adjusted spread (OAS) changes, 147
  long-term time series, 233–234
  prediction, 148
  regression, 151t
  usage, 149
Option adjusted spread duration (OASD), 82
Ordinary least squares (OLS) regression,
    52–53
Out-of-benchmark allocations (core-plus
    allocations), 157
Out-of-sample excess returns, 149–150
Out-of-sample months, usage, 148
Out-of-sample tests, 102–112
  IG sector, 103f
  occurrence, 106
Out-of-the-money puts, writing, 223–224

**P**

Pairs trades, market risk hedging, 197
Pan-European bonds
  duration-based bonds, 119–120
  fixed rate IG bonds, 121t–123t
  raw bid-ask spreads, 115
Pan-European credit bonds, LCS (usage),
    113–123
Pan-European credit indexes
  characteristics, 114t
  liquidity characteristics, 116t
  OAS time series, 115f
Pan-European credit market, European
    sovereign crisis, 117–118
Pan-European fixed rate HY bonds, LCS
    regression, 118t
Pan-European fixed rate IG bonds
  LCS distribution, 120f
  LCS regression, 118t
Pan-European IG bonds, quality (increase),
    113
Pan-European IG index, 115
Pan-European LCS
  regression, 119t
  U.S. LCS, comparison, 118–123
Pan-European non-quoted LCS model,
    117–118
Pan-European trader-quoted benchmark
    bonds, pooling, 118
Pan-Europe liquidity cost, increase, 118

Partition, sample, 35f
Passive carry trade, 222–223
Peer groups, population, 299
Performance
  attribution, 190, 202
    models, 32–33
  evaluation, hedge ratios (relationship),
      183–186
  forced selling, relationship, 297, 311–318
  metrics, difference, 184
  primary driver, 197
  statistics, hedging mechanism (usage), 201t
Pooled estimation, results, 45–46, 47t
Pooled idiosyncratic spread volatility, spread
    level (contrast), 18f
Population, sample (sector/year basis), 34f
Portfolio
  bond inclusion/exclusion criteria, 320t
  characteristics, 322–325
  company strategy, 133–134
  composition summary statistics, 323t
  concentrations, control, 249–250
  contribution-to-DTS exposure, 249–250
  credit bond portfolio, hedging, 149–150
  credit torpedoes, 32
  cumulative excess returns, 125
    difference, contrast, 127f
  flexible reversal, 321–322
  investor construction, 128
  LCS, 125f
  LCS-sorted portfolios
    summary statistics, 111t
    transition matrices, 112t
  management
    applications, empirical duration (usage),
        186–192
    tools, 32–33
  managers
    spread change, summary/implications,
        30–34
    TES liquidity usage, 130
  monthly performance, statistics, 150t
  MV, 128
  performance, 326t–327t
  rebalancing, 124–125
  structuring
    LCS, usage, 128
    realized downgrade losses, increase, 253
  TCX portfolio, properties, 339–342
  TEV details, 126f

Portfolio (*Continued*)
  three-month reversal, 321
  true duration, 157
  turnover
    example, 128f
    involvement, 128
Portfolio construction
  investor opportunity, persistence (impact),
    111
  LCS, usage, 123–129
  usage, 28
Position size ratios
  change, 255
  misinterpretation, 260
  setting, DTS (usage), 257–260
Post-rating event hedge ratios, 184f
Pre-crisis, relative/absolute spread volatility,
  233f
Pre-rating event hedge ratios, 184f
Price pressure, proxies, 311–314
Price-quoted bonds, 88
Probability density function, denotation,
  51–52
Profit and loss (P&L) volatility, 201, 203
Pro Forma DTS risk model, risk
  factors/exposures (description), 67t
Projected hedge ratios, empirical hedge ratios
  (comparison), 167f
Proxies, ratings downgrades (usage), 250

**Q**
Quarterly average returns, 304t
Quarterly TCX, turnover, 350f
Quasi-maximum likelihood (QML)
  approach, 39, 51–53
  estimation methodology, 52–53
  usage, 45t
Quoted bonds
  LCS/issue size/age, relationship, 95t
  LCS/OAS/DTS, relationship, 97t
Quoted universes, comparison, 101t

**R**
Random variable, probability density
  function (denotation), 51–52
Rates-only hedge, usage, 189
Rating event
  performance dynamics, 303–318
Rating event, defining, 179–180
Ratings downgrades, proxy usage, 250

Ratings transitions, historical frequency, 250
Raw bid-ask spreads, 115
Realized market betas, predictors, 206t
Recovery data, usage, 267–268
Regression
  coefficients, 13f
  fit, improvement, 147
  intercept, 143
Regression-based results, corroboration, 163
Relative cumulative performance,
  distribution, 308f
Relative OAS changes, long-term time series,
  233–234
Relative spread change
  stability, enhancement, 8
  volatility, 7f
    basis, 23
    comparison, 7–8, 8f
Relative spread volatilities, 64
  absolute spread volatility, contrast, 233f
Relative value opportunities (identification),
  spread decomposition (usage),
  147–148
Remaining maturity tolerant corporate
  index, 279
Replicating bond index (RBI), 351
  basket swap, 337–338, 357
Reported index excess return, 265
Return variance, source, 256
Return volatility
  estimation, 66–68
  result, 213–214
  sources, 256t
Risk-averse investors, risk premium demand,
  133
Risk factors, capture (absence), 127–128
Risk-free interest rate, assumption, 75
Risk management, DTS (benefits), 229
Risk measures, 220
Risk model construction, DTS usage
  (advantages), 244–246
Risk premium, contributions, 144f
Risk projection, usage, 235–236
Risk properties, 285t
Risk-return profile, 223–224
Risky Present Value (RPV), 242
Robustness tests, 328–330
Rolling TBA contracts, usage, 355
Rollover risk, 356–358
Roundtrip cost, 88

*R*-squared values, usage, 205
Rules-based portfolios,
    characteristics/performance, 298
Russian Crisis
    credit markets, change, 48
    evidence, 19
    response, 5–6

**S**
Same-industry CDS pairs, hedging
    mechanism performance, 243t
Sector buckets/breakpoints, 35f
Sector exposures, 32–33
Sector-level LCS, calculation, 83–84
Sector-specific risk, mitigation, 190
Sector-wise spread decomposition,
    default/liquidity contributions, 141f,
    146f
Securities
    market sensitivity, ex ante estimate, 199
    risk, increase, 253, 255
    trading on price, 165
Security-level analysis, impact, 13–14
Senior bonds, classification, 28
Seniority classes, DTS (usage), 27–30
SENIOR portfolios, 28
    notes/senior notes, inclusion, 29
    summary statistics, 29t
Shift/slope factors, regression coefficients,
    13f
Short bonds, sale, 190
Short-dated corporate bonds
    duration-matched treasuries, excess
        returns, 214
    excess returns, 216–217
    performance, 213
Short DTS exposures, 218
Short-duration Pan-European GE bonds,
    identification, 119–120
Short empirical duration strategy
    rates/performance, changes, 191f
    summary statistics, 191t
Shorter-maturity bonds, spread offering,
    215
Short-maturity bonds, exposures, 261
Short-term dislocations, 136
Short-term estimator, usage, 236
Single-issuer DTS steepener trade, return,
    220
Slope dependence, 77–79

Sovereign bonds, DTS, 55
Sovereign issuer, daily spread change
    (absolute/relative volatility), 63f
Sovereign risk (management), DTS (usage),
    66–70
Sovereign spreads
    increase, 61
    return volatility, embedding, 68
Spread
    absolute change, sensitivity, 4
    asset classes, results, 5
    basis, changes, 313
    behavior
        dynamics, examination, 56
        stability, 18–20
    buckets, summary statistics, 22t
    changes, neutralization, 149
    dependence, linear/nonlinear specification
        (usage), 46f
    increase, 170
    normalization, 12
    parallel shift, 73
    reversal, 307
    risk, components, 352
    spread volatility, linear relationship,
        17–18
    systematic change, exposure, 31
    volatility, 40–41
        prediction, risk projection (usage),
            235–236
        projections, 235
Spread-based constraint, adjustment, 32
Spread changes
    absolute/relative volatility, 63f
    assumption, 246
    autocorrelation, 63
    behavior, analysis, 9–10
    cross-sectional standard deviation,
        measurement, 256
    dynamics, 10–13
    models, regression estimates, 12t
    portfolio managers,
        summary/implications, 30–34
    return, calculation, 4
    spread level dependent model, regression
        estimates, 57t
    volatility, 5
        credit rating, 6f
        spread range, 6f
    volatility, contrast, 43f

Spread decomposition
  applications, 147–150
  expected default losses, alternative
      measure (usage), 145–147
  high-yield spread decomposition, 147
  Kraft, example, 136f
  methodology, 138–139
  model (month-by-month regression), CDP
      (usage), 152
  outlier-robust regression, 152t
  usage, 133–134, 147–148
Spread decomposition models
  alternatives, 150–152
  bond-level liquidity risk factor,
      incorporation, 150–151
  usage, 139
Spread duration, 20–21
  data, 22t
  inequality, 3–4
Spread duration-adjusted LCS quintile, 130
Spread level
  empirical duration, relationship, 171f
  hedge ratios, relationship, 161, 163
  pooled idiosyncratic spread volatility,
      contrast, 18f
  QML, usage, 45t, 47t
  systematic spread volatility
      relationship, 231
      volatility, contrast, 232f
  yearly regression, 19f
Spread premium, 265
  capture, 288–291
  constriction, index rules (impact), 278
  estimation, historical default data (usage),
      274
  measurement
      historical default/recovery data, usage,
          267–268
      index excess returns, usage, 268–274
      spread premium, usage, 268–274
Spread-quoted bonds, 88
Spread volatility, 261
  dependence, determination, 48
  idiosyncratic components, 63
  idiosyncratic spread volatility, 16–18
  linear growth, 73
  prediction, 46f
  projections test, 65f
  refinements/tests, 25
  regression, 58, 62

relationship, 78f
spread, zero level, 25–27
spread function, 76f, 77f
spread level, contrast, 59f
systematic components, 63
yearly regression, 19f
Stale pricing, impact, 158–159, 173–179
Standardized excess return, distribution, 24f
Standard & Poor's 500 (S&P500) Index,
      U.S. Corporate Index/Total Return
      Volatility (relative spread volatility
      contrast), 234f
Subordinated bonds, classification, 28
SUBORD portfolio, 28
  notes/senior notes, inclusion, 29
  summary statistics, 29t
Synthetic credit replication, 338
Synthetic replication
  arbitrage limits, impact, 356f
  tracking error
      arbitrage limits, impact, 355
      drivers, 352
Systematic market factors, impact, 143
Systematic risk, 198
  variance, 202
Systematic spread change
  measurement, 48
  representation, 14
  spread level
      relationship, 14
      volatility, contrast, 232f
  time series volatility, 15f
  volatility/spread level, relationship,
      15–16
Systematic spread volatility, 9, 13–16
  estimation, QML (usage), 49t, 50t
  spread level
      conditional relation, 45t
      contrast, 16f
      QML, usage, 45t
  spread level, relationship, 231
Systematic volatility, 42, 44

T
Tactical mark-to-market investors,
      distinctions, 136
Targeted portfolio LCS value, maintenance,
      128
Target index, investor replication, 186–187
TCX. *See* Cash credit replication

TED spread, 87
  LCS, relationship, 88f
Theoretical hedge ratio, calculation, 163
Three-month reversal portfolio
  monthly relative returns, distribution, 328f
  performance, 331t
  properties, 330
  rolling six-month average relative returns,
    329f
Total DTS exposure, evolution, 69f
Total economic value (TEV)
  estimation, 125
  monthly estimation, IG index (contrast),
    124f
  weighted average, 124–125
Total economic value (TEV), differential,
    188f
Total economic value (TEV), improvement,
    123–124
Total return swap (TRS), guarantee, 337
TRACE
  reports, 173–174
  usage, 90
TRACE volume, LCS (relationship), 98f
Tracking errors, 363f
  drivers, 352
Tracking error volatility (TEV)
  decline, 187
  details, 126f
  impact, 188f
Tracking portfolio, construction, 123
Tradable cash basket proxies, creation, 129
Trade efficiency scores (TESs), 129–130
  computation, 130
  creation, LCS value basis, 130
  liquidity ranking, 130
Trader-quoted bonds, LCS (usage), 92–96
Traders
  bid-ask indications, relationship, 91
  1-2-3 rankings, average LCS
    (correspondence), 108–109
  quotes, indicative only characteristic, 113
  rank categories, LCS distribution, 109f
Trades
  formation, 242
  performance, 197
  volatility, 204
Trading volume data, TRACE report, 173
Trailing 24-week empirical betas, poor
    quality, 203

Transactions costs
  control, quarterly rebalancing (usage),
    348–351
  performance net, 330–332
  volatility, 348
*t*-statistics, 317
  range, 18–19
  relationship, 44
Turnover
  constraint, rebalanced monthly subject,
    123
  costs, estimation, 129

U
Uncertainty, source, 74
Underperformance
  period, 317
    defining, 314
    standard deviation, 252
Unhedged portfolio
  excess returns, 149f
  out-of-sample excess returns, 149–150
United States, liquidity cost (increase), 118
Upgraded bonds, pre-rating/post-rating event
    regressions, 182
Upgraded issuers
  downgraded issuers, performance
    comparison, 306
  relative spreads, 307f
U.S. Aggregate Index, spread-to-swap levels,
    353f
U.S. bonds
  duration-based bonds, 119–120
  fixed rate IG bonds, comparison,
    121t–123t
U.S. corporate bonds, results, 5
U.S. Corporate Index
  credit ratings, 5
  data description, 34–35
  investor usage, 295
  quality subsets, DTS levels, 258
  rating event, 298
  relative OAS changes, long-term time
    series, 233–234
  span, 9
  systematic spread volatility estimation,
    QML usage, 49t
  total return volatility, relative spread
    volatility (contrast), 234f
  tracking, 253

U.S. credit bonds, Liquidity Cost Scores, 82–88
U.S. Credit Index
  aggregate credit steepener, performance contrast, 223t
  performance statistics, 222
  realized negative excess returns, 223
  TCX performance, contrast, 344–348
  tracking, 338
U.S. credit indexes
  characteristics, 114t
  liquidity characteristics, 116t
  OAS time series, 115f
U.S. credit markets, trading conventions, 113
U.S. fixed rate HY bonds, LCS regression, 118t
U.S. fixed rate IG bonds
  LCS distribution, 120f
  LCS regression, 118t
U.S. High Yield Indexes, 168f, 172f
  bonds, proportion, 296
  systematic spread volatility estimation, QML (usage), 50t
U.S. IG Credit Index, LCS segmentation, 92f
U.S. Investment Grade Corporate Index, 167, 171f
  monthly spread levels, time series, 229–230
U.S. investment-grade corporates, DTS results, 48
U.S. Investment Grade spreads, 230
U.S. LCS
  Pan-European LCS, comparison, 118–123
  regression, 119t
U.S. trader-quoted benchmark bonds, pooling, 118
U.S. Treasury hedge ratios, 162t

U.S. Treasury yield
  changes, return (sensitivity measurement), 160
  differences, 164

**V**
Value-weighted monthly relative returns, 303, 305
Vodafone, duration-based group, 120
Volatility
  drought, 235
  forecasts, comparison, 235f
  idiosyncratic volatility, 44–48
  quantification, 242
  systematic volatility, 42, 44
Volatility, observation problem, 40
Volatility Index (VIX), 87
  futures, 136–137, 351
  futures, possibilities, 357
  LCS, relationship, 88f
Volatility-to-spread slope, dependence, 78–79
Voluntary selling, 305

**W**
Washington Mutual defaults, impact, 236
WorldCom, downgrades, 218

**X**
Xtrakter, bond-level trading volume data, 117

**Y**
Yearly spread slope estimates, 18–19

**Z**
Zero-coupon bonds
  exclusion, 34
  Merton model, 74–77
  price, 75

Printed and bound by CPI Group (UK) Ltd, Croydon, CR0 4YY

23/04/2025

14661000-0004